Practical Derivatives

Dr. A.L. Saini

M.Com., Ph.D., L.L.B. (G), FCA

ISO 9001:2015 CERTIFIED

First Edition : 2014
Reprint : 2017
Reprint : 2023

Published by : Mrs. Meena Pandey
for **HIMALAYA PUBLISHING HOUSE PVT. LTD.,**
"Ramdoot", Dr. Bhalerao Marg, Girgaon, Mumbai - 400 004.
Phone: 022-23860170, 23863863; **Fax:** 022-23877178
E-mail: himpub@bharatmail.co.in; **Website:** www.himpub.com

Branch Offices :

New Delhi : "Pooja Apartments", 4-B, Murari Lal Street, Ansari Road, Darya Ganj, New Delhi - 110 002. Phone: 011-23270392, 23278631; Fax: 011-23256286

Nagpur : Kundanlal Chandak Industrial Estate, Ghat Road, Nagpur - 440 018. Phone: 0712-2721215, 2721216

Bengaluru : Plot No. 91-33, 2nd Main Road, Seshadripuram, Behind Nataraja Theatre, Bengaluru - 560 020. Phone: 080-41138821; Mobile: 09379847017, 09379847005

Hyderabad : No. 3-4-184, Lingampally, Besides Raghavendra Swamy Matham, Kachiguda, Hyderabad - 500 027. Phone: 040-27560041, 27550139

Chennai : No. 34/44, Motilal Street, T. Nagar, Chennai - 600 017. Mobile: 09380460419

Pune : "Laksha" Apartment, First Floor, No. 527, Mehunpura, Shaniwarpeth (Near Prabhat Theatre), Pune - 411 030. Phone: 020-24496323, 24496333; Mobile: 09370579333

Cuttack : Plot No 5F-755/4, Sector-9, CDA Market Nagar, Cuttack - 753 014, Odisha. Mobile: 09338746007

Kolkata : 3, S.M. Bose Road, Near Gate No. 5, Agarpara Railway Station, North 24 Parganas, West Bengal - 700 109. Mobile: 09674536325

DTP by : Priyanka Mahadik

Printed at : Trinity Academy, Mumbai. On behalf of HPH.

Preface

Due to globalisation and liberalisation processes initiated by the states all over the world, the international trade and financial activities have grown multifold resulting in rising level of all types of risks for market participants such as market risk, interest rate risk, foreign exchange risk, inflation risk and price risk. During the last few years, a number of new financial instruments have assumed significance in the Indian economy. With rapid globalisation, this trend is likely to accelerate in future. Derivatives are a kind of financial instruments whose values change in response to the change in specified interest rates, security prices, commodity prices, index of prices or rates, or similar variables. Typical examples of derivatives are futures and forward contracts, swaps and option contracts.

This book shows how to quantify financial risks and manage them. For a firm, the ability to manage risk is a source of competitive advantage. In particular, firms that manage risks well are better able to take advantages of growth opportunities. Derivatives are the instrument of choice to manage financial risks, and it is therefore, critical for managers to understand how derivatives can be used to manage risks.

Equity index futures, equity stock futures, equity index options and equity stock options are traded on some major stock exchanges. For instance, in case of equity index futures and equity index options, the National Stock Exchange of India Limited (NSE) and the Stock Exchange, Mumbai (BSE) have introduced trading in S&P CNX NIFTY index and BSE SENSEX, respectively. In the case of equity stock futures and equity stock options, NSE and BSE have introduced trading in certain securities specified by the Securities and Exchange Board of India (SEBI).

This book deals with accounting treatment of equity index futures, equity stock futures, equity index options and equity stock options (hereinafter collectively referred to as 'Equity Derivative Instruments') from the viewpoint of the parties who enter into such contracts as buyers or sellers.

Equity Derivative Instruments are a type of financial instruments, which are bought or sold with specific motives, e.g., speculation, hedging and arbitrage. The accounting treatment recommended in this book is applicable to all contracts entered into for Equity Derivative Instruments irrespective of the motive

Since the inceptions of Future and Option trading in 2001, it is observed that the people's interest and the volume in it are jumping by leaps and bounds. This book has been written in common man's language and with exhaustive details.

Second part of this book deals with accounting for financial instruments. Accounting for financial instruments under IFRS is complex. Entities should take the time to understand the requirements, including the impact on systems, processes and documentation. This book provides an overview of revised IAS 39 and IFRS 7 and Ind AS 39 on financial instruments.

The publication of this book comes at a time of heightened stress in the financial system and the global economy. The role that financial instruments have played in recent events is well documented. Write-downs in the value of loans and other asset-backed securities, extension of financial support to special purpose entities, fair valuation in less liquid markets, disclosure of undrawn loan commitments, liquidity risk and exposure to credit risk are to name but a few. A common understanding and consistent application of the financial reporting requirements in these areas are critical in alleviating uncertainty and enhancing confidence in reporting financial performance.

This book contains practical approach to understand Futures and Options and explains how to apply the complex standards on financial instruments.

The views expressed in this book are of author's own. This book is useful for those who do business in Futures and Options and Stock Exchanges, and for Brokers. This book is also useful for practicing Chartered Accountants/Cost Accountants/Company Secretaries/Professionals/Research Institutions/Companies/Businessmen and C.A. Final Students. This book is also useful for teachers and students of finance, commerce, and management like MBA, PGDBM, M.Com., MFC, MBE and MFM. This book is also useful for derivatives practitioners like equity researchers, portfolio managers, financial executives, analysts, investors, policymakers and risk managers.

I have taken help of the various International Financial Reporting Standards (IFRS) and Indian Standards while explaining the comparative position. I have also taken a few quotes against which I have given proper reference.

I am thankful to Mr. K.N. Pandey, Anuj Pandey and Niraj Pandey and all the editorial staff of M/s Himalaya Publishing House Pvt. Ltd. for bringing out this first edition of the book within a very short time.

I will be happy to welcome further suggestions from readers to improve this book. The readers may send their suggestions on e-mail: arjunsaini@rediffmail.com.

Dated 1st June, 2014 **Dr. A.L. Saini**

Practical Derivatives

Highlights

1. All Types of Derivatives Explained in Easy Language.
2. Easy Examples, Questions and Answers on Various Derivatives.
3. Detailed Study on Equity Derivative Instruments.
4. Practical Examples – How to Trade in Futures and Options.
5. Accounting for Derivatives.
6. Hedge Accounting.
7. Futures Options and Forward Contracts.
8. Taxation Aspect of Derivatives.
9. Commodity Derivatives.
10. Financial Derivatives.
11. Currency Options and Swaps.
12. Equity Derivatives.
13. Financial Instruments.
14. Practical Questions and Answers on Derivatives and Financial Instruments.

Dr. A.L. Saini

Contents

Part – I

Derivatives

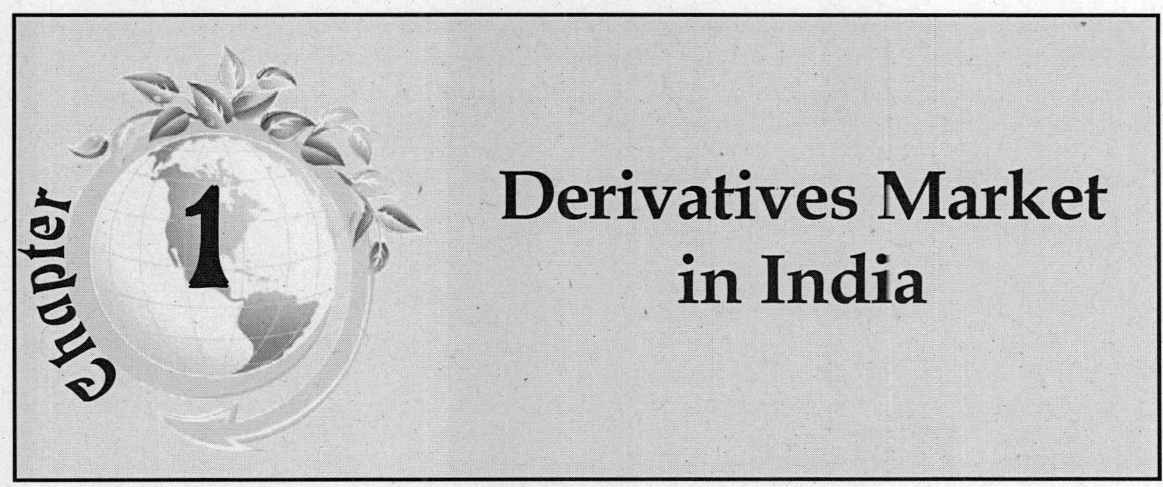

Derivatives Market in India

INTRODUCTION

A variant of secondary market is the forward market, also know as derivatives market, where securities are traded for future delivery and payment. Pure forward is however, not in practice in actual derivatives market, the versions of forward that are traded in derivatives market are futures and options.

In futures market, standardised securities are traded for future delivery and settlement. These futures can be on a individual securities or the index itself. In the case of options, securities are traded for conditional future delivery.

As early as seventeenth century Europe, when speculating traders used futures/ forward contracts to trade in agricultural commodities, of course the working was not at all sophistical, due to that there were frequent collapses in the systems.

But with these the evolution of the system at foward market came into existence.

Later, a group of Chicago businessmen formed the Chicago Board of Trade (CBOT) in 1848. The main purpose of the CBOT was to provide a centralised location known in advance for buyers and sellers to negotiate forward contracts. In the year 1865, the CBOT went one step further and listed the first "exchange traded" derivatives contract in the US, these contracts were called **"Futures Contracts".**

In 1919, Chicago Butter and Egg Board, a spin-off of CBOT, was reorganised to allow futures trading. Later, its name was changed to Chicago Mercantile Exchange (CME). The CBOT and the CME remain the two largest organised futures exchanges ("financial exchanges"), in the world today.

At Kansas City Board of Trade the first index futures contract was traded. Currently the most popular stock index futures contract in the world is based on S&P 500 index, traded on Chicago Mercantile Exchange. In the mid eighties, financial futures became the most active derivative instruments generating volumes many times more than the commodity futures. The three most popular futures contracts such as Index futures, futures on T-bills and Euro-Dollar futures are even traded today.

On September 1984, the Chicago Mercantile Exchange (CME), and the Singapore International Monetary Exchange (SIMEX) both set electronic link between them to provide the facility to trade, some contracts interchangeability round the clock to their traders.

DERIVATIVES MARKET IN INDIA

Till the mid-1990s equity stocks were transacted and they were in two categories,

1. Spot Transactions.
2. Carry forward Transactions (Badla).

Badla system was discontinued somewhere in December 1993. Due to discontinuation of Badla system of trade volumes fell sharply as existing system was requiring big amount of cash i.e., liquidity.

Due to fall in trading volumes some alternative system was required to be introduced. Securities and Exchange Board of India (SEBI) set up a 24-member committee under the chairmanship of Dr. L.C. Gupta on November, 18th 1996 to develop appropriate regulatory framework for derivatives trading in India.

On March 17, 1998 the committee submitted its report prescribing necessary pre-conditions for introduction of derivatives trading in India. The committee recommended that derivatives should be declared as 'securities' so that regulatory framework applicable to trading of 'securities' could also govern trading of derivatives. SEBI also set up a group in June 1998 under the Chairmanship of Prof. J.R. Varma, to recommend measures for risk containment in derivatives market in India. Later, the report, which was submitted in October 1998, worked out the operational details of margining system, methodology for charging initial margins, broker net worth, deposit requirement and real-time monitoring requirements.

Withdrawal of Prohibition on Options

Under the Securities Contracts Regulation Act (SCRA), 1956 as amended by the Act 1969 all options in securities were prohibited.

In the year 1995, the prohibitions on options were withdrawn under the Securities Contracts Regulations Act.

Arrival of Derivatives Trading in India

In December 1999, the SCRA was amended-to include the derivatives within the ambit of 'securities' and the regulatory framework was developed for governing derivatives trading. The act also made it clear that derivatives shall be legal and valid only if such contracts are traded on a recognised stock exchange, thus, precluding OTC derivatives. In March 2000, the government also rescinded the three-decade old notification, which prohibited forward trading in securities.

In June 2000, derivatives trading commenced in India after SEBI granted the final approval to this effect in May 2000. SEBI permitted the derivative segments of two stock exchanges, and approved derivatives contracts commence trading and settlement in NSE and BSE, and their clearing house/corporation.

To begin with, SEBI approved trading in index futures contracts based on S&P CNX Nifty and BSE - 30 (Sensex) index. Later, this was followed by approval for trading in options based on these two indexes and options on individual securities.

In June 2001, the trading in index options commenced and in July 2001 the trading in options on individual securities commenced. In November 2001 Futures contracts on individual stocks were launched. Trading and settlement in derivative contracts is done in accordance with the rules, byelaws, and regulations of the respective exchanges and their clearing house corporation duly approved by SEBI and notified in the official gazette.

Trading Mechanisms at NSE

The futures and options trading system of NSE, called NEAT-F&O trading system, provides a fully automated screen-based trading for Nifty futures and options and stock futures and options on a nationwide basis and an online monitoring and surveillance mechanism It supports an anonymous order-driven market, which provides complete transparency of trading operations and operates on strict price-time priority. It is similar to that of trading of equities in the Cash Market (CM) segment. The NEAT-F&O trading system is accessed by two types of users. The Trading Members(TM) have access to functions such as order entry, order matching order and trade management.

Trading Mechanisms at BSE

The Derivatives Trading at BSE takes place through a fully automated screen-based trading platform called as DTSS (Derivatives Trading and Settlement System). The DTSS is designed to allow trading on a real-time basis. In addition to generating trades by matching opposite orders, the DTSS also generates various reports for the member participants.

ADVANTAGES AND IMPORTANCE OF DERIVATIVES

Derivative is a product whose value is derived from the value of one or more basic variables, called bases (underlying asset, index, or reference rate), in a contractual manner. The underlying asset can be equity, forex, commodity or any other asset. For example, wheat farmers may wish to sell their harvest at a future date to eliminate the risk of a change in prices by that date. Such a transaction is an example of a derivative. The price of this derivative is driven by the spot price of wheat which is the "underlying".

In the Indian context the Securities Contracts Regulation Act, 1956 (SCRA) defines "derivative" to include:

1. A security derived from a debt instrument, share, loan whether secured or unsecured, risk instrument or contract for differences or any other form of security.
2. A contract, which derives its value from the prices, or index of prices, of underlying securities. Derivatives are securities under the SCRA and hence, the trading of derivatives is governed by the regulatory framework under the SCRA.

Derivatives are important financial instruments and perform a wide variety of functions. These functions range from hedging and insuring against adverse changes to ensuring market efficiency. Some of the important advantages that they bestow upon their users are as follows:

1. Hedging Risk

Derivatives are used to hedge risks. They can be used as hedging devices by retail investors, portfolio managers and borrowers hedging against interest rate rises. Index Futures can be used to hedge a portfolio against adverse movement in the stock market.

Through the process of hedging, the buyer of the instrument implicitly transfers the risk to those who want to assume it, for a consideration. To give an example, a company is worried that the price of their important raw material, tomatoes, will go up or fluctuate wildly. To avoid this, they can fix the price of tomatoes in the futures market now, with delivery to be taken in the future. This relieves the company of the uncertainty.

2. Widening Portfolio

Derivatives enable banks, traders or investors to bet on price movements without having to deal with actual assets. If the value of the underlying goes up or down, the difference is simply settled in cash. Derivatives are more flexible than the underlying products. The value is based on the price of the underlying product, and most contracts are settled in cash terms. Investors could gamble, for example, on the tobacco crop in Andhra Pradesh without having to buy a tobacco farm.

3. Leveraging

One of the most important uses of derivatives stems from the fact that they can be 'leveraged' i.e., geared up to be worth many times the value of the underlying. For instance, if the price of the asset moves ₹ 10, the value of derivative instrument can change by ₹ 100. Hence, an investor can put in only a small amount of money for a large transaction. This is not possible while trading, for instance, equities. Let is take the property owner with a mortgage as an example. A person buys a house for ₹ 1,00,000. He puts up ₹ 10,000 and borrows ₹ 90,000 from the bank. Six months later, the house is sold for ₹ 1,50,000. He pays back ₹ 90,000 to the bank (for these purposes we shall ignore interest payments, etc.) and keeps ₹ 60,000 – not bad for an original investment of just ₹ 10,000. The principle is exactly the same in many derivatives' investments – (Big Bang for a Little Buck.)

4. Facilitating Large International Investments

Another important area where derivatives come in useful is international investments. International investments often involve huge sums of money. To a large extent, derivatives make such investment possible. For instance, Japanese insurance companies fund housing loans in the US by buying into derivatives on real estate in the US. Without such use of derivatives, investment would be much more difficult.

Derivative users in the Market

1. Hedgers

Hedgers wish to eliminate or reduce price risk to which they are already exposed. To hedge is to enter into transactions that protect a business or assets against changes in the underlying commodity. The instruments bought as a hedge, tend to have the opposite value movements to the underlying asset. Financial and commodity markets are used to transfer risk from an individual or corporation to someone more willing and able to bear that risk.

To give an example, consider an American company, which discovers a rich deposit of oil near the Bay of Bengal. The management is afraid to develop the site because they are uncertain about the revenues that could accrue. Some of the uncertainties are:

(a) The price of oil could fall

(b) Interest rates could rise and

(c) Adverse currency movements.

The company does not have to bear all the risks. These risks can be hedged to an extent. For instance, the oil can be sold in the futures market, thus, providing a fixed price. The interest rate can be artificially fixed using the Forward Rate Agreement and interest Futures market. The currency risk can be limited using currency Forwards or Options.

The above case is a classic example of how risk-averse investors, can overcome many of the risks and uncertainties by the innovative use of derivatives.

2. Speculators

Speculators willingly take price risks to profit from price changes in the underlying. In contrast to hedgers, speculators buy or sell derivative contracts in an attempt to earn profits. They are willing to assume the risk of price fluctuations, hoping to profit from them. In the above case of the American company, they overcame the risk. This risk was taken over by the speculators. Speculators are essential to the proper functioning of the Futures market. They absorb the excess demand or supply generated by hedgers. Most importantly, they assume the risks of price fluctuations that hedgers are so eager to avoid. Speculators add to the liquidity of the market.

In general, the speculator takes a view on the market and plays accordingly. If one is bullish on the market, one can buy Futures, and *vice versa* for a bearish outlook.

3. Arbitrageurs

Arbitrageurs profit from price differentials existing in two markets by simultaneously operating in two different markets. An arbitrageur makes riskless profits by exploiting the price differentials on the same instrument or similar assets, often by trading on different exchanges. He buys the instrument at the lower price and promptly makes a resale at the higher price. Theoretically speaking, the price ought to be the same on two markets, but this is not always the case. Opportunities exist whereby one can buy a derivative instrument in one market, sell it in another and pocket the difference. Arbitrage plays a role in ensuring market efficiency, in the sense that it helps to eliminate pricing anomalies. Arbitageurs are on the lookout for market inefficiencies and quickly look to eliminate them.

All class of investors are required for healthy functioning of the market. Hedgers and investors provide the economic substance to any financial market. Without them, the markets would lose their purpose and become mere tools of gambling. Speculators provide liquidity and depth to the market. Arbitrageurs bring price uniformity and help price discovery.

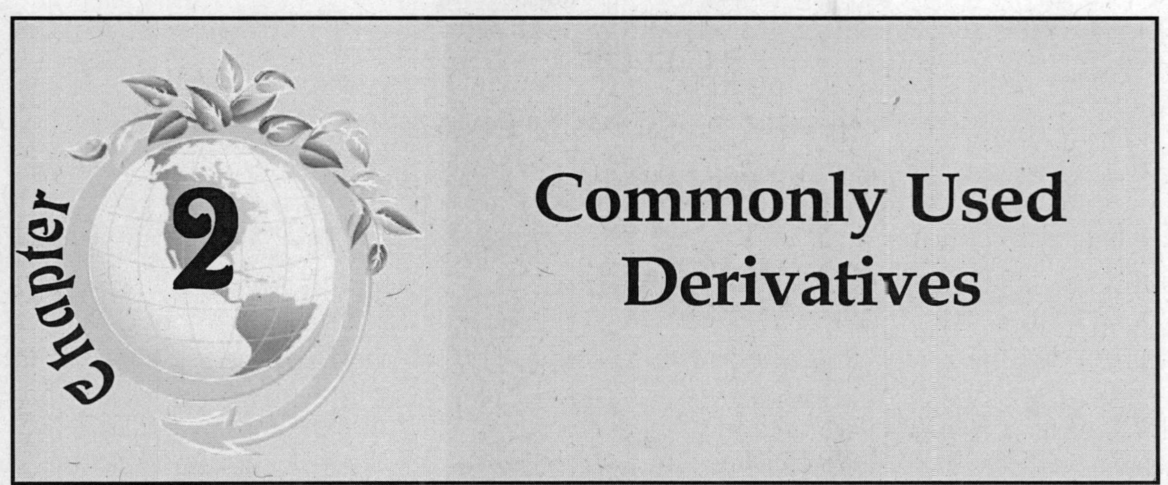

Commonly Used Derivatives

INTRODUCTION

The emergence of the market for derivative products, most notably forwards, futures and options, can be traced back to the willingness of risk-averse economic agents to guard themselves against uncertainties arising out of fluctuations in asset prices. By their very nature, the financial markets are marked by a very high degree of volatility. Through the use of derivative products, it is possible to partially or fully transfer price risks by locking-in asset prices. As instruments of risk management, these generally do not influence the fluctuations in the underlying asset prices. However, by locking-in asset prices, derivative products minimise the impact of fluctuations in asset prices on the profitability and cash-flow situation of risk-averse investors.

Definition/Meaning of Derivative

A derivative is a financial instrument or other contract with all three of the following characteristics:

(a) Its value changes in response to the change in a specified interest rate, financial instrument price, commodity price, foreign exchange rate, index of prices or rates, credit rating or credit index, or other variable, provided in the case of a non-financial variable that the variable is not specific to a party to the contract (sometimes called the 'underlying');

(b) It requires no initial net investment or an initial net investment that is smaller than would be required for other types of contracts that would be expected to have a similar response to changes in market factors; and

(c) It is settled at a future date.

Definitions and Meaning of Frequently Used Derivative Contracts

Forwards: A forward contract is a customised contract between two entities, where settlement takes place on a specific date in the future at today's pre-agreed price.

Futures: A futures contract is an agreement between two parties to buy or sell an asset at a certain time in the future at a certain price. Futures contracts are special types of forward contracts in the sense that the former are standardised exchange-traded contracts, such as futures of the Nifty index.

Options: An Option is a contract, which gives the right, but not an obligation, to buy or sell the underlying at a stated date and at a stated price. While a buyer of an option pays the premium and buys the right to exercise his option, the writer of an option is the one who receives the option premium and therefore, obliged to sell/buy the asset if the buyer exercises it on him. Options are of two types – **Calls** and **Puts**:

1. *'Calls'* give the buyer the right but not the obligation to buy a given quantity of the underlying asset, at a given price on or before a given future date.
2. *'Puts'* give the buyer the right, but not the obligation to sell a given quantity of underlying asset at a given price on or before a given future date. Presently, at NSE futures and options are traded on the Nifty, CNX IT, BANK Nifty and 116 single stocks.

Warrants: Options generally have lives of up to one year. The majority of options traded on exchanges have maximum maturity of nine months. Longer dated options are called Warrants and are generally traded over-the counter.

What is an 'Option Premium'?

At the time of buying an option contract, the buyer has to pay premium. The premium is the price for acquiring the right to buy or sell. It is price paid by the option buyer to the option seller for acquiring the right to buy or sell. Option premiums are always paid upfront.

What is 'Commodity Exchange'?

A Commodity Exchange is an association, or a company of any other body corporate organizing futures trading in commodities. In a wider sense, it is taken to include any organised market place where trade is routed through one mechanism, allowing effective competition among buyers and among sellers. This would include auction-type exchanges, but not wholesale markets, where trade is localised, but effectively takes place through many non-related individual transactions between different permutations of buyers and sellers.

What is meant by 'Commodity'?

Forward Contracts Regulation Act (FCRA), 1952 defines "goods" as "every kind of movable property other than actionable claims, money and securities". Futures' trading is organised in such goods or commodities as are permitted by the Central Government. At present, all goods and products of agricultural (including plantation), mineral and fossil origin are allowed for futures trading under the auspices of the commodity exchanges recognised under the FCRA.

What is Commodity derivatives market?

Commodity derivatives market trade contracts for which the underlying asset is commodity. It can be an agricultural commodity like wheat, soybeans, rapeseed, cotton, etc or precious metals like gold, silver, etc.

What is the Difference between Commodity and Financial Derivatives?

The basic concept of a derivative contract remains the same whether the underlying happens to be a commodity or a financial asset. However, there are some features, which are very peculiar to commodity derivative markets. In the case of financial derivatives, most of these contracts are cash-settled. Even in the case of physical settlement, financial assets are not bulky and do not need special facility for storage. Due to the bulky nature of the underlying assets, physical settlement in commodity derivatives creates the need for warehousing. Similarly, the concept of varying quality of asset does not really exist as far as financial underlyings are concerned. However in the case of commodities, the quality of the asset underlying a contract can vary at times.

Some Frequently Used Derivative Contracts are given below in Detail

Forward Contract

A forward contract is an agreement in which two parties agree to undertake an exchange of the underlying asset at some future date at a pre-determined price.

A forward contract is a customised contract between two parties, where settlement takes place on a specific date. The settlement date and price are agreed in advance by the parties concerned.

The main features of forward contracts are:

- They are bilateral contracts and hence exposed to counter-party risk.
- Each contract is custom designed, and hence is unique in terms of contract size, expiration date and the asset type and quality.
- The contract price is generally not available in public domain.
- The contract has to be settled by delivery of the asset on expiration date.
- In case, the party wishes to reverse the contract, it has to go to the same counter-party compulsorily. This can result in payment of an exit premium.

Today, forward markets exist in a whole host of commodities The most important forward market is the foreign exchange market in which billions of dollars worth of currency are traded each business day. Another sector where forward contracts are popular is the agriculture sector, where commodity prices fluctuate a great deal. Take the case of a factory interested in purchasing onions in bulk. Both, the producer and the factory would like to reduce the uncertainty in prices, as the delivery may be staggered over a period of time. One way to achieve this would be to reach an agreement with the producer to supply onions at various times in the future at fixed prices today. This example captures the very essence of forward trading.

Forward contracts are private agreements tailor made to meet the requirements of the parties. They are outside the regulation of any exchange. This, often, exposes the contracting parties to the risk of default. If a forward contract is closed before the scheduled closing date, a penalty may be charged. Hence, the drawbacks of forward contracts are lack of standardisation, which prevents trading on an exchange and the risk of default.

Futures

Futures are agreements between two parties to undertake a transaction at an agreed price on a specified future date. Futures contracts are exchange-based instruments, which are traded on a regulated exchange. In general, Futures contracts are related to various underlying assets such as commodities, market indices, interest rates and so on.

In futures, there is an agreement to buy or sell a specified quantity of financial instrument/commodity on a designated future date at a price agreed upon by the buyer and seller today. The contracts themselves are often traded on the Futures market, which is a market in which contracts for future delivery of a commodity or a share are bought or sold. For example, if you buy 100 Company X Futures at ₹ 100 for May 31 delivery, it means that on May 31, you would pay the seller ₹ 10,000 and get in return 100 shares of Company X. In general, there is no physical delivery of the underlying asset but the settlement is done by paying or receiving the difference of the actual price on May 31 and the contracted price. In the same example, if the shareprice of Company X was ₹ 150 on May 31, you would get ₹ 5,000 (100 × ₹ 150 – ₹ 100) and if the price of Company X was ₹ 50, then you would have to pay ₹ 5,000.

The standardised items in any Futures contract are as follows:

- Quantity of the underlying
- Quality of the underlying (not required in financial Futures)
- The date and month of delivery
- The units of price quotation and minimum change in price (tick size)
- Location of settlement

One of the most popular type of Futures is the one based on stock indices. Futures on individual stocks exist in some countries but are not very popular. Price volatility in individual stocks is much higher than that of an index. This results in higher risk and margin requirements. In addition, such instruments suffer from lack of depth and liquidity in trading. In most cases, Futures based on individual stocks often have a physical settlement resulting in more complex regulatory requirements.

The basic difference between commodity and financial Futures is the nature of the underlying asset. In commodity Futures, the underlying asset is a commodity, which may be wheat, cotton, pepper, turmeric, corn, oats, soybeans, orange juice, crude oil, natural gas, gold, and silver. In financial Futures, the underlying can be bonds, stocks, stock indices and currencies. Given the nature of the underlying, a financial Future is fairly standard and there are no quality issues while in a commodity Future, quality of the underlying asset matters.

In general, most Futures contracts are not held to expiry, and so delivery does not take place. Open positions are closed out on the last day of trading at a price determined by the spot/"cash" market price of the underlying asset. This price is called "Exchange Delivery Settlement Price" or EDSP.

The basic difference between a Forward and Futures contract is that one is customized and the other is standardized. To be more specific, the terms of a Forward contract are individually agreed between two parties, while Futures, are traded on exchanges where the terms of the contract are standardised by the exchange.

Other salient differences are:

(a) *Counter party risk:* In case of Futures, after a trade is confirmed by two members of an exchange, the exchange itself becomes the counter-party to that trade. The credit risk, which in the case of forward contracts was on the counter-party, gets transferred to the exchange, reducing the risk to almost nil.

(b) *Liquidity:* Futures contracts are more liquid and their pricing is more transparent due to standardisation and market reporting of volumes and price.

(c) *Squaring off:* A Forward contract can be reversed only with the same counter-party with which it was entered into. A Futures contract can be reversed with any member of the exchange.

Forward Rate Agreements (FRAs)

FRAs are instruments that are used to hedge future interest rate risk. The concerned two parties agree on a single future rate of interest. The actual rate of interest is compared with the rate agreed in the FRA and based on the difference, one party pays compensation to the other. Thus, two parties enter into an agreement between themselves to protect against a future adverse movement in interest rates.

For instance, a company ABC needs to borrow ₹ 3 million in three months time for a period of one year. The current rate of interest is 14 per cent. The company is worried that interest rates will rise in the future, To mitigate this risk, ABC enters into an agreement with a financial institution, XYZ, and purchases a FRA at 14 per cent. Suppose, after three months, interest rates are 17 per cent. Then, XYZ has to compensate ABC to the tune of 3 per cent (17 per cent less 14 per cent) of ₹ 3 million. Thus, XYZ pays ABC (0.17 – 0.14)*3 million = ₹ 90,000. Now suppose interest rates fall to 11 per cent. In such a case, ABC has to compensate XYZ to the tune of ₹ 90,000 i.e., (0.14 – 0.11)*3 millipn.

Note that there is no physical principal amount in the FRA transaction. It is still necessary to borrow or lend cash if the underlying need to do so exists, which will be a transaction distinct from the FRA. By transacting the FRA, the interest rate, for the period in question becomes fixed. FRAs are quoted like deposits, for varying currencies and duration. Customers with large requirements can enter into FRAs with their banks for virtually any future period.

The main reasons for the phenomenal success of this instrument lie in its basic structure and features.

These reasons are enumerated below:

- It is an extremely efficient method of meeting the widespread need to hedge, or trade, forward period interest rates. Virtually, every bank and business organisation with exposure to debt has a need for hedging tools like the FRA.
- There is no principal amount involved, and the only sums, which change hands are those which compensate for the movement in the interest rates. Hence, the credit risk is much smaller than traditional cash deposits.
- The markets in all major currencies and periods are extremely liquid.
- FRAs are *very* straight forward products as compared to complex derivative products like index options, and relatively simpler to administer. Also, standardised terms ensure that all participants know their exact positions.
- FRAs give the user flexibility with regard to amounts, periods and currencies.
- There are no margin requirements. With no up front outlay, minimal capital requirements, the gearing possibilities are almost limitless.

Caps

An interest rate Cap is a contract, which allows the purchaser to set the upper limit for interest rates payable. The buyer of the Cap receives compensation if interest rates rise above the agreed level. As a hedging technique, capping is often used in the case of long-term borrowing (usually three to five years). With this technique, an organisation can benefit from a fall in interest rates, but put a cap on the maximum interest rate payable.

For instance, XYZ Ltd. wants to borrow ₹ 30m. It arranges with bank A to borrow this over a period of 5 years at the Prime Lending Rate (PLR) +1.5 per cent. Assume that the current PLR is 14 per cent. XYZ Ltd. buys an interest rate Cap of 15.5 per cent. If, during the next 5 years, interest rates rise above 15.5 per cent, the Cap seller will compensate XYZ the amount of interest paid over 15.5 per cent. He will pay the differential interest over 15.5 per cent.

The buyer of a Cap needs to pay a premium to the seller. This premium depends on many factors like the current interest rates, the level at which the Cap comes into effect, the duration of the Cap and the expected volatility in interest rates.

Floors and Collars

Buyers of Caps have to pay a premium, which can be a large cash payment. To reduce this, some buyers simultaneously sell a Floor. Hence, they receive a premium.

If interest rates fall below an agreed level, they have to compensate the Floor buyer.

In the above example, XYZ can sell a Floor at the PLR (14 per cent). If rates fall below 14 per cent, it has to pay the Floor buyer, but it saves on the interest paid to the bank. The Floor premium received helps to offset the Cap premium paid.

The combination of selling a Floor at a low strike rate and buying a Cap at a higher strike rate, is called a Collar.

Swaps

A Swap can be defined as an exchange of obligations by two parties. For instance, in an Interest Rate Swap (IRS), one company arranges with another to exchange interest rate payments.

There are many types of Swaps like Asset Swaps, Currency Swaps and so on. However, the most important one is an Interest Rate Swap (IRS). One company may be paying fixed rate of interest but prefers floating rates. Another company may be paying a floating rate, but would find a fixed rate advantageous. Thus, it makes sense for both the companies to enter into an IRS agreement.

An important advantage of IRS is that different firms can access funds at varying rates and terms. They may not always find these terms beneficial. So when two parties find each other's terms beneficial, they enter into Swap agreements. IRS enables them to access sources of funding at better rates than what they would be able to achieve on a direct basis.

It is important to note that the principal amount is purely 'notional.' It exists only to facilitate the calculation of interest. There is no physical exchange of principal in single currency IRS. As per the agreement terms, the difference is settled in cash at the end of the stipulated period. The IRS is for a period that is agreed upon at the time of entering into the agreement.

Example

Companies A and B want to borrow the same amount. Company A can borrow @14 per cent fixed or @PLR+2 per cent Company B can borrow @12 per cent fixed or @PLR+1 per cent Company B has an absolute advantage in both areas. Still it makes sense for them to enter into an IRS. Company A prefers a fixed rate and Company B prefers a floating rate. They enter into an IRS whereby A pays B 13.5 per cent while B pays A PLR+2 per cent. Now, A pays PLR+2 per cent to the bank but receives the same from B. As a result, A has to pay only 13.5 per cent thus saving 0.5 per cent. B pays 12 per cent to the bank but receives 13.5 per cent from A. Hence, the net effect for B is PLR+0.5 per cent (2 per cent – 1.5 per cent). Thus, the IRS is advantageous to both.

There are various other types of IRS, prominent amongst which are:

- *Amortising swaps:* In these Swaps, the notional principal amount on which the interest calculations are based, decreases according to a pre-determined schedule. The main demand for this type of Swap is from customers of banks who wish to match repayment schedules on loans as precisely as possible
- *Accreting swaps:* These are similar to Amoritising Swaps, except that the notional principal amount increases according to a pre-determined schedule.
- *Roller coasters:* This type, which combines both features, are most often used in connection with long term project financing. The notional principal increases and reduces during the life of the transaction, going up and down according to a schedule agreed at the time of the deal.
- *Forward start:* These Swaps have become more, and more commonplace. They simply involve agreement of all the details, including the price, at the point when the deal is transacted – for an IRS that starts, say, 6 months' later.

Cross Currency Swaps

Cross Currency Swaps are similar to IRS and involve more than one currency. They are often undertaken as a result of some underlying transaction such as bonds.

Options

The buyer of an Option has the right, but NOT the obligation to buy or sell an agreed amount of a commodity on or before a specified future date.

The concept is somewhat similar to insurance where the buyer pays an amount of money, known as the premium, for certain rights. These can be taken up if you wish, but there is no obligation to do so.

Unlike insurance, however, there is no limit on the amount 'claimed'. You have an option to, for example, buy at a certain price and may do so, no matter how valuable the commodity in question may become.

An option to buy is known as a 'Call' Option while an option to sell is known as a 'Put' Option. The rate at which the buyer of the Option has the right to buy, or sell, is the 'strike' or 'exercise' price.

An Option, which can be 'exercised' at any time before it expires is described as an 'American' style Option. One, which can only be exercised on the 'expiry date' is called an 'European' style option.

Buying an Option protects against downside risk and at the same time gives upside potential. You establish the worst possible rate at which you will buy/sell a commodity, but still have the possibility of improving on this rate. The buyer, hence, has the best of both worlds.

Pay-off Profiles for Different Option Strategies

Pay-off profile implies the behavior of returns (profits) from adopting different strategies. Each pay-off profile illustrates graphically how the value of each position changes as the relationship between strike/spot rate changes. In an Option strategy, all the gains/losses of a buyer will be the losses/gains of a seller. Hence, the pay-off profile of a seller will be mirror image of the pay-off profile of a buyer.

Long Call Option: A long Call i.e., the purchase of a Call, is an option to buy an asset at strike price. The maximum profit for the buyer of a Call Option is unlimited and maximum loss is limited to the extent of Option premium.

Short Call Option: A Short Call Option is the right to sell an asset at the strike price. The pay-off to the Short Call is the mirror image of that of the Long Call. Profit for the long is loss for the short and *vice versa.*

Long Put Option: A Long Put Option is an option to sell an asset at the strike price. As with any long position, the loss is limited to the premium paid with an unlimited potential for profit.

Short Put Option: A Short Put Option gives an obligation to buy an asset at the strike price if the buyer chooses to exercise the option. The profit and loss profile for a Short Put mirrors that of the long Put option.

Hedging with Currency Options

The hedger has an opportunity to hedge the exchange risk by using a simple Call or Put Option or by acquiring positions in multiple Options so that the combination provides a unique pay-off profile. The selection of an appropriate alternative by the hedger depends on the risk profile and view about the future market prices of the underlying asset.

Hedging for exporter: An Indian company exported goods to the US and expects payment after three months. The amount is equal to US$ 10 million. The amount of rupees the exporter will be receiving will depend on the spot rate of exchange prevailing then. Here, the exporter is exposed to vagaries of currency rates which may result in reduction of profit in the transaction or even a loss. The exporter, therefore, wants to hedge his rupee inflows through options. The hedge can be obtained by selecting one of the following alternatives.

Alternative 1: Buy a Put Option on US dollar with a strike price of ₹ 43 by paying a premium of ₹ 0.50.

Alternative 2: Sell a Call Option on US dollar with a strike price of ₹ 43 by paying a premium of ₹ 0.60.

Alternative 1: Exporter bought a Put Option at a strike price of ₹ 43.00 per dollar by paying a premium of ₹ 0.50 per dollar. Maturity of the contract is 3 months from now.

The table 2.1 provides the rupee inflow to the exporter depending on spot rate prevailing at the time of realisation of the receivables.

Table 2.1: Rupee Inflows to the Exporter

Exchange Rate (3 months hence) ₹/$	Option exercised Yes/No	₹ Inflow	Outflow on a/c of premium	Net inflow
40.00	Yes	43.00	0.50	42.50
40.50	Yes	43.00	0.50	42.50
41.00	Yes	43.00	0.50	42.50
41.50	Yes	43.00	0.50	42.50
41.90	Yes	43.00	0.50	42.50
42.00	Yes	43.00	0.50	42.50
42.50	Yes	43.00	0.50	42.50
43.00	Indifferent	43.00	0.50	42.50
43.50	No	43.50	0.50	43.00
44.00	No	44.00	0.50	43.50
44.10	No	44.10	0.50	43.60
44.50	No	44.50	0.50	44.00
45.00	No	45.00	0.50	44.50
45.50	No	45.50	0.50	45.00

At a ₹ 0.50 premium, the effective delivery price after three months would be 42.50 (i.e., 43.00 – 0.50) or more. If the dollar appreciates relative to the rupee well beyond the 43.00 level, the exporter will be able to sell the dollar currency at a spot price and hence the Option is allowed to expire. If the spot price is less than or equal to ₹ 43 then the Option is exercised. Thus, the exporter is able to benefit from two advantages that the Option market offered over the Forward market, namely an opportunity to profit from a rally in the currency market and protection against a drop in the currency.

Alternative 2: Exporter has another choice to hedge the receivables by selling the Call Option at a strike price of ₹ 43.00/$ by receiving premium of say ₹ 0.60 per dollar, for the contract maturing 3 months from now. The table below provides the rupee inflows to the exporter depending on the spot prices prevailing at the time of realisation of receivables.

Table 2.2: Rupee Inflows to the Exporter

Exchange Rate (3 months hence) ₹/$	Option exercised Yes/No	₹ Inflow	Outflow on a/c of premium	Net inflow
40.00	Yes	40.00	0.60	40.60
40.50	Yes	40.50	0.60	41.10
41.00	Yes	41.00	0.60	41.60
41.50	Yes	41.50	0.60	42.10
41.90	Yes	41.90	0.60	42.50
42.00	Yes	42.00	0.60	42.60
42.50	Yes	42.50	0.60	43.10
43.00	Indifferent	43.00	0.60	43.60
43.50	No	43.00	0.60	43.60
44.00	No	43.00	0.60	43.60
44.10	No	43.00	0.60	43.60
44.50	No	43.00	0.60	43.60
45.50	No	43.00	0.60	43.60
45.50	No	43.00	0.60	43.60

Considering the premium of ₹ 0.60 per dollar received for selling a Call Option, the effective delivery price after three months would be 43.60 (i.e., 43 00 + 0.60) or less. If the dollar appreciates relatively to the rupee well beyond the 43.00 level, the Option buyer will exercise the Call Option, the exporter will be able to deliver the dollar, received from exports to the buyer.

As we see from both the tables, we find that rupee inflow under alternative 1 is higher than the inflow under alternative 2 when the spot rate is less than ₹ 41.90 and when the spot rate is more than ₹ 44.10. Whereas the inflow under alternative 2 is more than the inflow under alternative 1 when the spot rate lies between ₹ 41.90 and ₹ 44.10. The net gain from the Put Option will not exceed that of the Call Option until the rupee appreciates sufficiently to generate an intrinsic value for the Put Option of 0.50 (premium paid for put) plus 0.60 (premium received for call). So selling Call Option is superior to buying Put if the expected spot price at the maturity lies within the range of strike prices + the sum of two premiums. Thus, the selection of long Put or short Call depends on the expectation of the hedger about the spot prices that are likely to prevail at the timeof exercising the Option.

Hedging for importer: An Indian company is importing goods from a Gulf country after three months. The payment is expected to be made in dollars at the time of importing goods. The value of import is US$ 10 million. The amount of rupees the importer will be paying will depend on the spot rate of exchange prevailing then. Here, the importer is exposed to vagaries of currency rates, which may result in reduction of profit in the transaction or even resulting in a loss. He, therefore, wants to hedge his rupee outflows through currency Options. The hedge can be obtained by selecting one of the two alternatives.

Alternative 1: Buy Call Option on US$ with a strike price of ₹ 43 by paying premium of ₹ 0.60 per dollar.

Alternative 2: Sell Put Option on US$ with a strike price of ₹ 43 by receiving premium of ₹ 0.50 per dollar.

Alternative 1: Indian company bought Call Option at a strike price of ₹ 43.00 per dollar by paying a premium of ₹ 0.60 per dollar. Maturity of the contract is three months from now. The table 2.3 provides the rupee outflows to the importer depending on the spot price prevailing at the time of realisation of payables.

Table 2.3: Rupee Outflows to the Importer

Exchange Rate (3 months hence) ₹/$	Option exercised Yes/No	₹ Inflow	Outflow on a/c of premium	Net inflow
40.00	Yes	40.00	0.60	40.60
40.50	Yes	40.50	0.60	41.10
41.00	Yes	41.00	0.60	41.60
41.50	Yes	41.50	0.60	42.10
41.90	Yes	41.90	0.60	42.50
42.00	Yes	42.00	0.60	42.60
42.50	Yes	42.50	0.60	43.10
43.00	Indifferent	43.00	0.60	43.60
43.50	No	43.00	0.60	43.60
44.00	No	43.00	0.60	43.60
44.10	No	43.00	0.60	43.60
44.50	No	43.00	0.60	43.60
45.00	No	43.00	0.60	43.60
45.50	No	43.00	0.60	43.60

The effective price after three months would be 43.60 (i.e., 43.00 + 0.60) or less. If the dollar depreciates relative to the rupee below the 43.00 level, the company will be able to buy the dollar currency at a spot price and hence the Option is allowed to expire. If the spot price is more than ₹ 43.00 or equal then the Option is exercised.

Alternative 2: The Indian company has another alternative to hedge the dollar payables by selling the Put Option at a strike price of ₹ 43.00 per dollar by receiving premium of say ₹ 0.50 per dollar, for the contract maturing 3 months from now. The table 2.4 provides the rupee outflows to the importer depending on the spot-price prevailing at the time of realisation of payables.

Table 2.4: Rupee Outflow to the Importer

Exchange Rate (3 months hence) ₹/$	Option exercised Yes/No	₹ Inflow	Outflow on a/c of premium	Net inflow
40.00	Yes	40.00	0.50	42.50
40.50	Yes	40.50	0.50	42.50
41.00	Yes	41.00	0.50	42.50
41.50	Yes	41.50	0.50	42.50
41.90	Yes	41.90	0.50	42.50
42.00	Yes	42.00	0.50	42.50
42.50	Yes	42.50	0.50	42.50
43.00	Indifferent	43.00	0.50	42.50
43.50	No	43.00	0.50	42.50
44.00	No	43.00	0.50	43.00
44.10	No	43.00	0.50	43.50
44.50	No	43.00	0.50	43.60
45.00	No	43.00	0.50	44.00
45.50	No	43.00	0.50	45.50

Considering the premium of ₹ 0.60 per dollar received for selling a Call Option, the effective delivery price after three months would be 43.60 (i.e., 43.00 + 0.60) or less. If the dollar depreciates relative to the rupee well below the 43.00 level, the Option buyer will exercise the Put Option, the importer will be able to take delivery of the dollar, which will be used for import payments.

As we see from both the tables, rupee outflow under alternative 1 is less than the outflow under alternative 2 when the spot rate is less than ₹ 41.90 and or more than ₹ 44.10. The outflow under alternative 2 is less than the outflow under alternative 1 when the spot rate lies between ₹ 41.90 and ₹ 44.10. The net gain from the Call Option will not exceed that of the Put Option until the rupee depreciates sufficiently to generate an intrinsic value for the Put Option at 0.50 (premium received for put) plus 0.60 (premium paid for call). So selling Put Option is superior to buying Call if the expected spot price at the maturity lies within range of strike price + the sum of two premiums. The selection of long Call or Short put depends on the expectation of the hedger about the spot prices that are likely to prevail at the time of exercising the Option.

Query 1: What is a derivative?

Answer

A derivative is a financial instrument or other contract within the scope of this Standard with all three of the following characteristics:

(a) its value changes in response to the change in a specified interest rate, financial instrument price, commodity price, foreign exchange rate, index of prices or rates, credit rating or credit index, or other variable, provided in the case of a non-financial variable that the variable is not specific to a party to the contract (sometimes called the 'underlying');

(b) it requires no initial net investment or an initial net investment that is smaller than would be required for other types of contracts that would be expected to have a similar response to changes in market factors; and

(c) it is settled at a future date.

Query 2: Is it possible to use derivative to hedge risk?

Answer

Yes, Derivatives may be used for trading purposes as well as to hedge the risk.

Query 3: Explain an exotic feature in derivative called KIKO (knock-in-knock-out) and whether with these features in a derivative instrument, is it possible to apply hedge accounting?

Answer

One of the conditions for being able to apply hedge accounting is that the hedge instrument should not have features that make it very exotic or speculative. If the hedge instrument is speculative, then the mark-to-market gains/losses has to be compulsorily recognised in the income statement.

One such exotic arrangement is the barrier option with a knock in knock out feature. Ordinary FX options provide the buyer with an unlimited upside and a known downside, i.e., the premium. The knockout feature limits the upside given to the buyer and therefore makes the option considerably cheaper. When an investor purchases an ordinary FX option, the payout depends on where the spot rate closes on a particular day (the maturity). With the Knockout feature, if at any time up to and including the maturity, the Knockout level is reached, the option will expire worthless.

Query 4: Entity XYZ, whose functional currency is the Indian Rupees, sells products in France denominated in Euro. XYZ enters into a contract with an investment bank to convert Euro to Indian Rupees at a fixed exchange rate. The contract requires XYZ to remit Euro based on its sales volume in France in exchange for Indian rupees at a fixed exchange rate of 55.00. Is that contract a derivative?

Answer

Yes. The contract has two underlying variables (the foreign exchange rate and the volume of sales), no initial net investment or an initial net investment that is smaller than would be required for other types of contracts that would be expected to have a similar response to changes in market factors, and a payment provision. AS-30 does not exclude from its scope derivatives that are based on sales volume.

Query 5: The definition of a derivative requires that the instrument "is settled at a future date". Is this criterion met even if an option is expected not to be exercised, for example, because it is out of the money?

Answer

Yes. An option is settled upon exercise or at its maturity. Expiry at maturity is a form of settlement even though there is no additional exchange of consideration.

Query 6: Entity ABC enters into an interest rate swap with a counterparty (XYZ) that requires ABC to pay a fixed rate of 8 per cent and receive a variable amount based on three month LIBOR, reset on a quarterly basis. The fixed and variable amounts are determined based on a ₹ 100 million notional amount. ABC and XYZ do not exchange the notional amount. ABC pays or receives a net cash amount each quarter based on the difference between 8 per cent and three-month LIBOR. Alternatively, settlement may be on a gross basis. Determine whether an interest rate swap is a derivative financial instrument?

Answer

The definition of a derivative does not depend on gross or net settlement. The contract meets the definition of a derivative regardless of whether there is net or gross settlement because its value changes in response to changes in an underlying variable (LIBOR), there is no initial net investment, and settlements occur at future dates.Thus, an interest rate swap is a derivative financial instrument.

Query 7: Entity A makes a five-year fixed rate loan to Entity B, while B at the same time makes a five-year variable rate loan for the same amount to A. There are no transfers of principal at inception of the two loans, since A and B have a netting agreement. Is this a derivative?

Answer

Yes. This meets the definition of a derivative (that is to say, there is an underlying variable, no initial net investment or an initial net investment that is smaller than would be required for other types of contracts that would be expected to have a similar response to changes in market factors, and future settlement). The contractual effect of the loans is the equivalent of an interest rate swap arrangement with no initial net investment.

Query 8: Entity XYZ enters into a forward contract to purchase one million equity shares of T in one year. The current market price of T is ₹ 50 per share; the one-year forward price of T is ₹ 55 per share. XYZ is required to prepay the forward contract at inception with a ₹ 50 million payment. The initial investment in the forward contract of ₹ 50 million is less than the notional amount applied to the underlying, one million shares at the forward price of ₹ 55 per share, i.e., ₹ 55 million. Is the forward contract a derivative?

Answer

No. The initial net investment approximates the investment that would be required for other types of contracts that would be expected to have a similar response to changes in market factors because T's shares could be purchased at inception for the same price of ₹ 50. Accordingly, the prepaid forward contract does not meet the initial net investment criterion of a derivative instrument.

Query 9: In some markets the premium to be paid for deep in the money option is substantial (i.e., options are not leveraged). Would the option be a derivative instrument?

Answer

The premium paid on options generally fulfills the requirement of little or no initial investment as it is less than the amount required to obtain the underlying instrument outright, except when the option is so deep in the money that the premium paid is equivalent to making an investment in the underlying. In the latter case, the instrument is not a derivative but would be accounted as an investment in the underlying itself.

Query 10: Many derivative instruments, such as futures contracts and exchange traded written options, require margin accounts. Is the margin account part of the initial net investment?

Answer

No. The margin account is not part of the initial net investment in a derivative instrument. Margin accounts are a form of collateral for the counterparty or clearing house and may take the form of cash, securities or other specified assets, typically liquid assets. Margin accounts are separate assets that are accounted for separately.

Query 11: What is an embedded derivative?

Answer

An embedded derivative is a component of a hybrid (combined) instrument that also includes a non-derivative host contract – with the effect that some of the cash-flows of the combined instrument vary in a way similar to a stand-alone derivative.

Query 12: A lease contract contract contains a provision that rentals increase each year by ₹ 2 million. Is there an embedded derivative in this contract?

Answer

The price adjustment feature does not meet the definition of a derivative on a stand-alone basis since its value does not change in response to changes of some underlying. There is no underlying in this case; hence, there is no embedded derivative in the lease contract.

Query 13: How are embedded derivatives accounted for?

Answer

The accounting of embedded derivatives depends upon whether those embedded derivatives are closely related to the host contract or not. For example, if lease rentals in a lease contract are based on sales, the embedded derivative (ie. lease rentals deriving their value from sales) would be treated as closely related. Where the lease rentals are based on profits after tax, the embedded derivative would be treated as not closely related, since the risk correlation between profits after tax and lease rentals is not very high. In the former situation, the embedded derivative would not be separated and the entire lease contract would be accounted for in accordance with AS-19. In the latter situation, the embedded derivative would be separated and separately accounted for. It may be noted that embedded derivatives that are to be separated are accounted for like any other derivatives. This means that the fair value changes in the embedded derivative are recorded in the income statement.

Query 14: Can embedded derivatives be used for purposes of hedge accounting?

Yes, Embedded derivatives can also be used for purposes of hedge accounting, provided hedging conditions are fulfilled.

Query 15: One of the conditions for separating an embedded derivative from the host contract and accounting for as a derivative is that the economic characteristics and risks of the embedded derivative are not closely related to the economic characteristics and risks of the host contract. Explain it?

Answer

Generally, one has to evaluate if the risk involved in the embedded derivative and the host instruments are similar or dissimilar. Where the risks involved are similar then it is a closely related; where the risks are dissimilar then is not closely related. Whilst this is a general principle, one will have to be guided by the actual examples given in the standard, to conclude if the embedded derivative and the host are closely related or not.

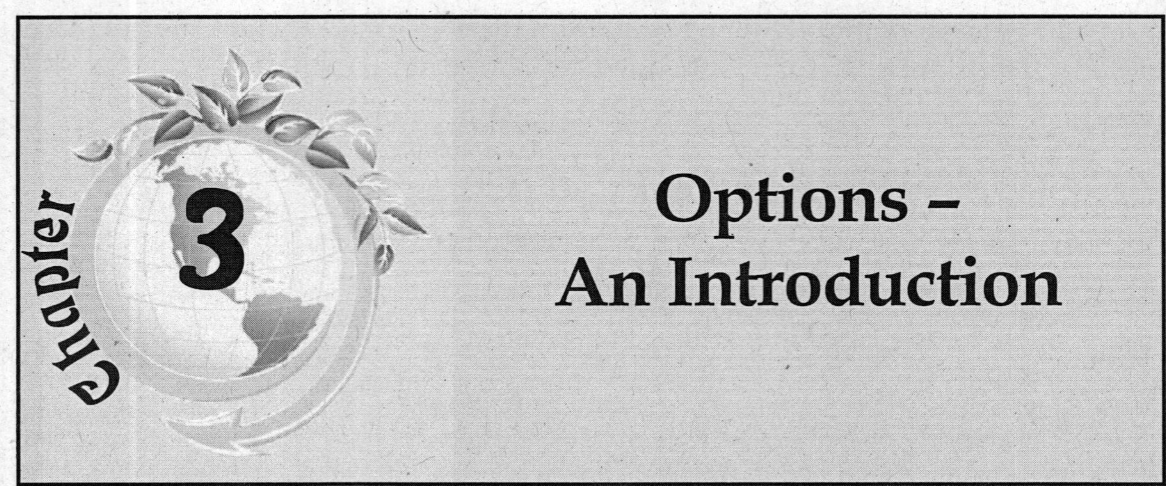

INTRODUCTION

Options are fundamentally different from forward and future contracts. An option gives the holder of the option the right to do something. The holder does not have to exercise this right. In contrast, in a forward or futures contract, the two parties have committed themselves to do something. Whereas it costs nothing (except margin requirements) to enter into a futures contract, the purchase of an option requires an upfront payment.

DIFFERENCE BETWEEN OPTIONS AND FUTURES

There are certain fundamental differences between a futures and an option contract.

Options	Futures
Only the seller (writer) is Obligated to perform. Premium is paid by thebuyer to the seller.	Both the parties areobligated to perform. No premium is paid by anyparty.
Loss is restricted while there is unlimited gain potential for the option buyer.	There is potential/risk forunlimited gain/ loss for thefutures buyer.
An option contract can be exercised any time during its currency by the buyer.	A futures contract has tobe honoured by both theparties only on the datespecified.

Types of Options

The options are of two types: a call option and put option.

Calls give the buyer the right but not the obligation to buy a given quantity of the underlying asset, at a given price on or before a given future date. In other words, a call option entitles the buyer to either seek delivery of shares from the writer if he so desires or let the call option lapse.

Puts give the buyer the right but not the obligation to sell a given quantity of the underlying asset at a given price on or before a given date. In other words a put option buyer is entitled to give delivery of shares to the writer if he so desires or let the put option lapse.

In brief, the right to purchase a specified stock is called call option, while the right to sell a specified stock is called a put option. Anyone is eligible to enter into an option contract as per the law of contract which can be writtenby a writer, who owns the stock and he is obliged to deliver upon exercise of the call. He has written, that is called a covered call writer and if the writer of call option does not own the stock, which he has written, is called uncovered or naked call writer and the option is called an uncovered or naked call option.

Obligation of the Option Writer and Option Buyer

Legally writer is obligated to perform to terms and condition of the option. In other words, the buyer of the option has bought a right to exercise the option and is under no obligation to exercise the option. Even he can let the option lapse an expiration date of the option.

Options Terminology

Index options: These options have the index as the underlying.

Stock options: Stock options are options on individual stocks. A contract gives the holder the right but no obligations to buy or sell shares at the specified price.

Buyer of an option: The buyer of an option is the one who by paying the - option premium buys the right but not the obligation to exercise his option on the seller/writer.

Writer of an option: The writer of a call/put option is the one who receives the option premium and is there by obliged to sell/buy the asset if the buyer wishes to exercise his option.

Call option: A call option gives the holder the right but not the obligation to buy an asset by a certain date for a certain price.

Put option: A put option gives the holder the right but not the obligation to sell an asset by a certain date for a certain price.

Option price: Option price is the price which the option buyer pays to the option seller. It is also referred to as the option premium.

Expiration date: The date specified in the options contract is known as the expiration date, the exercise date, the strike date or the maturity.

Strike price: The price specified in the options contract is known as the strike price or the exercise price.

American options: American options are options that can be exercised at any time upto the expiration date. Most exchange-traded options are American.

European options: European options are options that can be exercised only on the expiration date itself. European options are easier to analyse than American options, and properties of an American option are frequently deduced from those of its European counterpart.

In-the-money option: An in-the-money (ITM) option is an option that would lead to a positive cash-flow to the holder if it were exercised immediately. A call option on the index is said to be in-the-money when the current index stands at a level higher than the strike price (i.e., spot price > strike price). If the index is much higher than the strike price, the call is said to be deep ITM. In the case of a put, the put is ITM if the index is below the strike price.

At-the-money option: At-the-money (ATM) option is an option that would lead to zero cash-flow if it were exercised immediately. An option on the index is at-the-money when the current index equals the strike price (i.e., spot price = strike price).

Out-of-the-money option: An out-of-the-money (OTM) option is an option that would lead to a negative cash-flow it were exercised immediately. A call option on the index is out-of-the-money when the current index stands at a level which is less than the strike price (i.e., spot price – strike price). If the index is much lower than the strike price, the call is said to be deep OTM. In the case of a put, the put is OTM if the index is above the strike price.

Intrinsic value of an option: The option premium can be broken down into two components – intrinsic value and time value.

Intrinsic value refers to the value of a security which is intrinsic to or contained in the security itself. An option is said to have intrinsic value if the option is in-the-money. When out-of-the-money, its intrinsic value is zero. The intrinsic value for an in-the-money option is calculated as the absolute value of the differencebetween the current price of the underlying and the strike price of the option, floored to zero.

Time value of an option: The time value of an option is the difference between its premium and its intrinsic value. Both calls and puts have time value. An option that is OTM or ATM has only time value. Usually, the maximum time Value exists when the option is ATM. The longer the time to expiration, the greater is an option's time value, all else equal. At expiration, an option should have no time value.

Selection of Eligible Options for Trading

The following criteria will have to be met before a stock can be considered eligible for options trading.

- The stock should be amongst the top 200 scrips, on the basis of average market capitalisation during the last six months and the average free float market capitalisation should not be less than ₹ 750 crore. The free float market capitalisation means the non-promoter holding in the stock. The non-promoter holding in the company should be at least 30 per cent.
- The stock should be amongst the top 200 scrips on the basis of average daily volume (in value terms), during the last six months. Further, the average daily volume should not be less than ₹ 5 crore in the underlying cash market.
- The stock should be traded on at least 90 per cent of the trading days in the last six months.
- The ratio of the daily volatility of the stock vis-a-visthe daily volatility of the index should not be more than 4, at any time during the previous six months.
- The name of the company on whose stock the option contract has been derived.
- The quantity of the stock required to be delivered in the case of exercise of the option.
- The price at which the stock would be delivered, called the exercise price or the strike price.
- The date when the contract expires, called the expiration date.

Difference between American and European Options

The basic difference between an American and a European option lies in the exercise period/timing of each option. An American option can be exercised by the buyer any time during its currency, while European option may be exercised only during a limited period just before the expiry of the option.

Difference between Exchange Traded Options and Over-the-counter Options

Exchange traded options are standardised options and are traded on organised exchanges. By standardised, it means, the options which:

1. Have a uniform underlying asset,
2. Has a specified strike price and expiration date,
3. Has specified trading hours and **a specified** last trading day, and
4. Other features as may be desired.

Over-the-counter options or OTC options are customised options, sold directly by dealers instead of through an exchange. These are resorted to by, usually the institutional investors like banks, when they write customised interest rate and currency options for commercial clients. The parties to the contract negotiate the terms of these options.

Advantages of Buying Options

1. Risk is limited up to the amount of premium paid either for call or put options for the buyer, (while the risk is unlimited for seller of the option).
2. In the downward movement in the stock price, the buyer did not exercise the option and would allow it to lapse. In other words an option is not a liability of its holder (Or the buyer).
3. Buyer has a right to purchase exercise a specified number of shares of a particular company from the option writer (seller) at a exercise price at time up to the expiry of the option. The contract is only one way obligation i.e. the seller is obliged to deliver the contracted shares while the buyer has the choice to exercise the option or let the contract lapse (the buyer is not obligated to perform).

Disadvantages of Writing Options

The writer of an option is one who sells options, either call or put. It is generally advisable that investors should not write options, as the writer of option has limited upside i.e., the premium money and an unlimited downside.

PRICING OF OPTIONS

Option

Options are of two types – calls and puts. Calls give the buyer the right but not the obligation to buy a given quantity of the underlying asset, at a given price on or before a given future date. Puts give the buyer the right but not the obligation to sell a given quantity of the underlying asset at a given price on or before a given date.

Pricing of Option

There are various models which help us get close to the true price of an option. Most of these are variants of the Black Scholes model for pricing European option.

Black – Scholes Option Pricing Formulae

Black – Scholes Option Pricing Formulae is based on the following assumptions:

1. We are operating in a perfect market, i.e., there are no transaction costs or taxes, arbitrage opportunities do not exist, and there are no trading constraints
2. Funds can be borrowed and lent at the same risk less rate of interest of interest.
3. No dividends are paid on stocks
4. The option would be exercised only at expiration.
5. The price changes in the stock are continuous, i.e., smooth and not bumpy.

The Black and Scholes formula for computing a reasonable value of an option (C) is given as follows:

$$C = SN(d_1) - Ke^{l\text{-}rt)}N(d_2)$$

Where:

C = Theoretical call premium

S = Current Stock price

t = time until option expiration

K = option striking price

r = risk – free interest rate

N = Cumulative standard normal distribution

e = exponential term (2.7 183)

$$d_1 = \frac{\text{In } (S/K) + (R + S^2/2)t}{S\sqrt{t}}$$

s = standard deviation of stock returns

In = natural logarithm.

N (d_1) and N (d_2) represent the possibilities that deviation of less than d_1 and d_2 respectively will occur in a normal distribution that has a mean of 0 and a standard deviation of 1.

Example:

Consider a call option having the following features:

Price of share (*S*)	= ₹ 90
Exercise price (*k*)	= ₹ 100
Expiration period	= 3 months, i.e., 0.25 year
Risk factor (*s*)	= 50 per cent or 0.50
Exponential (*e*)	= 2.71828
*Risk-free int*erest rate (*r*)	= 10 per cent p.a.

On applying the above mentioned formulae of d_1, d_2 and *C* we get *C* = 5.03

If the call option is selling at a price more ₹ 5.03, then the investor should consider selling, i.e., writing thatcall option. However, in case the call option is selling for less than ₹ 5.03, then investor should buy that call option.

Factors Affecting Option Price

Various factors affect the price of options on stocks. We shall look at the impact of changes in each of these factors on option prices one at a time, assuming that all other factors remain the same. There are six factors affecting the price of a stock option:

The table 3.1 shows the effect of these factors on price of a stock option (Call/Put).

Table 3.1: Factors Effecting Price of a Stock Option

Factors	Call	Put
Current Stock Price	Increase in value of Stock Price results in increase in premium of call Options.	Increase in value of Stock Price results in decrease in premium of put options.
Expiration Time	Far off the expiration time, higher the premium of calloptions.	Far off the expiration time, higher the premium of putoptions.
Price Volatility	Higher the price volatility of the underlying stock ofthe call option, higher would be the premium.	Higher the price volatility of the underlying stock of the put option, higher would bethe premium.
Strike Price	As the Strike Price goes up, the chances of the option becoming profitable to exercise diminish and as such the premium on the option declines.	As the Strike Price goes up, the chances of the putoption yielding profit improve and accordingly the premium on the put option appreciates.
Interest Rates	Higher the interest rates, higher is the call option premium.	Higher the interest rates, higher is the put option premium.
Cash Dividends	Ex-dividend rate of the stock is usually lower than the cum dividend rate by an amount approximately equal to the cash dividend per share. The fall in the value of the stock decreases the value of the call option.	Ex-dividend rate of the stock is usually lower than the cum dividend rate by an amount approximately equal to the cash dividend per share. The fall in the value of the stock increases the value of the put option.

USING STOCK OPTIONS

Stock Option: Stock options are options on individual stocks. A contract gives the holder the right but no obligations to buy or sell shares at the specified price.

Using Stock Options: Stock Options are used by Speculators and Hedgers

Speculation: Stock futures can be used for speculation in following ways.

1. Bullish Stock, Buy Calls or Sell Puts

Consider a speculator who believes that a particular security is undervalued and expects its price to go up in next 2-3 months. Then he can buy that security in equity, or buy a futures contract. The same thing can be done by using options by buying calls or selling put options.

Example:

Take the case of a speculator who believes that the price of HLL will go up in the next three months. He could do any of the following:

He could buy the stock, hold it for two months and sell it off for a profit. Say for instance, he buys 200 shares of HLL at ₹ 150 a share, it would cost him ₹ 30,000. Assume that his belief proved correct and at end of three months HLL sells for ₹ 175. He would have earned ₹ 5,000 on an investment of ₹ 30,000, a return of 16.6 percent over a period of three months.

He could also have done the same thing by buying Call options or selling Put options on HLL.

Case I: Buy Calls

Let us assume that ATM calls on HLL with a strike of 150 trades at ₹ 18. He buys 200 calls which costs him ₹ 3,600. Assuming that his belief proves correct and three months later HLL trades at ₹ 175. After accounting for the call premium paid by him, he earns a net profit of ₹ 1,400, i.e., ([(175 – 150) – 18] × 200) on an investment of ₹ 3,600, a return of 38.8 per cent over three months.

Case II: Sell Puts

He can also sell 200 Puts of HLL with a strike price of 150 which is trading at ₹ 18 and received a premium of ₹ 3,600. Now, if his belief of rise in HLL price proves to be correct and HLL price rises to 175, then the buyer of the put will let the put expire and writer (seller) of the put gets to keep the premium, i.e., ₹ 3,600. However if his belief proves incorrect and HLL price comes down tosay 140, the buyer of the put will exercise on him, and the speculator would suffer a loss equal to difference between the spot price and the strike price less the premium received by the speculator earlier.

Thus, generally, it is advised that investors shall never sell/write options as the profits are limited to the extent of premium received but the losses can be unlimited.

2. Bearish Stock, Buy Puts or Sell Calls

Consider a speculator who believes that a particular is overvalued and expects its price to go down in next 2-3 months. In this code, he holds the same stock he can sell it and book profits and buy again at lower bands later.

If he does not hold the stock, then he can sell stock futures and buy again at lower levels. To execute this strategy using options he can buy put options or sell calls.

Example:

Take a case of Speculator who believes that the price of Maruti will go down in next three months. Then he can either buy put option or sell call option of Maruti

Case I: Buy puts

Assuming that Maruti trades of ₹ 800 in spot Market, he buys 100 ATM puts of Strike Price 800 available at a premium of ₹ 4. Which cost him ₹ 400. Now if his belief of fall in Maruti price proves to be correct and Maruti price does fall to ₹ 780 then the ATM puts that he had bought will now become ITM and will trade at ₹ 20, and he makes a profit of ₹ 1,600 [(20 – 4) × 100] in a period of three months.

Case II: Sell Calls

He sells 100 calls of strike price 800 available at a premium of ₹ 8 and receives a premium of ₹ 800 (6 × 100). Now if his belief of fall in Maruti price proves to be correct and Maruti price falls to ₹ 780 then the buyer of the calls will let the option expire and the writer (seller) of call gets to keep the premium, i.e., ₹ 800. However, if his belief proves to be incorrect and Maruti price rises to say 820, the buyer of the call option will exercise on him , and the speculator would suffer a loss equal to the difference between the spot price and the strike price less the premium received by the speculator earlier.

Thus, generally, it is advised that investors shall never sell/write options as the profits are limited to the extent of premium received but the losses can be unlimited.

Hedging: Have Stock, Buy Puts

If an investor is long on a security and he anticipates that the price of security may be volatile in near futures, then he can minimize his exposure to this unwanted risk due to volatile in stock price which he isanticipating, by hedging his position by selling that stock futures. The same strategy of hedging can be done by buying puts.

Example:

Consider an investor who holds 1000 shares of BHEL. He plans to sell the shares three months later as he would need the money to purchase a new flat. Today BHEL trades at ₹ 1,925 in the spot market. Investor worries about a fall in the price of BHEL in coming months, when he would actually need the money.

He could, of course, sell the shares today and get ₹ 1,925 for them. However, he does not want to lose on the possibility of an increase in share price in coming three months. Now, to ensure that he gets profit from increase in price of BHEL, but does not suffer losses due to decrease in price in BHEL, he buys put options on BHEL.

Consider that he buys put option with a strike price of ₹ 1,950 which trades of a premium of ₹ 30.

Case I: Price of BHEL falls to 1825

Now he suffers a loss of ₹ 100 per share but the put of strike price ₹ 1,950 which he bought at ₹ 30 now trades at ₹ 125. So this ensure that he practically lost only ₹ 5 [-100 + (125 - 30)] and he would get at least ₹ 1,920 per share of BHEL.

Case II: Price of BHEL rises to 2025

Now as the price of BHEL rises he lets his option to expire there by losing ₹ 30, but on other hand he gains ₹ 100 as he is able to sell BHEL shares at 2025, there by making net gain of ₹ 70 per share as compared to earlier price of ₹ 1,925.

OPEN INTEREST

Open interest is the total number of outstanding contracts that are held by market participants at the end of the day. In other words it can also be defined as the total number of futures contracts or option contracts that have not yet been exercised (squared off), expired, or fulfilled by delivery.

Generally, open interest applies to the futures market. Open interest, or the total number of open contracts on a security, is often helpful to confirm trends and trend reversals for futures and options contracts. It also helps to measure the flow of money into the futures market. For each seller of a futures contract there must be a buyer of that contract. Only one contract is created buy a seller and buyer.

So to determine the total open interest for any given market we need to know the totals from one side or the other, buyers or sellers, not the sum of both.

Each trading day at the end of the session open interest reports or represents the increase or decrease in the number of contracts for that day, and it is shown as a positive or negative number.

How to Calculate Open Interest?

Each trade completed on the exchange has an impact upon the level of open interest for that day. This we can understand by example given below.

Open interest will increase by one contract, if both parties to the trade are initiating a new position, one new buyer and one new seller.

Open interest will decline by one contract, if both traders are closing an existing or old position one old buyer and one old seller.

Open interest will not change if one old trader passing off his position to a new trader, one old buyer sells to one new buyer.

Benefits of Monitoring Open Interest

It is very important to monitor changes in the open interest figures at the end of each trading day, which indicates and concludes about the day's activity that has taken place.

Any Increasing open interest means that new money is flowing into the market place. The result will be that the present trend (up, down or sideways) will continue.

Any decrease in open interest means that the market is liquidating and implies that the prevailing price trend is coming to an end. FNO player is supposed to know open interest position daily which will help him in major market moves.

A leveling off an open interest is often an early warning of the end to an up trending or bull market.

Interpretation of Volume and Open Interest

Open interest is used in conjunction with volume, which represents the total number of shares or contracts that have changed hands in a one-day trading session in the commodities or options market. The greater the amount of trading during a market session, the higher the trading volume. A trader can easily see that the volume represents a measure of intensity or pressure behind a price trend. The greater the volume the more we can expect the existing trend to continue rather than reverse.

Sudden increase in volume precedes price, which means that the loss of either upside price pressure in an uptrend or downside pressure in a downtrend will show up in the volume figures before presenting itself as a reversal in trend on the bar chart.

Price	Open Interest	Volume	Interpretation
Rising	Rising	Rising	Market is Strong
Rising	Falling	Falling	Market is Weakening
Falling	Rising	Rising	Market is Weak
Falling	Falling	Falling	Market is Strengthening

So, price action increasing in an uptrend and open interest on the rise are interpreted as new money coming into the market reflecting new buyers and is considered as bullish in the market. If the price action isrising and the open interest is on the decline, short sellers covering their positions are causing the rally which brings bearishness and flow of money leaves the market.

If prices are in a downtrend and open interest is on the rise, chartists know that new money is coming into the market, showing aggressive new short selling. This scenario will prove out a continuation of a downtrend and a bearish condition. Lastly, if the total open interest is falling off and prices are declining, the price decline is being caused by disgruntled long position holders being forced to liquidate their positions. Technicians view this scenario as a strong position technically because the downtrend will end as all the sellers have sold their positions.

MARGINS – CLEARING AND SETTLEMENT (INF&O)

Margins for Futures

In order to have healthy competition among clearing members in reducing margins to attract customers, a mandatory minimum margin is obtained by the members from the customers. This saves the market against serious liquidity crisis arising out of possible defaults by the clearing members owing to insufficient margin retention.

In interest of smooth functioning of the market comprising the stock exchanges, clearing houses and the banks involved, the members collect margins from their clients as may be stipulated by the stock exchanges from time to time.

The members pass on the margins to the clearing house on the net basis, i.e., at a stipulated percentage of the net of purchase and sale position while they collect the margins from clients on gross basis, i.e., separately on purchases and sales. The stock exchange imposes margins as given below:

1. Buyer and seller have to pay initial margin.
2. Buyer and sellers have to settle their on marked to the market basis daily.

Marking to Market

All futures contracts for each member are marked-to-market (MTM) to the daily settlement price of the relevant futures contract at the end of each day. The profits/ losses are computed as the difference between:

1. The trade price and the day's settlement price for contracts executed during the day but not squared up.
2. The previous day's settlement price and the current day's settlement price for brought forward contracts.
3. The buy price and the sell price for contracts executed during the day and squared up.

The CMs who have a loss are required to pay the mark-to-market (MTM) loss amount in cash, which is in turn passed on to the CMs who have made a MTM profit. This is known as daily mark-to-market settlement. CMs are responsible to collect and settle the daily MTM profits/losses incurred by the TMs and their clients clearing and settling through them. Similarly, TMs are responsible to collect/pay losses/profits from/to their clients by the next day. The pay-in and pay-out of the mark-to-market settlement are affected on the day following the trade day.

Final Settlement for Futures

On the expiry day of the futures contracts, after the close of trading hours, NSCCL marks all positions of a CM to the final settlement price and the resulting profit/loss is settled in cash. Final settlement loss/profit amount is debited/credited to the relevant CM's clearing bank account on the day following expiry day of the contract.

Note:

Incase if the future Buy/Sell is not settled till expiry date, then it is automatically settled in profit or loss at end of expiry date as closing price and brokerage is not charged.

Settlement Price for Futures

Daily settlement price on a trading day is the closing price of the respective futures contracts on such day. The closing price for a futures contract is currently calculated as the last half an hour weighted average price of the contract in the F&O Segment of respective exchanges. Final settlement price is the closing price of the relevant underlying index/security in the capital market segment of respective exchanges, on the last trading day of the contract. The closing price of the underlying Index/security is currently its last half an hour weighted average value in the capital market segment of respective exchanges.

Settlement for Options

Options contracts have three types of settlements, daily premium settlement, exercise settlement, interimexercise settlement in the case of option contracts on securities and final settlement.

Daily Premium Settlement

Buyer of an option is obligated to pay the premium towards the options purchased by him. Similarly, the seller of an option is entitled to receive the premium for the option sold by him. The premium payable amount and the premium receivable amount are netted to compute the net premium payable or receivable amount for each client for each option contract.

Exercise Settlement

Although most option buyers and sellers close out their options positions by an offsetting closing transaction, an understanding of exercise can help an option buyer determine whether exercise might be more advantageous than an offsetting sale of the option. There is always a possibility of the option seller being assigned an exercise. Once an exercise of an option has been assigned to an option seller, the option seller is bound to fulfill his obligation, in other words pay the cash settlement amount in the case of a cash-settled option, even though he may not yet have been notified of the assignment.

Interim Exercise Settlement

Interim exercise settlement takes place only for option contracts on securities. An investor can exercise his in-the-money options at any time during trading hours, through his trading member. Interim exercise settlement is effected for such options at the close of the trading hours, on the day of exercise. Valid exercised option contracts are assigned to short positions in the option contract with the same series, i.e., having the same underlying, same expiry date and same strike price, on a random basis, at the client level. The CM who has exercised the option receives the exercise settlement value per unit of the option from the CM who has been assigned the option contract.

Final Exercise Settlement

Final exercise settlement is effected for all open long in-the-money strike price options existing at the close of trading hours, on the expiration day of an option contract. All such long positions are exercised and automatically assigned to short positions in option contracts with the same series, on a random basis. The investor who has long in-the-money options on the expiry date will receive the exercise settlement value per unit of the option from the investor who has been assigned the option contract.

Exercise Process

The period during which an option is exercisable depends on the style of the option. On NSE, index options are European style, i.e., options are only subject to automatic exercise on the expiration day, if they are m-the-money. As compared to this, options onsecurities are American style. In such cases, exercise is automatic on the expiration day, and voluntary prior to the expiration day of the option contract, provided they are in-the-money. Automatic exercise means that all in-the-money options would be exercised by NSCCL on the expiration day of the contract. The buyer of such options need not give an exercise notice in such cases. Voluntary exercise means that the buyer of an in-the-money option can direct his TM/CM to give exercise instructions to NSCCL. In order to ensure that an option is exercised on a particular day, the buyer must direct his TM to exercise before the cut-off time for accepting exercise instructions for that day. Usually, the exercise orders will be accepted by the system till the close of trading hours. Different TMs may have different cut-off times for accepting exercise instructions from customers, which may vary for different options.

An option, which expires unexercised, becomes worthless. Some TMs may accept standing instructions to exercise, or have procedures for the exercise of every option, which is in-the-money at expiration. Once an exercise instruction is given by a CM to NSCCL, it cannot ordinarily be revoked. Exercise notices given by a buyer at anytime on a day are processed by NSCCL after the close of trading hours on that day. All exercise notices received by NSCCL from the NEAT F&O system are processed to determine their validity. Some basic validation checks are carried out to check the open buy position of the exercising client/TM and if option contract is in-the-money. Once exercised contracts are found valid, they are assigned.

Assignment Process

The exercise notices are assigned in standardised market lots to short positions in the option contract with the same series (i.e., same underlying, expiry date and strike price) at the client level. Assignment to the short positions is done on a random basis. NSCCL determines short positions, which are eligible to be assigned and then allocates the exercised positions to any one or more short positions. Assignments are made at the end of the trading day on which exercise instruction is received by NSCCL and notified to the members on the same day.

It is possible that an option seller may not receive notification from its TM that an exercise has been assigned to him until the next day following the date of the assignment to the CM by NSCCL.

Exercise Settlement Computation

In case of index option contracts, all open long positions at in-the-money strike prices are automatically exercised on the expiration day and assigned to short positions in option contracts with the same series on a random basis. For options on securities, where exercise settlement may be interim or final, interim exercise for an open long in-the-money option position can be affected on any day till the expiry of the contract. Final exercise is automatically affected by NSCCL for all openlong in-the-money positions in the expiring month option contract, on the expiry day of the option contract. The exercise settlement price is the closing price of the underlying (index or security) on the exercise day (for interim exercise) or the expiry day of the relevant option contract (final exercise). The exercise settlement value is the difference between the strike price and the final settlement price of the relevant option contract.

For call options, the exercise settlement value receivable by a buyer is the difference between the final settlement price and the strike price for each unit of the underlying conveyed by the option contract, while for put options it is difference between the strike price and the final settlement price for each unit of the underlying conveyed by the option contract. Settlement of exercises of options on securities is currently by payment in cash and not by delivery of securities. It takes place for in-the-money option contracts.

The exercise settlement value for each unit of the exercised contract is computed as follows:

- Call options = Closing price of the security on the day of exercise – Strike price
- Put options = Strike price – Closing price of the security on the day of exercise

For final exercise the closing price of the underlying security is taken on the expiration day The exercisesettlement by NSCCL would ordinarily take place on 3rd day following the day of exercise. Members may ask for clients who have been assigned to pay the exercise settlement value earlier.

Client Margins

NSCCL intimates all members of the margin liability of each of their client. Additionally members are also required to report details of margins collected from clients to NSCCL, which holds in trust client margin monies to the extent reported by the member as having been collected form their respective clients.

CORPORATE ADJUSTMENTS

The basic premise for any adjustment for corporate actions is that the value of the position of the market participants, on the cum and ex-dates for the corporate action, should continue to remain the same as far as possible.

The corporate actions may be broadly classified under stock benefits and cash benefits. The various stock benefits declared by the issuer of capital are Bonus, Rights, Merger, De-merger, Amalgamation, Splits, Consolidations, Warrants, etc. The cash benefit declared by the issuer of capital is cash dividend.

The adjustment for corporate actions would be carried out on the last day on which a security is traded on a cum basis in the underlying equities market, after the close of trading hours.

The adjustments would be carried out on Strike price, Position and Market Lot, depending on type of corporate adjustment.

Adjustments due to Bonus and Stock Split

Table below shows the adjustment factor as applied to each of above mentioned Corporate Actions.

Corporate Actions	Adjustment Factor
Bonus (Ratio – A:B)	(A+B)/B
Stock Split (Ratio – A:B)	A/B

- *Strike Price:* The new Strike Price shall be calculated by dividing the old strike price by the adjustment factor, provided above.
- *Market Lot:* The new Market Lot shall be calculated by multiplying the old market lot by the adjustment factor, provided above.
- *Position:* The new Position shall be calculated by multiplying the old position by the adjustment factor, provided above.

Adjustments due to Right Issue

Consider Right Issue in Ratio A:B, at Premium – C, Face value of Shares being D, Exisitng Strike Price being X, existing lot being Y then,

- *Strike Price:* The new Strike Price shall be calculated as follows

  New Strike Price = ((B*X) +A*(C+D))/(A+B)

- *Market Lot:* The new Market Lot shall be calculated as follows

  New Market Lot = Y*(A+B)/B

Adjustments due to Dividends

Dividends which are below 10 per cent of the market value of the underlying stock would be deemed to be ordinarydividends and no adjustment in the Strike Price and Futures Price would be made for Ordinary Dividends. For extra-ordinary dividends, above 10 per cent of the market value of the underlying security, the Strike Price would be adjusted.

To decide whether the dividend is "extra-ordinary" (i.e., over 10 per cent of the market price of the underlying stock.), the market price would mean the closing price of the scrip on the day previous to the date on which the announcement of the dividend is made by the company after the meeting of the Board of Directors. However, in case where the announcement of dividend is made after the close of market hours, the same days closing price would be taken as the market price.

In case of declaration of "extra-ordinary" dividend by any company, the total dividend amount would be reduced from all the strike prices of the option contracts on that stock.

The revised Strike Prices would be applicable from the ex-dividend date specified by the exchanges.

Adjustments due to Mergers

On the announcement of the record date for the merger, the exact date of expiration (Last Cum-date) would be informed to members.

After the announcement of the Record Date, no fresh expiry month contracts on Futures and Options wouldbe introduced on the underlying, that will cease to exist subsequent to the merger.

Un-expired contracts outstanding as on the last cum-date would be compulsorily settled at the settlement price. The settlement price shall be the closing price of the underlying on the last cum-date.

Currency Options

OPTIONS

The buyer of an Option has the right, but NOT the obligation to buy or sell an agreed amount of a commodity on or before a specified future date.

The concept is somewhat similar to insurance where the buyer pays an amount of money, known as the premium – for certain rights. These can be taken up if you wish, but there is no obligation to do so.

Unlike insurance, however, there is no limit on the amount 'claimed'. You have an option to, for example, buy at a certain price and may do so, no matter how valuable the commodity in question may become.

An option to buy is known as a 'Call' Option while an option to sell is known as a 'Put' Option. The rate at which the buyer of the Option has the right to buy, or sell, is the 'strike' or 'exercise' price.

An Option, which can be 'exercised' at any time before it expires is described as an 'American' style Option. One, which can only be exercised on the 'expiry date' is called an 'European' style option.

Buying an Option protects against downside risk and at the same time gives upside potential. You establish the worst possible rate at which you will buy/sell a commodity, but still have the possibility of improving on this rate. The buyer, hence, has the best of both worlds.

Pay-off Profiles for Different Option Strategies

Pay-off profile implies the behaviour of returns (profits) from adopting different strategies. Each pay-off profile illustrates graphically how the value of each position changes as the relationship between strike/spot rate changes. In an Option strategy, all the gains/losses of a buyer will be the losses/gains of a seller. Hence, the pay-off profile of a seller will be mirror image of the pay-off profile of a buyer.

Long Call Option: A long Call i.e., the purchase of a Call, is an option to buy an asset at strike price. The maximum profit for the buyer of a Call Option is unlimited and maximum loss is limited to the extent of Option premium.

Short Call Option: A Short Call Option is the right to sell an asset at the strike price. The pay-off to the Short Call is the mirror image of that of the Long Call. Profit for the long is loss for the short and *vice versa*.

Long Put Option: A Long Put Option is an option to sell an asset at the strike price. As with any long position, the loss is limited to the premium paid with an unlimited potential for profit.

Short Put Option: A Short Put Option gives an obligation to buy an asset at the strike price if the buyer chooses to exercise the option. The profit and loss profile for a Short Put mirrors that of the long Put option.

Hedging with Currency Options

The hedger has an opportunity to hedge the exchange risk by using a simple Call or Put Option or by acquiring positions in multiple Options so that the combination provides a unique pay-off profile. The selection of an appropriate alternative by the hedger depends on the risk profile and view about the future market prices of the underlying asset.

Hedging for exporter: An Indian company exported goods to the US and expects payment after three months. The amount is equal to US$ 10 million. The amount of rupees the exporter will be receiving will depend on the spot rate of exchange prevailing then. Here, the exporter is exposed to vagaries of currency rates which may result in reduction of profit in the transaction or even a loss. The exporter, therefore, wants to hedge his rupee inflows through options. The hedge can be obtained by selecting one of the following alternatives.

Alternative 1: Buy a Put Option on US dollar with a strike price of ₹ 43 by paying a premium of ₹ 0.50.

Alternative 2: Sell a Call Option on US dollar with a strike price of ₹ 43 by paying a premium of ₹ 0.60.

Alternative 1: Exporter bought a Put Option at a strike price of ₹ 43.00 per dollar by paying a premium of ₹ 0.50 per dollar. Maturity of the contract is 3 months from now.

The table 4.1 provides the rupee inflows to the exporter depending on spot rate prevailing at the time of realisation of the receivables.

Table 4.1: Rupee Inflow to the Exporter

Exchange Rate (3 months hence) ₹/$	Option exercised Yes/No	₹ Inflow	Outflow on a/c of premium	Net inflow
40.00	Yes	43.00	0.50	42.50
40.50	Yes	43.00	0.50	42.50
41.00	Yes	43.00	0.50	42.50
41.50	Yes	43.00	0.50	42.50
41.90	Yes	43.00	0.50	42.50
42.00	Yes	43.00	0.50	42.50
42.50	Yes	43.00	0.50	42.50
43.00	Indifferent	43.00	0.50	42.50
43.50	No	43.50	0.50	43.00
44.00	No	44.00	0.50	43.50
44.10	No	44.10	0.50	43.60
44.50	No	44.50	0.50	44.00
45.00	No	45.00	0.50	44.50
45.50	No	45.50	0.50	45.00

At a ₹ 0.50 premium, the effective delivery price after three months would be 42.50 (i.e., 43.00 – 0.50) or more. If the dollar appreciates relative to the rupee well beyond the 43.00 level, the exporter will be able to sell the dollar currency at a spot price and hence the Option is allowed to expire. If the spot price is less than or equal to ₹ 43 then the Option is exercised. Thus, the exporter is able to benefit from two advantages that the Option market offered over the Forward market, namely an opportunity to profit from a rally in the currency market and protection against a drop in the currency.

Alternative 2: Exporter has another choice to hedge the receivables by selling the Call Option at a strike price of ₹ 43.00/$ by receiving premium of say ₹ 0.60 per dollar, for the contract maturing 3 months from now. The table 4.2 provides the rupee inflows to the exporter depending on the spot prices prevailing at the time of realisation of receivables.

Table 4.2: Rupee Inflow to the Exporter

Exchange Rate (3 months hence) ₹/$	Option exercised Yes/No	₹ Inflow	Outflow on a/c of premium	Net inflow
40.00	Yes	40.00	0.60	40.60
40.50	Yes	40.50	0.60	41.10
41.00	Yes	41.00	0.60	41.60

41.50	Yes	41.50	0.60	42.10
41.90	Yes	41.90	0.60	42.50
42.00	Yes	42.00	0.60	42.60
42.50	Yes	42.50	0.60	43.10
43.00	Indifferent	43.00	0.60	43.60
43.50	No	43.00	0.60	43.60
44.00	No	43.00	0.60	43.60
44.10	No	43.00	0.60	43.60
44.50	No	43.00	0.60	43.60
45.50	No	43.00	0.60	43.60
45.50	No	43.00	0.60	43.60

Considering the premium of ₹ 0.60 per dollar received for selling a Call Option, the effective delivery price after three months would be 43.60 (i.e., 43.00 + 0.60) or less. If the dollar appreciates relatively to the rupee well beyond the 43.00 level, the Option buyer will exercise the Call Option, the exporter will be able to deliver the dollar, received from exports to the buyer.

As we see from both the tables, we find that rupee inflow under alternative 1 is higher than the inflow under alternative 2 when the spot rate is less than ₹ 41.90 and when the spot rate is more than ₹ 44.10. Whereas the inflow under alternative 2 is more than the inflow under alternative 1 when the spot rate lies between ₹ 41.90 and ₹ 44.10. The net gain from the Put Option will not exceed that of the Call Option until the rupee appreciates sufficiently to generate an intrinsic value for the Put Option of 0.50 (premium paid for put) plus 0.60 (premium received for call). So selling Call Option is superior to buying Put if the expected spot price at the maturity lies within the range of strike prices + the sum of two premiums. Thus, the selection of long Put or short Call depends on the expectation of the hedger about the spot prices that are likely to prevail at the time of exercising the Option.

Hedging for importer: An Indian company is importing goods from Gulf country after three months. The payment is expected to be made in dollars at the time of importing goods. The value of import is US$ 10 million. The amount of rupees the importer will be paying will depend on the spot rate of exchange prevailing then. Here, the importer is exposed to vagaries of currency rates which may result in reduction of profit in the transaction or even resulting in a loss. He, therefore, wants to hedge his rupee outflows through currency Options. The hedge can be obtained by selecting one of the two alternatives.

Alternative 1: Buy Call Option on US$ with a strike price of ₹ 43 by paying premium of ₹ 0.60 per dollar.

Alternative 2: Sell Put Option on US$ with a strike price of ₹ 43 by receiving premium of ₹ 0.50 per dollar.

Alternative 1: Indian company bought Call Option at a strike price of ₹ 43.00 per dollar by paying a premium of ₹ 0.60 per dollar. Maturity of the contract is 3 months from now. The table 4.3 provides the rupee outflows to the importer depending on the spot price prevailing at the time of realisation of payables.

Table 4.3: Rupee Outflows to the Importer

Exchange Rate (3 months hence) ₹/$	Option exercised Yes/No	₹ Inflow	Outflow on a/c of premium	Net inflow
40.00	Yes	40.00	0.60	40.60
40.50	Yes	40.50	0.60	41.10
41.00	Yes	41.00	0.60	41.60
41.50	Yes	41.50	0.60	42.10
41.90	Yes	41.90	0.60	42.50
42.00	Yes	42.00	0.60	42.60
42.50	Yes	42.50	0.60	43.10
43.00	Indifferent	43.00	0.60	43.60
43.50	No	43.00	0.60	43.60
44.00	No	43.00	0.60	43.60
44.10	No	43.00	0.60	43.60
44.50	No	43.00	0.60	43.60
45.00	No	43.00	0.60	43.60
45.50	No	43.00	0.60	43.60

The effective price after three months would be 43.60 (i.e., 43.00 + 0.60) or less. If the dollar depreciates relative to the rupee below the 43.00 level, the company will be able to buy the dollar currency at a spot price and hence the Option is allowed to expire. If the spot price is more than ₹ 43.00 or equal then the Option is exercised.

Alternative 2: The Indian company has another alternative to hedge the dollar payables by selling the Put Option at a strike price of ₹ 43.00 per dollar by receiving premium of say ₹ 0.50 per dollar, for the contract maturing 3 months from now. The table 4.4 provides the rupee outflows to the importer depending on the spot price prevailing at the time of realisation of payables.

Table 4.4: Rupee Outflows to the Importer

Exchange Rate (3 months hence) ₹/$	Option exercised Yes/No	₹ Inflow	Outflow on a/c of premium	Net inflow
40.00	Yes	40.00	0.50	42.50
40.50	Yes	40.50	0.50	42.50
41.00	Yes	41.00	0.50	42.50
41.50	Yes	41.50	0.50	42.50
41.90	Yes	41.90	0.50	42.50
42.00	Yes	42.00	0.50	42.50
42.50	Yes	42.50	0.50	42.50
43.00	Indifferent	43.00	0.50	42.50
43.50	No	43.00	0.50	42.50
44.00	No	43.00	0.50	43.00
44.10	No	43.00	0.50	43.50
44.50	No	43.00	0.50	43.60
45.00	No	43.00	0.50	44.00
45.50	No	43.00	0.50	45.50

Considering the premium of ₹ 0.60 per dollar received for selling a Call Option, the effective delivery price after three months would be 43.60 (i.e., 43.00 + 0.60) or less. If the dollar depreciates relative to the rupee well below the 43.00 level, the Option buyer will exercise the Put Option, the importer will be able to take delivery of the dollar which will be used for import payments.

As we see from tables 4.3 and 4.4, rupee outflow under alternative 1 is less than the outflow under alternative 2 when the spot rate is less than ₹ 41.90 and or more than ₹ 44.10. The outflow under alternative 2 is less than the outflow under alternative 1 when the spot rate lies between ₹ 41.90 and ₹ 44.10. The net gain from the Call Option will not exceed that of the Put Option until the rupee depreciates sufficiently to generate an intrinsic value for the Put Option at 0.50 (premium received for put) plus 0.60 (premium paid for call). So selling Put Option is superior to buying Call if the expected spot price at the maturity lies within range of strike price + the sum of two premiums. The selection of long Call or Short put depends on the expectation of the hedger about the spot prices that are likely to prevail at the time of exercising the Option.

Example: Strategy with call Option.

X = $ 0.68/DM

C = 2.00 cents/DM

On expiry date of Option (assuming European type), the gain or loss will depend on the then Spot rates (S_t) as shown in the Table No. 4.5.

Table 4.5: Spot Rates and Financial Impact of Call Option

S_t	Gain (+)/Loss (-)for the buyer of call option
$ 0.6000	- $ 0.02
$ 0.6200	- $0.02
$ 0.6400	- $ 0.02
$ 0.6500	- $ 0.02
$ 0.6600	- $ 0.02
$ 0.6700	- $ 0.02
$ 0.6800	- $ 0.02
$ 0.6900	- $0.01
$ 0.7000	$0.00
$0.7100	+ $0.01
$ 0.7200	+ $ 0.02
$ 0.7400	+ $ 0.04
$ 0.7600	+ $ 0.06

- For S_t < $ 0 68/DM, the Option is allowed to lapse. Since DM can be bought at a lower price than X, the loss is lim-ited to the premium paid, i.e., $ 0.02.
- At S_t > 0.68, the Option will be exercised.
- Between 0.68 < S_t < 0.70, a part of loss is recouped.
- At S_t > 0.70, net profit is realised.

Reverse profit profile is obtained for the writer of call Option.

Example: Strategy with put Option.

Spot rate at the time of buying put Option: $ 1.7000/E

X = $ 1.7150/£

p = $ 0.06/E

The gain/loss for the buyer of put Option on expiry are given n Table 4.6

- For S_t > 1.7150, the Option will not be exercised since Pound sterling has higher price in the market. There will be net loss of $ 0.06.
- For 1.6550 < S_t < 1.7150, Option will be exercised, but there will be net loss.

- For S_t < 1.6550, the Option will be exercised and there will be net gain.

Table 4.6: Spot Rate and Financial Impact of Put Option

S_t	Gain (+)/Loss (-)
1.6050	+0.050
1.6150	+0.040
1.6250	+0.030
1.6350	+0.020
1.6450	+0.010
1.6500	+0.005
1.6550	+0.000
1.6600	- 0.005
1.6650	-0.010
1.6750	- 0.020
1.6850	- 0.030
1.6950	- 0.040
1.7050	-0.050
1.7150	-0.060
1.7250	- 0.060
1.7350	- 0.060

The reverse will be the profit profile of the seller of Option.

Example: A straddle is bought with the following data: X = \$ 1.7495/E, c = \$ 0.0031/£, p = \$ 0.0091/£ Prepare the profit profile.

Solution: Table gives the profit profile.

Table 4.7: Profit Profile with Straddle

S_1	Gain/loss on call	Gain/loss on put	Net gain/lost
1.7065	-0.0031	0.0339	0.0308
1.7145	-0.0031	0.0259	0.0228
1.7155	-0.0031	0.0249	0.0218
1.7265	-0.0031	0.0139	0.0108
1.7373	-0.0031	0.0031	0.0000
1.7425	-0.0031	-0.0021	-0.0052
1.7440	-0.0031	-0.0036	-0.0067
1.7455	-0.0031	-0.0051	-0.0082

1.7475	-0.0031	-0.0071	-0.0102
1.7495	-0.0031	-0.0091	-0.0122
1.7516	-0.0010	-0.0091	-0.0101
1.7545	0.0019	-0.0091	-0.0072
1.7575	0.0049	-0.0091	-0.0042
1.7605	0.0079	-0.0091	-0.0012
1.7617	0.0091	-0.0091	0.0000
1.7635	0.0109	-0.0091	0.0018
1.7665	0.0139	-0.0091	0.0048
1.7695	0.0169	-0.0091	0.0078
1.7725	0.0199	-0.0091	0.0108
1.7755	0.0229	-0.0091	0.0138
1.7785	0.0259	-0.0091	0.0168
1.7815	0.0289	-0.0091	0.0198
1.7855	0.0329	-0.0091	0.0238
1.7885	0.0359	-0.0091	0.0268
1.7925	0.0399	-0.0091	0.0308

Butterfly Spread

Long butterfly spread means buying two calls with middle strike price (X_1) and selling each with lower (X_1) and higher (X_3) strike price respectively. Likewise, a short butterfly in-volves selling two calls with middle strike price (X_2) and simul-taneously buying each with lower (X_1) and higher (X_2) strike prices respectively.

Example: Tabulate and draw graphically the profit profile of a long butterfly with the following data:

X, = \$ 0.7450/SFr; c, = \$ 0.0155/SFr

X_2 = \$ 0.7550/SFr; c_2 = \$ 0.0115/SFr

X_3 = \$ 0.7650/SFr; c_3 = \$ 0.0080/SFr

Solution: The cost of butterfly spread = 2 × c_2 – (c, + c_3)

= 2 × 0.0115 – (0.0155 + 0.0080) = – 0.0005

Thus, the investor in fact receives a sum = \$ 0.0005/SFr in the beginning. There are four scenarios when the options matures

(a) $S_t < X_1$

In this case none of the options are exercised and the investor makes a profit equal to the initial amount received by him, i.e., \$ 0.0005/SFr.

(b) $X_1 < S_t < X_2$

In this case, the call with exercise price X_p, i.e., \$ 0.745C is exercised, while the other two are not exercised. The profit of the investor is given by

Profit = – $(S_t - X_1)$ + initial amount received or

Profit = – $(S_t - X_1)$ + 0.0005 (7.7a)

Profit has been calculated for various values S_t between X_1 and X_2 in Table 4.8

Table 4.8: Profit Profile for Long Butterfly Spread for $X_1 < S_t < X_2$

S_1 (\$/£)	Profit/Loss (\$/£)
0.7450	0.0005
0.7460	(0.0005)
0.7470	(0.0015)
0.7480	(0.0025)
0.7490	(0.0035)
0.7500	(0.0045)
0.7510	(0.0055)
0.7520	(0.0065)
0.7530	(0.0075)
0.7540	(0.0085)
0.7550	(0.0095)

(c) $X_2 < S_t < X_3$

In this case, the calls with prices 0.7450 and 0.7550 are exercised.

The profit is given = – $(S_t - X_1) + 2(S_t - X_2)$ + initial amount received

$= - S_t + X_1 + 2\,S_t - 2\,X_2 + 0.0005$

(7.7b) $= S_t + X_1 - 2X_2 + 0.0005$

Profit has been calculated for various values of S_t between X_2 and X_3 in the table 4.9:

Table 4.9: Profit Profile for Long Butterfly Spread for $X_1 < S_t < X_3$

S_1 ($/£)	Profit/Loss ($/£)
0.7650	0.0005
0.7640	(0.0005)
0.7630	(0.0015)
0.7620	(0.0025)
0.7610	(0.0035)
0.7600	(0.0045)
0.7590	(0.0055)
0.7580	(0.0065)
0.7570	(0.0075)
0.7560	(0.0085)
0.7550	(0.0095)

(d) $S_t > X_3$

In this case all the three options are exercised and is given by

$= -(S_t - X_1) + 2(S_t - X_2) - (S_t - X_1) +$ Initial pay received

$= -S_t + X_1 + 2S_t - 2X_2 - S_t + X_3 + 0.0005$

$= X_1 - 2X_2 + X_3 + 0.0005$

$= 0.7450 - 2(0.7550) + 0.7650 + 0.0005$

$= 0.0005$

Thus, the investor makes a constant profit of $ 0.0005 this case.

Example: The exporter Vikrayee knows that he would receive US $ 5,00,000 in three months. He buys a put option of three months maturity at a strike price of ₹ 43.00/US $. Spot rate is ₹ 43.00/US $. Forward rate is also ₹ 43.00/US $. Premium to be paid is 2.5 per cent.

Show various possibilities of how Option is going to be exer-cised.

Solution: The exporter pays the premium immediately, that is, a sum of 0.025 × $ 5,00,000 × ₹ 43.00 = ₹ 5,37,500. Now let us examine different possibilities that may occur at the time of settlement of the receivables.

(a) The rate becomes ₹ 42/US $. That is, the US dollar has depreciated. In this situation, put Option holder would like to make use of his Option and sell his dollars at the strike price, ₹ 43.00 per dollar. Thus, net receipts would be:

₹ 43 × $ 5,00,000 – ₹ 43.00 × 0.025 × $ 5,00,000

= ₹ 43 × $ 5,00,000 (1 – 0.025)

= ₹ 41.925 × 5,00,000 = ₹ 2,09,62,500

If he had not covered, he would have received ₹ 42 × 5,00,000 or ₹ 21,00,000. But he would not be certain about the actual amount to be received until the date of maturity.

(b) Dollar rate becomes ₹ 43.50. This means that dollar has appreciated a bit. In this case, the exporter does not stand to gain anything by using his Option. He sells his dollars directly in the market at the rate of ₹ 43.50. Thus, the net amount that he receives is:

₹ 43.50 × $ 5,00,000 × ₹ 43.00 × 0.025 × $ 5,00,000

= ₹ (43.50 – 43.00 × 0.025) × $ 5,00,000

= ₹ 42.425 × $ 5,00,000

= ₹ 2,12,12,500

If he had not covered, he would have got ₹ 43.50 × $ 5,00,000 or ₹ 21,750,000.

(c) Dollar rate, on the date of settlement, becomes ₹ 43.00, that is, equal to strike price. In this case also, the exporter does not gain any advantage by using his option. Thus, the net sum that he gets is:

₹ 43.00 × 5,00,000 – ₹ 43 × 0.025 × 5,00,000

= ₹ (43 – 43 × 0.025) × 5,00,000

= ₹ 2,09,62,500

It is apparent from the above calculations that irrespective of the evolution of the exchange rate, the minimum amount that he is sure to get is ₹ 2,09,62,500 and any favourable evolution of exchange rate enables him to reap greater profit.

Note: Covering with put option becomes more beneficial than forward cover if the appreciation of dollar is greater than the amount of premium. In the above example, if US dollar becomes more than ₹ 44.075 (43 + 43 × 0.025), covering with options turns out to be better than covering with forward.

Example: A French exporter, Robin, has exported his product to UK for an amount of £ 5,00,000. He is to receive payment after three months. He wants to cover his receivables. The following data is available. Indicate what Robin should do.

Spot rate: Euro 1.4000/E

Put option strike price: Euro 1.4000/E

Premium: 2.80 per cent

Option Maturity: 3 months

Solution: At the beginning, Robin pays upfront premium of £ 0.028 × £ 5,00,000 or Euro 0.028 × £ 5,00,000 × 1.4000 or Euro 19,600.

Thus, Robin ensures for himself a minimum amount of Euro 5,00,000 × (1 – 0.028) × 1.400 or Euro 6,80,480.

This also means that Robin ensures for himself a minimum rate of Euro 6,80,400/ 5,00,000 per pound or Euro 1.3608/E. This rate is called break-even point.

If on the date of settlement, Pound sterling depreciates to, say Euro 1.37/E, Robin exercises his Option and receives Euro 6,80,400.

In case Pound sterling appreciates to, say, Euro 1.43, Robin does not use his put Option and sells Pounds directly to the market.

Example: An American company has sold put Option. Strike price is \$ 1.1607/ Euro and premium \$ 0.0 I/Euro. Complete

By indicating profits that the company would make for the following spot rates on the date of maturity.

Table 4.10: Spot Rate Data

S_t	1.1507	1.1520	1.1607	1.1615	1.1620	1.1720
Profit or Loss						

Solution: Since the company has sold a put Option on Euro, it has received the premium amount upfront. Thus, its profit will be:

$$-(X - S_t - p) \text{ for } X > S_t\}$$

or

$$p \qquad \text{for } X < S_t\}$$

Therefore, the profit of the seller of the option is

$$\text{Profit } S_t + p - X = S_t + 0.01 - 1.1607$$

$$= S_t - 1.1507 \text{ for } X > S_t \text{ or}$$

$$\text{Profit } = p = 0.01 \text{ for } X < S_t$$

Table will look like as follows:

S_t	1.1507	1.1520	1.1607	1.1615	1.1620	1.1720
Profit or Loss	0.00	0.0013	0.01	0.01	0.01	0.01

Example: An American speculator has purchased a put Option on Pound sterling with a premium of \$ 0.04/£. Exercise price is \$ 1.65. At the time of the exercise of the Option, spot rate is \$ 1.50. The standard size of the put Option is £ 31250. What is the profit made on this Option ?

Solution: Premium paid p = \$ 0.04/£

Profit per unit pound seteting = X – St

= \$ 1.65 – \$ 1.50

= \$ 0.15

Net Profit = \$ 0.15 – 0.04

= \$ 0.11

Total profit on the option = \$ 0.11 × £ 31250 = \$ 3437.50

Example: An importer, Krayee, is to pay one million US dollars in two months. He wants to cover exchange risk will call Option. The data are as follows:

Spot rate, forward rate and strike price are ₹ 43.00 per do lar. The premium is 3 per cent. Discuss various possibilities that may occur for the importer.

Solution: The importer pays the premium amount immediate That is, a sum of ₹ 43 × 0.03 × 10,00,000 or ₹ 1.290.00C paid as premium.

Let us examine the following three possibilities.

(a) Spot rate on the date of settlement becomes ₹ 42.50 That is, there is slight depreciation of US dollar. In such a situation, the importer does not exercise his Option and buys US dollars from the market directly. The net amount that he pays is:

₹ (42.50 × \$ 10,00,000 + 43 × 0.03 × \$ 10,00,000)

or

₹ 4,37,90,000

(b) Spot rate, on the settlement date, is ₹ 43.75 per US dollar. Evidently, the US dollar has appreciated. In this case, the importer exercises his Option. Thus, the net sum that he pays is:

₹ 43 × \$ 10,00,000 + ₹ 43 × 0.03 × \$ 1,00,000

or

₹ 43 × 1.03 × \$ 10,00,000

or

₹ 4,42,90,000

(c) Spot rate, on the settlement, is the same as the strike price. In such a situation, the importer does not exercise Option, or rather, he is indifferent between exercise and non-exercise of the Option. The net payment that he makes is:

₹ 43 × 1.03 × \$ 10,00,000

or

₹ 4,42,90,000

Thus, the maximum rate paid by the importer is the exercise price plus the premium.

Example: An importer of France has imported goods worth US \$ 1 million from USA. He wants to cover against the likely appreciation of dollors against Euro. The data are as follows:

Spot rate: Euro 0.9903/US $

Strike price: Euro 0.99/US $

Premium: 3 per cent

Maturity: 3 months

What are the operations involved?

Solution: While buying a call Option, the importer pays upfront the premium amount of:

$ 10,00,000 × 0.03

or

Euro 10,00,000 × 0.03 × 0.9903

or

Euro 29,709

Thus, the importer has ensured that he would not have to pay more than

Euro 10,00,000 x 0.99 + Euro 29709

or

Euro 10,19,709

On maturity, following possibilities may occur:

(a) US dollar appreciates to, say, Euro 1.0310. In this case, the importer exercises his call Option and thus pays only Euro 10,19,709 as calculated above.

(b) US dollar depreciates to, say, Euro 0.9800. Here, the importer abandons the call Option and buys US dollar from the market. His net payment is Euro (0.9800 × 10,00,000 + 29,709) or Euro 10,09,709.

(c) US dollar remains at Euro 0.99. In this case, the importer is indifferent. The sum paid by him is Euro 10,19,709.

Example: A company bids for a contract for a sum of 1 million US dollars. While the period of response is 6 months, the current exchange rate is ₹ 43.50 per US dollar. Six month forward rate is ₹ 44.50 per US dollar.

Premium for a put option of 6 months maturity is 3 per cent with a strike price of ₹ 43.50.

Discuss various possibilities of losses/gains in case the enterprise decides to cover or not to cover.

Solution:

(a) If the enterprise does not cover and the dollar rate decreases, the potential loss is unlimited.

(b) If the enterprise covers on forward market and if its bid is not accepted and the dollar rate increases, its potential loss is unlimited, since the enterprise will be required to deliver dollars to the bank after buying them at a higher rate.

(c) If the enterprise buys a put option, it pays the premium amount of ₹ 0.03 × $ 10,00,000 × 43.50 or ₹ 13,05,000.

Now, there may be two situations:

1. The bid is accepted and the rate on the date of acceptance is ₹ 42.00 per dollar, i.e., the US dollar has depreciated. In this case, the put option is resold (exercised) with a gain of ₹ (43.50 – 42.00) × $ 10,00,000 or ₹ 15,00,000.

   After deducting the premium amount, the net gain works out to be ₹ 1,95,000 (₹ 15,00,000 – ₹ 13,05,000). And, future receipts are sold on forward market.

   Other possibility is that the bid is accepted but the US dollar has appreciated to ₹ 44.00. In that case, the Option is abandoned. And, the future receipts are sold on forward market.

2. The bid is not accepted and the US dollar depreciates to ₹ 42.00. In that case, the enterprise exercises its put option and makes a net gain of ₹ 1,95,000.

In case the bid is not accepted and US dollar appreciates, the enterprise simply abandons its Option and its loss is equal to the premium amount paid.

Example: An American football team plans to come to France to play the following year. The team will receive Euro 2 million in addition to all other expenses. The team anticipates a depreciation of Euro against dollar. Besides, the National Football League will take three months to decide on whether to play in France or not. How can the Football team cover its foreign exchange position?

Solution: The team can buy put Option on Euro, with maturity of 3 months. If National League does not give permission to play in France and Euro appreciates in the meantime, the team will let the put Option expire and suffer the loss equal to the premium paid. 'If League gives permission to play and Euro depreciates, the team can resell (exercise) its put Option with a profit and it can sell forward its receipt of Euro 2 million.

Example: The data below give hypothetical tunnels with narrow as well as wide ranges:

Maturity	**Narrow range**	**Wide range**
One month 3 months	₹ 42.50 – 43.50	₹ 41.50 – 44.60
6 months	₹ 42.80 – 43.90	₹ 41.60 – 44.80
	₹ 42.90 – 44. 10	₹ 41.75 – 45.00

An exporter wants to cover against a decline in the US dollar. Suppose he is to receive one million US dollars in 3 months and he covers by selling a tunnel (a combination of selling a call and buying a put) of wide range (anticipating wider fluctuations in exchange rate) that is, a tunnel with the range of ₹ 41.60 – 44.80. If on the maturity date, the dollar rate is lower than ₹ 41.60, he will sell his dollars at the rate of ₹ 41.60. On the other hand, if the dollar rate is higher than ₹ 44.80, he will get only ₹ 44.80. However, if the dollar rate happens to be between the tunnel boundaries on the date of maturity, he will sell at the actual spot rate.

An importer will buy a tunnel (i.e., combine buying of call and selling of put).

What is the significance of buying a tunnel? It signifies that the buyer of the tunnel is ready to accept a potential loss of up to ₹ 41.60 in the hope of buying his dollars at the rate of ₹ 44.80. And, the seller of a tunnel is ready to accept potential loss beyond the rate of ₹ 44.80 in the hope of buying the dollars at a rate of ₹ 41.60.

Example: A classical FFr/US dollar call Option is bought at a premium of 2 per cent while the average rate option is bought at a premium of 1.8 per cent. The spot rate is FFr 6.10. The other rates are given below:

	Classical Option	Average rate Option
Exercise price	FFr 6.20	FFr 6.20
Rate at maturity	FFr 6.40	—
Average rate for maturity period	—	FFr 6.38

The amount covered is one million US dollars. Compare the gains in the two cases.

Solution: In the case of classical call Option, the net gain is:

FFr (6.40 - 6.20) – (6.10 × 0.02) per US dollar

or

FFr 0.078 per US dollar

Total net gain is FFr 0.078 × $ 10,00,000

or

FFr 78,000

And, the gain in the case of average rate option is:

FFr (6.38 – 6.20) – (6.10 × 0.018) per US dollar

or

FFr 0.0702 per US dollar

Total net gain with average rate option is:

FFr 0.0702 × 10,00,000

or

FFr 70,200

The main advantage of average rate option over the classical one is that premium demanded on the former is lower. The net gain may be lower or higher than the classical one, depending on how the rate up to/at maturity has moved.

It is obvious that, if the option is out of money at the maturity date, the option holder does not receive anything. His loss is limited to the amount of the premium.

Average rate options may be used to cover a continuing flow of cash in a particular currency.

Example: Using the following data, find out the value of call option premium:

p = \$ 0.024; X = \$ 0.70/DM

3-m forward rate S_f = \$ 0.7 I/DM

3-m US interest rate t_n = 10 per cent per annum.

Solution: Here, DM is being treated as foreign currency. The following equation can be used to find c.

$$p = c + B_h [X - S_f]$$

$$0.024 = c + \frac{1}{1+0.1\times\frac{3}{12}} [0.70 - 0.71]$$

$$\Rightarrow c = 0.024 \times \frac{0.01}{1.025}$$

or

$$c = \$\ 0.03375/DM$$

Currency Swaps

INTRODUCTION

A Swap can be defined as an exchange of obligations by two parties. For instance, in an Interest Rate Swap (IRS), one company arranges with another to exchange interest rate payments.

There are many types of Swaps like Asset Swaps, Currency Swaps and so on. However, the most important one is an Interest Rate Swap (IRS). One company may be paying fixed rate of interest but prefers floating rates. Another company may be paying a floating rate, but would find a fixed rate advantageous. Thus, it makes sense for both the companies to enter into an IRS agreement.

An important advantage of IRS is that different firms can access funds at varying rates and terms. They may not always find these terms beneficial. So when two parties find each other's terms beneficial, they enter into Swap agreements. IRS enables them to access sources of funding at better rates than what they would be able to achieve on a direct basis.

It is important to note that the principal amount is purely "notional." It exists only to facilitate the calculation of interest. There is no physical exchange of principal in single currency IRS. As per the agreement terms, the difference is settled in cash at the end of the stipulated period. The IRS is for a period that is agreed upon at the time of entering into the agreement.

Example

Companies A and B want to borrow the same amount. Company A can borrow @14 per cent fixed or @PLR + 2 per cent Company B can borrow @12 per cent fixed or @PLR + 1 per cent Company B has an absolute advantage in both areas. Still it makes sense for them to enter into an IRS. Company A prefers a fixed rate and Company B prefers a floating rate. They enter into an IRS whereby A pays B 13.5 per cent while B pays A PLR + 2 per cent. Now, A pays PLR + 2 per cent to the bank but receives the same from B. As a result, A has to pay only 13.5 per cent, thus, saving 0.5 per cent. B pays 12 per cent to the bank but receives 13.5 per cent from A. Hence, the net effect for B is PLR + 0.5 per cent (2 per cent – 1.5 per cent). Thus, the IRS is advantageous to both.

There are various other types of IRS, prominent amongst which are:

- *Amortising Swaps:* In these Swaps, the notional principal amount on which the interest calculations are based, decreases according to a pre-determined schedule. The main demand for this type of Swap is from customers of banks who wish to match repayment schedules on loans as precisely as possible
- *Accreting Swaps:* These are similar to Amoritising Swaps, except that the notional principal amount increases according to a pre-determined schedule.
- *Roller coasters:* This type, which combines both features, are most often used in connection with long-term project financing. The notional principal increases and reduces during the life of the transaction, going up and down according to a schedule agreed at the time of the deal.
- *Forward start:* These Swaps have become more, and more commonplace. They simply involve agreement of all the details, including the price, at the point when the deal is transacted - for an IRS that starts, say, and 6 months' later.

CROSS CURRENCY SWAPS

Cross Currency Swaps are similar to IRS, and involve more than one currency. They are often undertaken as a result of some underlying transaction such as bonds.

The market of currency swaps has been developing at rapid pace for the last fifteen years. As a result, this is no the second most important market after the spot currency market. In fact, currency swaps have succeeded parallel loan which had developed in countries where exchange control was in operation. In parallel loans, two parties situated in two different countries agreed to give each other loans of equal value and same maturity, each denominated in the currency of the lender. While initial loan was given at spot rate, reimbursement of principal as well as interest took into account forward rate.

However, these parallel loans presented a number of difficulties. For instance, default of payment by one party did not free the other party of its obligations of payment. In contrast, in a swap deal, if one party defaults, the counterparty is automatically relieved of its obligation. Likewise, despite the Impanation of loans, they figured in balance sheets of enterrises. Owing to these limitations, currency swaps gained in importance. Currency swaps can be divided into three categories: (a) fixed-to-fixed currency swap, (b) floating-to-floating currency swap, and (c) fixed-to-floating currency swap.

A fixed-to-fixed currency swap is an agreement between two parties who exchange future financial flows denominated in two different currencies. A currency swap can be understood as a combination of simultaneous spot sale of a currency and a forward purchase of the same amounts of currency. This double separation does not involve currency risk. In the beginning of exchange contract, counterparties exchange specific amount of two currencies. Subsequently, they settle interest according to an agreed arrangement. During the life of swap contract, each party pays the other the interest streams and finally they reimburse each other the principal of the swap. A simple currency swap enables the substitution of one debt denominated in one currency at a fixed rate to a debt denominated in another currency also at a fixed rate. It enables both parties to draw benefit from the differences of interest rates existing on segmented markets. A similar operation is done with regard to floating-to-floating rate swap.

A fixed-to-floating currency coupon swap is an agreement between two parties by which they agree to exchange financial flows denominated in two different currencies with different type of interest rates, one fixed and other floating. Thus, a currency coupon swap enables borrowers (or lenders) to borrow (or lend) in one currency and exchange a structure of interest rate against another fixed rate against variable rate and *vice versa*. The exchange can be either of interest coupons only or of interest coupons as well as principal. For example, one may exchange US dollars at fixed rate for French francs at variable rate. These types of swaps are used quite frequently.

Participants in Swap Deals

Participants in swap markets are: (a) Financial institutions, (b) Big enterprises, and (c) International organisations and public sector institutions.

Financial institutions play a very important role in swap operations. They influence, to a very great extent, the structure of operations and price of swaps. Currency swaps are useful to financial institutions as they enable them to make loans and accept deposits in the currency of their customers' choice. A financial institution may participate in the swap deal either as a broker, counterparty or an intermediary.

When the financial institution acts as a broker only, it is not a counter party in the deal. It should search for counterparties, facilitate negotiations, while preserving the anonymity of counterparties.

In the role of a counterparty, the financial institution incurs various risks —credit risk, market risk and delivery risk. When the bank or financial institution is a counterparty to a swap, it tries to arrange another swap having symmetrical features against another company so as to balance its flows and reduce its own risk. Thus, if it has entered into a Dollar-Euro fixed-to-fixed swap with a German company, it will try to find an American company that would like a Euro-Dollar fixed-to-fixed swap involving the same amount and for the same duration.

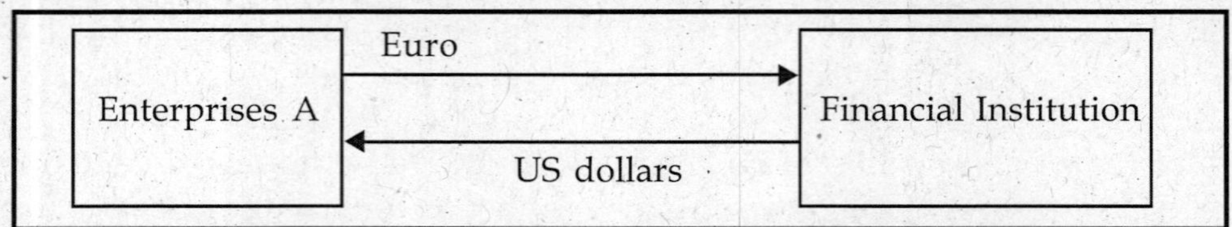

Fig. 5.1: Financial Institution as Counterparty

As an intermediary, the financial institution or the bank plays the role of a counterparty as well as a broker at the same time. When the bank is a counterparty or an intermediary, it is required to make quite complex arrangements in terms of several counterparties so as to reduce its own risks.

Margins on swaps have diminished. They are lower even for currencies that are highly traded. Depending on the currencies involved in a swap, a bank may gain 5 to 12 basis points.

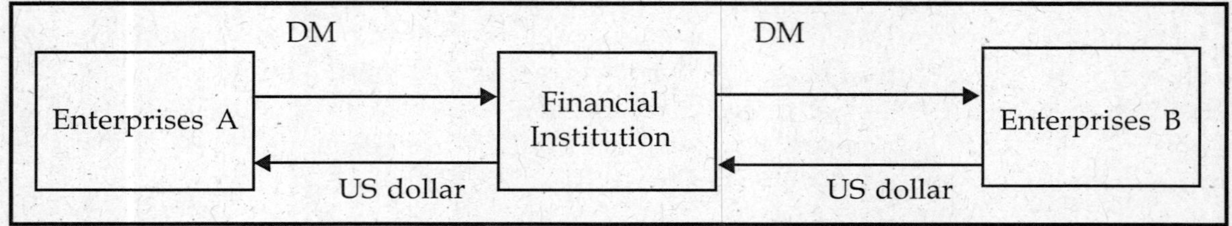

Fig. 5.2: Financial Institution as Intermediary

The second category of participants are enterprises. They are mostly multinationals, but there may also be big and medium enterprises with good ratings. French public enterprises such as SNCF (French Railways) and EDF (French Electricity Company) take recourse to swap markets in order to obtain more favourable interest rates. For example, in May 1994, SNCF issued bonds worth 150 billion Italian lira on international capital market which it exchanged with an American enterprise for French francs through a swap contract. Currency swaps involve a long position in one bond, combined with a short position in another bond. They may also be considered as portfolio of forward contracts. Enterprises use them when they have excess in one currency and shortage in another. Sometimes, subsidized loans available for promoting exports may be swapped for a desired foreign currency.

Thirdly, other institutions such as World Bank, and nation states also often take recourse to currency swaps and currency coupon swaps.

IMPORTANT FEATURES OF SWAP CONTRACTS

Minimum size of a swap contract is of the order of 5 million US dollar or its equivalent in other currencies. But there are swaps of as large a size as 300 million US dollar, specially in the case of Eurobonds. The US dollar is the most sought-after currency in swap deals. The dollar-yen swaps represent 25 per cent of the total while dollar-deutschemark swap account for 20 per cent of the total. The swaps involving Euro are also likely to be widely prevalent in European countries.

Life of a swap is between two and ten years. As regards the rate of interest of the swapped currencies, the choice depends on the anticipation of enterprises. Interest payments are made on annual or semi-annual basis.

Process of Swap Deals

If there are two enterprises, which have symmetrical requirement of capital in two different currencies, a swap is possible.

Fixed-to-fixed Rate Currency Swap

A company FSA is in need of US dollar loan but its rating on the American financial market is not very high. Similarly, an American company ACL needs a Euro loan of equivalent amount but it is less favourably placed on the Euro financial market. The market rates are given as follows:

	FSA	ACL	Difference
Dollar rate	6 per cent	5 per cent	1 per cent
Euro rate	9 per cent	9 per cent	0 per cent

As the interest rates indicate, there is net difference of 1 per cent, which the two companies can share between themselves. How is it possible? It is possible through the use of dollar-euro swap. The two companies FSA and ACL agree to enter into a swap deal. The company FSA will borrow on European market at a rate of 9 per cent. The company ACL will borrow on American market at 5 per cent. And, then they exchange their principal sums. The steps involved are given below:

(i) The company FSA places at the disposal of the company ACL, the sum borrowed in Euros against the equivalent sum of US dollars borrowed by the ACL For this exchange, an exchange rate is defined. Normally, this rate can be an average of buying and selling rate. Figure 5.3(a) represents this step of the Swap deal.

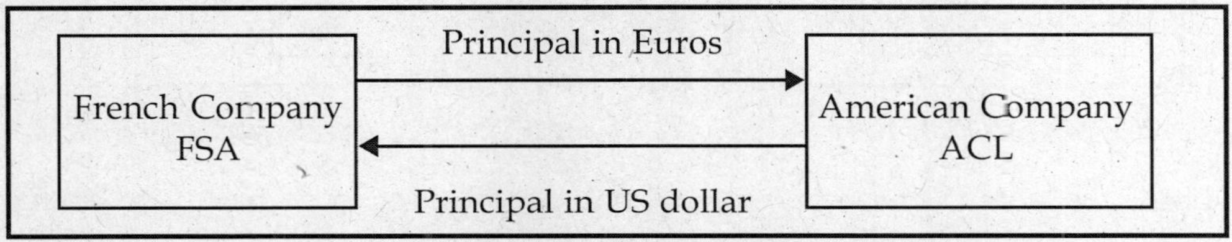

Fig. 5.3(a): Fixed-to-Fixed Rate Swap

(ii) Interest rates are determined in the beginning of the transaction. Interest amount are paid on fixed dates. After negotiations the two companies decide that the company FSA will pay 5Vi per cent interest in dollars to the company ACL which in turn will pay 8¾ per cent interest in Euro to the company FSA. Thus, the net rate to be paid by each company is:

FSA: 9 per cent (paid to the market) + 5½ per cent
(paid to the company ACL) – 8¾ per cent
(received from the comp ACL) = 5¾ per cent.

ACL: 5 per cent (paid to the market) + 8¾ per cent
(paid to the company FSA) – 5½ per cent
(received from the comp FSA) = 8¼ per cent.

Thus, both the companies have ensured the rates for themselves which are less than their respective borrowing rates. The FSA makes a gain of ¼ per cent while the ACL makes a gain of per cent per cent. The sum of the gains is equal to the net difference between the rates for the two companies. This step is depicted by Figure 5.3(b).

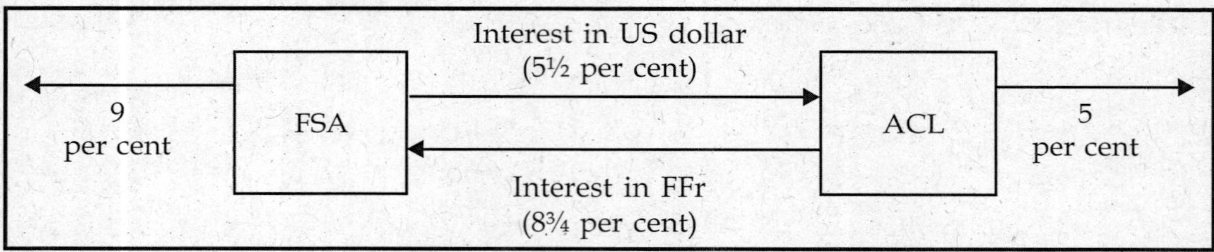

Fig. 5.3(b): Interest Payments during the Life of the Swap

(iii) In the end, the company FSA reimburses the amount in dollars to the American company ACL and in exchange, it receives its principal in Euros from the ACL. Thus, the amount that had been exchanged in the beginning has been re-exchanged between the two companies. Figure 5.3(c) shows this transaction.

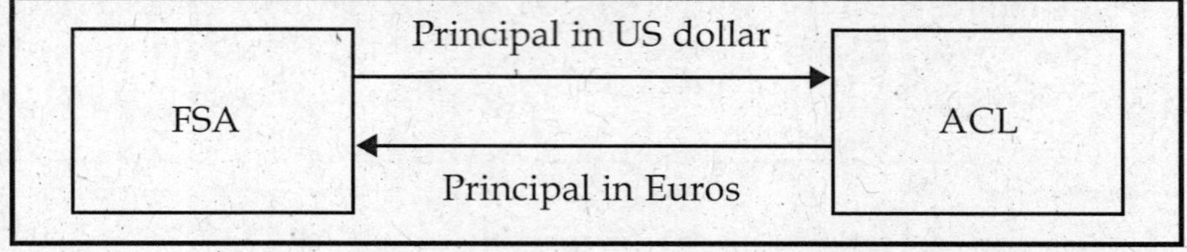

Fig. 5.3(c): Reimbursement of the Principal on Maturity

It should be noted, that a swap has enabled the French company to exchange a debt denominated in Euros at a fixed rate into another debt, denominated in US dollar at fixed rate. A swap may be compared to a combination of borrowing and lending. The rights and obligations of the two counterparties are interlinked. If one party defaults, the other is exonerated of its obligations. A swap operation offers a good deal of flexibility in terms of interest rate, date of maturity and its life.

If a French enterprise borrows US dollars for 5 years and it wants to cover against exchange rate risks, it needs to do the following: make 4 forward purchases of dollar to pay the interest due and one forward purchase to cover final reimbursement of principal and the last instalment of interest. That is, purchase 5 forward contracts at different rates.

In the case of breach of Swap contract, penalties are attracted, which may be provided for in the contract at the beginning.

The swap operations are quite fast and transaction costs are relatively low. They may be settled prematurely by paying a penalty, which is a function of the evolution of interest rates, exchange rates and the period remaining before maturity.

Fixed-to-floating Rate Currency Swap

Fixed-to-floating rate swaps also follow the same sequence of steps as do fixed-to-fixed rate swaps, with the difference that one currency has fixed rate while the other has floating rate. While the fixed rate is charged over the entire period of the Swap, the floating rate is re-calculated every six months. Thus, if a French company can raise capital at fixed rate on French market but prefers to obtain dollars at floating rate, it may take recourse to swaps. It may find a borrower who is highly rated on American market and who can borrow on that market at floating rate with better conditions but who would like to borrow francs at fixed rate. The two borrowers may swap their borrowings and draw a benefit from the operation.

For example, the American company ACL wants to borrow 600 million French francs at variable or floating rate. After having borrowed 100 million US dollars on American market at fixed rate, it enters into a swap deal with its bank. This swap is represented by Figure 5.4.

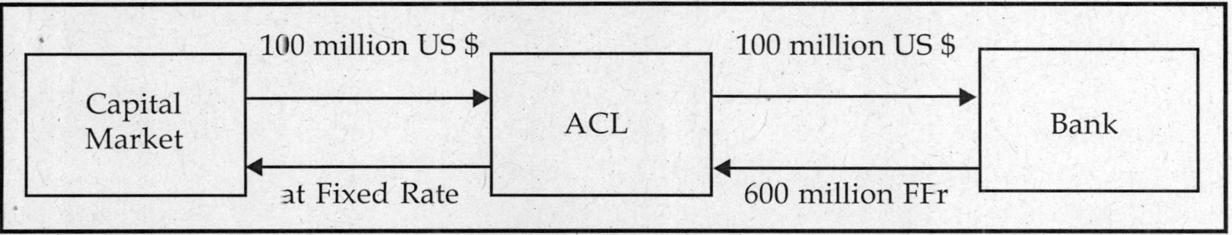

Fig. 5.4: Swap Contract Agreement

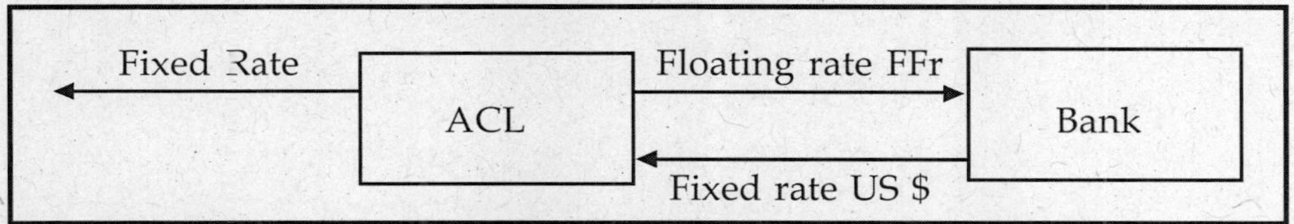

Fig. 5.5: Interest Payments During the Life of Contract

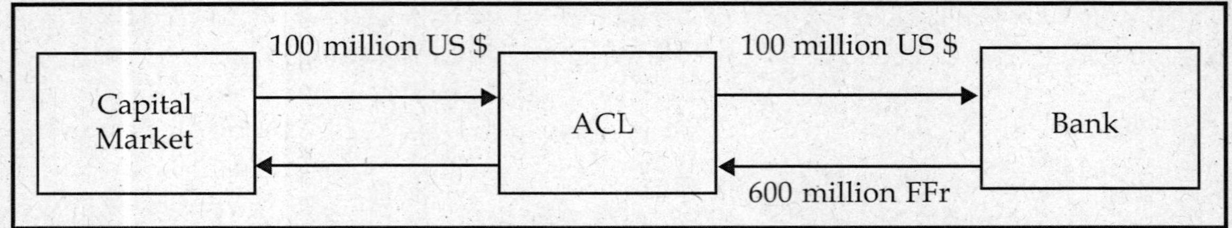

Fig. 5.6: Reimbursement of the Principal on Maturity

On the date of the contract, there is an exchange of the principal. The company ACL pays to its bank 100 million US dollar and receives from it 600 million French frans. The spot rate is FFr 6.00/US dollar.

During the life of the swap contract, the ACL will pay floating rate on the French francs and the bank will pay to it the fixed rate on US dollars. At the end of the contract life, there will be a re-exchange of the principal.

Question: Firm A is a US-based multinational whereas firm B is a France-based multinational. Both companies till now have borrowed exclusively from their base countries. Now, both firms need to raise capital for their new ventures. Due to scarcity and saturation, firm A can issue 5-year US $ bonds at 7.5 per cent and 5-year French franc bonds in French market at 11 per cent fixed. Firm B can issue 5-year US $ bond in US market at 7 per cent and 5-year FFr bond in French market at 12 per cent. Firm A requires US $ 100 million whereas firm B needs FFr 550 million. Current exchange rate is FFr 5.5 = US $ 1.

What kind of swap can firm A and B enter into?

What will be the total cost and saving for each party?

What risks are involved?

Solution: Firm A and firm B can enter into a currency swap.

In the US $ market firm B has 0.5 per cent interest rate advantage over firm A while in FFr market, firm A has 1.0 per cent interest rate advantage over firm B. Thus, it is possible for A and B to engage in mutually beneficial trade.

Swap is as follows:

Firm A borrows 550 million francs at 11 per cent

Firm B borrows $ 100 million at 7 per cent

Firm A lends 550 million FFr to firm B, charging 11.25 per cent

Firm B lends US $ 100 million to firm A, charging 7 per cent

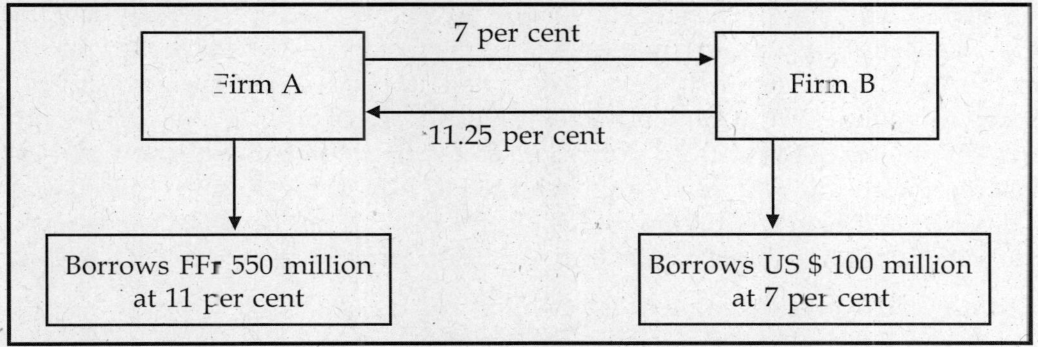

Net cost to firm A = 11 per cent + 7 per cent – 11.25 per cent
= 6.75 per cent

Net cost to firm B = 7 per cent +11.25 per cent – 7 per cent
= 11.25 per cent

Savings for firm A = 0.75 per cent (= 7.50 – 6.75)

Savings for firm B = 0.75 per cent (= 12.00 – 11.25)

Total savings = 1.5 per cent

This can also be obtained as follows:

	Firm A	Firm B	Difference
US Bond	7.5 per cent	7 per cent	0.5 per cent
FFr Bond	11 per cent	12 per cent	(1.0 per cent)
Net Difference			
Difference			1.5 per cent

Biggest risk for the parties involved is default by the counterparty. If the parties retain right of offset, then default under such conditions implies that the mutual exchanges for remaining period will not occur. If there is no default, the Swap allows the firms to obtain financing at known costs.

Pricing a Currency Swap

As is clear from its definition, a Swap is equivalent to borrowing and lending simultaneously. So, the value (or price) of a swap should be equal to the difference between the present values of all inflows and all outflows. Pricing problem of a swap is essentially to find out as to what rate should be quoted so that the two series of cash-flows have equal present value. For example, a bank is willing to swap 10 per cent fixed on French franc with 8 per cent fixed on an equivalent US dollar principal for 3 years. This means that the present value of franc payments at 10 per cent is equal to the present value of the dollar payments at 8 per cent, both expressed in a common currency.

Question: There is an existing six-year deal where a 6 million French frans floating liability was swapped with a 1 million US dollar fixed rate liability by a French firm. Under this deal, the French firm pays fixed dollar 10 per cent per annum semiannually and receives floating FFr at 6 month LIBOR. The swap is already 1 year 9-month old. The market rate for a 4-year fixed dollar versus 6-month FFr LIBOR is now 11 per cent. The last reset date was 3-months ago when the FFr LIBOR for the current semester was set at 9 per cent. The current 3-month LIBOR for FFr is 8 per cent and exchange rate is FFr 5.70/US $. At what price can the firm sell this swap at the moment?

Solution: The present value of the floating FFr leg is:

$$\text{FFr}\ \frac{6.00\times\left(1+\frac{0.09}{2}\right)}{\left(1+\frac{0.09}{2}\right)} = \text{FFr 6.1470 million.}$$

Here, the discount rate has been taken as 8 per cent (i.e. the current 3-month FFr LIBOR rate).

The remaining dollar cash-flows are as follows:

Table 5.8: Remainig Dollar Cash-flows

Months	.3	9	15	21	27	33	39	45	51
Cash now (US$)	50,000	50,000	50,000	50,000	50,000	50,000	50,000	50,000	50,000
PV (at II per cent)	48,661	46,125	43,720	41,441	39,281	37,233	35,292	33,452	6,65,867

PV of dollar cash-flow at 5.5 per cent $(=\frac{11}{2})$ semi-annually works out to: $ 9,91,072

At the current exchange rate, it is equal to: FFr 9,91,072 × 5.70 = FFr 5.6491 million.

Selling the current swap contract implies selling a fixed dollar liability and a floating rate FFr asset. The net value of the Swap is FFr (6.1470 – 5.6491) million or FFr 4,97,889. In other words, the firm can sell this swap for FFr 4,97,889.

❀ ❀ ❀

Futures – An Introduction

INTRODUCTION

Futures markets were designed to solve the problems that exist in forward markets. A futures contract is an agreement between two parties to buy or sell an asset at a certain time in the future at a certain price. But unlike forward contracts, the futures contracts are standardized and exchange traded. To facilitate liquidity in the futures contracts, the exchange specifies certain standard features of the contract. It is a standardised contract with standard underlying instrument, a standard quantity and quality of the underlying instrument that can be delivered, (or which can be used for reference purposes in settlement) and a standard timing of such settlement. A futures contract may be offset prior to maturity by entering into an equal and opposite transaction. More than 99 per cent of futures transactions are offset this way.

The standardised items in a futures contract are:

- Quantity of the underlying
- Quality of the underlying
- The date and the month of delivery
- The units of price quotation and minimum price change
- Location of settlement

MARK-TO-MARKET

Mark-to-market is a concept whereby the accounts of members are settled on a daily basis. On Futures markets all over the world, profits are paid by the clearing house on a daily basis, just like losses are paid to the clearinghouse by members. The fundamental here is, the losses of one party are the profits of another. Since the clearing house is the counter party to all transactions, it has to insist on settlement each trading day.

MARGIN MONEY

Margin money is like a security deposit or insurance against a possible future loss of value. This is the money deposited with your broker or exchange to mitigate default risk. Suppose you buy 100 shares of Company X at ₹ 100, you have an exposure of ₹ 10,000. In the unlikely event of you failing to honor your commitment, your broker would incur a loss of ₹ 10,000. To avoid this, the exchange or broker would insist on a margin of a percentage of the exposure, generally 10-25 per cent. The per cent margin is decided on the basis of the maximum price change permitted in a given period. If the margin is inadequate to cover the. exposure, the exchange can demand additional funds because of adverse price movement.

The aim of margin money is to minimize the risk of default by either counter-party. The payment of margin ensures that the risk is limited to the previous day's price movement on each outstanding position. However, even this exposure is offset by the initial margin holdings. Given below is an Example of Margining and Mark-to-market.

Table 6.1: Marging and Mark-to-market

	MON	TUE	WED	THU	FRI
Value of Futures	60000	59000	53000	60000	52000
Buyer					
Initial Margin	6000				
Variation Margin (+credit) (-debit)	0	-1000	-6000	+7000	-8000
Profit/Loss	0	-1000	-7000	0	-8000
Seller					
Initial Margin	6000				
Variation Margin (-credit) (-debit)	0	+1000	+6000	-7000	+8000
Profit/Loss	0	+1000	+7000	0	+8000

Different types of Margins

There are different types of margins called Initial margin, Variation (or mark-to-market) margin, Maintenance margin and Additional margin.

Initial Margin

The basic aim of Initial margin is to cover the largest potential loss in one day. Both, the buyer and seller, have to deposit margins. The initial margin is deposited before the opening of the day of the Futures transaction.

Normally, this margin is calculated on the basis of variance observed in daily price of the underlying (say the index) over a specified historical period (say, immediately preceding one year).

The margin is kept in a way that it covers price movements more than 99 per cent of the time. Usually, three sigma (standard deviation) is used for this measurement. This technique is also called value at risk (or VAR). Variation or Mark-to-market margin.

All daily losses must be met by depositing of further collateral - known as variation margin, which is required by the close of business, the following day. Any profits on the contract are credited to the client's variation margin account.

Maintenance Margin

Some exchanges work on the system of maintenance margin, which is set at a level slightly less than initial margin. The margin is required to be replenished to the level of initial margin, only if the margin level drops below the maintenance margin limit.

For example, if initial margin is fixed at 100 and Maintenance margin is at 80, then the broker is permitted to trade till such time that the balance in this initial margin account is 80 or more.

If it drops below 80, say to 70, then a margin of 30 (and not 10) is to be paid to replenish the levels of initial margin.

Additional Margin

In case of sudden higher than expected volatility, additional margin may be called for by the exchange. This is generally imposed when the exchange fears that the markets have become too volatile and may result in some crisis, like payments crisis. This is a preemptive move by exchange to prevent breakdown.

Cross Margining

This is a method of calculating margins after taking into account combined positions in Futures, Options and cash market. Hence, the total margin requirement reduces due to cross-hedges.

Settlement

Historically, the Futures market developed on the basis of the physical delivery of the underlying, which often was a commodity. However, now in most Futures markets, only a small proportion of contracts result in physical delivery. Majority of them are settled by buying a contract of an opposite nature, which squares the transaction.

Pricing of Futures

The theoretical way of calculating any Future is to factor in the current price and holding costs, i.e., interest expenses. If not, then there is an arbitrage opportunity. Arbitrage is risk-less profit earned by buying and selling the same security at different prices and exchanges. The other subjective things that enter the pricing mechanism are sentiments and event expectations.

Clearing House

The clearing house is an organisation that acts as counterparty to all buy/sell transactions. It does this by imposing itself between the two counterparties thereby replacing the original contract (for instance between X and Y) by two new contracts (between X and Clearing house/corporation and between Y and Clearing house/ corporation). Alternatively the Clearing House, instead of acting as counterparty, guarantees all trades executed through the Exchange. The latter has the same effect in terms of reducing credit risk as the former.

Another very important function of the clearing house is the fixation and enforcement of margin requirements. The margin amounts remain with the clearing house and are used to pay investors if any party defaults. Thus, there is, no danger of default as the clearing house effectively guarantees all transactions. This enables trading of huge volumes as two parties can trade with each other free of the worry that the other will default.

The volume of Futures traded and the value of the underlying is huge. If a small fraction of the participants default, it could run into hundreds of millions of dollars (worldwide). Hence, the clearing house operates a margining system.

Long/short Positions

In simple terms, long and short positions indicate whether you have a net over-bought position (long) or over-sold position (short).

Market Maker

A dealer is said to make a market when he quotes both bid and offer prices at which he stands ready to buy and sell the security. Thus, he is a person who brings buyers and sellers together. He lends liquidity in the system by making trading feasible.

Gearing

Gearing (or leveraging) is akin to funding an asset by taking a loan. To put it simply, suppose you want to buy an asset of ₹ 100 and have only ₹ 50. You need to borrow ₹ 50 to own the desired asset. In such an event, the gearing is 2. Inmost cases, the higher the gearing, the higher is the risk.

Basis

The difference between spot price and Futures price is known as basis. Although the spot price and Futures price generally move in line with each other, the basis is not constant. Generally basis will decrease with time. And on expiry, the basis is zero and Futures price equals spot price.

Contango

Under normal market conditions, Futures contracts are priced above the Spot price. This is known as the Contango market.

Backwardation

It is possible for the Futures price to prevail below the spot price. Such a situation is known as backwardation. This may happen when the cost of carry is negative, or when the underlying asset is in short supply in the cash market but there is an expectation of increased supply in future – for example, agricultural products.

APPLICATION OF FUTURES

Understanding Beta

The index model suggested by William Sharpe offers insights into portfolio diversification. It expresses the excess return on a security or a portfolio as a function of market factors and non-market factors. Market factors are those factors that affect all stocks and portfolios. These would include factors such as inflation, interest rates, business cycles etc. Non-market factors would be those factors which are specific to a company, and do not affect the entire market. For example, a fire breakout in a factory, a new invention, the death of a key employee, a strike in the factory, etc. The market factors affect all firms. The unexpected change in these factors causes unexpected changes in the rates of returns on the entire stock market. Each stock however responds to these factors to different extents. Beta of a stock measures the sensitivity of the stocks responsiveness to these market factors. Similarly, beta of a portfolio measures the portfolio's responsiveness to these market movements. Given stock betas, calculating portfolio beta is simple. It is nothing but the weighted average of the stock betas.

The index has a beta of 1. Hence, the movements of returns on a portfolio with a beta of one will be like the index. If the index moves up by ten per cent, my portfolio value will increase by ten per cent. Similarly, if the index drops by five per cent, my portfolio value will drop by five per cent. A portfolio with a beta of two, responds more sharply to index movements. If the index moves up by ten per cent, the value of a portfolio with a beta of two will move up by twenty per cent. If the index drops by ten per cent, the value of a portfolio with a beta of two will fall by twenty per cent. Similarly, if a portfolio has a beta of 0.75, a 10 per cent movement in the index will cause a 7.5 per cent movement in the value of the portfolio. In short, beta is a measure of the systematic risk or market risk of a portfolio. Using index futures contracts, it is possible to hedge the systematic risk. With this basic understanding, we look at some applications of index futures.

We look here at some applications of futures contracts. We refer to single stock futures. However, since the index is nothing but a security whose price or level is a weighted average of securities constituting an index, all strategies that can be implemented using stock futures can also be implemented using index futures.

Hedging: Long Security, Sell Futures

Futures can be used as an effective risk-management tool. Take the case of an investor who holds the shares of a company and gets uncomfortable with market movements in the short run. He sees the value of his security falling from ₹ 450 to ₹ 390. In the absence of stock futures, he would either suffer the discomfort of a price fall or sell the security in anticipation of a market upheaval. With security futures he can minimise his price risk. All he need do is enter into an offsetting stock futures position, in this case, take on a short futures position. Assume that the spot price of the security he holds is ₹ 390. Two-month futures cost him ₹ 402. For this he pays an initial margin. Now if the price of the security falls any further, he will suffer losses on the security he holds. However, the losses he suffers on the security will be offset by the profits he makes on his short futures position. Take for instance that the price of his security falls to ₹ 350. The fall in the price of the security will result in a fall in the price of futures. Futures will now trade at a price lower than the price at which he entered into a short futures position. Hence his short futures position will start making profits. The loss of ₹ 40 incurred on the security he holds, will be made up by the profits made on his short futures position.

Index futures in particular can be very effectively used to get rid of the market risk of a portfolio. Every portfolio contains a hidden index exposure or a market exposure. This statement is true for all portfolios, whether a portfolio is composed of index securities or not. In the case of portfolios, most of the portfolio risk is accounted for by index fluctuations (unlike individual securities, where only 30-60 per cent of the securities risk is accounted for by index fluctuations). Hence a position LONG PORTFOLIO + SHORT NIFTY can often become one-tenth as risky as the LONG PORTFOLIO position!

Suppose we have a portfolio of ₹ 1 million which has a beta of 1.25. Then a complete hedge is obtained by selling ₹ 1.25 million of Nifty futures.

Warning: Hedging does not always make money. The best that can be achieved using hedging is the removal of unwanted exposure, i.e., unnecessary risk. The hedged position will make less profits than the unhedged position, half the time. One should not enter into a hedging strategy hoping to make excess profits for sure; all that can come out of hedging is reduced risk.

Speculation: Bullish Security, Buy Futures

Take the case of a speculator who has a view on the direction of the market. He would like to trade based on this view. He believes that a particular security that trades at ₹ 1,000 is undervalued and expects its price to go up in the next two-three months. How can he trade based on this belief? In the absence of a deferral product, he would have to buy the security and hold on to it. Assume he buys a 100 shares which cost him one lakh rupees. His hunch proves correct and two months later the security closes at ₹ 1,010. He makes a profit of ₹ 1,000 on an investment of ₹ 1,00,000 for a period of two months. This works out to an annual return of 6 per cent.

Today a speculator can take exactly the same position on the security by using futures contracts. Let us see how this works. The security trades at ₹ 1,000 and the two-month futures trades at 1006. Just for the sake of comparison, assume that the minimum contract value is 1,00,000. He buys 100 security futures for which he pays a margin of ₹ 20,000. Two months later the security closes at 1010. On the day of expiration, the futures price converges to the spot price and he makes a profit of ₹ 400 on an investment of ₹ 20,000. This works out to an annual return of 12 per cent. Because of the leverage they provide, security futures foreman attractive option for speculators.

Speculation: Bearish Security, Sell Futures

Stock futures can be used by a speculator who believes that a particular security is over-valued and is likely to see a fall in price. How can he trade based on his opinion? In the absence of a deferral product, there wasn't much he could do to profit from his opinion. Today all he needs to do is sell stock futures.

Let us understand how this works. Simple arbitrage ensures that futures on an individual securities move correspondingly with the underlying security, as long as there is sufficient liquidity in the market for the security. If the security price rises, so will the futures price. If the security price falls, so will the futures price.

Now take the case of the trader who expects to see a fall in the price of ABC Ltd.

He sells one two-month contract of futures on ABC at ₹ 240 (each contact for 100 underlying shares). He pays a small margin on the same. Two months later, when the futures contract expires, ABC closes at 220. On the day of expiration, the spot and the futures price converges. He has made a clean profit of ₹ 20 per share. For the one contract that he bought, this works out to be ₹ 2,000.

Arbitrage: Overpriced Futures: Buy Spot, Sell Futures

As we discussed earlier, the cost-of-carry ensures that the futures price stay in tune with the spot price. Whenever the futures price deviates substantially from its fair value, arbitrage opportunities arise.

If you notice that futures on a security that you have been observing seem overpriced, how can you cash in on this opportunity to earn riskless profits?

For instance, ABC Ltd., trades at ₹ 1,000. One-month ABC futures trade at ₹ 1,025 and seem overpriced. As an arbitrageur, you can make risk less profit by entering into the following set of transactions.

1. On day one, borrow funds, buy the security on the cash/spot market at 1000.
2. Simultaneously, sell the futures on the security at 1025.
3. Take delivery of the security purchased and hold the security for a month.
4. On the futures expiration date, the spot and the futures price converge. Now unwind the position.
5. Say the security closes at ₹ 1,015. Sell the security.
6. Futures position expires with profit of ₹ 10.
7. The result is a risk less profit of ₹ 15 on the spot position and ₹ 10 on the futures position.
8. Return the borrowed funds.

When does it make sense to enter into this arbitrage? If your cost of borrowing funds to buy the security is less than the arbitrage profit possible, it makes sense for you to arbitrage. This is termed as cash-and-carry arbitrage. Remember however, that exploiting an arbitrage opportunity involves trading on the spot and futures market. In the real world, one has to build in the transactions costs into the arbitrage strategy.

Arbitrage: Under Priced Futures: Buy Futures, Sell Spot

Whenever the futures price deviates substantially from its fair value, arbitrage opportunities arise. It could be the case that you notice the futures on a security you hold seem under priced. How can you cash in on this opportunity to earn risk less profits? For instance, ABC Ltd. trades at ₹ 1,000. One month ABC futures trade at ₹ 965 and seem under priced. As an arbitrageur, you can make risk less profit by entering into the following set of transactions.

1. On day one, sell the security in the cash/spot market at 1,000.
2. Make delivery of the security.

3. Simultaneously, buy the futures on the security at 965.
4. On the futures expiration date, the spot and the futures price converge. Now unwind the position.
5. Say the security closes at ₹ 975. Buy back the security.
6. The futures position expires with a profit of ₹ 10.
7. The result is a risk less profit of ₹ 25 on the spot position and ₹ 10 on the futures position.

If the returns you get by investing in riskless instruments is more than the return from the arbitrage trades, it makes sense for you to arbitrage. This is termed as reverse-cash-and-carry arbitrage. It is this arbitrage activity that ensures that the spot and futures prices stay in line with the cost-of-carry. As we can see, exploiting arbitrage involves trading on the spot market. As more and more players in the market develop the knowledge and skills to do cashed-carry and reverse cash-and-carry, we will see increased volumes and lower spreads in both the cash as well as the derivatives market.

HOW INDEX FUTURES WORK?

Once a grain trader went to his stockbroker with bags of money. Those were the pre-derivative days. He asked his broker for advice on which shares to buy. The market was very volatile and so the broker told the simpleton, "I can't say exactly which shares will rise and by how much, but the market will definitely go up." The trader then said, "Great Excellent Buy 100 Sensex." The broker laughed out and advised the grain trader to go back to his village.

This story captures the very essence of index Futures. Index Futures are derivatives whose underlying asset is the stock market index. This is of great help when one wants to take a position on market movements. Suppose you feel that the markets are bullish and the Sensex would shoot by 300 points. Instead of buying shares that constitute the index, you can buy the market by taking a position on the Index Futures. Index Futures can be used as hedging devices, for speculation, arbitrage, cash-flow management and asset allocation.

Basics of Index

An index is a representative of a set, and is generally the indicator of the status of the set. In a stock market context, index is an indicator of the broad market. For instance, by tracking the changes of the BSE Sensex, one can effectively gauge stock market moods in India.

Any index is an average of its constituents. For example, the BSE Sensex is a weighted average of prices of 30 select stocks, where the weight is the market capitalisation of individual stocks. Market capitalisation is the product of stock price and number of shares issued by the company.

Suppose there are 2 stocks, A and B, details of which are included below.

Company	Shares outstanding (mn)	Price (₹)
A	10	100
B	1	150

The market capitalisation (also known as market cap) for A is ₹ 1,000mn (10*100) and for B is ₹ 150mn (1*150). If we were to create a market cap weighted index, then the index is defined as:

Index (i) = Sum of market cap on day (ii)* 100/Sum of market cap on day (0)

Where is the day on which index has to be calculated; And day (0) is the base date or initial date.

So on day (0), the index is 100. On day 5, if A is trading at ₹ 200 and B at ₹ 200, the index (5) would become:

Index (5) = (10*200 + 1*200)*100/(10*100 + 1*150) Index (5) = 191.3

Importance of Market Index

A market index is important because of the following reasons:

- It acts as a good barometer of market behavior.
- It is used to benchmark portfolio performance.
- It is used in instruments derivatives like Index funds and Index derivatives

Different indices can exist at the same time. Their properties would depend on the sponsor and its constituents. For example, in India, there exist the BSE Sensex of the Bombay Stock Exchange and the National Stock Exchange sponsored S&P CNX Nifty. The most important (and usually popular) type of market index is the broad market index, which comprises large and liquid stocks of the country.

In addition, there are specialised indices like sector specific indices, which track the performance of individual sectors. Similarly, different types of indices can be created depending on the companies included in the set.

In general, index movements reflect changes in the set properties. We are all used to seeing changes in BSE Sensex, which, as explained earlier, is the index for the stock prices on the Bombay Stock Exchange. This reflects changing expectations of the stock market about future performance of Indian economy and hence the corporate sector. Whenever the Sensex rises, it means that prices of the stocks constituting the Sensex have risen. Stock prices rise when perception about future performance of economy and company improves. Thus, the index is a barometer of the market at that instant.

In general, the reported market index figure is actually the price index, which reflects only the change in prices. To calculate the total returns of any index, we have to factor in the dividends announced by the companies comprising the index. The Total Return Index is the correct index for benchmarking mutual fund performance as they earn dividends.

Contract Specifications for Index Futures

NSE trades Nifty, CNX IT, BANK Nifty, CNX Nifty Junior, CNX 100, Nifty Madcap 50 and Mini Nifty 50 futures contracts having one-month, two-month and three-month expiry cycles. All contracts expire on the last Thursday of every month. Thus a January expiration contract would expire on the last Thursday of January and a February expiry contract would cease trading on the last Thursday of February. On the Friday following the last Thursday, a new contract having a three-month expiry would be introduced for trading. Thus, as shown in Figure 5.5 at any point in time, three contracts would be available for trading with the first contract expiring on the last Thursday of that month. Depending on the time period for which you want to take an exposure in index futures contracts, you can place buy and sell orders in the respective contracts. The Instrument type refers to "Futures contract on index" and Contract symbol – NIFTY denotes a "Futures contract on Nifty index" and the Expiry date represents the last date on which the contract will be available for trading. Each futures contract has a separate limit order book. All passive orders are stacked in the system in terms of price-time priority and trades take place at the passive order price (similar to the existing capital market trading system). The best buy order for a given futures contract will be the order to buy the index at the highest index level whereas the best sell order will be the order to sell the index at the lowest index level.

Example: If trading is for a minimum lot size of 100 units. If the index level is around 2000, then the appropriate value of a single index futures contract would be ₹ 2,00,000. The minimum tick size for an index future contract is 0.05 units. Thus a single move in the index value would imply a resultant gain or loss of ₹ 5.00 (i.e., 0.05*100 units) on an open position of 100 units.

Contract Specifications for Index based Futures

Index futures are futures contracts on an index, like the Nifty. The underlying asset in case of index futures is the index itself. For example, Nifty futures traded in NSE track spot Nifty returns. If the Nifty index rises, so does the pay off of the long position in Nifty futures. Apart from Nifty other indices such as CNX IT, Bank Nifty etc. are also traded on the NSE. They have one-month, two-month, and three-month expiry cycle: a one-month Nifty futures contract would expire in the current month, a two-month contract the next month, and a three-month contract the month after. All contracts expire on the last Thursday of every month, or the previous trading day if the last Thursday is a trading holiday. Thus, a September 2009 contract would expire on the last Thursday of September 2009, which would be the final settlement date of the contract.

HOW WE DO PRICING OF FUTURES?

In general, the Futures Price = Spot Price + Cost of Carry

Cost of carry is the equivalent of interest costs or carrying costs. This depends on opportunity cost, cost of storage and insurance. The largest component is the opportunity cost of capital, which is the equivalent of interest costs.

Apart from the theoretical value, the actual value may vary depending on demand and supply of cash and Futures contract. In this context, this is also similar to how other instruments in any market behave.

In general, the Futures price is greater than the spot price. In special cases, when cost of carry is negative, the futures price may be lower than Spot prices.

The difference between spot price and Futures price is known as basis. Although the Spot price and Futures price generally move in line with each other, the basis is not constant. Generally, basis will decrease with time. And on expiry, the basis is zero and futures price equals spot price.

Under normal market conditions, Futures contracts are priced above the spot price. This is known as the Contango market.

It is possible for the Futures price to prevail below the spot price. Such a situation is known as backwardation. This may happen when the cost of carry is negative, or when the underlying asset is in short supply.

Cost of carry is the sum of all costs incurred if a similar position is taken in cash market and carried to maturity of the Futures contract. The typical costs are interest in case of financial Futures (also insurance and storage costs in case of commodity futures). The revenues that may accrue can be dividends in case of index Futures.

The above is only a theoretical model. In reality, the actual value may vary depending on demand and supply of the underlying at present and investors' expectations about the future.

Cost of Carry Model with Dividends

A drawback of the conventional cost of carry model mentioned above used for pricing Futures is the ignorance of dividends. This follows from the fact that most stock indices are pure price indices; they do not take dividends into account. In real world, holding a stock gives the owner dividends.

To fit stock index Futures, we must include dividends that would be received between the present and expiration of the Futures. The chance to receive dividends lowers the cost of carrying the stocks. Carrying stocks requires that a trader finance the purchase price of the stock from the present until the Futures expiration. However, the trader will receive dividends which will lower the value of the stocks. This contrasts with the cost of carry of holding a commodity like gold, which does not generate any cash-flow.

For stocks, the cost of carry is the financing cost for the stock less the dividends received while the stock is being carried.

As an example, assume the present is time zero and a trader decides to engage in a self financing cash and carry transaction. The trader decides to buy and hold one share of ABC Ltd., currently trading for ₹ 100. Thus, he borrows ₹ 100 and buys the stock. We assume that the stock pays a dividend of ₹ 2 in six months and the trader will invest the proceeds for the remaining six months at a rate of 12 per cent. The table below shows the trader's cash-flows. The stock costs ₹ 100, but the value after one year, say V is unknown. From the table, the trader's cash-flow after one year is the future value of the dividend, ₹ 2.12 plus the current value of the stock, V less the repayment of the loan, ₹ 112.

Thus, the stock index Futures price must equal or exceed the cash inflows at the Futures expiration. In other words, the stock index Futures price must equal the cost of the stocks underlying the stock index, plus the cost of carrying those stocks to expiration, S(1 + C), minus the future value of all the dividends to be received, D(1 + r). The future value of dividends is measured at the time the Futures contract expires. Thus,

$$F = S(1 + C) - D(1 + r)$$

where:

F = stock index Futures price

S = the value of the stocks underlying the stock index

C = the percentage cost of carrying the stocks

D = the dividend

R = the interest earned on carrying the dividend.

Table 6.2: Cash-flows

T = 0 Borrow ₹ 100 for 1 year at 13 per cent + 100 Buy 1 share of ABC Ltd., –100 T = 6 months Receive dividend of ₹ 2 Invest ₹ 2 for 6 months at 12 per cent	 + 2 – 2
T = 1 year Collect proceeds from dividend investment Sell ABC Ltd for V Repay debt	 + 2.12 + V – 113
Total Profit = V + 2.12 – 113	

❀ ❀ ❀

INTRODUCTION

In Financial market derivatives play very important role and hence, future and option are, in recent times, actively traded on many exchanges and also the forward contracts on the OTC market. Hence, we shall study in detail about forward, and futures.

FORWARD CONTRACTS

A forward contract is an agreement between two parties irrevocably agree buy or sell an asset at a specified date for a specified price.

For example one of the parties to the contract assumes a long position and agrees to buy the underlying asset on a certain specified future date for a certain specified price. The other party assumes a short position and agrees to sell the asset on the same date for the same price. Other contract details like delivery date, price and quantity are negotiated bilaterally by the parties to the contract. The forward contracts are normally traded outside the exchanges. General Terms and Conditions are as follows:

- They are bilateral contracts and hence exposed to counter-party risk.
- Each contract is custom designed, and hence is unique in terms of contract size, expiration date and the asset type and quality.
- The contract price is generally not available in public domain.

  On the expiration date, the contract has to be settled by delivery of the asset.
- If the party wishes to reverse the contract, it has to compulsorily go to the same counterparty, which often results in high prices being charged.

Example:

Suppose Amit (a buyer) and Rahul (a seller) agree to undergo a trade in 100 grams of gold on 31 Dec. 2006 at ₹ 9,000/tola. Here, ₹ 9,000/tola is the "forward price of 31 Dec. 2006 Gold".

Amit the buyer is said to be long and Rahul the seller is said to be short. Once the contract has been entered into, Amit is obligated to pay Rahul ₹ 9,00,000 on 31 Dec. 2006, and take delivery of 100 tolas of gold. Similarly, Rahul is obligated to be ready to accept ₹ 9,00,000 on 31 Dec. 2006, and give 100 tolas of gold in exchange.

Problems & Limitations of Forward Contracts:

- Forward market tends to be afflicted by poor liquidity and from unreliability deriving from credit risk.
- Lack of centralisations of trading.
- Very much flexibility and generating.

FUTURES CONTRACTS

Futures markets came into the existence to solve the problems that use to occur in forward market. A futures contract is an agreement between two parties to buy or sell an asset at a certain time in the future at a certain price. But unlike forward contracts, the futures are standardised and exchange traded. To facilitate liquidity in the futures contracts, the exchange specifies certain standard features of the contract. It is a standardised contract with standard underlying instrument, a standard quantity and quality of the underlying instrument that can be delivered. In other words, this can be used for reference purposes in settlement and a standard timing of such settlement. A futures contract can be offset prior to maturity by entering into an equal and opposite transaction. Most of the future transactions are offset in this manner. The general norms of futures contract are:

- Quality of the underlying
- Quantity of the underlying
- The date and the month of delivery
- The units of price quotation and minimum price change
- Location of settlement.

Difference between Forwards and Futures Contracts

There is always misconception between forward contracts and future contracts because primarily both serve essentially the same financial functions of allocating risk in the presence of future price uncertainty. However, futures are considered a significant improvement over the forward contracts as they eliminate counterparty risk and also offer more liquidity

Table 7.1: Difference between Futures and Forwards Contracts

Futures	Forwards
Trade on an organized exchange	OTC in nature
Standardized contract terms	Customized contract terms
Hence more liquid	Hence less liquid
Requires margin payments	No margin payment
Follows daily settlement	Settlement happens at end of period

FUTURES TERMINOLOGY

Spot Price: The price at which an asset trades in the spot market.

Futures Price: The price at which the futures contract trades in the futures market.

Contract Cycle: The period over which a contract trades. The index futures contracts on the NSE have one month, two-month and three-month expiry cycles which expire on the last Thursday of the month. Thus a January expiration contract expires on the last Thursday of January and a February expiration contract ceases trading on the last Thursday of February. On the Friday following the last Thursday, a new contract having a three-month expiry is introduced for trading.

Expiry Date: It is the date specified in the futures contract. This is the last day on which the contract will be traded, at the end of which it will cease to exist.

Contract Size: The amount of asset that has to be delivered under one contract. For instance, the contract size on NSE's futures market is 50 Nifties.

Basis: In the context of financial futures, basis can be defined as the futures price minus the spot price. There will be a different basis for each delivery month for each contract. In a normal market, basis will be positive. This reflects that futures prices normally exceed spot prices.

Cost of Carry: The relationship between futures prices and spot prices can be summarized in terms of cost of carry. This measures the storage cost plus the interest that is paid to finance the asset less the income earned on the asset.

Initial Margin: The amount that must be deposited in the margin account at the time a futures contract is first entered into is known as initial margin.

Marking-to-market: In the futures market, at the end of each trading day, the margin account is adjusted to reflect the investor's gain or loss depending upon the futures closing price. This is called marking-to-market.

Maintenance Margin: This is somewhat lower than the initial margin. This is set to ensure that the balance in the margin account never becomes negative. If the balance in the margin account falls below the maintenance margin, the investor receives a margin call and is expected to top up the margin account to the initial margin level before trading commences on the next day.

Discount: The difference between the shares spot price and the futures price, if the futures price is below the spot price, is known as discount, and the future is said to be trading at a discount. This generally happens if traders anticipate a fall in share price in near future.

Premium: The difference between the shares spot price and futures price, if the futures price is above the spot price, is known as premium, and the future is said to be trading at a premium. This generally happens if traders anticipate a rise in share price in near future.

Beta: It is a measure of the volatility, or systematic risk, of a security or a portfolio in comparison to the market as a whole, and is calculated using regression analysis.

You can think of beta as the tendency of a security's returns to respond to swings in the market. A beta of 1 indicates that the security's price will move with the market. A beta of less than 1 means that the security will be less volatile than the market. A beta of greater than 1 indicates that the security's price will be more volatile than the market.

Pricing Futures

We expect that the spot price of an asset converges to that of the futures price as the delivery date of the contract approaches otherwise an arbitrage opportunity exists.

If the future price stays above the spot price, we can buy the asset now and short a futures contract (i.e., agree to sell the asset later at the future price). Then we delivery and clear a profit. If the futures price stays below the spot price, anyone who wants the asset should go long on a futures contract and accept delivery instead of paying the spot price.

To understand this, you need to know the Cost-of-carry model, to understand the dynamics of pricing that constitute the estimation of fair value of futures.

Before we examine the pricing issue, we must make the important distinction between futures contract price at this moment and the actual price of the scrip on a future date. Futures price is the current price of the futures contract whereas future price is the spot price that will prevail on a specified date in future.

Cost-of-carry Model

Cost-of-carry model is an arbitrage-free pricing model. Its central theme is that futures contract is so priced as to preclude arbitrage profit. In other words, investors will be indifferent to spot and futures market to execute their buying and selling of underlying asset because the prices they obtain are effectively the same. Expectations do influence the price, but they influence the spot price and, through it, the futures price. They do not directly influence the futures price. According to the cost-of-carry model, the futures price is given by:

Futures price = Spot Price + Carry Cost – Carry Return

Carry Cost (CC) is the interest cost of holding the underlying asset (purchased in spot market) until the maturity of futures contract. Carry Return (CR) is the income (e.g., dividend) derived from underlying asset during holding period. Thus, the futures price (F) should be equal to spot price (S) plus carry cost minus carry return. If it is otherwise, there will be arbitrage opportunities as follows.

Example:

Say, the price of VSNL stock on 31 December 2005 was ₹ 220 and the futures price on the same stock on the same date, i.e., 31 December 2005 for March 2006 was ₹ 230. Other features of the contract and related information are as follows:

Time to expiration	3 months (0.25 year)
Borrowing rate	1 0 per cent p.a.
Annual dividend on the stock	25 per cent payable before 31.03.2006

Based on the above information, the futures price for VSNL stock on 31 December 2005 should be: = 220 + (220*0.10*0.02) – (0.25*10) = 223.00

Where ₹ 10 is the Face Value.

Thus, as per the 'cost of carry' criteria, the futures price is ₹ 223, which is less than the actual price of ₹ 230 in February 2006. This would give rise to arbitrage opportunities and consequently the two prices will tend to converge.

When **F > (S + CC – CR):** Sell the (overpriced) futures contract, buy the underlying asset in spot market and carry it until the maturity of futures contract. This is called "cash-and-carry" arbitrage.

When **F < (S + CC – CR):** Buy the (under priced) futures contract, short-sell the underlying asset in spot market and invest the proceeds of short-sale until the maturity of futures contract. This is called "reverse cash-and-carry" arbitrage.

USING INDEX FUTURES

Index

An index is barometer for measuring the performance of fund managers and is a comprehensive measure of market trends, intended for investors who are concerned with general stock market price movements. An Index comprises stocks that have large liquidity and market capitalization. Each stock is given a weight age in the Index equivalent to its market capitalisation.

Both NSE and BSE has launched index futures based on the S and P, CNX Nifty and BSE Sensex respectively.

Mentioned below are the significant uses of the index:

1. As a barometer for market behaviour,
2. As a benchmark portfolio performance,
3. As an underlying in derivative instruments like index futures, and
4. In passive fund management by index funds

Sensex

BSE – 30 sensex, which is the benchmark index of Indian Capital Market, comprises 30 scrips. This is the first index constructed by the Bombay Stock Exchange. Sensex measures the floating capitalisation of its constituents. SENSEX is calculated using the "Free-float Market Capitalisation" methodology.

Nifty

This is the first index constructed by the National stock Exchange. Its construction is slightly different form that of SENSEX. As we have seen before, SENSEX measures the floating capitalisation of its constituents. However, NIFTY is a step behind. It takes the full capitalisation of its 50 constituents.

Index Futures

Index derivatives are derivative contracts which have the index as the underlying. The most popular index derivatives contract the world over are index futures and index options.

NSE's market index, the S&P CNX Nifty was scientifically designed to enable the launch of index-based products like index derivatives and index funds. The first derivative contract to be traded on NSE's market was the index futures contract with the Nifty as the underlying. This was followed by index options.

Uses of Index Futures

Index futures are used by speculators, hedgers and arbitragers.

Speculators

Index futures can be used for speculation in following ways:

Bullish Index, Buy Nifty Futures

Consider a speculator who believes that market will rise and wishes to make profit out of it. Then he has two alternatives for this:

1. Buy selected liquid securities which move with the index, and sell them at a later date
2. Buying the entire index portfolio by using index futures and then selling it at a later date.

Although first alternative is widely used, it is cumbersome and expensive in terms of transactions costs, and requires a large capital. By using the second alternative an investor can "buy" the entire index by trading on one single security. Once a person is LONG NIFTY using the futures market, he gains if the index rises.

Example:

When you think the index will go up, buy the Nifty futures. The minimum market lot is 50 Nifties. Hence, if Nifty is at 5200, the investment is done in units of ₹ 2,60,000. When the trade takes place, the investor is only required to pay up the initial margin, which is ₹ 26,000 (10 per cent Margin). Hence, by paying an initial margin of ₹ 26,000, the investor gets a claim on the index worth ₹ 2,60,000.

Now if Nifty future rises from 5,200 to 5,300 you make gains of ₹ 5,000 ([5,300 – 5,200] × 50) on an investment of ₹ 26,000, i.e., approx 19 per cent.

Bearish Index, Short Nifty Futures

Consider a speculator who believes that market will fall and wishes to make profit out of it. Then he has two alternatives for this:

1. Sell selected liquid securities (if already holding it) which move with the index, and buy them at a later date.
2. Selling the entire index portfolio by using index futures and then buying it at a later date.

If he does not hold the stock, he can not do any thing in stock equities. In this case he can sell nifty futures and buy again at lower levels.

Example:

When you think the index will go down, buy the Nifty futures. The minimum market lot is 50 Nifties. Hence, if Nifty is at 5200, the investment is done in units of ₹ 2,60,000. When the trade takes place, the investor is only required to pay up the initial margin, which is ₹ 26,000 (10 per cent Margin). Hence, by paying an initial margin of ₹ 26,000, the investor gets a claim on the index worth ₹ 2,60,000.

Now if Nifty future falls from 5,200 to 5,100 you make gains of ₹ 5,000 ([5,200 – 5,100] × 50) on an investment of ₹ 26,000, i.e., approx 19 per cent.

Hedging:

Index futures can be used for hedging in following ways:

1. Long Security, Short Nifty Futures

An investor studying the market often come across a security which he believes is undervalued. He purchases securities based on a sense that they are worth more than the prevailing market price. When doing so, he faces two kinds of risks:

1. His understanding might go wrong, and the company is really not worth more than the prevailing market price.
2. The entire market moves against him (come down) and generates losses even though his belief about the security was correct.

He can minimise his exposure to above mentioned risks by hedging his position by selling Nifty futures.

Example:

A LONG Reliance position generally gains if Nifty rises and generally loses if Nifty drops. In this sense, a LONG Reliance position is not a focused play on the valuation of Reliance. It carries a LONG Nifty position along with it, as incidental baggage. An investor may be thinking he wants to take a LONG Reliance position, but a long position on Reliance effectively forces him to have LONG Reliance + LONG Nifty. This is because Reliance is one of the components of Nifty index

Thus every time you adopt a long position on a security, you should sell some amount of Nifty futures. This offsets the hidden Nifty exposure that is inside every long-security position. Once this is done, you will have a position, which is purely about the performance of the security. The position LONG Reliance + SHORT Nifty is a pure play on the value of Reliance, without any extra risk from fluctuations of the market index.

The amount of Nifty that requiring to be shorted depends on per cent weight age of Reliance in Nifty and the risk factor value (beta) of Reliance.

A Speculator adopts a position of ₹ 10,00,000 LONG Reliance on 3rd Sep. 2007. He plans to hold the position till 27th. Assuming the beta of Reliance as 1.2, he needs a short position of ₹ 12,00,000 on the index futures market to totally remove his Nifty exposure.

On 3rd Sep. 2007, Nifty trades at 4800 and the nearest futures contract (expiring on 27th Sep. 2007) is trading at about 4820. Hence, each market lot of the futures (50 Nifties) is worth ₹ 2,41,000. To sell ₹ 12,00,000 of Nifty, he needs to sell 5 lots (by rounding off to the nearest market lot).

He sells 5 market lots of Nifty (250 Nifties) to get the Position:

LONG Reliance ₹ 10,00,000 SHORT Nifty ₹ 12,00,000 15 days later, Nifty crashed because of instability in the government and it trades at 4255 in futures.

Speculator now unwinds both the positions. His position on Reliance lost ₹ 1,20,000 since Reliance had dropped to 8,80,000. His short position on Nifty Sept futures earned ₹ 1,41,250. Overall, he earned ₹ 21,250.

2. Short Security, Long Nifty Futures

An investor studying the market often come across a security, which he believes is overvalued. He sells securities based on a sense that they are worth less than the prevailing market price. When doing so, he faces two kinds of risks:

1. His understanding might go wrong, and the company is really worth more than the prevailing market price.
2. The entire market moves against him (goes up) and generates losses even though his belief about the security was correct.

He can minimise his exposure to above mentioned risks by hedging his position by buying Nifty futures.

Example:

A SHORT Reliance position generally gains if Nifty falls and generally loses if Nifty rises. In this sense, a SHORT Reliance position is not a focused play on the valuation of Reliance. It carries a SHORT NIFTY position along with it, as incidental baggage. An investor may be thinking he wants to take a SHORT Reliance position, but a short position on Reliance effectively forces him to have SHORT Reliance + SHORT Nifty. This is because Reliance is one of the components of Nifty index

Thus, every time you adopt a short position on a security, you should buy some amount of Nifty futures. This offsets the hidden Nifty exposure that is inside every short-security position. Once this is done, you will have a position which is purely about the performance of the security. The position SHORT Reliance + LONG Nifty is a pure play on the value of Reliance, without any extra risk from fluctuations of the market index.

The amount of Nifty that requiring to be bought depends on per cent weight age of Reliance in Nifty and the risk factor value (beta) of Reliance.

A Speculator adopts a position of ₹ 10,00,000 Short Reliance on 3rd Sep. 2007. He plans to hold the position till 27th. Assuming the beta of Reliance as 1.2, he needs a long position of ₹ 12,00,000 on the index futures market to totally remove his Nifty exposure.

On 3rd Sep. 2007, Nifty trades at 4800 and the nearest futures contract (expiring on 27th Sep. 2007) is trading at about 4820. Hence, each market lot of the futures (50 Nifties) is worth ₹ 2,41,000. To sell ₹ 12,00,000 of Nifty, he needs to sell 5 lots (by rounding off to the nearest market lot).He buys 5 market lots of Nifty (250 Nifties) to get the position:

Short Reliance ₹ 10,00,000 + Long Nifty ₹ 12,00,000.

Using Index Futures 15 days later, Nifty rose because of stable political outlook and it trades at 5340 in futures

Speculator now unwinds both the positions. His position on Reliance lost ₹ 1,20,000 since Reliance had increased to 11,20,000. His long position on Nifty Sept futures earned ₹ 1,30,000. Overall, he earned ₹ 10,000.

Have Portfolio, Short Nifty Futures

The only certainty about the capital market is that it fluctuates! A lot of investors who own portfolios experience the feeling of discomfort about these fluctuations.

Sometimes, they may have a view that market will fall in the near future. At other times they may feel market will remain very volatile, and they do not have an appetite for this kind of volatility.

This is particularly a problem if you need to sell shares in the near future, for example, in order to finance a purchase of a house/car. This planning can go wrong if at the time when you want to sell shares, Nifty has dropped sharply.

In such a scenario investor generally does two things:

1. He sells shares immediately. This sentiment generates "panic selling".
2. Does nothing, i.e., suffer the pain of the volatility. Due to presence of index futures market, a third and remarkable alternative becomes available.
3. Remove your exposure to index fluctuations temporarily by selling index futures. This allows an investor to be in control of his risk, instead of doing nothing and suffering the risk.

Hence, a position LONG PORTFOLIO + SHORT NIFTY can often become one-tenth as risky as the LONG PORTFOLIO position.

Suppose we have a portfolio of ₹ 1 million which has a beta of 1.25. Then a complete hedge is obtained by selling ₹ 1.25 million of Nifty futures.

Example:

A Speculator has a portfolio composed of five securities as shown the table below:

Security	No of Shares	Market Value	Beta Value
A	100	125.5	0.59
B	200	98.5	0.90
C	450	847.65	0.75
D	200	450.65	1.13
E	300	325.5	1.10
Total Value		601,472.50	

Now the portfolio Beta is Calculated as follows:

Portfolio Beta = [(100 × 125.5 × 0.59) (200 × 98.5 × 0.90) (450 × 847.65 × 0.75) (200 × 450.65 × 1.13) (300 × 325.5 × 1.10)]/6,01,472.50 = 0.865.

This means for complete hedging he will need to sell futures worth 0.865 × 6,01,472.50 = ₹ 5,20,478.275. On 3rd Sept 2007, Nifty is at 4825. So he decides to sell 100 Nifties (2 Nifty Contracts).

Now as sensed by the speculator, the index crashes and his Portfolio value comes down, but he gains in Nifty short position as shown in table below:

Security	Market Value (3rd Sept 07)	Market Value (27th Sept 07)	Profit/loss
A	125.5	117.5	0.59
B	98.5	90.40	0.90
C	847.65	810.25	0.75
D	450.65	440.85	1.13
E	325.5	298.65	1.10
Total Value	6,01,472.50	5,72,207.5	29,265
Nifty	4,825	4,535	+ 29,000

His profits on the futures hedging were ₹ 29,000 and his losses on the portfolio were ₹ 29,265. Thus the net loss is ₹ 265. If he had not hedged, he would have lost ₹ 29,265.

In this example, as there was drop in Nifty, the short position on the futures market generated profits. If Nifty would have risen, then the investor would have gained money on his securities portfolio, and lost money on the futures position. In either event, he would be hedged, i.e., he would neither gain nor lose from index fluctuations.

Note: Example deliberately uses a small portfolio of small securities, in practice; the effectiveness of hedging would be greater with larger portfolios of larger securities.

Hedging does not remove losses. The best that can be achieved using hedging is the removal of unwanted exposure, i.e. unnecessary risk. The hedged position will make less profit than the un-hedged position, half the time. One should not enter into a hedging strategy hoping to make excess profits for sure. All that can come out of hedging is reduced risk.

Arbitrage: Index Futures can be used for arbitrage as explain below:

Have Funds, Lend them to the Market

Most people would like to lend funds into the security market, without suffering the risk. Traditional methods of loaning money into the security market suffer from (a) Price risk of shares and (b) credit risk of default of the counter-party. What is new about the index futures market is that it supplies a technology to lend money into the market without suffering any exposure to Nifty, without bearing any credit risk.

The basic idea is simple. The lender buys all 50 securities of Nifty on the cash market, and simultaneously sells them at a future date on the futures market. It is like a repo. There is no price risk since the position is perfectly hedged. There is no credit risk since the counterparty on both legs is the NSCCL which supplies clearing services on NSE. It is an ideal lending vehicle for entities which are shy of price risk and credit risk, such as traditional banks and the most conservative corporate treasuries.

Example:

5th Sep 2007 trades 4,800 and the nearest futures contract (expiring on 27th Sep 2007) is trading at about 4,840. A speculator wants to earn this return for 22 days.

He buys ₹ 10,00,000 of Nifty on spot market (Buys portfolio of shares in Nifty in proportion of their weightage). In doing so he places Buy orders for 50 scrips in Nifty per their weightage in Nifty, and ends up paying slightly more. His average cost of purchase is 0.15 per cent higher (considering impact cost) i.e., he has obtained Nifty spot at 4,807.2.

He sells ₹ 10,00,000 of Nifty futures at 4,840. He sells 4 lots of Nifty to get position of approx ₹ 10,00,000.

Now during the period from 5th Sep – 27* Sep 2007 he receives few dividends on the 50 scrips of Nifty that he is holding, total dividend amount being ₹ 8,500.

On 27th Sep. at 3.15 he puts sells off his Nifty portfolio of 50 shares. Nifty happens to close to 4,820 and his sell order goes through at 4,813 (considering impact cost @ 0.15 per cent).

The futures position expires on 27th Sep at 4,810, i.e., it converges with spot price. Now speculator gains ₹ 6 per unit. Spot transaction and ₹ 20 on per unit future transaction. In addition to this he earned 8,500 as dividends.

USING STOCK FUTURES

Stock Futures

Stock derivatives are derivative contracts which have the Stocks as the underlying. The most popular stock derivatives contracts in the world over are stock futures and stock options.

Difference between Trading Securities and Trading Futures on Individual Securities:

1. To trade securities, a customer must open a security trading account with a securities broker and a demat account with a securities depository. Whereas to trade future, customer must open a future trading account with a derivatives broker.
2. Buying security involves putting up all the money upfront. Buying futures simply involves putting in the margin money. They enable the futures traders to take a position in the underlying security without having to open an account with a securities broker.
3. With the purchase of shares of a company, the holder becomes a part owner of the company. The shareholder typically receives the rights and privileges associated with the security, which may include the receipt of dividends,

invitation to the annual shareholders meeting and the power to vote. With the purchase of futures on a security, the holder essentially makes a legally binding promise or obligation to buy the underlying security at some point in the future (the expiration date of the contract). Security futures do not represent ownership in a corporation and the holder is therefore not regarded as a shareholder.

4. Selling securities involves buying security before selling it. In cases where short selling is permitted, it is assumed that the securities broker owns the security and then "lends" it to trader so that he can sell it. Besides, even if permitted, short sales on security can only be executed on an up-tick. A futures contract represents a promise to transact at some point in the future. In this light, a promise to sell security is just as easy to make as a promise to buy security. Selling security futures without previously owning them simply obligates the trader to selling a certain amount of the underlying security at some point in the future. It can be done just as easily as buying futures, which obligates the trader to buying a certain amount of the underlying security at some point in the future.

USING OF STOCK FUTURES

Stock futures are used by speculators, hedgers and arbitragers.

Speculation

Stock futures can be used for speculation in following ways:

1. Bullish Security, Buy Futures

Consider a speculator who believes that a particular security is undervalued and expects its price to go up in next 2-3 months. Then he can buy that security and hold it till price rises. He can also do the same thing by buying the futures contract instead of buying in equity, and can take advantage of leverage that derivatives market provides and increase his returns.

Example:

Consider a Security ABC which is currently trading at ₹ 1,000 and its future trades at ₹ 1,010. If a speculator is bullish on this scrip and thinks that the script will rise in coming weeks. He can make profit in two ways.

1. He buys 200 shares of ABC at 1,000 and sells at 1,050 after 30 days, thus, making gains of 10,000 on investment of 2,00,000, i.e., 5 per cent in a month.
2. He buys a future at 1010 and sells the same at 1050 (When spot price is 1050) after 30 days. Assuming lot size 200, as min contract value, i.e., 2 lack then to buy one contract he needs approx ₹ 40,000 (assuming 20 per cent Margin). Thus he makes gain of ₹ 8,000 [(1,050 – 1,010) × 200] on investment of 40,000, i.e., 20 per cent in a month.

2. Bearish Security, Sell Futures

Consider a speculator who believes that a particular is overvalued and expects its price to go down in next 2-3 months. In this case, he holds the same stock he cancels it and book profits and buy again at lower bands later on.

If he does not hold the stock, he can not do any thing in stock equities. In this case he can sell stock futures and buy again at lower levels.

Example:

Consider a Security XYZ which trading at ₹ 500 and Its future trades at ₹ 495. If a speculator is bearish on the scrip and thinks that the script will fall in coming weeks. He can make profit by selling XYZ futures of ₹ 495 and buy the same back when price of XYZ falls to say 475, and at same time corresponding future price becomes 480. Assuming lot size of 500, as min contract value is 2 lack. He needs a margin of ₹ 50,000 to sell one contract. He makes gain of ₹ 7,500 [(495 – 480) × 500] on investment of 50,000, i.e., 15 per cent.

Hedging

Stock futures can be used for hedging in following ways:

1. Long Security, Sell Futures

If an investor is long on a security and he anticipates that the price of security may be volatile in near futures, then he can minimize his exposure to this unwanted risk due to volatity in stock price which he is anticipating by hedging his position by selling that stock futures.

Example:

Consider an investor holding shares of ABC Company quoting of ₹ 800. If he anticipates the price of a security fall due to any reason then he can hedge his long position in the security by selling a future contract of ABC say quoting at ₹ 802, by paying an initial margin. Now if the price of security falls to say ₹ 750 he suffers a loss of ₹ 50 on the security. But this loss will be offset by the profits he makes on his short position as the future will also come down to 750 or nearby levels

Note: Hedging does not remove losses. The best that can be achieved using hedging is the removal of unwanted exposure, i.e., unnecessary risk. The hedged position will make less profit than the un-hedged position, half the time. One should not enter into a hedging strategy hoping to make excess profits for sure; all that can come out of hedging is reduced risk.

Arbitrage

Stock futures can be used for arbitrage in following ways:

1. Overpriced Futures: Buy Spot, Sell Futures

As we discussed earlier, the cost-of-carry ensures that the futures price stay in tune with the spot price.

Whenever the futures price deviates substantially from its fair value, arbitrage opportunities arise.

If you notice that futures price on a security seems to be much more then its fare value and futures seems to be over price, i.e., **F > (S + CC – CR):** Sell the (overpriced) futures contract, buy the underlying asset in spot market and carry it until the maturity of futures contract. This is called "cash-and-carry" arbitrage.

Example:

Consider Stock ABC trade @ ₹ 1,000 and its one month future trade @ ₹ 1,025 which seems to be overpriced As an arbitrageur, you can make risk less profit in following manner:

On day one, you borrow funds to buy the security in the cash/spot market at 1,000. Simultaneously, sell the futures on the security at 990.Now take delivery of the security purchased and hold the security for a month. On the futures expiration date, the spot and the futures price converge. Now unwind the position.

Say the security closes at ₹ 1,010. Sell the security and the future position expires with profit of ₹ 15. The result is a risk less profit of ₹ 10 on the spot position and ₹ 15 on the futures position. Now return the borrowed funds.

2. Under priced Futures: Buy Futures, Sell Spot

If you notice that the futures price on a security seems to be well below its fare value and futures seems to be under price, i.e., **F < (S + CC – CR):** Buy the (under priced) futures contract, short-sell the underlying asset in spot market and invest the proceeds of short-sale until the maturity of futures contract. This is called "reverse cash-and-carry" arbitrage.

Example:

Consider Stock XYZ trade @ ₹ 1,000 and its one month future trade @ ₹ 955, which seems to be under priced As an arbitrageur, you can make risk less profit in following manner:

On day one, sell the security in the cash/spot market at 1000 and simultaneously, buy the futures on the security at 965. On the futures expiration date, the spot and the futures price converge. Now unwind the position.

Say the security closes at ₹ 985. Buy back the security. The futures position expires with a profit of ₹ 20. The result is a risk less profit of ₹ 15 on the spot position and ₹ 20 on the futures position.

❀ ❀ ❀

Forward Contract

INTRODUCTION

A forward contract is an agreement to buy or sell an asset on a specified date for a specified price. One of the parties to the contract assumes a long position and agrees to buy the underlying asset on a certain specified future date for a certain specified price. The other party assumes a short position and agrees to sell the asset on the same date for the same price. Other contract details like delivery date, price and quantity are negotiated bilaterally by the parties to the contract. The forward contracts are normally traded outside the exchanges.

The salient features of forward contracts are:

- They are bilateral contracts and hence exposed to counter-party risk.
- Each contract is custom designed, and hence is unique in terms of contract size, expiration date and the asset type and quality.
- The contract price is generally not available in public domain.
- On the expiration date, the contract has to be settled by delivery of the asset.
- If the party wishes to reverse the contract, it has to compulsorily go to the same counter-party, which often results in high prices being charged.

However, forward contracts in certain markets have become very standardised, as in the case of foreign exchange, thereby reducing transaction costs and increasing transactions volume. This process of standardisation reaches its limit in the organised futures market.

Forward contracts are very useful in hedging and speculation. The classic hedging application would be that of an exporter who expects to receive payment in dollars three months later. He is exposed to the risk of exchange rate fluctuations. By using the currency forward market to sell dollars forward, he can lock on to a rate today and reduce his uncertainty. Similarly an importer who is required to make a payment in dollars two months hence can reduce his exposure to exchange rate fluctuations by buying dollars forward.

If a speculator has information or analysis, which forecasts an upturn in a price, then he can go long on the forward market instead of the cash market. The speculator would go long on the forward, wait for the price to rise, and then take a reversing transaction to book profits. Speculators may well be required to deposit a margin upfront. However, this is generally a relatively small proportion of the value of the assets underlying the forward contract. The use of forward markets here supplies leverage to the speculator.

LIMITATIONS OF FORWARD MARKETS

Forward markets world-wide are afflicted by several problems:

- Lack of centralisation of trading,
- Illiquidity, and
- Counterparty risk

In the first two of these, the basic problem is that of too much flexibility and generality. The forward market is like a real estate market in that any two consenting adults can form contracts against each other. This often makes them design terms of the deal which are very convenient in that specific situation, but makes the contracts non-tradable. Counterparty risk arises from the possibility of default by any one party to the transaction. When one of the two sides to the transaction declares bankruptcy, the other suffers. Even when forward markets trade standardized contracts, and hence avoid the problem of illiquidity, still the counterparty risk remains a very serious issue.

A Forward contract is an agreement in which two parties agree to undertake an exchange of the underlying asset at some future date at a pre-determined price.

A Forward contract is a customised contract between two parties, where settlement takes place on a specific date. The settlement date and price are agreed in advance by the parties concerned.

Today, Forward markets exist in a whole host of commodities. The most important Forward market is the foreign exchange market in which billions of dollars worth of currency are traded each business day. Another sector where forward contracts are popular is the agriculture sector where commodity prices fluctuate a great deal. Take the case of a factory interested in purchasing onions in bulk. Both, the producer and the factory would like to reduce the uncertainty in prices, as the delivery may be staggered over a period of time. One way to achieve this would be to reach an agreement with the producer to supply onions at various times in the future at fixed prices today. This example captures the very essence of forward trading.

Forward contracts are private agreements tailor made to meet the requirements of the parties. They are outside the regulation of any exchange. This, often, exposes the contracting parties to the risk of default. If a Forward contract is closed before the scheduled closing date, a penalty may be charged. Hence, the drawbacks of Forward contracts are lack of standardization which prevents trading on an exchange and the risk of default.

FORWARD RATE AGREEMENTS (FRAS)

FRAs are instruments that are used to hedge future interest rate risk. The two concerned parties agree on a single future rate of interest. The actual rate of interest is compared with the rate agreed in the FRA and based on the difference. One party pays compensation to the other. Thus, the two parties enter into an agreement between themselves to protect against a future adverse movement in interest rates.

For instance, a company ABC needs to borrow ₹ 3 million in 3 months time for a period of one year. The current rate of interest is 14 per cent. The company is worried that interest rates will rise in the future, to mitigate this risk, ABC enters into an agreement with a financial institution, XYZ, and purchases a FRA at 14 per cent. Suppose after three months, interest rates are 17 per cent. Then, XYZ has to compensate ABC to the tune of 3 per cent (17 per cent less 14 per cent) of ₹ 3 million. Thus XYZ pays ABC (0.17 - 0.14)*3 million = ₹ 90,000. Now suppose interest rates fall to 11 per cent. In such a case, ABC has to compensate XYZ to the tune of ₹ 90,000, i.e., (0.14 - 0.11)*3 millipn.

Note that there is no physical principal amount in the FRA transaction. It is still necessary to borrow or lend cash if the underlying need to do so exists, which will be a transaction distinct from the FRA. By transacting the FRA, the interest rate, for the period in question becomes fixed. FRAs are quoted like deposits, for varying currencies and duration. Customers with large requirements can enter into FRAs with their banks for virtually any future period.

The main reasons for the phenomenal success of this instrument lie in its basic structure and features.

These reasons are enumerated below:

- It is an extremely efficient method of meeting the widespread need to hedge, or trade, forward period interest rates. Virtually every bank and business organisation with exposure to debt has a need for hedging tools like the FRA.
- There is no principal amount involved, and the only sums, which change hands are those which compensate for the movement in the interest rates. Hence, the credit risk is much smaller than traditional cash deposits.
- The markets in all major currencies and periods are extremely liquid.

- FRAs are *very* straightforward products as compared to complex derivative products like index Options, and relatively simpler to administer. Also, standardized terms ensure that all participants know their exact positions.
- FRAs give the user flexibility with regard to amounts, periods and currencies.
- There are no margin requirements. With no up front outlay, minimal capital requirements, the gearing possibilities are almost limitless.

Formation of Forward Rates

Currency Forward rate links exchange market and money market. In order to know forward buying and selling rates, it is necessary to know interest rates. Forward rate is based on Spot rate and differential of interest rates of two currencies. If currency A has a rate of interest higher than currency B, currency A will be quoted at Forward discount in relation to currency B or inversely, currency B will be at Forward premium with respect to currency A.

Question 1: Following interest rates are given:

	Borrowing rate (per cent)	Lending rate (per cent)
US $ (1 year)	4 per cent p.a.	4.25 per cent p.a.
FFr (1 year)	5.50 per cent p.a.	5.75 per cent p.a.

Spot rate: FFr/US $: 5.2550/2600

Calculate the Forward buying and selling rates.

Solution: Let us say the bank engages itself to buy US $ 1 million against French francs after one year. While buying US dollars, how many French francs will it have to give out? It would take the following steps:

(a) Borrows a certain amount of US dollars on the money market, the sum being such that it would become $ 10,00,000 after one year (capital and interest). The amount borrowed, therefore, is the present value of $ 10,00,000 of one year hence. So borrowed amount is:

$$\frac{10,00,000}{(1 + 4.25 \text{ per cent})}$$

(b) Transform this amount in FFrs at market buying rate to get

$$\frac{10,00,000}{(1 + 4.25 \text{ per cent})} \times 5.2550 \text{ FFr}$$

(c) Place these French francs on the money market at a rate of 5.50 per cent. So after one year, it will have a sum of French francs as given below:

$$\frac{10,00,000}{(1 + 4.25 \text{ per cent})} \times 5.2550\ (1 + 5.5 \text{ per cent})\ \text{FFr}$$

(d) Give these French francs to buy \$ 10,00,000. Thus the buying rate becomes

$$\frac{1,10,00,000}{10,00,000\ (1 + 4.25 \text{ per cent})} \times 5.2550\ (1 + 5.5 \text{ per cent})$$

or

$$\frac{5.2550 \times 1 + 5.5 \text{ per cent}}{(1 + 4.25 \text{ per cent})} \text{ FFr per US \$}$$

FFr 5.3180/US \$

Next, suppose the bank engages itself to sell US \$ 10,00,000 against French francs. The bank borrows a sum of French francs such that their conversion in US dollar and subsequent placement of these dollars in the money market will result into \$ 10,00,000 after one year. The following steps would be involved:

(a) Borrowing of a sum, say X of French francs.

(b) Conversion of X French francs into US dollars at the market selling rate, to get

$$\frac{X}{5.2600} \text{ US dollar}$$

(c) Placing of these US dollars in the money market. After one year this will give,

$\frac{X}{5.2600}$ (1 + 4 per cent) US dollars. This should be equal to US \$ 10,00,000.

(d) Reimbursing of the Frency franc loan along with interest. The reimbursed amount would be X (1 + 5.75 per cent).

This should equal to \$ 10,00,000 or

$$\$\ 10,00,000 = X\ (1 + 5.75 \text{ per cent})\ \text{FFr}$$

Or

$$\$\ \frac{X}{5.26} (1 + 4 \text{ per cent}) = X\ (1 + 5.75 \text{ per cent})\ \text{FFr}$$

Or

$$\$\ 1 = 5.2600 \times \frac{1 + 5.75 \text{ per cent}}{1 + 4 \text{ per cent}} \text{ FFr}$$

$$= \text{FFr } 5.3485/\text{US \$}$$

This is the selling rate.

Thus, one year forward FFr-US $ quotation would be 5.3180/4385.

Alternatively, the above steps are given in a simple way;

To find forward buying rate for dollar

Borrow $ 1 at a rate of 4.25 per cent

Sell $ 1 at spot to get FFr 5.2250

Place FFr 5.2250 in money market to receive

1 × 5.2550 (1 + 5.5 per cent)

By dollar forward such that principal and interest, both are covered. That is,

$ 1 × (1 + 4.25 per cent) = FFr 1 × 5.2550 (1 + 5.50 per cent)

$$= \$ 1 = \text{FFr } 5.2550 \times \frac{1 + 5.50 \text{ per cent}}{1 + 4.5 \text{ per cent}}$$

Borrow FFr 1 at 5.75 per cent

Sell FFr at spot to get $ 17(5.2600)

Place $ 17(5.2600) at 4 per cent to get

$ 1/(5.2600) [1+4 per cent]

Sell US $ amount forward to pay the FFr debt. Therefore,

$$\$ \frac{1}{5.2600} \; 1 + 4 \text{ per cent} = \text{I } 1 + 5.75 \text{ per cent}$$

$$\$ 1 = 5.2600 \; \frac{1 + 5.75 \text{ per cent}}{1 + 4 \text{ per cent}}$$

It is seen that the rate of interest on US dollar is lower, it being quoted at Forward premium with respect to French franc.

Premium or Discount

At times, the difference between Forward and Spot market i; given in percentage terms. This percentage difference is referred to as premium or discount. Mathematically,

$$\text{Premium or Discount} = \frac{\text{Forward rate} - \text{Spot rate}}{\text{Spot rate}} \times \frac{12}{\text{N}} \times 100$$

Where N is the number of months forward.

Question 2: Following Rupee-US dollar rates are given:

Spot: ₹ 43.5050/6090

3-months forward: ₹ 43.6030/7100

What are premium/discount on buying and selling ra respectively?

Solution: As is clear from the quoted figures, US dollar is quoted: Forward premium.

$$\text{Premium on buying rate} = \frac{43.6030 - 43.5050}{43.5050} \times \frac{12}{3} \times 100 \text{ per cent}$$

Or

0.9014 per cent

$$\text{Premium on selling rate} = \frac{43.7100 - 43.6090}{43.6090} \times \frac{12}{3} \times 100 \text{ per cent}$$

Or

0.9264 per cent

EQUILIBRIUM IN THE FORWARD CURRENCY MARKET

The Forward rates and Spot rates are linked through interest rates. In practice, Forward rates do not fully incorporate the interest rates. As a result, Forward rate may be either overstated or understated *vis-a-vis* what it should be as per the prevailing interest rates. As long as Forward rates do not correspond to what is dictated/warranted by interest rates, there is disequilibrium. The arbitrageurs obviously would like to benefit from this disequilibrium. The arbitrage process involving forward rates and money market interest rates is known as covered interest arbitrage.

Question 3: Find the possible arbitrage gain from the data given below:

₹ 40.1000/US $ (Spot)

₹ 40.4000/US $ (3-m forward)

Interest rates (3-month)

Re: 11.5 per cent p.a.

US $: 8 per cent p.a.

Solution: Here US $ is at forward premium. The premium is

$$= \frac{40.4000 - 40.1000}{40.1000} \times \frac{12}{3} \times 100 \text{ per cent}$$

Interest rate differential = 11.5 – 8.0 = 3.5 per cent

Now, we take the following steps:

(a) Borrow \$ 1,000 at 8 per cent p.a. for 3 months and con-vert this sum into rupees to get ₹ 1,000 × 40.1000 or ₹ 40,100.

(b) Place these rupees so obtained for 3 months in the money market. At the end of three months, this place-ment will yield

$$₹\ 40{,}100 \times \left(1 + \frac{11.5}{100} \times \frac{3}{12}\right) \text{ Or } ₹\ 41{,}258.75$$

(c) Sell these rupees 3-month forward to get US \$ at the maturity date. The amount obtained will be:

$$\text{US } \$ \frac{41{,}258.75}{40.4000} \text{ Or } \$\ 1021.1110$$

(d) Refund the US \$ loan with the interest due. The amount to be refunded is

$$\$\ 1{,}000 \times 1 + \frac{8}{100} \times \frac{3}{12} \text{ Or US } \$\ 1{,}020$$

Thus, net gain = \$ 1,021.1110 – \$ 1020

= \$ 1.111 The gain is 0.11 per cent.

Question 4: Calculate the arbitrage gain from the following data:

DM 1.6000/US \$ (spot)

DM 1.5840/US \$ (6-m forward)

6-month interest rates

US \$: 6 per cent p.a. DM: 4.5 per cent p.a.

Solution: From the data, it is seen that US \$ is at Forward discount. The discount is:

$$\frac{1.5840 - 1.6}{1.6} \times \frac{12}{6} \times 100 = 2 \text{ per cent}$$

Interest rate differential = 6 – 4.5 = 1.5 per cent

Now, we take the following steps:

(a) Borrow US \$ 1,000 for 6 months. Convert this sum in DM at the spot rate to obtain

DM 1,000 × 1.6 Or DM 1,600

(b) Place these DMs in money market for 6 months at a rate of 4.5 per cent p.a. This will result in

$$\text{DM } 1{,}600 \times 1 + \frac{4.5}{100} \times \frac{6}{12} \text{ Or DM } 1{,}636$$

(c) Sell the sum of DM 1,636 six-month Forward to get back US $. The sum obtained would be

$$\text{US\$ } \frac{1{,}636}{1.584} \text{ Or \$ } 1{,}032.83$$

(d) Refund the US $ loan with interest at the end of six-months. The refunded amount is:

$$\text{US \$ } 1{,}000 \times 1 + \frac{6}{100} \times \frac{6}{12} \text{ Or \$ } 1{,}030$$

Net gain = $ 1,032.83 – $ 1,030 or $ 2.83

Gain is 0.283 per cent.

Question 5: Given the following data, at what Forward rate will there be no arbitrage gain possible?

₹ 22.00/DM (spot)

6-month interest rates

Re: 11.5 per cent p.a.

DM: 6.5 per cent p.a.

Solution: In order to have no arbitrage gain in the Forward exchange market, it is necessary that interest rate differential be equal to the Forward premium or discount. Here,

the interest rate differential = 11.5 per cent – 6.5 per cent

= 5 per cent p.a.

$$\text{Forward premium} = \frac{S_f - 22}{22} \times \frac{12}{6} \times 100$$

where S_f is the 6-month Forward exchange rate.

For no arbitrage,

$$\frac{S_f - 22}{22} \times \frac{12}{6} \times 100 = 5 \text{ per cent}$$

$$S_f = 22 + 5 \times 22/200$$

$$= 22.55$$

In this way, at a 6-month Forward rate of ₹ 22.55/DM, there will be no arbitrage gain.

Quoting Prices of Goods Exported

Forward exchange rates can be made use of in quoting prices of goods—merchandise or equipment — to be sold to foreigners. These rates can be specially useful when the amount due is to be received or paid in installments.

Question 6: An Indian company is negotiating the price of equipment that it is selling to an American buyer. It wants to receive ₹ 5,00,000 (risk free) for this equipment. The American buyer will pay in 3 equal dollar installments, with first installment to be paid after 3 months. What dollar price should the Indian company quote? The following information is available:

Re/US $

Spot	3-month forward	6-month forward	9-month forward
40.1020/41.2000	40.4050/41.5200	40.7200/41.8400	40.95 10/42.0620

Solution: The Indian company is to receive the installments of US dollars. Further, it wants to have a risk-free inflow of rupees. For the purpose, it would do well to sell the dollars Forward. Suppose each installment is of 'D' dollars, the total rupee value (ignoring the time value of money) is going to be:

$$D\ [40.4050 + 40.7200 + 40.9510] = ₹\ 5,00,000$$

$$122.076\ D = ₹\ 5,00,000 \text{ or } D = ₹\ 4,095.8091$$

Therefore, the Indian seller should quote a dollar price of 3D (3 × $ 4,095.8091) or $ 12,287.43.

Question 7: In Example 5.9, if the Indian seller desires four equal rupee instalments, how much should the quoted price in US dollars be if the first instalment is to be received immedi-ately and other data remains the same?

Solution: Since each installment is to be equal in rupee terms, the sum of each one will be:

$$\frac{₹\,5,00,000}{4} \text{ or } ₹\ 1,25,000$$

Dollar-equivalent of this sum will be

$$D_1 = \frac{\$1,25,000}{40.1020} = \$3,117.05$$

Similarly,

$$D_2 = \frac{\$1,25,000}{40.4050} = \$\ 3,093.67$$

$$D_3 = \frac{\$1,25,000}{40.7200} = \$\ 3,069.74$$

$$D_4 = \frac{\$1,25,000}{40.9510} = \$\ 3,052.43$$

Therefore, the total dollar price is $D_1 + D_2 + D_3 + D_4$

Or

$ 12,332.88

Covering Exchange Risk on Forward Market

Often, the enterprises that are exporting or importing take recourse to covering their operations in the Forward market. If an importer anticipates eventual appreciation of the currency in which imports are denominated, he can buy the foreign currency immediately and hold it up to the date of maturity. This means he has to block his rupee cash right away. Alternatively, the importer can buy the foreign currency forward at a rate known and fixed today. This will do away with the problem of blocking of funds/ cash initially. In other words, Forward purchase of the currency eliminates the exchange risk of the importer as the debt in foreign currency is covered. Likewise, an exporter can eliminate the risk of currency fluctuation by selling his receivables forward.

Question 8: An Indian importer has bought merchandise for $ 1 million from an American company. The payment is due in 3-months. The exchange rates are as follows:

Spot: ₹ 42.50/US $

3 months forward: ₹ 43.00/US $

Suggest what the importer can do.

Solution: As is clear from the data, the US dollar is quoting at forward premium. The course available to the importer is to buy dollars forward and engage himself to pay in three months, an amount of ₹ 43 million irrespective of the Spot rate in three months.

By covering himself on the Forward market, the importer has had to pay the amount of the premium also. that is, he has paid a little dearer for the dollar than the Spot rate. There is, thus, a cost associated with covering.

If, on the other hand, US dollar was at Forward discount with respect to the domestic currency, the importer would have been required to pay less than Spot rate. In that case, there would be a gain for the importer.

Question 9: An Indian company has sold merchandise for DM 1 million, payable in six months, to its German client. The exchange rates are as follows:

Spot: ₹ 22.00/DM

6-months forward: ₹ 21.70/DM

What should the exporter do?

Solution: Since Deutschmark is at discount with respect to the Spot rate, the exporter will cover itself through forward sale of DM. At the end of the maturity (or at the date of settlement), the company will get ₹ 21.70 million. It is obviously less than what it would have got had the settlement been done on the spot. However, if the foreign currency (DM) was at premium, the Forward sale would have brought a gain to the enterprise.

For a large number of currencies, it is difficult to obtain covers for periods longer than one year but it is possible to renew the contracts regularly at the end of each period (year). This facilitates the coverage of the required total period. In this situation, the cost of covering only for the first period is known by the hedger.

PRECAUTIONS TO USE DERIVATIVES

We saw how useful derivatives are as hedging and risk management tools. However, derivatives do not come without their share of problems and dangers. Derivatives are highly sophisticated instruments and users with inadequate information and understanding expose themselves to all the risks inherent in using derivatives. Spectacular losses have been made and some companies have even come to the point of collapse after using derivative instruments. Some examples of the unfortunate use of derivatives are:

- In 1994, American consumer products giant Procter and Gamble (P&G), lost an estimated US$ 200 million on a complex interest rate Swap. The Swap was intended to lower funding costs for P&G if interest rates moved in a certain manner. However, the Swap turned out to be a sophisticated bet on future interest rate changes. It was the result of speculation and lax controls. The company ought not to have betted on interest rate changes. This case can be viewed as a classic case of how not to use derivatives.
- Sumitomo lost 1.17 billion pounds on copper and copper derivative instruments from 1995-1996.
- Nat West Markets, in 1997, announced it had lost 77m pounds as a result of mispriced interest rate Options and Swaps.
- The German metals and services group, Metallge sells haft, came to the verge of destruction in 1994 after losses on energy derivatives exceeded DM 2.3 billion
- Barings, Britain's oldest merchant bank lost 900m pounds sterling on Nikkei Index contracts on the Singapore and Osaka Derivatives Exchanges, ultimately leading to the bank's near collapse in 1995. The main person involved was Nick Leeson, the bank's derivatives trader.
- In 1994, Orange County, USA's richest local authority went bankrupt after trading in high risk derivatives. On the advice of Merrill Lynch, county treasurer, Robert Citron invested the county's assets in interest sensitive derivatives. The market moved against him and the county faced losses of around US$ 1.6

billion. Afterwards, Merrill Lynch agreed to pay Orange County over US$ 400m rather than face trial, in a friendly agreement.

The above-cited examples are enough to make any potential user of derivatives apprehensive. However, the stories not told about derivatives represent the majority of cases where derivatives effectively reduce risk. Today, almost all large, non financial organisations use financial derivatives and the number of users is fast increasing. Derivatives are no different than the majority of modern inventions: if used m a proper way they are powerful and, indeed valuable tools. In wrong hands, they can cause tremendous destruction as the above examples testify. The function of a corporate financial officer is to reduce risk by using derivatives and not to speculate. Yet, in any derivative disaster, an element of speculation seems to be present. Another cause of losses is decisions taken by people with inadequate knowledge and who do not fully understand the complex structure of derivatives. The case of the Orange County derivatives amply demonstrates this. It is dear that the derivative products used by the county treasurer were not fully comprehended by him.

Barings – What Went Wrong?

A careful study of the Barings case brings to light several issues. Extensive data obtained by Singapore inspectors show that Nick Leeson lost 4.8m pounds sterling between July and October 1992. Leeson covered all the losses by July '93. But it appeared that Leeson recovered his losses by selling options in a way that stored up trouble. He used a strategy called "Straddling". Simply put, Leeson traded in a way that he was severely exposed to the market movement and a slight movement against him would lead to huge losses. After the Kobe earthquake, the volatility of the Nikkei increased sharply and Leeson and Barings' were left facing huge losses.

Leeson did not take the relatively small losses he would have made had he sold the contracts when the market started to go against him, but waited in the hope that the situation would reverse and he would make good the losses. But this was not to be, and the rest, as they say, is history.

What Leeson did was to engage in highly speculative trading. He primarily used derivatives, not as risk mitigating instruments, but as means of earning speculative profits. The downside risk was huge and the risk of losses was great.

Derivatives – Irreplaceable Tools or Weapons of Destruction?

Derivatives have acquired a myth of danger and mystery. One reason is the sensational media coverage of the derivatives disasters. However, what often escapes notice is that these disastrous transactions involve speculation (intentional risks to make profits) or inadequate controls, poorly implemented regulations or oversight. Derivatives as an instrument do not cause harm or otherwise, it is the way it is put to use that determines the consequences. It is to be noted that most companies use derivatives for risk reduction and only very few businesses with poor management hurt themselves.

As explained earlier, derivative contracts can be geared to many times their value. In other words, contracts, which may be worth millions, if the market moves in a certain way, cost only a fraction of that value.

Usually, the market will not move that much and the contract will be settled or sold to somebody else for a small gain or loss. However, if it does shift significantly, big losses can be incurred, which are magnified due to the gearing effect.

Banks have complex computer programmes to tell them how much they could lose if the market moves by a certain amount. Regulations require them to put money aside to protect against possible losses.

On exchanges, traders have to pay any losses incurred on their position at the end of each day. This "margin" payment is to prevent risks getting out of hand.

Making Derivatives Use Safer

It is very important to prevent disasters of the kind mentioned above. Investors, both retail and corporate ought to be reassured so as to ensure a thriving derivatives market. If the investors are to place their faith in derivatives, measures have to be taken at various levels. Some ways to streamline the functioning of the derivatives market are:

At the exchange level, position limits and surveillance procedures should be sound. Regulations should be modified as and when new incidents come to light. Enforcement of regulations must be sound.

At the clearing house level, margin requirements must be stringently enforced, even while dealing with large institutions.

At the level of individual companies with positions on the market, extensive modern risk measurement systems should be put in place. The basic concept that should not be lost sight of is that, while thinking about returns is great, risk measurement also merits serious consideration.

Serious attempts have to be made to educate potential investors about derivatives, their intricacies and their dangers if not used properly. Investors, on their part, must get information on derivatives and seriously consider all aspects before investing.

Brokers and other institutions, who get investors to buy derivatives, must warn them of potential dangers, if any. To make money, they should not sell derivative products that the client may not be comfortable with.

While introducing derivatives in countries where they do not exist, regulators must do so in a phased manner and introduce new types as the market matures. Complex products, when the market and people are not ready, could cause more harm than good.

❋ ❋ ❋

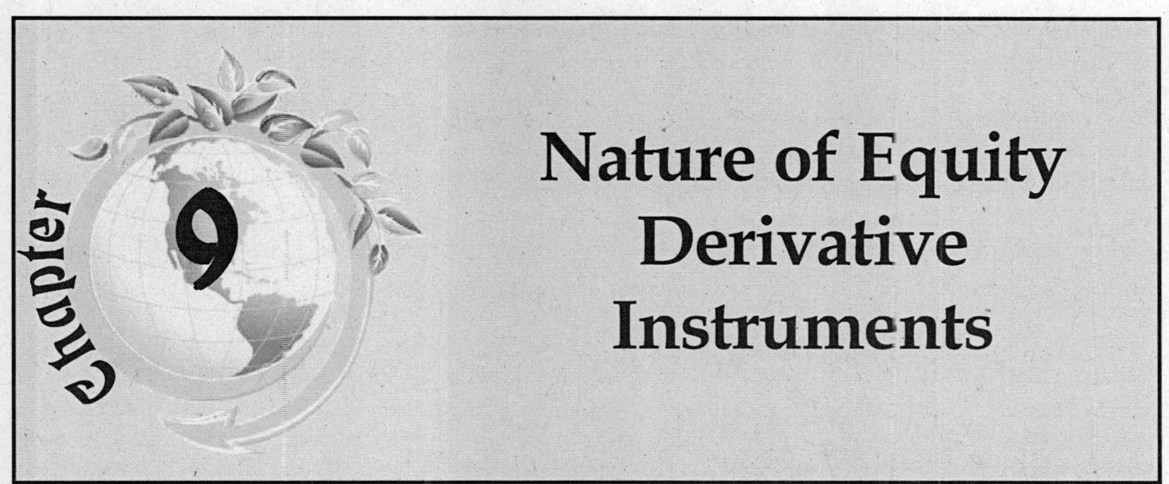

Nature of Equity Derivative Instruments

INTRODUCTION

During the last few years, a number of new financial instruments have assumed significance in the Indian economy. With rapid globalisation, this trend is likely to accelerate in future. Derivatives are a kind of financial instrument which values change in response to the change in specified I is "interst", security prices, commodity prices, index of prices or rates, or similar variables. Typical example to derivatives are futures and forward contracts, swaps and option contracts. Equity Derivative Instrument serotypes of financial instruments, which are bought or sold with specific motives, e.g., speculation, hedging and arbitrage.

In order to understand a true of various Equity Derivative Instruments, it is essential first to understand the meaning of the terms 'forward contract', 'futures contract' and 'options contract'.

A forward contract is an agreement between two parties where by one party agrees to buy from, or sell to, the to her party an acetate future time for an agreed price (usually referred to as the 'contract price'). The parties to forward contracts may be individuals, corporate or financial in situations. At maturity, a forward contracts settled by delivery of the asset by the seller to the buyer in return for payment of the contract price. For example, a person (X) may enter to a forward contract with other person (Y) on June 15, 2003 to buy 10 kgs. of silver at the end of 90 days at a price of ₹ 8,200 per kg. At the end of the 90 days, Y will deliver 10 kgs. of silver to X against payment of ₹ 82,000. If the price of silver, at the end of the 90 days, is ₹ 8,300 per kg., X would make a profit of ₹ 1,000 and Y would lose ₹ 1,000, as X could sell silver bought at ₹ 82,000 for ₹ 83,000, where as Y would have to buy silver for ₹ 83,000 and sell for ₹ 82,000. On the other hand, if the price of silver at the end of the 90 days is ₹ 7,800 per kg., X would lose ₹ 4,000, where as Y would make a profit of ₹ 4,000, as X would have to sell silver bought at ₹ 82,000 for ₹ 78,000, where as Y would buy silver for ₹ 78,000, which he would sell to X at ₹ 82,000.

A futures contract, like a forward contract, is an agreement between two parties to buy or sell an a asset at a certain time in future for an agreed price. Futures contracts are normally traded on an exchange. To make trading possible, the exchange specifies certain standard diced features of the contract. The exchange may also provide for guarantee mechanism to ensure that each party to the contrate tract meats its etsits obligations and, consequently, risk from default by parties is minimised.

An Option is a type of derivative instrument where by a person gets the right to buy or sell at an agreed amount an underlying asset nor be fore the specified future date. He is not under any obligation to do so. The person who gets such right is called 'Option Buyer' or 'Option Holder'. The person again at whom the buyer/holder can exercise his right is called 'Option Seller' or 'Option Writer'. Un like a buyer/holder, the seller/writer of an option has no right but has an obligation to sell or buy the under lying asset as and when the buyer/holder exercises his right. In order to acquire the right of Option, the buyer/holder pays to the seller/writer an Option Premium, which is the price, paid for the right. Every option contract is for a specific period of time. On the expiry of the specified period, the contract also expires. On the basis of the rights of the buyer with regard to the time of settlement, the Options can be classified in to two broad categories, viz., American-style options and European-style options. In case of American-style options, the buyer/holder can exercise his right at any time be fore the contract expires or on the Expiry Date, where as in case of European-style options, the buyer/holder can exercise his right only on the Expiry Date.

An Option can either be a 'Call Option' or a 'Put Option'. In case of Call Option, buyer/holder of the Option gets the right to purchase the under lying asset where as in case of Put Option buyer/holder gets the right to sell the under lying asset. In market terminology, a person buying a Call Option is considered to have made a 'long call' and a person buying a Put Option is considered to have made a 'long put'. Similarly, a person selling a Call Option or a Put Option is considered to have made a 'short call' or a 'short put', respectively. In a Call Option the seller/writer of the Option has an obligation to sell the under lying asset, where as in a Put Option the seller/writer has an obligation to buy the under lying asset. The rights and the obligations of the parties involved in option contract can be summarised in a tabular form as below:

Table 9.1: Obligation of the Parties Involved

Option Type	Buyer/Holder	Seller/Writer
Call	Right but not an obligation to buy the under lying asset.	Obligation but no right to sell the under lying asset.
Put	Right but not an obligation to sell the under lying asset.	Obligation but no right to buy the under lying asset.

The price at which the buyer/holder has the right to buy or sell and the seller/writer has an obligation to sell or buy is known as the 'Strike' or 'Exercise' price.

It may be noted that the buyer/holder of an option can make a loss of no more than the Option Premium paid to the seller/writer but the possible gain is unlimited. On the other hand, the Option Seller/Writer's maximum gain is limited to the Option Premium charged by him from the buyer/holder but can make unlimited loss.

In market terminology, an option contract can be 'at the money', 'in the money' or 'out of the money'. 'At the money' means that the current market value of the under lying asset is the same as the Exercise Price of the Option. A Call Option is said to be 'in the money' if the current market value of the under lying asset is above the Exercise Price of the Option. A Put Option is said to be 'in the money' if the current market value of the under lying asset is below the Exercise Price of the Option. A Call Option is said to be 'out of the money' if the current market value of the under lying asset is below the Exercise Price of the Option. A Put Option is said to be 'out of the money' if the current market value of the under lying asset is above the Exercise Price of the Option.

Futures and options are both standardised derivative instrument stranded on a stock exchange. The difference between these two types of derivative in strumpets is in respect of the rights and obligations of the parties involved in such contracts. In case of a futures contract, both the parties are under obligation to complete the contract on the specified date. However, in case of options contract, the buyer/holder has aright, but no obligation to exercise the Option, whereas the seller/writer has an obligation but no right to complete the contract.

There can be futures and options on commodities, currencies, securities, stock index, individual stock, etc. In India, SEBI has permitted trading in futures and options in two equity indexes, viz., BSE SENSEX and S&P CNX NIFTY and certain specified securities listed on the stock exchanges. Currently, these futures and options contracts are traded on The Stock Exchange, Mumbai and the National Stock Exchange of India Limited.

EQUITY INDEX FUTURES AND EQUITY STOCK FUTURES

An equity index futures contract is a futures contract in which the under lying asset is an equity index, e.g., S&P CNX NIFTY or BSE SENSEX. In other words, it is a contract to buy or sell equity index at an agreed a mount on a specified future date.

An equity stock futures contract is a futures contract in which the under lying asset is a security, e.g., equity shares of ABC Limited, equity shares of PQR Limited, etc. In other words, it is a contract to buy or sell a security at an agreed amount on a specified future date.

The following are the basic differences between these two types of equity futures:

(a) *The under lying asset:* In case of equity index futures, the under lying asset is equity index itself (e.g., BSE SENSEX, S&P CNX NIFTY), where as in case of equity stock futures, the under lying asset is a security (e.g., equity shares of a company).

(b) *The mode of settlement:* By its very nature, the index can not be delivered on maturity of the contract. As such, the settlement of an equity index futures contract takes the form of payment of the difference between the price as agreed in the contract (contract price) and the value of the index on the maturity date (Settlement Date), in cash. In contrast, an equity stock futures contract can be settled either through delivery of security for which the contract was entered in to or by receipt/payment of the difference between contract price and the value of the security for which the contract was entered into, in cash, just like equity index futures. At present, in India, equity stock futures contracts are settled through cash. However, in near future, equity stock futures may be settled through physical delivery of shares.

Examples of Equity Index Futures

(i) In July, Mr. A enters into an equity index futures contract to buy 100 units of BSE SENSEX of September 2003 series at a price of, say, ₹ 3,650 per unit. As a result, Mr. A is under obligation to buy 100 units of BSE SENSEX on the Settlement Date at the rate of ₹ 3,650 per unit. On the Settlement Date, if the price of BSE SENSEX is higher than ₹ 3,650, say, ₹ 3,680 per unit, Mr. A will receive ₹ 30 per unit (the difference between the price on the Settlement Date and the contract price). On the other hand, if, on the Settlement Date, the price of BSE SENSEX is lower than ₹ 3,650, say, ₹ 3,610 per unit, Mr. A will pay ₹ 40 per unit.

(ii) In July, Mr. B enters into an equity index futures contract to sell 200 units of S&P CNX NIFTY of September 2003 series at a price of, say, ₹ 1,100 per unit. As a result, Mr. B is under obligation to sell 200 units of S&P CNX NIFTY on the Settlement Date at the rate of ₹ 1,100 per unit. On the Settlement Date, if the price of the S&P CNX NIFTY is higher than ₹ 1,100, say, ₹ 1,125 per unit, Mr. B will pay ₹ 25 per unit (the difference between the price on the Settlement Date and the contract price). On the other hand, if, on the Settlement Date, the price of S&P CNX NIFTY is lower than ₹ 1,100, say, ₹ 1,050 per unit, Mr. B will receive ₹ 50 per unit.

Examples of Equity Stock Futures

(i) In July, Mr. A enters into an equity stock futures contract to buy 1,000 equity shares of XYZ Limited of September 2003 series at a price of, say, ₹ 250 per share. As a result, Mr. A is under obligation to buy 1,000 equity shares of XYZ Limited on the Settlement Date at the rate of ₹ 250 per share. On the Settlement Date, Mr. A will have to settle the contract either through purchase of shares or by payment/receipt of the difference between the contract price of ₹ 250 per share and the price of the shares of XYZ Limited on that date, depending upon whether the contract is delivery-settled or cash-settled. If the contract is delivery-settled, on the Settlement Date, Mr. A will buy 1,000 equity shares of XYZ Limited at a price of ₹ 250 per share. On the other hand, if the contract is cash-settled, on the Settlement Date, if the price of the shares of XYZ Limited is higher than ₹ 250, say, ₹ 280 per share, Mr. A will receive ₹ 30 per share (the difference between the price on the Settlement Date and the contract price). However, if, on the Settlement Date, the price of the shares of XYZ Limited is quoted lower than ₹ 250, say, ₹ 210 per share, Mr. A will pay ₹ 40 per share.

(ii) In July, Mr B enters into an equity stock futures contract to sell 500 equity shares of PQR Limited of September 2003 series at a price of, say, ₹ 500 per share. A saresult, Mr. B is under obligation to sell 500 equity shares of PQR Limited on the Settlement Date at the rate of ₹ 500 per share. On the Settlement Date, Mr. B will have to settle the contract either through sale of shares or by payment/receipt of the difference between the contract price of ₹ 500 per share and the price of the shares of PQR Limited on that date, depending upon whether the contract is delivery-settle dorcash-settled. If the contract is delivery-settled, on the Settlement Date, Mr. B will sell 500 equity shares of PQR Limited at a price of ₹ 500 per share. On the other hand, if the contract is cash-settled, on the Settlement Date, if the price of the shares of PQR Limited is higher than ₹ 500, say, ₹ 525 per share, Mr. B will pay ₹ 25 per share (the difference between the price on the Settlement Date and the contract price).

However, if, on the settlement Date, the price of the shares of PQR Limited is lower than ₹ 500, say, ₹ 450 per share, Mr. B will receive ₹ 50 per share.

EQUITY INDEX OPTIONS AND EQUITY STOCK OPTIONS

Equity index options are a type of derivative instruments whereby a person gets the right to buy or sell an agreed number of units of equity index on a specified future date. Equity stock options are a type of derivative instruments where by a person gets the right to buy or sell an agreed number of units of a security on or before a specified future date. At present, in India, trading inequity index options is allowed in two indexes, viz., BSE SENSEX and S&P CNX NIFTY and equity stock options are allowed in certain specified securities listed on the stock exchanges.

The following are the basic differences between these two types of equity options:

(a) *The underlying asset:* In case of equity index options, the underlying asset is equity index itself (e.g., BSE SENSEX, S&P CNX NIFTY), where as in case of equity stock options, the underlying asset is a security (e.g., equity shares of a company).

(b) *The time of settlement:* Equity index options are of European style, i.e., buyer/holder can exercise his option only on the day on which the option expires, where as equity stock options are of American style, i.e., the buyer/holder can exercise his option at any time before the Expiry Date or on the date of expiry it self.

(c) *The mode of settlement:* By its very nature, the index can not be delivered on maturity of the contract. As such, the settlement of an equity index options contract takes the form of payment of the difference between the Strike/Exercise Price and the value of the index on the Expiry Date, in cash. In contrast, equity stock options contract can be settled either through delivery of security for which an options contract was entered into or by payment of the difference between the Strike/Exercise Price and the value of the security for which the options contract was entered into, in cash, just like equity index option. At present, in India, equity stock options are settled through cash. However, in near future, equity stock options may be settled through physical delivery of shares.

Examples of Equity Index Options

Call Options: In July, Mr. A (buyer/holder) enters into an equity index options contract to buy a Call Option for 200 units of S&P CNX NIFTY of September 2003 series at a price of ₹ 1,100 per unit. As result, Mr. A obtains the right to buy 200 units of S&P CNX NIFTY on the Expiry Date at ₹ 1,100 per unit. For this right, Mr. A pays premium of ₹ 10 per unit of index to the seller/writer of the option. If, on the Expiry Date, the price of S&P CNX NIFTY is higher than ₹ 1,100, Mr. A will exercise his right to call. By exercising the right to call, he will receive the difference between the price on the Expiry Date and the Strike Price. On the other hand, if the price is below ₹ 1,100, he will not exercise his Call Option.

Put Options: In July, Mr. B (buyer/holder) enters into an equity index options contract to buy a Put Option for 100 units of BSE SENSEX of September 2003 series at a price of ₹ 3,650 per unit. As a result, Mr. B obtains a right to sell 100 units of BSE SENSEX on the Expiry Date at ₹ 3,650 per unit. For this right, Mr. B pays a premium of ₹ 25 per unit of index to the seller/writer of the option. If, on the Expiry Date, the price of BSE SENSEX is lower than ₹ 3,650, Mr. B will exercise his right to put. By exercising the right to put, he will receive the difference between the Strike Price and the price on the Expiry Date. On the other hand, if the price is above ₹ 3,650, he will not exercise his Put Option.

Examples of Equity Stock Options

Call Options: In July, Mr. A (buyer/holder) enters into an equity stock options contract to buy a Call Option for 1,000 equity shares of XYZ Limited of September 2003 series at a price of ₹ 250 per share. As a result, Mr. A obtains a right to buy 1,000 equity shares of XYZ Limited at the rate of ₹ 250 per share on or before the Expiry Date. For this right, Mr. A pays a premium of ₹ 5 per equity share to the seller/writer of the option. If, at any time on or before the Expiry Date, the price of the equity shares is quoted higher than ₹ 250, Mr. A may exercise his right to call. In case the contract is delivery-settled, by exercising the right to call, Mr. A will acquire 1,000 equity shares of XYZ Limited at ₹ 250 per share and since the prevailing market price is higher, he can make a profit by selling these shares in the market. In case the contracts cash-settled, by exercising the right to call, Mr. A will receive the difference between the prevailing market price and the Strike Price. On the other hand, if the market price is below ₹ 250 per share, he will not exercise his Call Option.

Put Options: In July, Mr. B (buyer/holder) enters into an equity stock options contract to buy a Put Option for 500 equity shares of PQR Limited of September 2003 series at a price of ₹ 500 per share. As a result, Mr. B obtains a right to sell 500 equity shares of PQR Limited on or before the Expiry Date at the rate of ₹ 500 per share. For this right, Mr. B pays a premium of ₹ 15 per equity share to the seller/writer of the Option. If, at any time on or before the Expiry Date, the price of the equity shares is quoted lower than ₹ 500, Mr. B may exercise the right to put. In case the contract is delivery-settled, by exercising his right to put, Mr. B will sell equity shares of PQR Limited at ₹ 500 per share and since the prevailing market price is lower, he can make a profit by buying theses hares in the market. In case the contract is cash-settled, by exercising the right to put, Mr. B will receive the difference between the Strike Price, i.e., ₹ 500 per share and the prevailing market price. On the other hand, if the market price is above ₹ 500 per share, Mr. B will not exercise his Put Option.

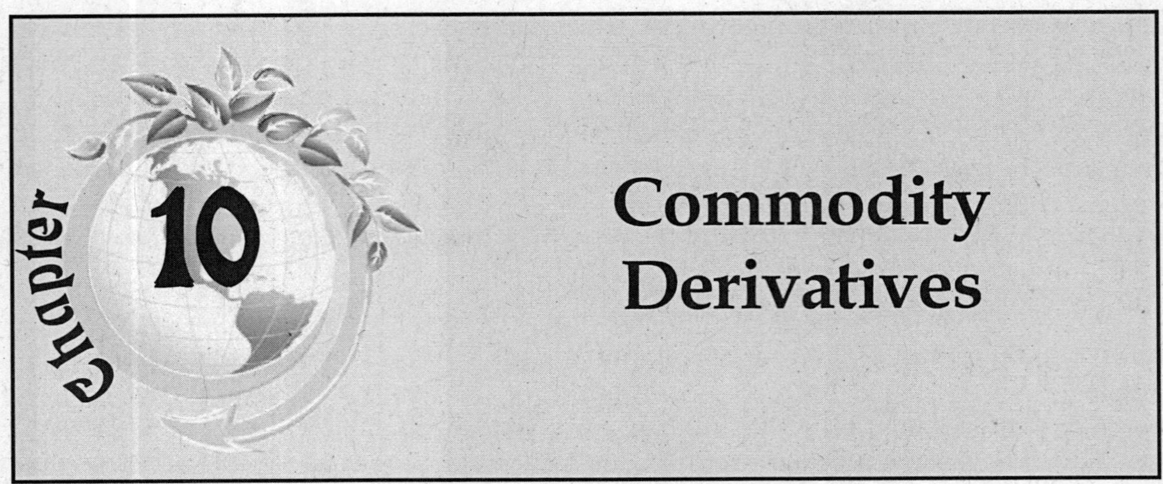

Commodity Derivatives

INTRODUCTION

As of now there is no accounting standard in India which specifically addresses the issue of commodity derivatives. As there is no accounting standard in India which specifically addresses the issue of commodity derivatives, the easiest approach is to treat derivatives as off balance sheet items and account them on the date of their settlement. Any realised gain or loss in respect of settled contracts is to be recognised in the income statement along with the underlying transaction.

However, derivatives have high leverage and the value of a derivative generally changes over the duration of its life because of market developments. Shareholders should be aware of these developments, and companies should report changes in the value of their derivative holdings on a periodic basis. Changes in the value of derivatives should be reflected both on the balance sheet and in earnings. Mark-to-market should be the basis for valuing derivatives. When a derivative is used to hedge the value of an asset, liability, or fixed commitment, the effects of price changes on the derivative and the hedged item should be reported.

In the absence of specific Accounting Standard in India, IFRS - 39 provides acceptable basis of accounting, as ICAI is committed to adopt IFRS. The accounting treatment prescribed henceforth is in accordance with this IFRS - 39.

Types of Commodity Derivatives from accounting perspective are: 1. For Speculation and 2. For Hedging: (a) Fair Value Hedge, (b) Hedge Cash-flow.

Derivatives Used for Speculation (Held for Trading)

Derivatives used for trading purposes are intended to gain from market price changes of these instruments. They are held with the objective of gaining from speculation.

Accounting Treatment: They are initially measured at cost, which is the fair value of whatever was paid or received to acquire the financial asset or liability. Transaction costs can either be included in the initial measurement of financial instruments or be expensed as and when incurred. Subsequent to initial measurement, at each reporting date, all such instruments are re-measured to fair value (mark-to-market) with gains and losses recognised in the income statement immediately.

Example: Accounting for a Simple Speculative Position.

Suppose in August a company expects the price of sponge iron to fall below ₹ 4.50 per kg. by the end of the year. So it enters into a futures contract to sell 1,00,000 kg. of sponge iron in December for ₹ 4.50 per kg. The transaction is speculative in that the company is assumed not to produce or hold the metal for sale.

Next, suppose that in September the value for December sponge iron futures rises to ₹ 5.00 per kg. At the end of September, the company has a potential liability equal to the ₹ 0.50 rise in price times the 1,00,000 kg. in the December sales contract, or ₹ 50,000. The drop in market value of the company's derivative holdings should be reported as a liability of ₹ 50,000 in the company's third-quarter financial statements. The company's earnings for the third quarter should be reduced by ₹ 50,000.

Suppose, then, that in December the company's expectations are vindicated, and the spot price of sponge iron falls to ₹ 4.00 per kg. The company can settle the contract or, alternatively, purchase 1,00,000 kg for ₹ 4.00 per kg and sell the 1,00,000 kg to the contract's counterparty for ₹ 4.50 per kg. Either way, the company realizes a profit of ₹ 50,000 on its derivatives trade. The effect on shareholders' equity in the fourth quarter is a positive ₹ 1,00,000 (cash increases by ₹ 50,000 in the fourth quarter at the same time that ₹ 50,000 in liabilities carried from the third quarter is eliminated). For the entire year, the impact on earnings is ₹ 50,000, the positive ₹ 1,00,000 recognised in the fourth quarter plus the negative ₹ 50,000 recognised in the third quarter.

Issue Involved: Guidance Note on Accounting for Equity Index and Equity Stock Futures and Options issued by ICAI for equity derivatives suggest that while all mark-to-market losses should be recognised, mark-to-market gains should be deferred till maturity of the derivative contract. This is based on the Principle of Prudence. Hence, recognition of both mark-to-market.

Profit and loss (as recommend under IAS and US GAAP) may not be possible under Indian GAAP. However, after declaration of the date of Ind-ASS implementation, the recognition of unrealised gain/profits are possible.

Derivatives Used for Hedging (Non Trading Derivatives)

Hedging is the attempt to mitigate the impact of economic risks on an entity's performance. Derivatives used for hedging are intended to manage exposures or risk. Hedge accounting means designating a hedging instrument, normally a derivative, as an offset to changes in the fair value or cash-flows of a hedged item. Hedge accounting attempts to match the offsetting effects of the fair value changes in hedged items and hedging instruments, and recognise them in net profit or loss at the same time.

Hedge accounting is an exception to the usual rules for financial instruments; there are strict criteria that must be met before it can be used. Management must identify, document and test effectiveness of those transactions that are intended to reduce risk.

The requirements are:

(a) The hedged item and the hedging instrument are specifically identified;

(b) The hedging relationship is formally documented;

(c) The documentation of the hedged relationship must identify the hedged risk and how the effectiveness of the hedge will be assessed;

(d) At the inception of the hedge, it must be expected to be highly effective, that is, the gains and losses on the hedged item and the hedging instrument should almost fully offset over the life of the hedge;

(e) Effectiveness of the hedge must be tested regularly throughout its life. Effectiveness should fall within a range of 80 to 125 per cent over the life of the hedge. This leaves some scope for short-term ineffectiveness, provided that overall effectiveness will fall within this range;

(f) One-to-one designation is normally required between a single external asset, liability or forecast transaction and a single external derivative instrument; and

(g) Hedges of forecast transactions are allowed if the forecast transaction is 'highly probable'. Further, the expected transaction must be within a third party.

An enterprise that elects to apply hedge accounting the method it will use for evaluatingthe effectiveness of the hedging derivative and the measurement approach for determining the ineffective portion of the hedge. Those methods must be consistent with the entity's approach to managing risk is required to establish at the inception of the hedge. Thus, the criteria to achieve hedge accounting are onerous. Management should always consider the costs and benefits of using hedge accounting.

Hedge accounting can be divided into two general categories as follows:

1. Hedging of existing assets or liabilities (Fair Value Hedges); and
2. Hedging of future/anticipated transactions (Cash-flow Hedges).

Fair Value Hedge: It is a hedge of the exposure to changes in fair value of a recognised asset or liability or a previously unrecognised firm commitment to buy or sell an asset at a fixed price (or part thereof), that is attributable to a particular risk and could affect profit or loss.

Accounting Treatment: The gain or loss from the change in fair value of the hedging instrument is recognised currently in earnings. At the same time the gain or loss (that is, the change in fair value) on the hedged item attributable to the hedged risk shall adjust the carrying amount ofthe hedged item and be recognised currently in earnings. If the fair value hedge is fully effective, the gain or loss on hedging instrument would exactly offset the loss or gain on the hedged item attributable to the hedged risk. Any difference that does arise, would be the effect of hedge ineffectiveness, which consequently is recognised currently in earnings.

Unrecognised Firm Commitments: A firm commitment is one in which price, quantity, and delivery dates have been fixed (our term contracts with National Oil Companies do not fall in this category). Cumulative changes in the fair value of the firm commitment is to be recognised as an asset or liability with corresponding effect on profit and loss. Upon acquisition of assetor assuming a liability, initial carrying amounts are to be adjusted by cumulative changes in fair value.

Example: Accounting for a Fair Value Hedging Position.

Suppose the situation is identical to that described above, except that the company has an inventory of 1,00,000 kg of sponge iron that it plans to sell in December. The company's cost of the inventory is, for this example, ₹ 4,00,000 (fair value being ₹ 4,50,000). The company includes this amount of ₹ 4,00,000 as inventory on its balance sheet. The company wants to protect the value of its inventory until its sale in December. In this case the company uses the futures contract (sale of 1,00,000 kg in December for ₹ 4.50 per kg) to protect the value of itsinventory. As before, the contract sales price for December is ₹ 4.50, the December sponge iron futures price rises to ₹ 5.00 in September, and the December spot price turns out to be ₹ 4.00. Additionally, suppose the spot price of sponge iron rises to ₹ 4.95 in September.

Following the mark-to-market valuation method in the first example, at the end of September, the value of the derivative declines by ₹ 50,000, increasing the company's liabilities by that amount. However, with the spot price of sponge iron at ₹ 4.95 in September, the inventory has increased in value by ₹ 45,000 (₹ 4.95 times 1,00,000 in liquidation value of the inventoryminus ₹ 4,50,000 in initial fair value of the inventory). If both the derivative position and inventory are marked-to-market, the effect on shareholders' equity is the gain in value on the inventory (₹ 45,000) less the increase in liabilities (₹ 50,000) or a negative ₹ 5,000. A negative ₹ 5,000 would also be the effect on earnings in the third quarter. The impacts on reported earnings and the balance sheet should include the change in value of the hedged item as well as the change in value of the derivative used to hedge the value of the item.

In December, when the inventory is actually sold, the company can settle its contract and sell its sponge iron inventory of 1,00,000 kg, realising ₹ 4,50,000 in cash. Recalling that the inventory was marked to market at ₹ 4,45,000 at the end of September, the net effect on the company's assets in its fourth-quarter financial report is a positive ₹ 5,000 (i.e., an increase in cash of ₹ 4,50,000 less the elimination of ₹ 4,45,000 in inventory). On the liabilities side, the ₹ 50,000 from the third quarter is eliminated when the December contract is settled. The net effect on earnings in the fourth quarter is a positive ₹ 55,000: a positive ₹ 5,000 in asset value change plus a ₹ 50,000 reduction in liabilities. For the year, the total effect on earnings is a positive ₹ 50,000: a negative ₹ 5,000 from the third quarter plus a positive ₹ 55,000 from the fourth quarter. The intended effect of the hedge was just to maintain inventory value from August until sale in December, which it did.

Issue Involved: As per Accounting Standard-2, inventory should be measured at cost or fair value whichever is lower. Hence, any adjustment of gain on hedged item (inventory) to carrying cost of inventory, as suggested above, may not be possible under Indian GAAP.

Cash-flow Hedge: A cash-flow hedge uses a derivative to hedge the anticipated future cash-flow of a transaction that is expected to occur but whose value is uncertain. This contrasts with a firm commitment, where price, quantity, and delivery date have been fixed. Hedging thevalue of a firm commitment is a fair value hedge. A cash-flow hedge differs from a fair value hedge in the following way. In a fair value hedge, the hedged item is an asset, liability, or fixed commitment. Assets and liabilities are carried on the balance sheet, and changes in the fair value of a fixed commitment are carried on the balance sheet during the duration of the hedge. With a cash-flow hedge, it is the cash-flow from an expected future transaction that is being hedged, and so there is no balance sheet entry for the hedged item.

Accounting Treatment: In other words when a cash-flow hedge exists, the fair value movements, on the part of the hedging instrument that is effective, are recognised in equity (under the head "other comprehensive income") until such time as the hedged item affects profit or loss. Any ineffective portion of the fair value movement on the hedging instrument is recognized in profit or loss. When the expected transaction does take place, gain or loss recognised in equity can either be charged to profit or loss in the period during which forecasted transactions affect earnings or be adjusted to the initial carrying amount of the corresponding asset or liability.

Example: Accounting for a Cash-flow Hedging Position.

An example of a cash-flow hedge is a metal company that, in August, fully intends to purchase 1,00,000 kg of sponge iron in December and wants to protect its cash-flow from an unforeseen rise in the purchase price of sponge iron. In order to hedge its exposure to rising sponge iron prices, the company can, in August, enter into a contract to purchase 1,00,000 kg at the December futures price of, say, ₹ 4.50 per kg. By this action, hedging is used to lock in the amount of cash-flow to be paid for sponge iron in December. The company documents that it will be using a futures contract to stabilize cash-flow associated with this purchase, and so it is a cash-flow hedge. In August, the company enters into a futures contract for the purchase of 1,00,000 kg of sponge iron in

December at ₹ 4.50 per kg. If the December contract price rises to ₹ 5.00 per kg by the end of September, the value of the contract will increase by ₹ 50,000, and that amount will be included as an asset in the company's third-quarter report to shareholders. The effect on reported third-quarter earnings will be zero. Here, the hedge was fully effective.

A perfectly effective hedge is one in which changes in the value of the derivative exactly offsetchanges in the value of the hedged item or expected cash-flow of the future transactions. The part of the change in the value of the derivative that is not effective in offsetting undesired changes in expected cash-flow is recognised in the income statement. For example, the expected transaction might be a sponge iron delivery in London, but the hedge is for sponge iron delivered at Singapore. In this case, the delivery location of the item being hedged is different from the delivery point of the hedging instrument. To the extent that changes in the price of sponge iron in London differ from changes in the value of the Singapore-based hedge, there will be hedge ineffectiveness.

The above discussion clearly conveys the number of accounting complexities involved in the issue. Unless the ICAI comes with clear guidelines on the subject the confusion is here to stay.

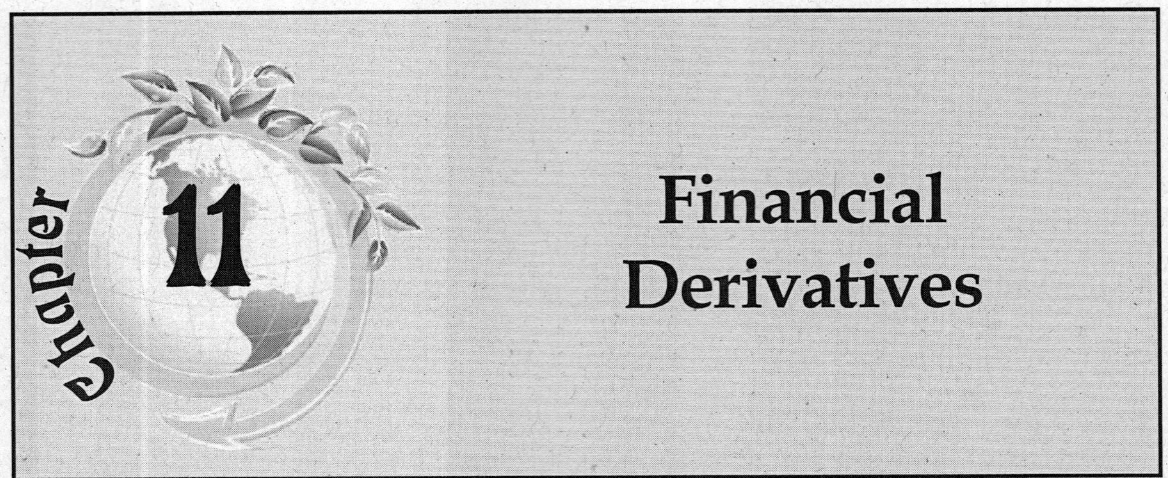

Financial Derivatives

INTRODUCTION

Derivative products initially emerged as hedging devices against fluctuations in commodity prices. These offer organisations the opportunity to break financial risks into smaller components to best meet specific risk management objectives. A derivative is an instrument where payoffs are derived from a more primitive or fundamental good. A financial derivative is a financial instrument, whose payoffs depend on another financial instrument underlying the transaction. Derivatives offer benefits such as risk management and efficiency in trading etc. to its users. Financial derivatives should be considered for inclusion in any organisation's risk-control arsenal. The most common financial derivative products can be classified as forwards, futures, options and swaps. Derivatives also have a darker side. Without a clearly defined risk management strategy, excessive use of financial derivatives can cause serious losses and can threaten the firm's long-term objectives. Derivatives being an important risk management tool necessitate its users to understand the intended function and the safety precautions before being put to use for the benefit of the society at large.

An entity that recognises gains from derivative transactions would be deemed to have adopted AS 30 early. Selective application of AS 30 is not possible. Hence, there is no prohibition on entities recognising gains on derivative transactions provided they also apply the categorisation, recognition, derecognition, initial and subsequent measurement, impairment and all other provisions of AS 30.

Emergence of financial derivative products Derivative products initially emerged as hedging devices against fluctuations in commodity prices, and commodity - linked derivatives remained the sole form of such products for almost three hundred years. Financial derivatives came into spotlight in the post-1970 period due to growing instability in the financial markets. However, since their emergence, these products have become very popular and by 1990s, they accounted for about two-thirds of total transactions in derivative products. In recent years, the market for financial derivatives has grown tremendously in terms of variety of instruments available, their complexity and also turnover. In the class of equity derivatives the world over, futures and options on stock indices have gained more popularity than on individual stocks, especially among institutional investors, who are major users of index-linked derivatives. Even small investors find these useful due to high correlation of the popular indexes with various portfolios and ease of use. The lower costs associated with index derivatives *vis-a-vis* derivative products based on individual securities is another reason for their growing use.

Derivatives remain a type of financial instruments that few of us understand and fewer still fully appreciate, although many of us have invested indirectly in derivatives by investing in a Mutual Fund whose underlying assets may include derivative products. Even, the financial derivatives have changed the face of finance by creating new ways to understand measure and manage financial risks. Derivatives offer organisations the opportunity to break financial risks into smaller components and then to buy and sell those components to best meet specific risk management objectives. Using derivatives should be considered as a part of any organisation's risk management strategy to ensure that value enhancing investment opportunities can be pursued.

What is a Derivative?

All the following conditions:

1. Whose value changes in response to changes in an underlying price or index: an interest rate, foreign exchange rate, a commodity price, a security price, a credit rating, or an index of any of the above;
2. This requires no initial investment or significantly, less than the investment required to purchase the underlying instrument; and
3. That is settled at a future date.

Some commodity-based derivatives are not considered a derivative under AS 30. A commodity contract is treated as an AS 30 instrument if any of the following three conditions is satisfied:

1. The entity has a practice of settling similar contracts net in cash, or by entering in offsetting contracts, or by selling the contracts; or
2. The entity has a practice of taking a delivery and margin; or
3. Where the contract permits either party to settle net in cash, through other financial instruments, by exchanging financial instruments, by selling the contracts or through the non financial items that are the subject of the contract and are readily convertible to cash, unless the contract is entered into and continues to be held for the purpose of receipt or delivery in accordance with the entity's normal purchase sale or usage requirements.

A derivative is an instrument whose payoffs depend on a more primitive or fundamental good. It is a contractual relationship between parties where pay-offs are derived from some agreed upon benchmark. These do not have independent existence without underlying product or commodity. Even, derivatives do not have their own value and rather they derive their value from some underlying product or commodity.

A financial derivative is a financial instrument, whose payoffs depend on another financial instrument or we can say a financial derivative is a financial instrument, whose value is linked in some way to the value of another instrument, underlying the transaction. The underlying instrument could be securities, currencies or indices. For example an option on a share of stock depends on the value of the underlying share.

FINANCIAL DERIVATIVES

Some of the benefits that financial derivatives bring to its users may be enumerated as:

Risk Management

Risk management is not about the elimination of risk. Rather it is about the management of risk. Financial derivatives provide a powerful tool for limiting risks that individuals and organisations face in the ordinary conduct of their businesses. Successful risk management with derivatives requires a thorough understanding of the principles that govern the pricing of financial derivatives. Used correctly, derivatives can save costs and increase returns.

Trading Efficiency

Derivatives allow for the free trading of individual risk components, thereby improving market efficiency. Traders can use a position in one or more financial derivatives as a substitute for a position in the underlying instruments. In many instances traders find financial derivatives to be a more attractive instrument than the underlying security. Reason being, the greater amount of liquidity in the market offered by the financial derivatives and lower transaction costs associated with trading a financial derivative as compared to the costs of trading the underlying instrument.

Speculation

Serving as a speculative tool is not the only use, and probably not the most important use, of financial derivatives. Financial derivatives are considered to be risky. However, these instruments act as a powerful instrument for knowledgeable traders to expose themselves to properly calculated and well understood risks in pursuit of a reward, i.e., profit.

FORWARD CONTRACTS

These are the simplest form of derivative contracts. A forward contract is an agreement between parties to buy/sell a specified quantity of an asset at a certain future date for a certain price. One of the parties to a forward contract assumes a long position and agrees to buy the underlying asset at a certain future date for a certain price. The other party to the contract assumes a short position and agrees to sell the asset on the same date for the same price. The specified price is referred to as the delivery price. The contract terms like delivery price and quantity are mutually agreed upon by the parties to the contract. No margins are generally payable by any of the parties to the other.

Features

Salient features of forward contracts may be enumerated as:

- Each contract is custom designed, and hence is unique in terms of contract size, maturity date and the asset type and quality,
- On the expiration date, the contract is normally settled by the delivery of the asset,
- Forward contracts being bilateral contracts are exposed to counter party risk, and
- If the party wishes to cancel the contract or change any of its terms, it has necessarily to go to the same counter party.

Illustration: On 1st April, Mr. 'X' enters into a forward contract with Mr. 'Y' and agrees to purchase 1,000 shares of 'TCS Ltd.' for a pre-determined price of ₹ 10 three months forward. Here on the fixed future date, Mr. 'X' will get the 1,000 shares and will pay the price i.e., ₹ 10,000 and Mr. 'Y' will deliver the shares and will receive the money.

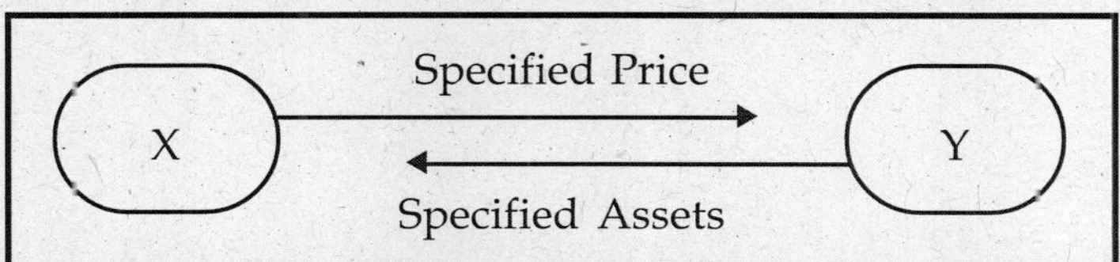

The contract is settled at maturity date. The holder of the short position delivers the asset to the holder of the long position in return for a cash amount equivalent to the delivery price. Forwards contracts are traded over the counter and are not dealt with on an exchange. These have certain flexibility and are self-regulatory. Forwards markets afford privacy that is not there in the exchange trading. Lack of liquidity and counter party default risks are the main drawbacks of a forward contract

FUTURES CONTRACTS

A futures contract is one by which one party agrees to buy from/sell to the other party at a specified future time, a specified asset at a price agreed at the time of the contract and payable on maturity date. The agreed price is known as the strike price. The underlying asset can be a commodity, currency, debt or equity security etc. Unlike forward contracts, futures are usually performed by the payment of difference between the strike price and the market price on the fixed future date, and not by the physical delivery and the payment in full on that date.

Features

Futures contracts can be characterised by:

- An organised exchange,
- Standardised contract terms viz., the underlying asset, the time of maturity and the manner of maturity etc.,
- Associated clearing house to ensure smooth functioning of the market,
- Margin requirements and daily settlement to act as further safeguard, and
- Existence of a regulatory authority.

Futures contracts being traded on organised exchanges impart liquidity to a transaction. The clearing house, being the counter party to both sides of a transaction, provides a mechanism that guarantees the honoring of the contract and ensuring very low level of default.

Types of Futures

Few types of financial futures are:

- Currency futures
- Interest futures
- Stock index futures

Illustration: On 1st September, Mr. 'X' enters into a futures contract to purchase 100 equity shares of 'TCS Ltd.' at an agreed price of ₹ 100 in December. If on the maturity date (as determined by the rules of the exchange for the month of December) the price of the equity stock rises to ₹ 120 , Mr. 'Y' will receive ₹ 20 per share and otherwise if the price of the share falls to ₹ 90, Mr. 'X' will pay ₹ 10 per share.

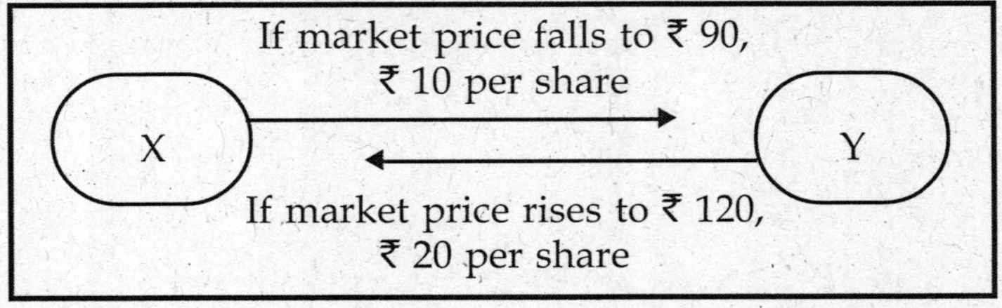

As compared to a forward contract the futures are normally settled only by the difference between the strike price and the market price as on maturity date.

OPTION CONTRACTS

The literal meaning of the word 'option' is 'choice' or we can say 'an alternative for choice'. In derivatives market also, the idea remains the same. An option contract gives the buyer of the option a right (but not the obligation) to buy/sell the underlying asset at a specified price on or before a specified future date. As compared to forwards and futures, the option holder is not under an obligation to exercise the right. Another distinguishing feature is that, while it does not cost anything to enter into a forward contract or a futures contract, an investor must pay to the option writer to purchase an option contract. The amount paid by the buyer of the option to the seller of the option is referred to as the premium. For this reward i.e. the option premium, the option seller is under an obligation to sell/buy the underlying asset at the specified price whenever the buyer of the option chooses to exercise the right. Option contracts having simple standard features are usually called plain vanilla contracts. Contracts having non-standard features are also available that have been created by financial engineers. These are called exotic derivative contracts. These are generally not traded on exchanges and are structured between parties on their own. The relevance of exotic options can be understood from these lines:

"Exotic products come about for a number of reasons. Sometimes they meet a genuine hedging need in the market; sometimes there are tax, accounting, legal, or regulatory reasons why corporate treasures find exotic products attractive; sometimes the products are designed to reflect a corporate treasurer's view on potential future movements in particular market variables; occasionally an exotic product is designed by an investment bank to appear more attractive than it is to an unwary corporate treasurer." John C. Hull

Illustration: Mr. 'X' pays $ 2,000 to buy a 'December 103' call option on a $ 100,000 US Treasury bond at an exercise price of $ 103. If the price rises above $ 103, Mr. 'X' will gain from the difference and if the price falls below $ 103, the maximum amount which Mr. 'X' may lose is the amount of premium paid.

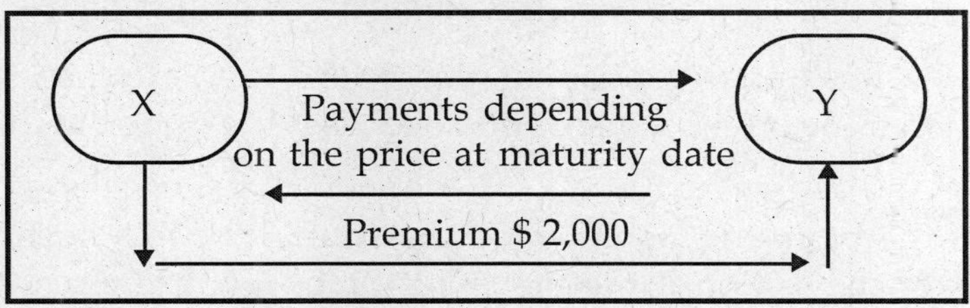

American Option and European Option

It is essential to be aware of the distinction between an American Option and a European Option. An American option can be exercised at any time up to the expiration date, a European option can be exercised only on the expiration date itself. Most of the option contracts traded on exchanges are of the type of American option.

Call Option and Put Option

Basically there are two types of options viz., Call Option and Put Option. A call option gives the buyer of the option the right (but not the obligation) to buy the underlying asset on or before a certain future date for a specified price whereas a put option gives the buyer of the option the right (but not the obligation) to sell the underlying asset on or before a certain future date for a specified price. As stated earlier, the option writer is under an obligation to sell/buy the underlying asset at the specified price whenever the buyer of the option chooses to exercise the right. The specified price is known as the strike price or the exercise price and the specified date is known as the exercise date, maturity date or the expiration date.

Money ness of an Option

Options can also be characterised in terms of their money ness. Using notations, the money ness of an option for the buyer of the option can be summarised as:

	Call Option	**Put Option**
In-the-money	M>E	M<E
At-the-money	M=E	M=E
Out-of-the-money	M<E	M>E

Where M is the prevalent market price for the option contract, and E is the exercise price of the option contract. For a seller/writer of the option the >, < signs will reverse. In words, the money ness of the option for the buyer of the option can be stated as:

- An in-the-money option is one that would lead to a positive cash-flow to the buyer of the option if the buyer of the option exercises the option at the current market price.
- An at-the-money option is one that would lead to a zero cash-flow to the buyer of the option if the buyer of the option exercises the option at the current market price.
- An out-of-the-money option is one that would lead to a negative cash-flow to the buyer of the option if the buyer of the option exercises the option at the current market price.

Cap, Floor and Collar

Limits can be set on the strike price for an option contract. If an upper limit on the strike price is set, it is called a 'cap'. If a lower limit on the strike price is fixed, it is called a 'floor'. If a combination of both, i.e., 'cap' and 'floor' is used, i.e., a range is fixed for the strike price, it is called a 'collar'. If the market price as on maturity date is higher than the cap price, then the cap price will be the strike price, otherwise the market price will be the strike price. Similarly, if the market price as on maturity date is lower than the floor price, then the floor price will be the strike price otherwise the market price will be the strike price. In other words we can conclude that in case of a collar, the strike price can not be higher than the cap price and lower than the floor price. Similar to a futures contract, the exercise of the option, normally, results in a contract to pay the difference between the strike price and the market price on the date of exercise of the option. As mentioned earlier, the buyer of the option has to pay a premium for purchasing the option. Hence, on the maturity date, the maximum loss that the buyer may suffer is the amount of the premium paid and the gain depends on the difference between the strike price and the market price as on maturity date. On the other hand, the gain to the seller of the option is limited to the amount of the premium received but the risk of loss is unlimited, depending upon the strike price and the market price as on maturity date.

SWAPS

A swap can be defined as a barter or exchange. A swap is a contract whereby parties agree to exchange obligations that each of them have under their respective underlying contracts or we can say a swap is an agreement between two or more parties to exchange sequences of cash-flows over period in the future. The parties that agree to the swap are known as counter parties.

Types of Swaps

There are two basic kinds of swaps:

- Interest rate swaps
- Currency swaps

Today, interest rate swaps account for the majority of banks' swap activity and the fixed-for-floating rate swap is the most common interest rate swap. In such a swap, one party agrees to make fixed-rate interest payments in return for floating-rate interest payments from the counterparty, with the interest rate payment calculations based on a hypothetical amount of principal called the notional amount. Notional amount typically does not change hands and it is simply used to calculate payments. Currency swaps involve exchange of currencies at specified exchange rates and to make a series of interest payments for the currency that is received at specified intervals.

Illustration: Mr. 'A' has borrowed from Mr. 'X' at LIBOR (London Interbank Offered Rate) + 2 per cent. Mr. 'A' to cover the transaction from unanticipated fluctuations in the interest rate, agrees to pay a fixed rate of 9 per cent to Mr. 'B' and in return Mr. 'B' agrees to pay a floating rate, i.e., LIBOR + 2 per cent to Mr. 'A'. Although the actual payments between Mr. 'A' and Mr. 'B' will take place only on a net basis. The net result of the transaction for each of the parties will be as follows:

- Mr. 'X' will receive the amount at LIBOR + 2 per cent.
- Mr. 'A's liability is fixed at 9 per cent.
- Mr. 'B's liability depends on the fluctuating rate, i.e., LIBOR.

Let us take two cases:

(1) LIBOR = 10 per cent

In this case Mr. 'A' will pay to Mr. 'X' at the rate of 12 per cent. Mr. 'B' will pay to Mr. 'A' at the rate of 3 per cent. Hence the net liability of Mr. 'A' is 9 per cent only.

(2) LIBOR = 5 per cent

In this case Mr. 'A' will pay to Mr. 'X' at the rate of 7 per cent and Mr. 'A' will pay to Mr. 'B' at the rate of 2 per cent. Hence the net liability of Mr. 'A' remains the same at 9 per cent.

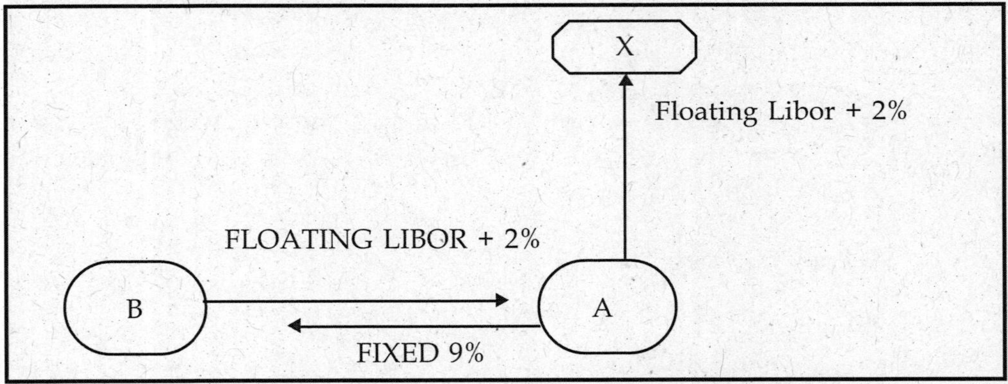

Swaps are not traded on organised exchanges and have an informal market among the dealers. As distinguished from futures and options, swaps market affords privacy that may not be there in exchange trading. The inherent limitations of a swaps market may be summarised as follows. First, a party has to find a counter party willing to take the opposite side of the transaction. Second, a swap agreement, being between two counter parties cannot be altered or terminated early without the agreement of both the parties. Third, parties to the swap must be certain of the creditworthiness of the counter party as the risk of counter party default is always there.

In the earlier versions of US standards the derivatives were defined by their classification (e.g., in FAS 80, 105, 1 19). This impeded wide applicability and caused accounting problems. The current standards of both the Financial Accounting Standards Board (FASB) as well as.

International Accounting Standards Board (IASB) take care of this problem. The approach of the relevant standards, namely FAS 133 (Accounting for Derivative Instruments and Hedging Activities) and IAS 39 (Financial Instruments: Recognition and Measurement) exhibits a convergence in thinking. Both these standards consider the intention and the nature more important than the classification of a derivative. This approach is in keeping with the basic accounting principles. Moreover, a separate treatment need not be prescribed for each of the plethora of derivative instruments by their name and classification.

As there is always an other side of the coin, derivatives also have a darker side. Organisations like Procter & Gamble, Long Term Capital Management, Barings Bank, etc., experienced huge losses from derivatives trading in the early 1990's. Barings Bank lost around $1 billion just because one trader whose job was to carry out low-risk arbitrage switched from being an arbitrageur to a speculator. The hedge fund named Long-term Capital Management lost about $4 billion in 1998. The treasury department of Procter & Gamble lost about $90 million trading highly exotic interest rate derivatives contracts. These losses warn the users against excessive use of financial derivatives. Without a clearly defined risk management strategy, excessive use of financial derivatives can be risky. They can cause serious losses and can threaten the firm's long-term objectives. Hence, it is important that users of derivatives fully understand the complexity of financial derivative contracts and accompanying risks. Derivatives being an important risk-management tool necessitate its users to understand the intended function and the safety precautions before being put to use. The use of derivatives should be integrated into an organisation's overall risk-management strategy and should be in harmony with its objectives. Hence, the users of derivatives can use these instruments for their benefit and for the benefit of the society at large.

Financial derivatives should be considered for inclusion in any organisation's risk-control arsenal. Using derivatives allows risk to be broken into pieces that can be managed independently. The viability of financial derivatives rests on the principle of comparative advantage i.e., the relative cost of holding specific risks. Whenever comparative advantage exists, trade can benefit all parties involved. From a market-oriented perspective financial derivatives offer free trading of individual risk components.

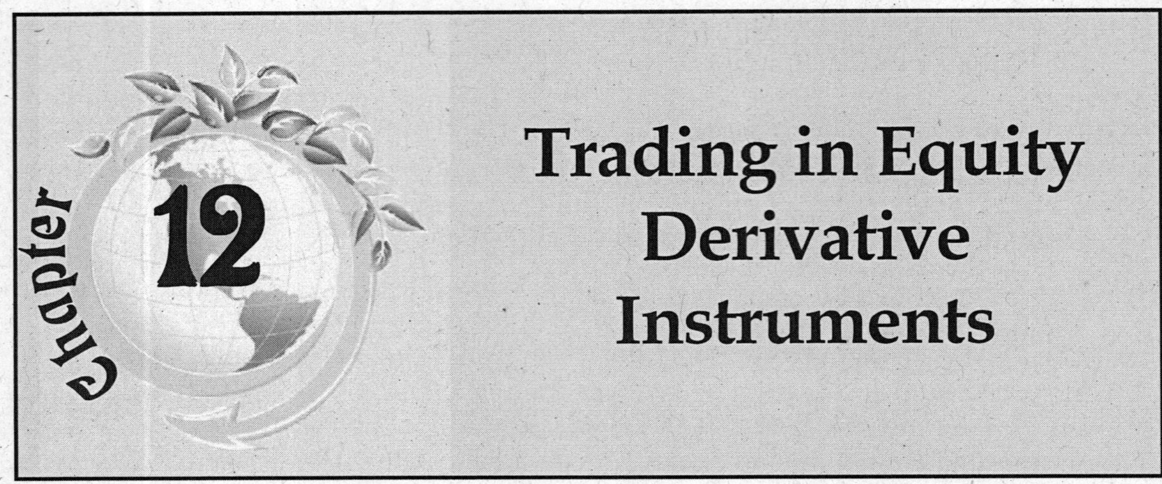

Trading in Equity Derivative Instruments

INTRODUCTION

Trading in Equity Derivative Instruments has commenced in India in a separate segment of existing stock exchanges known as 'Derivatives Segment'. The Clearing Corporation/House of the exchange may act as legal counter-party to all deals or may provide an unconditional guarantee for all the deals in Equity Derivative Instruments on the exchange. Thus, for all practical purposes, both the parties to an Equity Derivative Instruments contract would be assured that the obligations of the other party would bemet-either by the party itself for, in the event of default on the part of the party, by the Clearing Corporation.

A Client can trade in Equity Derivative Instruments only through a Trading Member of the exchange. A Clearing Member can also act as a Trading Member. The process of trading is similar to screen-based trading insecurities like shares on an exchange.

The exchanges, allowing trading in Equity Derivative Instruments contracts, introduce standardised contracts where the Settlement Date/Expiry Date, as the case may be, is specified by the stock exchange and the Clients can enter into contracts with different contract/Strike Prices, as the case may be, and different premiums, if relevant. The Settlement Date/Expiry Date adopted by BSE and NSE is the last Thurs day of a Contract Month. For example, the Equity Derivative Instruments contracts of August 2003 series will expire on 28th August 2003 (being the last Thursday of August 2003). In both BSE and NSE, the Equity Derivative Instruments contracts will have a maximum of three-month trading cycle – the near month (one), the next month (two) and the far month (three). Thus, in August 2003, one would be able to enter into futures contracts for the months of August 2003, September 2003 and October 2003. On 28th August, 2003 (last Thurs day of August 2003) the Equity Derivative Instruments contracts for August 2003 series will be finally settled/will expire and the re-after trading in November 2003 series will start.

Each exchange permitting Equity Derivative Instruments trading also provides the contract specifications. For example, the NSE has decided to permit contract multiplier of 200 for the S&P CNX NIFTY futures/options contracts, where as the BSE has decided that the contract multiplier would be 50 for trading in BSE SENSEX. Similarly, for each individual stock, market lot has been decided. A person can trade in Equity Derivative Instruments only in the multiples of the market lot.

In order to minimise the risk of failure of parties to a contract in fulfilling the irrespective obligations under the contract, the Clearing Corporation, from time to time, prescribes margin requirements for Clearing/Trading Members. Margins are required to be paid by Clearing/Trading Members, who, in turn, collect margins from the irrespective Clients. Margins can be paid in cash orb provided by way of a bank guarantee or by deposit receipts or securities or such there mode and would be subject to such terms and conditions as the Clearing Corporation may specify from time to time. There is a continuing obligation, during the contract period, to maintain margins at the levels specified by the Clearing Corporation, from time to time.

Every Client is required to pay an initial margin to the Trading Member/Clearing Member at the time of entering in to an Equity Derivative Instruments contract. Such a margin is calculated by using a Software called 'Standard Portfolio Analysis of Risk' (SPAN). SPAN calculates risk arrays for all the open positions on an over all basis and gives the out put in the form of a risk parameters file. This risk parameters file is made available to all the participants of Derivatives Segment. Members and Clients use the data from SPAN risk file, together with their position data, to calculate SPAN margin requirements on their respective positions on daily basis. SPAN calculates the margin by determining the worst possible loss using 16 risk scenarios. The Clients pay the deficit margin to, or receive the refund of excess margin from, the Trading Member/Clearing Member on **daily basis.**

EQUITY INDEX FUTURES AND EQUITY STOCK FUTURES

In addition to the payment of the Initial Margin, both the parties to the equity index/stock futures contract are required to pay daily 'Mark-to-Market Margin'. For computation of 'Mark-to-Market Margin', all out standing contracts, whether Long or short, of a Clearing Member in an equity index/stock futures contract are deemed to have been settled at the Daily Settlement Price. Such a member would be liable to pay to, or been titled to collect from, the Clearing House the difference between the price at which such contract was bought or sold and the Daily Settlement Price of that day, or the Settlement Price of the previous trading day and the Settlement Price of the contract at the end of the trading day, as the case may be. The Mark-to-Market Margin would be paid only in cash. After such settlement with the Clearing House, the member would be deemed to be Long or Short, as the case may be, in contracts at the Daily Settlement Price. Supposing 'X' buys one unit of an equity index future of one month maturity (say, April) on March 29 for ₹ 1,420. If at the end of the day (i.e., March 29) the Daily

Settlement Price of the equity index futures has fallen to ₹ 1,400, he would pay ₹ 20 to the Clearing House. The position for the sub sequent day sup to March 31 would be as follows:

Table 12.1: Assumed Daily Settlement Price

	(₹)	
March 30	1,435	Receive ₹ 35
March 31	1,430	Pay ₹ 5

Such differences would be directly debited/credited to the separate bank account required to be maintained by the Clearing Member with the Clearing Corporation. The Clearing Member would, in turn, debit/credit the bank account of the Trading Member, who, in turn, would debit/credit the account of the Client.

Each party to an equity index/stock futures contracts under an obligation to meet its commitment at the maturity of the contract. However, either party can, at any time during the currency of the contract, square pits future obligations under the contract by enter in gin to a reverse contract. For example, a person who is a buyer of 300 units of Stock of LMN Co. Limited September 2003 series can enter into an other contract of September 2003 series for sale of 300 units of Stock of LMN Co. Limited. Any gain or loss on the original contract arising after the date of entering in to the second contract would be offset by an equivalent loss or gain on the second contract. On entering in to are verse contract, the purchase and sales contracts offset each other automatically.

In case of non-payment of daily settlement dues by the Client, before the next trading day, the Clearing Member would be at liberty to close out transactions by selling or buying the futures contracts, as the case may be. The loss incurred in this regard would be met from the margin money of the Client and the gains, if any, would accrue to the Client. In case of shortfall caused by loss being in excess of the margin money, the amount would be recovered from the Client.

EQUITY INDEX OPTIONS AND EQUITY STOCK OPTIONS

In case of equity index options and equity stock options contracts, Option Buyer/ Holder is required to pay Option Premium to the Option Seller/Writer to acquire the right in the Options. When a person buys or sells Options, the premium amount will be debited or credited to the separate bank account of the Clearing Member with the Clearing Corporation. At the BSE and the NSE, this premiums normally debited or credited on then extra ding day (T + 1 Basis).

After entering in to an option contract, a Client can square off his position by entering in to are verse contract of the same series with the same Strike Price. For example, a buyer/holder having bought S&P CNX NIFTY Call Option of September 2003 series with Strike Price of ₹ 1,150 can square off his position by selling/writing S&P CNX NIFTY Call Option of September 2003 series with ₹ 1,150 as Strike Price. In such a case, the gain or loss of the Client will be the difference between Option Premium received and paid after reducing/adding the brokerage charged by the Clearing Member. Thus, profit can be earned by or loss can be reduced to the difference in the premium a mounts by squaring-up the position, before the Expiry Date.

On the expiry of a Call Option, if the market price of the underlying asset is lower than the Strike Price, the call would expire unexercised. Like wise, if on the expiry of a Put Option, the market price of the underlying asset is higher than the Strike Price, the Put Option would expire unexercised. When an Option Buyer/Holder decides to exercise his Option, he gives the exercise notice through the trading network during the time specified by the Clearing Corporation. The Clearing Corporation assigns the exercise notice to the Option Seller/Writer through the Trading Member.

Practically, all those Options, which are favourable to the buyer/holder on Expiry Date, are deemed to be exercised. No special notice is required to be sent by the buyer/holder. However, the buyer/holder can let favourable Option expire un exercised, if he so desires, upon intimation to the stock exchange.

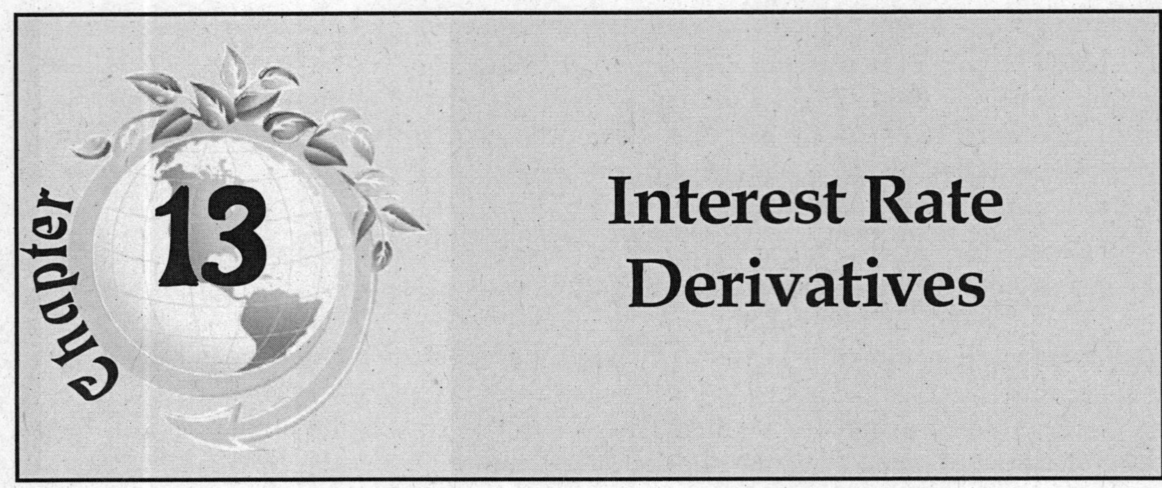

INTRODUCTION

Now that we have understood the basics of bonds, let us try and understand interest rate derivatives, which are investment products that derive their profits and losses based on the movement of bond prices (equivalently on movements in interest rates).

Derivative is a product whose value is derived from the value of one or more basic variables, called bases (underlying asset, index, or reference rate). The bases can be equity, currency, commodity, any asset or interest rate. Depending on the base, derivatives can be classified as equity derivatives, foreign exchange derivatives, commodity derivatives, and interest rate derivatives. In this chapter, we give a brief overview of various interest rate derivative products. These products can be broadly classified as either OTC or Exchange traded products.

As per Securities Exchange Board of India (SEBI) guidelines, derivatives include:

(a) a security derived from a debt instrument, share, loan, whether secured or unsecured, risk instrument or contract for differences or any other form of security;

(b) a contract which derives its value from the prices, or index of prices, of underlying securities;

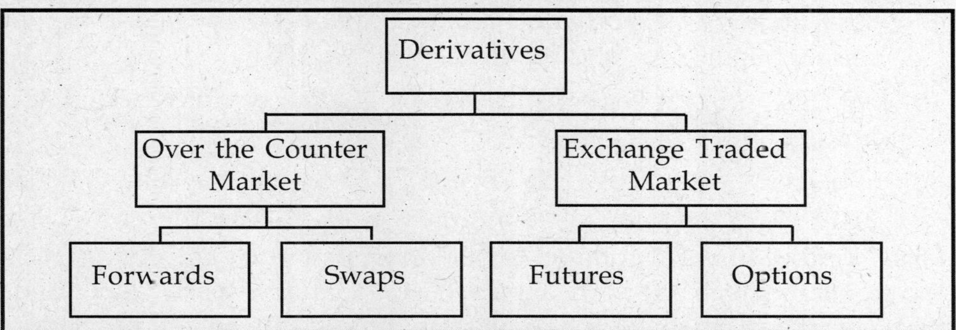

Fig 13.1: Derivalives

OTC DERIVATIVES

Over-the-counter (OTC) derivatives are private, bilateral contracts in which two parties agree on how a particular trade or agreement is to be settled in the future. OTC contracts on Interest Rate instruments have been prevalent in the Indian market since 1999 and have been used by institutions mainly to hedge their interest rate exposure. OTC trading is mostly done through the telephone. For OTC derivatives, the agreements are usually designed under the framework of an International Swaps and Derivatives Association (ISDA) agreement.

Only derivatives in the form of forwards and swaps are allowed by the RBI in the OTC market. Some of the popular derivatives traded globally in the OTC market are discussed below:

Forwards

A forward contract is the simplest derivative instrument. It is a private agreement between two parties in which one party (the buyer) agrees to buy from other party (the seller) an underlying asset, on a future date at a price established at the start of the contract. Therefore it is a commitment by two parties to engage in a transaction at a later date with price set in advance. The buyer is called the long and the seller is called the short.

When a forward contract expires, there are two possible arrangements that can be used to settle the obligation of the parties. These two settlements are following:

1. *Physical Delivery:* In this mechanism, the forward contract is settled by the physical delivery of the underlying asset by the seller to the buyer on the agreed upon price while entering into the contract.
2. *Cash Settlement:* An alternative procedure, called cash settlement permits the long and short to pay the net cash value of the position on the delivery date. There are three scenarios possible. Depending on what scenario prevails on the expiry date, the net pay-offs are determined for both the parties:

(a) Spot Price (ST) > Forward Price (FT): Short will pay long the difference between spot price and forward price, i.e., ST-FT.

(b) Spot Price (ST) = Forward Price (FT): The net payoff is zero, i.e., no party needs to pay other party.

(c) Spot Price (ST) < Forward Price (FT): Long will pay Short the difference between forward price and spot price, i.e., FT-ST.

A special kind of forward contract is called forward rate agreement (FRA). FRA is a forward contract in which one party agrees to lend to another party a specified amount at a future date for a specific period of time at an interest rate agreed upon today. FRAs are used more frequently by banks for hedging their interest rate exposures, which arise from mismatches in their tenure of their assets and liabilities. FRAs are also used widely for speculative activities.

Interest Rate Swap

In an interest rate swap, each counter party agrees to pay either a fixed or floating rate denominated in a particular currency to the other counterparty at regular intervals (say six months) over a defined period of time (say five years). The fixed or floating rate is multiplied by a notional principal amount (say, ₹ 1 crore). This notional amount of ₹ 1 crore is generally not exchanged between counter parties, but is used only for calculating the size of cash-flows to be exchanged.

The most common interest rate swap is one where one counterparty A pays a fixed rate (the swap rate) to counterparty B, while receiving a floating rate (usually pegged to a reference rate such as London Inter-Bank Offer Rate or LIBOR). Thus, A pays fixed rate to B (A receives variable rate) and B pays variable rate to A (B receives fixed rate).

Consider the following swap in which Party A agrees to pay Party B periodic fixed interest rate payments of 8.65 per cent, in exchange for periodic variable interest rate payments of LIBOR + 70 basis points (0.70 per cent). Note that there is no exchange of the principal amounts and that the interest rates are on a 'notional' (i.e., imaginary) principal amount. Also note that the interest payments are settled in net; for example, Party A pays 8.65 per cent – (LIBOR + 0.70 per cent). The fixed rate (8.65 per cent in this example) is referred to as the swap rate.

At the point of initiation of the swap, the swap rate is fixed so that the sum of the present value of the cash inflows for A is equal to sum of the present value of the cash outflows for A. This kind of swap is called a **Plain Vanilla Swap**.

Interest rate swaps can be used by hedgers to manage their fixed or floating assets and liabilities. They can also be used by speculators to profit from changes in interest rates. Interest rate swaps are very popular and highly liquid instruments. In India, one counterparty of the transaction has to be a bank and banks can offer these derivatives to corporates only for hedging the underlying exposures of the corporate. Also, neither of the parties involved in the transaction is allowed to have any options (put or call) embedded in the contract. In India, aside from Plain vanilla Swaps, the following swaps are currently allowed by the RBI:

- Cross-Currency Swaps
- G-Sec Linked Swaps

Discussions on these two swaps are beyond the scope of this book.

EXCHANGE TRADES CONTRACTS

Exchange-traded derivatives (ETD) are those derivative products that are traded via, Exchanges, which may or may not be specialised in derivatives trading. For Exchange traded derivatives, the Exchange acts as an intermediary to all transactions. Exchange provides a platform where buyers and sellers can come together and the orders are matched. Once the orders are matched, the Exchange becomes the buyer to the seller and the seller to the buyer. Thus, it protects both the parties to the transaction against counter party risk. To be able to do so, it takes initial margin from both sides as collateral. As time passes, the margin required from the parties changes on a day to day basis depending on the price movement of the transaction. Like OTC derivatives, the Exchange traded derivatives can be used for hedging or speculation. Exchange traded derivatives are usually in the form of a future or an option contracts on equity stocks, indices, currency and interest rates.

Futures

Like a forward contract, a futures contract is an agreement between two parties in which the buyer agrees to buy an underlying asset from the seller at a future date at a price that is agreed upon today. However, unlike a forward contract, a futures contract is not a private transaction but gets traded on a recognized Stock Exchange. In addition, a futures contract is standardised by the Exchange. All the terms, other than the price, are set by the Stock Exchange (rather than by the individual parties as in the case of a forward contract). Also, both the buyer and the seller of the futures contracts are protected against the counter party risk by an entity called the Clea ring Corporation. Currently in India futures are being traded on equities, commodities, FX and interest rate products. The next chapter explains the mechanism of interest rate futures in India.

Options

Like forwards and futures, options are derivative instruments that provide the opportunity to buy or sell an underlying asset on a future date. An option is a derivative contract between a buyer and a seller, where one party gives to the other the right, but not the obligation, to buy from (or sell to) the First Party the underlying asset on or before a specific day at an agreed - upon price (called the strike price). In return for granting the option, the party granting the option collects a payment from the other party. This payment collected is called the "premium" or price of the option. As of now, trading in options on interest rate products is not allowed in India.

KEY TERMINOLOGY FOR FUTURES MARKET

To understand the futures market well, one needs to know certain terminology associated with it. The following gives a brief description of the same:

Cash Market/Spot Market/Physical Market: It is the market for underlying securities (bonds in the current case). This can be an exchange traded market or an over the counter market. Settlement in cash market typically happens in one or two days.

Futures Price: Price at which a market participant can buy/sell the underlying at a future date.

Expiry Date: Last day of settlement for a derivative contract.

Mark to Market: In the futures market, at the end of each trading day, the margin account is adjusted to reflect the investor's gain or loss depending upon the futures closing price. This is called the mark-to-market process.

For example, if an Investor A agrees to buy 2000 bonds from another investor B on 30th June 2011. If on December 10, 2009, the futures price falls to ₹ 99 from ₹ 100 on December 9, 2009, the mark to market loss for A on December 10, 2009 is (100 – 99) × 2,000 = ₹ 2,000 (loss). A's loss is B's profit. So, the profit for B is ₹ 2000.

INTEREST RATE FUTURES IN INDIA

Like any other financial product, the price of IRF is determined by demand and supply, which in turn are determined by the individual investor's views on interest rate movements in the future. If an investor is of the view that interest rates will go up, he would sell the IRF. This is so, because interest rates are inversely related to prices of bonds, which form the underlying of IRF. So, expecting a rise in interest rates is same as expecting a fall in bond prices. An expectation of rising interest rates (equivalently of falling bond prices) would, therefore, lead the investor to sell the IRF. Similarly, if an investor expects a decline in interest rates (equivalently, a rise in bond prices), he would buy interest rate futures.

Rationale of IRFs

It is not just the financial sector, but also the corporate and household sectors that are exposed to interest rate risk. Banks, insurance companies, primary dealers and provident funds bear significant interest rate risk on account of the mismatch in the tenure of their assets (such as loans and Govt. securities) and liabilities. These entities, therefore, need a credible institutional hedging mechanism. Interest rate risk is becoming increasingly important for the household sector as well, since the interest rate exposure of several households are rising on account of increase in their savings and investments as well as loans (such as housing loans, vehicle loans etc.). Moreover, interest rate products are the primary instruments available to hedge inflation risk, which is typically the single most important macroeconomic risk faced by the household sector. It is, therefore, important that the financial system provides different agents of the economy a greater access to interest rate risk management tools such as exchange-traded interest rate derivatives.

Benefits of Exchange traded IRF

Interest rate futures provide benefits typical to any Exchange-traded product, such as:

Standardisation: Only contracts with standardised features are allowed to trade on the exchange. Standardisation improves liquidity in the market. The following features are standardised:

- Only certain expiry dates are allowed in India *viz.*, last working day of the months of March, June, September and December.
- The size of contract can only be in multiples of a certain number called the lot size. The lot size currently in India is ₹ 2 lakhs.
- Only some specific bonds can be used for delivery.

Transparency: Transparency is ensured by dissemination of orders and trades for all market participants. Also, competitive matching of orders of buyers and sellers boosts transparency. Transparency improves the efficiency of the market in terms of discovery of competitive price and liquidity.

Counter party Risk: Counter party risk is mitigated by the exchange as explained in the previous chapter (section 4.2). The credit guarantee of the clearing house addresses counter party risk thereby improving the confidence of investors leading to wider participation.

IRF: Contract Specifications

As stated earlier, only the standardised IRF contracts can be traded on the Exchange. Standardisation is done both in terms of the features of the product and the mechanism of its trading and settlement. Various features of standardisation are discussed in this section.

Product Features

The features of the product are as follows:

- *Underlying bond:* Underlying bond is a notional 10 year, 7 per cent coupon-bearing Government of India bond.
- *Lot size:* The minimum amount that can be traded on the exchange is called the lot size. All trades have to be a multiple of the lot size. The interest rate futures

contract can be entered for a minimum lot size of 2000 bonds at the rate of ₹ 100 per bond (Face Value) leading to a contract value of ₹ 2,00,000.

- *Contract cycle:* New contracts can be introduced by the Exchange on any day of a calendar month. At the time of introduction, the duration of any contract can vary from 1 month to 12 months. The expiry has to be on one of the four specific days of a year, specified by the regulator. Expiry cannot happen on any other date. The set of expiry dates available in a year constitute the expiry cycle or contract cycle. The expiries specified in the current contract cycle are the last business days of March, June, September and December. (Contracts are referred to by their respective expiry months. For example, December 2009 contract means a contract expiring in December 2009.) These four contract expiries have been chosen as they coincide with the quarterly financial accounting closure followed by Indian companies. Thus, at any given time, a maximum of four contracts can be allowed for trading on the exchange (*viz.*, March, June, September and December contracts). Currently, at NSE only two contracts are allowed to be traded.

Trading Aspects

- *Tick size:* The tick size of the futures contract is ₹ 0.0025. Tick size is the minimum price movement allowed for a futures contract.
- *Trading hours:* Interest Rate Futures are available for trading from 9 am till 5 pm on all business days.
- *Last Trading Day:* The last trading day for a futures contract is two business days before the expiry date (i.e., the last business day of the expiry month). For example the last trading date for December 2009 contract is 29th Dec 2009, because the last business day of December 2009 is the 31st.

Settlement Aspects

- *MTM Settlement and Physical Settlement:* For IRF, settlement is done at two levels: mark-to-market (MTM) settlement which is done on a daily basis and physical delivery which happens on any day in the expiry month. These two concepts have been explained in detail in next section.
- *Final Settlement Dates:* Final settlement which involves physical delivery of the bond can happen only the expiry date. If an investor wants to liquidate his position (i.e., sell if they have bought already or *vice versa*), however they can do so on any trading day before the last trading day, which has been defined above. All investors with an open short position as of the expiry day are assumed to be delivering the bond on the expiry day, which is two business days after the last trading day.
- *Delivery Basket of Bonds:* As stated earlier, the underlying notional bond may not exist in reality and, therefore, a basket of bonds is identified which qualify

for delivery, any one of which can be used for delivery in lieu of the notional bond. The seller of the futures has the option to choose which particular bond to deliver. Only certain identified bonds can be used for delivery. We elaborate on this in the next section. The eligibility criteria for the basket of bonds are:

- They have to be Central Government securities,
- Maturing at least 7.5 years but not more than 15 years from the first day of the delivery month. The Exchange can decide on any maturity basket within this period.
- With a minimum total outstanding stock of ₹ 10,000 crore.

The Table 13.1 summarises the contract specifications.

Table 13.1: A Summary of Contract Specification

Symbol	10YGS7
Market Type	Normal
Instrument Type	FUTIRD
Unit of trading	1 lot – 1 lot is equal to notional bonds of FV ₹ 2 lacs
Underlying	10 Year Notional Coupon bearing Government of India (GOI) security. (Notional Coupon 7 per cent with semiannual compounding.) ₹ 0.0025 or 0.25 paise
Tick size	Monday to Friday (On all business days) 9:00 a.m. to 5:00 p.m.
Trading hours	Four fixed quarterly contracts for entire year, expiring in March, June, September and December.
Contract trading cycle	Two business dayspreceeding the last business day of the delivery month. Last business day of delivery month
Last trading day Delivery day	Daily Settlement – Marked to market daily
Settlement	Final Settlement – Physical settlement in the delivery month

SETTLEMENT AND RISK MANAGEMENT

In case of exchange traded derivative contracts, the Clearing Corporation acts as a central counterparty to all trades. This principle is called 'novation'. This means that for settlement, the parties entering into a futures contract have obligations not towards each other, but towards the exchange on which the contract is traded. Thus, the exchange becomes the seller to all contract buyers and the buyer to all contract sellers. Novation, thus, entails risk of either party to contract defaulting. To mitigate this risk, the exchange imposes (a) margin requirements and (b) puts position limits on both the parties. The margin requirement. the position limits and settlement methods are discussed below.

Margin Requirement

Broadly two types of margins are required from each investor entering into a futures contract; namely, Initial Margin and Extreme Loss Margin. When the investors enter into a futures contract, they have to deposit cash or liquid assets equal to the total of these two margins. The initial margin is arrived at by taking various scenarios of market price movements to protect the exchange against the default risk of the parties and is subject to a minimum of 2.33 per cent of the value of the futures contra ct. Extreme loss margin on the other hand is equivalent to 0.3 per cent of the contract amount. When an IRF contract enters into the expiry month, the investors are required to post additional margin. This is done because the potential default amount increases during the expiry month and the Exchange has to protect itself against such rise in risk. More elaborate discussions on margin requirements are beyond the scope of this book.

Position Limits

As a risk management strategy to guard against heavy build-up of positions with one particular entity, the exchange imposes limits on the size of positions that can be taken by various entities.

Client Level: The gross open positions of a client across all contracts should not exceed 6 per cent of the total open interest or ₹ 300 crore, whichever is higher.

Trading Member Level: The gross open positions of the trading member across all contracts should not exceed 15 per cent of the total open interest of the entire market or ₹ 1,000 crore, whichever is higher.

Clearing Member Level: No separate position limit is prescribed at the level of the clearing member. However, the clearing member should ensure that his own trading position and the positions of each trading member clearing through him is within the limits specified above.

FIIs: The sum of gross long position in (a) the debt market and (b) the IRF market should not exceed their individual permissible limit for investment in government of India securities as prescribed from time to time. Further, short position in Interest Rate Futures contract should not exceed the sum stated above.

Settlement Methods

As discussed above settlement is done at two levels, viz., MTM settlement which is done on a daily basis and physical settlement which is done during the expiry month.

Mark-to-market (MTM) Settlement

To cover for the risk of default by the counterparty for the clearing corporation, the futures contracts are marked-to-market on a daily basis by the Exchange. Mark-to-market settlement is the process of adjusting the margin balance in an investor's account each day for the change in the value of the contract from the previous day. This process helps the clearing corporation in managing the counterparty risk of the future contracts by requiring the party incurring a loss due to adverse price movements to part with the loss amount on a daily basis. Simply put, the party in the loss position pays the clearing corporation the margin money to cover for the shortfall in cash.

To ensure a fair mark-to-market process, the clearing corporation computes and declares the official price for each day for determining daily gains and losses. This price is called the "daily settlement price" and represents the closing price of the futures contract for a given day. The daily settlement price (i.e., closing price for any IRF contract of any given day) is the weighted average trading price of the contract at the end of the day (See Box 5.2). The MTM gains and losses are calculated everyday by computing the difference between the futures settlement price of that day and of the preceding day. These gains (or losses) of each client are credited into (or debited from) that particular client's account.

Daily Settlement Price

The Daily Settlement Price would be the closing price of the 10 year notional coupon bearing GoI securities futures contract on the trading day.

Daily Settlement price is the Volume Weighted Average Price (VWAP) of:

- Trades in the last 30 minutes subject to at least 5 trades for a minimum aggregate notional Face value of ₹ 10 cr, failing which.
- Trades in the last 60 minutes subject to at least 5 trades for a minimum aggregate notional Face value of ₹ 10 cr, failing which.
- Trades in the last 120 minutes subject to at least 5 trades for a minimum aggregate notional Face value of ₹ 10 cr.

In the absence of trading in the above stipulated time frame the theoretical price, to be determined by the Exchanges, would be considered as Daily Settlement Price. Theoretical pricing is calculated on the basis of the prices of bonds from the delivery basket.

Physical Settlement

During the expiry month, the contract is settled by physical delivery of deliverable grade securities using the electronic book entry system of the existing Depositories (NSDL and CDSL) and Public Debt Office (PDO) of the RBI. The delivery of the deliverable grade securities takes place on the last business day of the delivery month. The short position holder in an expiring futures contract holds the right to decide which security to deliver from the basket.

AN EXPLANATION OF KEY CONCEPTS IN IRF

Why a Notional Bond is being used as Underlying?

We have already seen that the underlying for bond futures in India is a notional 10 year government bond with a coupon payment of 7 per cent per annum. Such a bond may not actually exist. So, let us understand why such a notional underlying has been selected.

If futures were to be introduced on each of the government bonds, then there would be a large number of interest rate futures contracts trading on each bond and as a result, the liquidity would be poor for many of these futures. So, a single bond futures has been identified which pays 7 per cent per annum as coupon rate and has maturity of 10 years. All bonds have been assigned a multiplier called 'conversion factor' which brings that bond on par with the theoretical bond available for trading. We will learn more about the conversion factor in subsequent sections.

If the bond future were to be based on an actual bond issue, it could potentially raise the activity in the futures market to such a large extent as to cause severe shortages of this actual bond for delivery at expiry. To avoid this danger of shortages to meet the delivery requirement, the Exchange allows a specific set of bonds – rather than a single bond – with different coupons and expiry dates to be used for satisfying the obligations of short position holders in a contract. Thus, while the purpose of a notional underlying bond is to ensure liquidity, the purpose of having a basket of bonds is to ensure that there delivery is not affected by short supply, which would have arisen in case of a single bond.

Now, why choose a bond with a 7 per cent coupon rate? The coupon rate of 7 per cent has been chosen for the hypothetical bond because the yields on government bonds are generally close to 7 per cent and hence there would not be much difference in yield between the delivered bond and the hypothetical underlying.

Conversion Factor

As stated earlier, the Reserve Bank of India has identified a set of bonds to be allowed for delivery by the investor having short position in the IRF to the long position holder on the settlement day. These are called deliverable bonds. All these bonds have differing maturities and coupon rates. To facilitate delivery, however, it is necessary to make them comparable with each other and all of them comparable with the notional bond as of the first day of the expiry month. For achieving this, the RBI has specified the use of conversion factor. The NSE publishes 'conversion factor' for each of the deliverable bond and for each expiry at the time of introduction of the contract. For a particular expiry month, the conversion factors do not change over time.

Conversion factor when multiplied by the futures price (whose underlying is the notional bond) converts it to the actual delivery price for a given deliverable bond. Thus conversion factors are used to take care of the differences between various bonds and thereby bring all the bonds at par for settlement.

Invoice Price

Following the short futures position holder's intimation to the Exchange of his intent to give delivery of the bond, the physical settlement of the trade is conducted. In physical settlement, the short investor gives one of the bonds from the basket of deliverable bonds and gets cash amount from the buyer of the bond. When futures are traded, they are quoted in clean price terms; accrued interest is not included in the traded futures price. But for the purpose of settlement dirty price is taken into account, which includes accrued interest.

Thus, on any given day, the futures settlement price of that day multiplied by the conversion factor gives the clean price of the bond for that day; this value plus the accrued interest value gives the invoice price or dirty price of the bond for that day. The buyer has to pay this price to the seller for getting delivery of the bond.

Invoice price = (Futures settlement price × Conversion factor) + Accrued Interest.

Illustration:

For a futures contract on bonds with face value of ₹ 100, suppose:

Futures settlement price is ₹ 90,

Conversion factor for the bond to be delivered is 1.3800,

Accrued interest on this bond at the time of delivery is ₹ 3.

The cash received by the party with the short position (and paid by the party with the long position) is then,

Invoice price = (1.3800 × 90.00) + 3.00 = ₹ 127.20.

Cheapest to Deliver Bond

The short position holders of IRFs are allowed to decide which bond they would like to give to the buyers on the settlement date. They have a choice to deliver different grades of underlying bonds at specific delivery or expiry points. The sellers will choose that bond from the basket which leads to maximum profit or minimum loss for them. This bond is called the cheapest to deliver bond (CTD) because it is the least expensive bond in the basket of deliverable bonds.

The sellers of the IRF have to acquire bonds to deliver them to the buyers. For them, the cost of acquiring the bonds for delivery = Quoted price of the bond + Accrued Interest. On the other hand, when they deliver these bonds to the buyers of the IRF, the price that they receive = (Futures settlement Price × Conversion factor) + Accrued interest.

The difference between the two accounts for the profit/loss of the seller of futures.

Profit of seller of futures = (Futures settlement Price × Conversion factor) – Quoted Spot Price of delivered bond.

Loss of seller of futures = Quoted Spot Price of delivered bond – (Futures settlement Price x Conversion factor).

Clearly, the cheapest to deliver bond is identified by calculating the profits/losses using the formulas given above, for each of the deliverable bonds and choosing that bond which maximises the profit (in case there is at least one profit making deliverable bond) or minimises the loss (in case all deliverable bonds are loss making).

Illustration: Determining Cheapest to Deliver Bond

Consider a party with a short position in IRF having to deliver a bond and there are three options available to it with spot prices as mentioned below. Let us assume that the current futures settlement price is ₹ 110.

Determining cheapest to deliver bond: An Example

Table 13.2: Futures settlement Price (A):110

Deliverable Bond (B)	Quoted Spot Price (C)	Conversion Factor (D)	Profits of Seller = (A × D) – C
1	109.55	0.88	= (110 x 0.88) – 109.55 = –12.75
2	106.01	0.84	= (110 x 0.88) – 106.01 = –13.61
3	102.09	0.83	= (110 x 0.88) – 102.09 = –10.79

As can be seen from the last column in Table 13.2, the difference between futures settlement price (after adjusting by the conversion factor) and the bond price is resulting in a loss for all the three bonds under consideration. This loss is lowest for bond 3 and hence, bond 3 will be the cheapest to deliver bond. Typically, all market participants know what the cheapest to deliver bond is at any given point of time and so the futures price tracks the price of the cheapest to deliver bond (after adjusting for conversion factor).

Bond Basis

'Bond basis' provides a way to track the movement in the IRF prices relative to the movement in CTD's price. The bond basis is defined as the difference between a bond's price in the cash market and the converted futures price. The converted futures price is the current futures price multiplied by conversion factor of the bond in consideration.

This value of bond basis is also called Gross bond basis.

Gross bond basis = Bond price – (Futures price × conversion factor for that bond).

If we add the cost of carry to the gross bond basis, we get net basis for a bond. Thus,

Net Bond Basis = Gross Bond basis + Cost of Carry till the delivery date.

Where Cost of Carry = Cost of financing the bond – Coupon payment receivable from the bond.

Net basis for a bond is typically greater than or equal to zero. If it is lower than zero, then there is an arbitrage opportunity, which is discussed in next chapter.

APPLICATION AND TRADING OF IRS

Illustration: View Based Trading

A trader expects a long term interest rate to rise.

- On 5th Oct 2009, the trader sells 250 contracts of the Dec. 2009 10 Year futures on NSE at ₹ 93.50.

Closing out the Position:

- 15th Oct 2009 – Futures market Price – ₹ 92.75.
- Trader buys 250 contracts of Dec. 2009 at ₹ 92.75 and squares off his position.
- Therefore total profit for trader is 250 × 2000 × (93.5000 – 92.75) or ₹ 3,75,000.

Arbitrage strategy

Frequently, the price of a bond in spot market and price of futures may not be aligned with each other because of some distortions in the supply/demand factors. The arbitrage strategy employed to gain risk-free profits by exploiting the non-alignment (or mis-pricing of futures relative to spot bond prices) is called cash/futures arbitrage. Cash/Futures arbitrage is also called basis arbitrage or cash and carry arbitrage.

Smart market participants take advantage of such situations to make risk free profits. It involves buying a bond in cash (spot) market and selling futures simultaneously or *vice versa*. It should be noted that the cost of carry has to be considered while calculating the profits. Net basis is an important parameter to track arbitrage in IRF market. As mentioned in the last chapter, net basis is typically positive. If net basis turns negative, however, an arbitrage opportunity arises, which can be exploited to make risk-free profits. The example below illustrates one such opportunity.

Illustration: Trading involving arbitrage

Suppose on Oct 5, 2009, 7.94 per cent 2021 G-Sec is trading at ₹ 99. The interest rate futures, which has a notional 7 per cent 10 year G-Sec as underlying is trading at ₹ 93.50. Following details are available:

- Last Coupon was paid on 24th May 2009, i.e., 131 days back in 30/360 convention.
- Next Coupon will be paid on 24th Nov. 2009, i.e., after 49 days (30/360 convention).
- Accrued Interest as of 5th Oct. 2009 is ₹ 2.89 (7.94 × 131/360).
- Conversion factor is 1.0722.
- Futures Expiry: 31st December 2009.
- Number of days for futures settlement after next coupon date: 37 days.
- Actual number of days from trade date to futures settlement date: 87.
- Number of days from trade date to futures settlement date in 30/360 convention: 86.
- Interest to accrue between the next coupon payment and the futures' expiry will be ₹ 0.82 (= 7.94 × 37/360).
- Assume that money market rate is 4 per cent per annum.
- Assume that cost of short-term financing is 4.5 per cent per annum.

Does an arbitrage opportunity exist?

The net basis here is:

Spot price – (futures price × conversion factor) + cost of carry = 99 – (93.5 × 1.0722) + (99 × 4.5 per cent × 87/365) – (100 × 7.94 per cent × 86/365) = –2.06

Since net basis is negative, there is an arbitrage opportunity that can be exploited through simultaneous trades in the spot bond market and the IRF market. The arbitrageur buys the G-sec in cash market and sells an IRF with an underlying notional bond simultaneously as described above.

Cash outflow at the beginning = Bond's Price + Accrued Interest = 99 + 2.89 = 101.89.

Cash inflow at the expiry = (Futures Settlement Price × Conversion Factor) + Accrued Interest till futures' expiry + Future Value of Interim Coupon = (93.5 × 1.0722) + 0.85 + 3.97 × {1 + 4 per cent × (37/365)} = 105.09.

(**Note:** If there is a coupon between settlement of the bond and the futures' expiry date, one has to take into account the future value of the coupon amount, which is equal to the coupon amount plus the interest arising from reinvesting the coupon amount.)

Here ₹ 3.97 (i.e., 7.94/2) is the coupon amount and the future value of the coupon is 3.97 × (1 + 4 per cent × 7/365). We are assuming that the coupon amount of the bond can be reinvested at the money market rate of 4 per cent. It may be noted that we are using actual/365 notation to work out the future value of the coupon amount, because money market operates under that convention.

Implied return = (105.09 – 101.89)/101.89 × (365/87) = 13 per cent per annum, which is higher than the cost of financing the investment (4.5 per cent) and hence, there is an arbitrage opportunity.

It can also be shown with another example that if the net basis for a bond is positive, there would no arbitrage opportunity.

Number of days for futures settlement after next coupon date: 7 days.

- Interest to accrue between the next coupon payment and the futures' expiry will be ₹ 0.15 (7.94 × 7/360).
- Assume that money market rate is 4 per cent per annum.
- Assume that cost of short term financing is 4.5 per cent per annum.

References

1. John C. Hull, *Options, Futures and Other Derivatives* (6th ed.), (Prentice-Hall, 2005).
2. Frank Fabozzi and Moorad Choudhry, *The Handbook of European Fixed Income Securities,* (John Wiley, 2004).
3. Report of the RBI - SEBI Standing Technical Committee on Interest Rate Futures. (June 2009): http://rbidocs.rbi.org.in/rdocs/PublicationReport/Pdfs/IRFF_170609.pdf

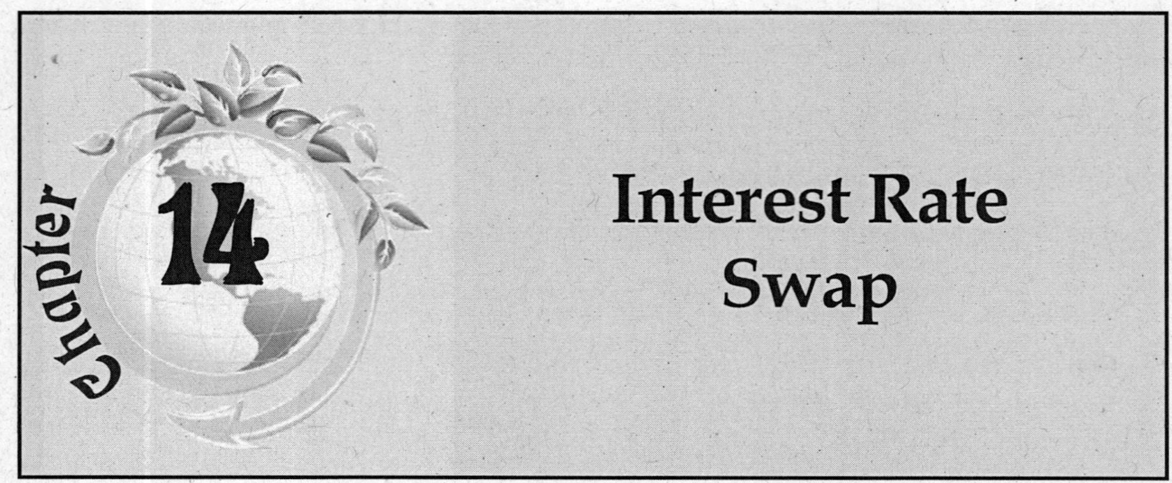

Interest Rate Swap

INTRODUCTION

In an interest rate swap, the parties to the agreement, termed the swap counter parties, agree to exchange payments indexed to two different interest rates. Total payments are determined by the specified notional principal amount of the swap, which is never actually exchanged. Following are important terms associated with the Interest Rate Swaps:

(a) *Swap Dealers:* They are the intermediaries.

(b) *Swap Market Conventions:* There are many different variants of interest rate swaps. The most common is the fixed/floating swap.

(c) *Timing of Payments:* A swap is negotiated on its 'trade date' and takes effect two days later on its initial 'settlement date.'

(d) *Price Quotation:* The price of a fixed/floating swap is quoted in two parts: a fixed interest rate and an index upon which the floating interest rate is based. The floating rate can be based on an index of short-term market rates (such as a given maturity of LIBOR) plus or minus a given margin.

(e) *Generic Swap:* Fixed interest payments on a generic swap typically are based on a 30/360 day-count convention whereas Floating-rate payments are based on an actual/360 day-count.

(f) *Day count Conventions:* Fixed payments can be quoted either on an actual/365 (bond equivalent) basis or on an actual/360 basis. Floating-rate payments indexed to private-sector interest rates typically follow an actual/360 day-count convention commonly used in the money market.

(g) *Swap Valuation:* Following are two methods used for the valuation of fixed/ floating swaps

- Pricing the Variable Rate Note
- Pricing the Fixed Rate Note

(h) *Non-par Swap:* A swap may be priced such that one party owes money to the other at the initial settlement.

Swap Dealers

Early interest rate swaps were brokered transactions in which financial intermediaries with customers interested in entering into a swap would seek counter parties for the transaction among their other customers. The intermediary collected a brokerage fee as compensation, but did not maintain a continuing role once the transaction was completed. The contract was between the two ultimate swap users, who exchanged payments directly.

Swap Market Conventions

There are many different variants of interest rate swaps. The most common is the fixed/floating swap in which a fixed-rate payer makes payments based on a long-term interest rate to a floating-rate payer, who, in turn, makes payments indexed to a short-term money market rate to the fixed-rate payer. A fixed/floating swap is characterized by:

- a fixed interest rate;
- a variable or floating interest rate which is periodically reset;
- a notional principal amount upon which total interest payments are based; and the term of the agreement, including a schedule of interest rate reset dates (that is, dates when the value of the interest rate used to determine floating-rate payments is determined) and payment dates.

The fixed interest rate typically is based on the prevailing market interest rate for Treasury securities with a maturity corresponding to the term of the swap agreement. The floating rate is most often indexed to three-or six-month LIBOR, in which case the swap is termed a "generic" or "plain vanilla" swap, but can be indexed to almost any money market rate such as the Treasury bill, commercial paper, federal funds, or prime interest rate. The maturity, or "tenor," of a fixed/floating interest rate swap can vary between 1 and 15 years. By convention, a fixed-rate payer is designated as the buyer and is said to be long the swap, while the floating-rate payer is the seller and is characterised as short the swap.

Timing of Payments

A swap is negotiated on its "trade date" and takes effect two days later on its initial "settlement date." If the agreement requires the exchange of cash at the outset, as in the case of a "no-par" swap, the transaction takes place on the initial settlement date. Interest begins accruing on the "effective date" of the swap, which usually coincides with the initial settlement date. (Forward swaps, in which the effective date of the swap is deferred, are an exception to this rule.). Floating-rate payments are adjusted on periodic "reset dates" based on the prevailing market-determined value of the floating-rate index, with subsequent payments.

SWAPTIONS

An interest rate swaption is simply an option on an interest rate swap. It gives the holder the right but not the obligation to enter into an interest rate swap at a specific date in the future, at a particular fixed rate and for a specified term. For an up-front fee (premium), the customer selects the strike rate (the level at which it enters the interest rate swap agreement), the length of the option period, the floating rate index (Prime, LIBOR, C.P.), and tenor.

Swaptions fall into three main categories:

(a) European Swaptions give the buyer the right to exercise only on the maturity date of the option.

(b) American Swaptions, on the other hand, give the buyer the right to exercise at any time during the option period.

(c) Bermudan Swaptions give the buyer the right to exercise on specific dates during the option period.

Question 1: Suppose a dealer quotes 'All-in-cost' for a generic swap at 8 per cent against six-month LIBOR flat. If the notional principal amount of swap is ₹ 5,00,000.

(i) Calculate semi-annual fixed payment.

(ii) Find the first floating rate payment for (i) above if the six month period from the effective date of swap to the settlement date comprises 181 days and that the corresponding LIBOR was 6 per cent on the effective date of swap.

(iii) In (ii) above, if the settlement is on 'Net' basis, how much the fixed rate payer would pay to the floating rate payer?

Generic swap is based on 30/360 days basis.

Answer

(i) ₹ 20,000/- (ii) ₹ 15,090 or 15,083 (iii) ₹ 4,917 = (20,000 – 15,083)

Illustration: Explain the concept of interest rate swap by giving appropriate examples.

Solution: An interest rate swap is an exchange of interest rate commitments, such as a fixed-rate commitment is exchanged for a floating-rate commitment. The parties to a swap retain their obligations to the original lenders, which means that the parties must accept counter-party risk.

Example: Lockwood Company has a high credit rating. It can borrow at a fixed rate of 10 per cent or at a variable interest rate of LIBOR + 0.3 per cent. It would like to borrow at a variable rate. Thomas Company has a lower credit rating. It can borrow at a fixed rate of 11 per cent or at a variable rate of LIBOR + 0.5 per cent. It would like to borrow at a fixed rate. Using the principle of comparative advantage, both parties could benefit from a swap arrangement, whereby.

(i) Lockwood Company borrows at a fixed rate of 10 per cent.

(ii) Thomas Company borrows at a variable rate of LIBOR+ 0.5 per cent.

(iii) The parties agree a rate for swapping their interest commitments, with perhaps: Thomas Company paying a fixed rate of 10.1 per cent to Lockwood Company. The outcome would be

Lockwood Company	
Borrows at	10 per cent
Receives from Thomas Company	(10.1 per cent)
Pays to Thomas Company	LIBOR
Net interest cost	LIBOR – 0.1 per cent (a saving of 0.4 per cent)
Thomas Company	
Borrows at	LIBOR + 0.5 per cent
Receives from Lockwood Company	(LIBOR)
Pays to Lockwood Company	10.1 per cent
Net interest cost	10.6 per cent (a saving of 0.4 per cent)

In this example, both companies benefit from lower costs.

Question 2: ABC Bank is seeking fixed rate funding. It is able to finance at a cost of six months LIBOR + 1/4 per cent for ₹ 200 million for 5 years. The bank is able to swap into a fixed rate at 7.5 per cent versus six-month LIBOR treating six months as exactly half a year.

(a) What will be the "all in cost" funds to ABC Bank?

(b) Another possibility being considered is the issue of a hybrid instrument which pays 7.5 per cent for first three years and LIBOR –1/1 per cent for remaining two years.

Given a three year swap rate of 8 per cent, suggest the method by which the bank should achieve fixed rate funding.

(c) What do you know about swaptions and their uses?

(d) What are the reasons for stock index futures becoming more popular financial derivatives over stock futures segment in India?

Answer

(a) ABC Bank pays LIBOR + 0.25 per cent p.a. for 5 years. The swap involves payment of 7.5 per cent p.a. and receipt of LIBOR.

In flow	Out flow
LIBOR	LIBOR + 0.25 per cent + 7.5 per cent

Net interest payment 7.75 per cent

Cash flows per six month period

In flow	Out flow
(LIBOR/2) × ₹ 200 million	(LIBOR/2) × ₹ 200 million
	+ ₹ 2,50,000 + ₹ 75,00,000

Therefore All in cost of funds = ₹ 77,50,000.

Alternatively it can also be calculated as follows:

₹ 200 million × 7.75 per cent × –12 = ₹ 7.75 millions or ₹ 77,50,000

(a) ABC Bank issues hybrid and enters both the five year and three year swaps.

First three years:

Bank pays on hybrid	7.5 per cent p.a.
Bank pays on five year swap	7.5 per cent p.a.
Bank receives on three year swap	8 per cent p.a.
Bank receives on five year swap	LIBOR
Bank pays on three year swap	LIBOR
Net interest payment	7 per cent p.a.

Final two years:

Bank pays on hybrid	LIBOR – 0.25 per cent
Bank received on five year swap	LIBOR
Bank pays on five year swap	7.5 per cent p.a.
Net interest payment	7.25 per cent p.a.

Therefore, the arrangement in (b) compared to (a) saves 0.75 per cent p.a. over the first three years and 0.5 per cent p.a. over final two years.

(i) Swaptions are combination of the features of two derivative instruments, i.e., option and swap.

(ii) A swaption is an option on an interest rate swap. It gives the buyer of the swaption the right but not obligation to enter into an interest rate swap of specified parameters (maturity of the option, notional principal, strike rate, and period of swap). Swaptions are traded over the counter, for both short and long maturity expiry dates, and for wide range of swap maturities.

(iii) The price of a swaption depends on the strike rate, maturity of the option, and expectations about the future volatility of swap rates.

(iv) The swaption premium is expressed as basis points.

USES OF SWAPTIONS

(a) Swaptions can be used as an effective tool to swap into or out of fixed rate or floating rate interest obligations, according to a treasurer's expectation on interest rates. Swaptions can also be used for protection if a particular view on the future direction of interest rates turned out to be incorrect.

(b) Swaptions can be applied in a variety of ways for both active traders as well as for corporate treasures. Swap traders can use them for speculation purposes or to hedge a portion of their swap books. It is a valuable tool when a borrower has decided to do a swap but is not sure of the timing.

(c) Swaptions have become useful tools for hedging embedded option which is common in the natural course of many businesses.

(d) Swaptions are useful for borrowers targeting an acceptable borrowing rate. By paying an upfront premium, a holder of a payer's swaption can guarantee to pay a maximum fixed rate on a swap, thereby hedging his floating rate borrowings.

(e) Swaptions are also useful to those businesses tendering for contracts. A business, would certainly find it useful to bid on a project with full knowledge of the borrowing rate should the contract be won.

Accounting for interest rate swap

Question 3: Raj Limted wants to borrow 5 year fixed rate rupee funding to finance an expansion project. Its credit rating is BBB (not very high). It finds that it will have to pay interest @ 11 per cent if it borrows at fixed interest rate. In the floating rate market, it can issue floating rate notes at margin of 0.75 per cent over the prime rate, which is 10 per cent.

On the other hand, Vijay Ltd., a large unit is looking for floating rate note but finds that it will have to pay prime rate, while in the fixed rate market it can raise 5 Year funds at 9.50 per cent due to AAA rating and BBB rating is 150 bp in fixed rate segment and 75 bp in floating rate segment. The requirements and access of the two parties are summarised below:

Particulars	Raj Ltd. (BBB Rating)	Vijay Ltd. (AAA Rating)
Cost of fixed Loan	11 per cent	9.50 per cent
Cost of Floating Loan	Prime rate+ 0.75 per cent	Prime rate (10 per cent)

Give the accounting treatment for interest rate swaps. Assume equal sharing of gains between swap bank and the parties to the swap arrangement, and an underlying principal of ₹ 100 Lakhs is exchanged at the beginning. At the end of the year, fair value of the swap is estimated as ₹ 1.25 lakhs, net gain to Vijay Ltd.

Answer

1. How can the swap arrangement be structured?: An effective swap arrangement can be structured, only if Vijay Limited.(the stronger company) opts for an interest rate scheme in which it has maximum comparative advantage. Therefore, Vijay Limited should opt for fixed loan (advantage of 1.5 per cent vs. 0.75 per cent in floating rate), and Raj Limited would go for a floating rate scheme at prime rate + 0.75 per cent.
2. Sharing of gain: Total gain = difference between swap points of fixed rate and floating rate = 1.50 per cent - 0.75 per cent = 0.75 per cent. Therefore, each party will gain 0.25 per cent.
3. Effective Interest rate and structure of swap can be presented through diagram:

9.50 per cent Vijay's Source	PR-0.25 per cent Vijay Ltd.	PR-0.25 Swap Bank 9.50 per cent	PR+0.75 per cent Raj Ltd. 9.75 per cent	Raj's Source

Effective Rate	Effective Rate
PR-0.25 per cent	10.75 per cent

Journal entries in the books of Vijay Limted

	Particulars		Debit	Credit
1.	Cash A/c To Loan A/c (Being amount borrowed from Financial Institutions)	Dr.	1,00,00,000	 1,00,00,000
2.	Interest A/c To Bank A/c (Being interest liability for the year paid for 100 lakhs * 9.50 per cent)	Dr.	9,50,000	 9,50,000
3.	Interest A/c To Swap Bank A/c (Being Interest payable to swap bank under swap arrangement made due = 100 lakhs * 9.75 per cent, e.g., PR-0.25 per cent)	Dr.	9,75,000	 9,75,000
4.	Swap Bank A/c To Bank (Being interest paid to swap bank)	Dr.	9,75,000	 9,75,000
5.	Swap bank A/c To Interest A/c (Being Interest payable by swap bank under the swap arrangement = ₹ 100 Lakhs * 9.50 per cent)	Dr.	9,50,000	 9,50,000
6.	Bank A/c To Swap Bank A/c (Being interest received from swap bank under swap arrangenment (950000 * 5)	Dr.	47,50,000	 47,50,000
7.	Swap Asset A/c To gain on Swap A/c (Profit and Loss)	Dr.	1,25,000	 1,25,000

Question 4: Accounting for Interest Rate Swap- Gain/ Loss

On April 1, 2006, A Ltd borrowed ₹ 10 lakhs at annual fixed interest rate of 7 per cent payable half-yearly. The life of the loan is 4 years with no pre-payment permitted. The Company expected the interest rate to fall and on the same day, it entered into an Interest Rate swap arrangement, whereby the company would pay 6-Month LIBOR and would receive annual fixed interest of 7 per cent every half year The swap effectively converted the Company's fixed rate obligation to floating rate obligation. The value of swap and debt are ₹ 0.2 Lakhs (positive) and 10.2 lakhs on 1.10.2006 and (₹ 0.1 lakhs) and ₹ 9.9 Lakhs on 31.03.2007 respectively. Six month LIBOR on April 1, 2006 was 6 per cent and that on October 1, 2006 was 8.5 per cent. Show important accounting entries for the first year.

Journal Entries in the books of A Ltd

Date	Particulars		Debit	Credit
01.04.06	Bank A/c To 7 per cent Term Loan A/c (Term loan borrowed at 7 per cent annual interest rate payable half yearly)	Dr.	10,00,000	10,00,000
30.09.06	Interest A/c To Bank (Interest on Term Loan for the first half year = ₹ 10 lakhs * 7 per cent* 6/12 months)	Dr.	35,000	35,000
30.09.06	Loss on Valuation of Debt A/c To 7 per cent Term Loan A/c (Increase in value of debt recognized due to restatement based on fair value. Fair value ₹ 10, 20,000 Less book value ₹ 10,00,000)	Dr.	20,000	20,000
30.09.06	Swap Hedge A/c To Gain on swap hedge A/c (Increase in value of swap recognized)	Dr.	20,000	20,000
30.09.06	Bank A/c To Interest A/c (Swap settlement received for first half year 2006-07. Gain on underlying principal received ₹ 10 lakhs * 6/12 * (7 per cent contracted rate – 6 per cent swap agreed interest rate.)	Dr.	5,000	5,000
31.03.07	Interest A/c To Bank A/c (Interest on term Loan for the second half year = ₹ 10 lakhs * 7 per cent * 6/12)	Dr.	35,000	35,000
31.03.07	Loan A/c To Gain on Valuation of debt A/c (Decrease in value of debt recognised due to restatement based on fair value. Fair value ₹ 9,90,000-Book value ₹ 10,20,000)	Dr.	30,000	30,000
31.03.07	Loss on Swap Hedge A/c To Swap Hedge A/c (Cumulative loss on swap recognised. Value as at 31.03.07 ₹ 20,000 loss Less	Dr.	30,000	30,000

	value already recognized gain ₹ 10,000 = 20,000 – 10,000)			
31.03.07	Interest A/c To Bank A/c (Swap settlement paid for second half year 2006-07. ₹ 10 lakhs * (8.5 per cent – 7 per cent)* 6/12	Dr.	7,500	7,500

Example: XYZ enters into an interest rate swap that requires XYZ to pay a fixed rate of interest and receive a variable rate of interest. The fixed interest rate amount is 7.5 per cent, while the variable interest rate amount is three-month LIBOR, reset on a quarterly basis. The notional amount of the swap is CU100 million. The underlying is an interest rate index, three-month LIBOR. Net regular settlements are calculated by applying the difference between 7.5 per cent and three-month LIBOR to the notional of CU100 million.

Hedge of Foreign Exchange Risk

INTRODUCTION

Hedging is a risk management technique, primarily done to protect the foreign exchange exposures against the volatility of exchange rates, by using derivatives like Currency Options, Currency Futures, Forward Contracts, Currency Swaps, Money Markets etc., by taking off-setting positions against the underlying asset. The treasury manager should completely understand the firm's exposure and risk policy before applying hedging techniques. Minimum hedge ratio may be calculated to minimise risk in case of future contracts. This ratio allows the hedger to determine the number of contracts that must be employed in order to minimise risk of the combined cash futures position. In hedging, to strike a balance between uncertainty and risk opportunity loss is a challenge. Hedging itself is a risk, and disastrous if it is applied incorrectly and with the intent of speculation.

The Concept of Risk

Risk is the possibility of actual outcome being different from the expected outcome. It includes both downside and upside potential. Downside potential is the possibility of actual results being adverse compared to the expected results and upside potential is the possibility of actual results being better than the expected results.

Foreign Exchange Exposure and Risk

It is the change in the domestic currency value of assets and liabilities to the changes in the exchange rates. This may be positive or negative. Positive exposure gives rise to Gain and negative exposure gives rise to loss.

How it is Measured?

Foreign exchange risk is measured by the variance of the domestic currency value of asset, liability or an operating income, which can be related to unexpected changes in the exchange rates.

HEDGING FOREIGN EXCHANGE RISK

Hedging refers to process, whereby one can protect the price of financial instrument at a date in the future by taking an opposite position in the present by using derivatives like Currency Options, Currency Futures, Forward Contracts, Currency Swaps, Money Markets, etc. It refers to technique of protecting the financial exposures in the underlying asset or liability due to volatility in the exchange rates by taking offsetting positions through derivatives to offset the losses in the cash market by a corresponding gain in the derivatives market.

Hedging Involves

- Foreign exchange exposure identification
- Value of exposure
- Creation of offsetting positions through derivatives.
- Measurement of Hedge ratio.
- Degree of Risk acceptable to management
- Expectations regarding future movement of exchange rates.

Derivatives are hypothetical assets; they derive their value from the underlying assets.

One very fundamental question – why do we need derivatives?

For risk management, there should be negative correlation between the assets in a portfolio. Risks can still be managed, even if there is a positive correlation between the asset in the portfolio and that is through creation of hypothetical assets against those assets i.e., (underlying asset).

Currency Options – are instruments, which give the buyer of the option the right but not the obligation to execute a specified transaction in the underlying currency pair. This gives the buyer the flexibility to execute settlement or not.

They are different from other derivatives in that they provide downside protection against risk and also an upside benefit from favourable movements in the underlying exchange rates.

Forward Contracts – are a commitment to settle at a fixed forward price. This provides only upside benefit from a favourable movement in the underlying exchange rates, but not downside protection.

Currency Futures – are one of the derivatives, where exporters and importers can hedge theirpositions by selling and buying future contracts. It provides a means to hedge the trader's position who wishes to lock in exchange rates on futures currency transactions. By purchasing (long hedge) or selling (short hedge) currency futures, a firm can fix the incoming and outgoing cash flows in one currency with respect to others.

HEDGING, IS IT NECESSARY?

To hedge or not to hedge is, thus, a very difficult question. For applying any hedging strategy Treasury managers must have correct answers to these fundamental questions.

I. How well he understands and knows the firms risk exposure.

II. If identified, would hedging these risks make cash flows positive?

III. Correct application and timing of hedging strategies must be in line with exchangerate movement.

IV. If yes, is it possible to hedge these risks adequately?

Hedging, How could it be Destructive? Speculation and Hedging

When speculation is mixed with hedging, it is destructive. There is a thin line of difference between hedging and speculative activity. Speculation means dealing in a commodity or financial asset with a view to obtaining profit on the prospective changes in the market value of the item under consideration. It involves contemplation of future expectations and taking positions to gain, unlike hedging in which offsetting positions are taken, but not with the objective of earning a profit. Speculation involves forecasting the evolution of supply and demand, i.e., if exchange rate rises, when speculators are long and fall when they are short, then they gain. They lose when forecasts turn out to be wrong. Hedgers offset their risks by taking offsetting positions; it is speculators who bear the risk transferred by the hedgers. It is for this risk borne by them that they get a reward in the form of speculative profits. Therefore, the nature of speculative activity is such that to earn speculative rewards, they must bear risk. Hedging and speculation are not similar answers to a problem. They cannot be used interchangeably for getting desired results or to meet similar objectives. Hedging is a risk-management or reducing technique, where the objective is not to earn profits, unlike speculation. Hedging, when mixed with speculation, can be disastrous for the hedger.

Uncertainty and Risk of Opportunity Loss

How to strike a balance between uncertainty and the risk of opportunity loss?

The problem of settling an effective hedge ratio has two dimensions.

1. **Uncertainty:** If a firm does not hedge the transaction, it cannot know with certainty at what rate of exchange it can lock its exposures. It could be a better rate or a worse rate.
2. **Opportunity:** If firms enter into hedge transactions like forward contracts, currency options etc, they would of course be certain at a rate at which they are locking their exposures. But now they have taken an infinite risk of 'opportunity' loss.

Hedgers offset their risks by taking offsetting positions. It is speculators who bear the risk transferred by the hedgers. It is for this risk borne by them that they get a reward in the form of speculative profits. Therefore, the nature of speculative activity is such that, to earn speculative rewards, they must bear risk

Perfect Hedge Ratio – So, construction of an exact opposite position to the existing risk exposure results, in a perfect hedge, which is a challenge.There is yet another dimension to hedging. Hedging has a cost. If the expected risk does not materialise, hedging will prove an ineffective way of doing business. All these complexities associated with hedging through derivatives pose a great challenge to arrive at a right Hedge ratio. Various real life instances of how hedging has proved to be destructive are enumerated alongside.

(A) Forward Contracts taken by an Importer

During 2004 and early 2005, various short-term forward contracts were taken in USD by a leading automobile importer, to hedge its imports. At the time of maturity, USD depreciated substantially to the extent of ₹ 3 per USD, below the rate at which forward contracts were taken. It resulted in opportunity loss of approximately ₹ 15 crore for the firm, in spite of the fact that the firm had hedged its exposure. In the above case, the firm may have taken currency call options or currency long futures as a hedging instrument to hedge its imports.

Currency call options provide downside protection against risk and upside benefit from favourable movements. Alternatively, forward contracts may have been cancelled, when exchange rate has started moving in opposite direction for minimising the loss. So, selection and timing of right hedging strategy is of utmost importance and it should be in line with the exchange rate movement.

(B) Currency Call options taken by an Importer

During 2005, a Fortune 500 consumer electronics MNC, had taken call options to buy USD and sell INR, to hedge its imports. The options were taken at a higher strike rate to save call premium, as it has a negative relationship between call premium and strike rate, as strike rate increases call premium decreases. The other objective of the hedger was to earn profits, since it expected USD to depreciate against rupee. But USD appreciated against rupee, instead of depreciating, unlike the hedger's expectation. Firm lost heavily in terms of opportunity loss of ₹ 2 per USD, since it remained exposed to risk by selecting a very higher Call option strike rate. Hedger instead of doing hedging by selectinga Call option strike rate equivalent to forward contract rate for the same maturity period, speculated, by selecting a very high Call option strike rate.Under-mentioned pay off Table may be used for hedging a currency call option for importtransactions.

E.g., - On 1st May 2005, a firm bought a 3-month currency call option contract to buy USD

Call, sell INR @ 43.70 at a premium of 20 paise.

Contract Size = USD $2 million.

Expiry period - 31st July 2005.

3-month Forward Contract rate - 43.70

Spot rate on 1st May 2005 - 43.50

Table 15.1: OPTION v/s FORWARD COMPARISON (INR RS)

MARKETRATE USD	FORWARDUSD @43.70	OPTIONUSD @43.70 +.20P
42.70	-20,00,000	16,00,000
43.00	-14,00,000	10,00,000
43.10	-12,00,000	8,00,000
43.20	-10,00,000	6,00,000
43.30	-8,00,000	4,00,000
43.40	-6,00,000	2,00,000
43.50	-4,00,000	0
43.60	-2,00,000	-2,00,000
43.70	0	-4,00,000
43.80	2,00,000	-2,00,000
44.00	6,00,000	2,00,000
44.20	10,00,000	6,00,000
44.50	16,00,000	12,00,000
44.70	20,00,000	16,00,000

(C) Purchased Call Option and Sold Put Option at Different Strike Prices to Hedge Imports

A leading petrochemical importer, purchased currency call option and sold put option to hedge its imports. The firm expected the USD to appreciate.

E.g., – On 1st May 2005, a firm bought 3 month currency call option contract to buy USD call, sell INR @ 43.70 at a premium of 20 paise. It sold a 3-month currency put option @ 43.80 at a premium of 10 paise.

Contract Size = 2 million USD.

Expiry period - 31st July 2005.

3-month Forward Contract rate - 43.70

Spot rate on 1st May 2005 - 43.50

There were two-fold objectives of the firm to adopt this strategy. Firstly to reduce the premium from 20 paise to 10 paise and secondly it expected the USD to appreciate.

But actually, the USD depreciated to ₹ 43.45 on the maturity date, and the firm lost an additional 35 paise per USD, instead of reducing its premium cost from 20 paise to 10 paise. Ideally, the firm may have kept its PUT strike price lessthan 43.70. It adopted an aggressive speculative strategy to bring down its premium cost.

There is of course no 'set of rules' that can provide perfect hedging strategies, and thereby guarantees that there would be no wild fluctuations in company's cash flows. By using un-speculative strategies, one can hedge itsrisk. With the increased volume of international trade and financing, increase in volatility of exchange rates and increased exposure of foreign exchange gain and losses, hedging foreign exchange risk has gained importance.

So, deciding to hedge is one thing, and getting it right is quite another. Hedging should also be done without speculation. Further, in-correct application of hedging strategies along with notrade off between uncertainties associated with exchange rate and opportunity loss, makes a hedging foreign exchange risk itself a risk.

Manage Currency Risk by Derivatives

'Profit is the reward of risk'. An entrepreneur is always said to be a risk-taker. But In today's technology-driven global village, unanticipated fluctuations in financial or business derivates may change the whole scenario unless the enterprise takes appropriate steps to identify, measure the said risk and take defensive steps to minimise the losses.

Currency Risk (Exposure)

The currency exposure is a measure of the sensitivity of real value (adjusted for inflation) of enterprise's assets and income (or liability/loss) expressed in functional currency (an nterprise's operational currency) to unanticipated risk. A project has currency exposure when the currencies for its expenditures and revenues are not the same.

Higher Currency Exposure to Financial Risk Leads to:

1. Financial distress and possible bankruptcy, as manager may compromise to quality and safety of workers.
2. The customers will start thinking of after-sales service and sale volume will decrease.
3. Suppliers will tighten credit terms.
4. Cost of running the enterprise will be high.
5. Conflict between stakeholders and debt-holder (debt-holders are given more interest; therefore, stakeholder may lose interest)
6. Tax may be more as tax on book profit will be payable and in the period of loss the compensation is not available.

HOW TO MANAGE CURRENCY RISK?

The devices (derivatives) available: Forward market hedge: In this the Net Liability is covered by Forward contract of specific period at a premium or discount.

Roll over contracts: These are similar to Forward contract but rolled over after specified period at premium or discount.

Financial Swaps: It is the exchange of one set of financial obligation to another for specific period. These are mainly currency swap or interest rate swap.

Money Market Hedge: In this the exposed position of currency is covered through borrowing or lending in money market.

Currency options: Option is right (but not obligation) given by the seller (writer) to buyer (holder) to buy or sale (depend on put or call option) at predetermined price in the specific period. The writer sells the product at the price that changes on the basis of the time factor and the movement (fluctuation) in the currency. These are the options where physical currency is not being transferred but only the difference is being settled.

How to Manage Currency Risk More Efficiently?

1 **Select your currency:** It is desirable to hedge but all part of it, as the favourable side may generate great benefits. You may put different currencies in order of your requirement and hedge in order of preference. Suppose an enterprise is exposed to payables in dollar and euro, one may find euro to be less strong than dollar for specific period so while hedging the currency, it may hedge euro first.

2. **Seek more quotations:** Different Banks or dealers may have different rates, so it is always better to get two or more quotations from different dealers. Even quotation from same dealer at different times also differs. Currencies are always quoted in pairs. One unit of the base currency (first currency in the pair) represents the number of units of the second currency of the pair as indicated by the exchange rate.

   Example: USD/CHF@1.4000. This means 1 US dollar purchases 1.4000 Swiss francs.

3. **Knowing the Spread:** It is the difference between the price you buy at (also known as theask) and the price you sell at (also known as the bid). The enterprise should develop theability to sell the buy price (ask)and the sell price (bid) at alltimes. Spread has historically been a 'hidden' cost. However, by using technology such as the Internet, the market has become more transparent. An enterprise can see the spread and, thus, can know exactly what the cost of the trade is prior to entering a position.

4. **Try to minimise dependence on one currency hedge:** An enterprise should try to expose to different currencies and hedge accordingly. Firms exposed to dollar in early nineties suffered a lot by using Risk Profiling, the method of worst case and best case through scenario management on performance measure of individual currency.

5. **Shift:** Firms should shift from one 'instrument' to another or one currency to another depending upon the changing market conditions or changing economy indicators (which are key factors of currency rates).

6. **Exchange rate predictions:** Based on Economic forecasting models (PPP-relative purchasing power parity, balance of payment, interest rate parity), exchange rate may be predicted and acted accordingly.

Rate expected = spot rate (1 + diff inflation rate) year

Suppose inflation in 'A' currency is 6 per cent and 'B' currency 3 per cent, and the spot rate is 48.25 after 5 years, the predicted rate would be:

$48.25 (1 + (.06 - .03))5 = 55.93$

Other methods like economic indicators, oscillators, currency and other investment ratings may also be used to predict or forecast the currency rates.

7. **Internal derivatives 'currency concentration':** Where a 'hedging affiliate' (member of group having asked to use the derivates for the group having net exposure in particular currency) using the derivative for 'issuing affiliate' (member of group, having declined to use the derivates for the group having net exposure in particular currency) to enter into a contract with unrelated party to netting off the consolidated exposure. FABS (US GAAP) have facilitated to use internal derivatives by issuing the statement 138(amending statement 133).

Ronald Fink, in CFO Magazine described this as 'Natural Hedge', matching revenues and costs for the same currency or offsetting losses in one currency with gains in another. There are two main reasons for this shift, and probably a third. One, most multinationals have centralised their treasury operations, at least on a regional basis. With access to data from inter-company and third-party transactions within the various countries in which a multinational operates, risk managers can better understand how transactions in one currency offsets those in another and, thus, erects natural hedges.

The owner of the enterprise may also cover the exposure in currency in the firm by changing his investment portfolio. This is backed by theory given by some analysts like Modigiliani-Miller.

The devices (derivatives) available at present for managing currency risk, include Forward market hedge, Roll over contracts, Financial Swaps, Money Market Hedge and Currency Options.

ACCOUNTING OF CURRENCY DERIVATIVES

Currency risk can be managed efficiently by careful selection of the currency; seeking more quotations from different dealers; knowing the Spread; minimising dependence on one currency hedge; shifting from one 'instrument' to another or one currency to another; careful prediction of Exchange rates and through internal derivatives.

- Any premium or discount arising at the inception of a forward exchange contract is accounted for separately from the exchange differences on the forward exchange contract.
- Exchange difference on a forward exchange contract is the difference between (a) the foreign currency amount of the contract translated at the exchange rate at the reporting date, or the settlement date where the transaction is settled during the reporting period, and (b) the same foreign currency amount translated at the latter of the date of inception of the forward exchange contract and the last reporting date.

For enterprises entering into contract for trading or speculation purpose: A gain or loss on a forward exchange contract to which paragraph the above not apply should be computed by multiplying the foreign currency amount of the forward exchange contract by the difference between the forward rate available at the reporting date for the remaining maturity of the contract and the contracted forward rate (or the forward rate last used to measure a gain or loss on that contract for an earlier period).

- The gain or loss so computed should be recognised in the statement of profit and loss for the period.
- The premium or discount on the forward exchange contract is not recognised separately.

An example of accounting of derivatives under IAS 39

Business Event: Sales of Cotton to the value of £100000 by enterprise in Germany to a customer in UK on 30.06.2003. The value of the order is immediately hedged by means of a forward exchange contract. Goods are shipped to the customer on 31st August, 2003. Payment for the goods is due on 31st October 2003.

Basic Data	6/30/2003	7/31/2003	8/31/2003	9/30/2003	10/31/2003
Spot Rate (GBP-EURO)	0.610	0.620	0.610	0.600	0.620
Forward rate of cover transaction (GBP-EURO)	0.590	0.590	0.590	0.590	0.590
Forward rate for delivery on 31/10/2003 (GBP-EURO)	0.590	0.595	0.600	0.610	[0,620]

JOURNAL ENTRIES

Date	Particulars	Debit	Credit
June 30 2003	No Entry When the derivative transaction is entered into on 30/6/2003, the forward rate for 31/10/2003 is identical with the forward rate at which hedging transaction is concluded. Since current forward rate and settlement rate are identical, the derivative has zero value.		
July 31 2003	Derivatives A/c Dr. To Valuation reserve IAS 39 (The rise in the exchange rate renders a forward currency sale lessfavourable vis-à-vis the position on 30/6/2003. Since the original position was hedged by the forward contract, fair value accrues to the latter.)	1424.30	 1424.30
August 31, 2003	Derivatives A/c Dr. To Valuation reserve IAS 39 (Likewise at the end of the following month the exchange rate rises. The fair value of the derivative rises further. A hedge of a future payment stream is deemed to be a cash-flow hedge, variationsin the value of which are accounted over reserves.)	1400.56	 1400.56
August 31, 2003	Receivables A/c Dr. Valuation Reserve Dr. To Foreign Sales (Invoicing the customer gives rise to an asset to which the hedge transaction continues to be related. The cash-flow hedge is now regarded as a hedge of the current value of the asset (fair value hedge). The amount held in Valuation Reserve IAS 39 is now related to the measurement of the asset.)	161,109.57 2824.86	 163,934.43
Sept, 30, 2003	Receivables A/c Dr. To Gain From Value variation IAS 39 underlying (Measurement of receivable at current spot rate accounted toprofit and loss.)	5557.10	 5557.10
Sept, 30, 2003	Derivatives A/c Dr. To Gain From Value variation IAS 39 underlying	2732.24	 2732.24

	(Measurement of the forward exchange contract by comparing the current forward rate for the settlement date with the forward rate of the contract actually booked. The difference is taken to Profit & Loss.)		
Oct, 31, 2003	Expenses (receivable value fluctuation) Dr. To Receivables (Follow-up re-measurement of receivable at spot rate as at date.)	5376.34	 5376.34
Oct, 31, 2003	Derivatives A/c Dr. To Income (value fluctuation forward Contract) (Follow-up remeasurement of forward exchange contract)	2644.10	 2644.10
Oct, 31, 2003	Bank A/c Dr. To Receivables (Payment received from customer measured at spot rate, which equals the amount of the receivable since the latter has already been marked to market)	161,290.32	 161,290.32
Oct, 31, 2003	Bank A/c (EURO balance) Dr. To Bank (GBP balance) To Derivatives (The foreign currency amount received is exchanged into euros at the contracted forward rate as per the forward contract. The difference in value of the foreign currency amount *vis-à-vis* the spot rate is equivalent to the value of the forward contract at the moment of settlement.)	169,491.53	 161,290.32 8,201.21
Oct, 31, 2003	Gain From Value variation IAS 39 underlying Dr. Gain from value variation Hedge Receivable Dr. To Expense (Value fluctuations IAS 39 underlying) To Foreign Sales (The net sum of the value fluctuations booked to Profit Loss is reversed since the hedging relationship is concluded. The contra entry is to Sales since as a result of the hedging transaction, the proceeds from the sale of goods could be locked in.)	5557.10 5376.34	 5376.34 5557.10

As per standard practice under IND AS 39 (which is equivalent to IAS 39): In the case of Fixed assets related forward contracts, the accounting treatment will be the same for forward booking, valuation of contracts before actual delivery of fixed assets will be from valuation reserve. On actual delivery the Fixed assets be capitalised and the value in valuation reserve will be transferred to Fixed assets. Subsequent valuation will be at mark-to-market and shown in Profit and loss account and on capitalisation transferred to Fixed assets. Any premium or discount arising at the inception of a forward exchange contract is accounted for separately from the exchange differences on the forward exchange contract.

In case Hedge relationship is broken like purchase deal is being concealed or otherwise Balances of valuation reserve being transferred to Gain/loss in profit and loss account.

Since we are committed to go inline with IAS, similar type of guidelines are sought for growing demand of derivatives which are buzzword of today's and tomorrow's financial markets.

QUESTIONS AND ANSWERS ON CURRENCY FUTURES

Question 1: An operator buys on Monday a Pound future at the rate of US $ 1.6900. Closing rates are US $ 1.7000, 1.7200 and 1.7150 on Monday, Tuesday and Wednesday respectively. The contract is closed on Wednesday. Indicate the marking-to-market operations and net result for the operator.

Solution: The standard size of the Pound future is £ 62,500.

(a) Monday closing rate is US $ 1.7000. Therefore, the gain for investor is

$ 62,500 (1.70 – 1.69) or $ 625

(b) Tuesday closing rate is US $ 1.72. Therefore, the investor gains

$62,500 × (172 – 1.70) or $ 1,250

(c) Wednesday closing rate is $ 1.7150. Therefore, the investor makes a loss of

$ 62,500 × (1.72 – 1.7150) or $ 321.50

Net result = $ 625 + $ 1,250 – $ 312.50 = $ 1,562.50

or

net result = $62,500 × (1.7150 – 1.6900)

= $ 1,562.50

Question 2: An operator has a long position of £ 2,50,000 and sells a Future contract to cover his position. The rates are given below:

	Spot rate (\$/£)	Future rate (\$/£)	Basis
Initial	1.5070	1.5001	-0.0069
One month later	1.4845	1.4834	-0.0011
Variation	0.0225	0.0167	-0.0058

Solution: Since the basis has changed over the month, it is clear that the cover is not perfect. The loss on Spot position is: £ 2,50,000 (1.5070 – 1.4845) = 5,625 US dollar

The profit on Futures market is

£ 2,50,000 (1.5001 – 1.4834) = 4,175 US dollar

So, net loss is 5,625 – 4,175 = 1,450 US dollar

The loss of 1,450 US dollar, is much less than what it would have been (5,625 US dollar) if the position had been left uncovered.

Question 3: An American importer has negotiated in March to buy goods worth DM 5,00,000, payable in 3 months. Fearing an appreciation of Deutschemark against US dollar, he decides to cover his exposure through futures contracts. Following data is available:

Spot rate: DM 1.6735/US \$

June future: \$ 0.5915/DM

The importer buys DM future contracts to cover the probable loss. On June 05 (the date of settlement), two possibilities can present themselves: (a) appreciation of DM or (b) depreciation of DM.

(a) June future: \$ 0.5980/DM]

Spot rate: DM 1.6540/US \$

The number of contracts bought = $\frac{5,00,000}{1,25,000}$ = 4.

Since the Future rate has increased from \$ 0.5915 to \$ 5,980, the gain made by the importer is:

4 × (0.5980-0.5915) × \$ 1,25,000 = \$ 3250

But on the Spot market, his loss would be

$$\$\ 5,00,000\ \frac{1}{1.6540} - \frac{1}{1.6735}$$

= \$ 5,00,000 (0.60459 – 0.5975) = US \$ 3520

So, the importer has been able to compensate 92.33

per cent $\frac{3,250}{3,250}$ × 100 per cent of his loss by covering on market.

(b) June Future rate on June 05 is $ 0.5900/DM and spot rate is DM 1.6800. That is, there is a marginal depreciation of Deutschemark as against the anticipation. Here, the American importer incurs a loss on the Futures market. His loss is

4 × (0.5915 – 0.5900) × 1,25,000 = US $ 750

At the same time his gain on the Spot market is

$$\$\ 5{,}00{,}000\ \frac{1}{1.6735} - \frac{1}{1.6800}$$

$$= \$\ 5{,}00{,}000\ (0.59755 - 0.59523)$$

$$= \$\ 1{,}160$$

Thus, hedging on Futures market has reduced the volatility of total payments to be made by the American importer as the loss (or gain) on Spot market is partly neutralised by the gain (or loss) on Futures market

Question 4: An American exporter has sold in January, goodsworth DM 5,00,000 to a German client. The settlement is to take place in 6-months. The following data is given:

Spot rate: $ 0.6024/DM

June Futures: $ 0.5880/DM

He wants to cover in Futures market.

Since he has a long position in Deutschmark (i.e., he is to receive DM 5,00,000 from his German client), he takes a short position on Futures market. That is, he sells DM Futures. The number of contracts sold is 4 (= 5,00,000/1,25,000).

Solution: Two possibilities may occur:

(a) The first possibility is that on 05 June, the June Future is $ 0.5840 and Spot rate is 0.5980.

As the June Future rate has passed from $ 0.5880 to $ 0.5840, the exporter makes a gain of:

4 × (0.5880 – 0.5840) × $1,25,000 = $2,000 But at the same time, on the spot market, the loss is

$ 5,00,000 (0.6024 – 0.5980) = $ 2,200

So, the loss of opportunity has been substantially covered on the Futures market. The cover is to the extent of 90.9 per cent

$$\frac{2{,}000}{2{,}000} \times 100 \text{ per cent.}$$

(b) The second possibility is that the DM undergoes an appreciation and the Spot rate on 05 June is 0.6040 while June Future is 0.5895.

Now the exporter makes a loss on the Futures market. It is equal to

4 × (0.5895 – 0.5880) × $1,25,000 = $ 750.

On the other hand, there is a gain of opportunity on the Spot market. The amount of gain is:

$ 5,00,000 × (0.6040 – 0.6024) = $ 800.

The gain covers more than the loss on Futures market.

Question 5: The following data is given:

3-month interest rate of Eurodollar: 5 per cent

3-month interest rate of Euro franc: 5.25 per cent

Spot rate: S0.1940/FFr Days before maturity: 91

What is basis and franc future price?

Solution: Basis as per the equation 6.3 is

= 0.1940 [0.05 – 0.0525] × 91/360 = –0.0001 US dollar

Hence Future price = $ 0.1940 – $ 0.0001 = $ 0.1939.

If franc future was lower than this price, an arbitrageur could sell francs spot and buy franc futures. And, if franc future was higher than this price, the arbitrageur could buy franc spot and sell franc futures to make gain.

A perfect coverage on Futures market is difficult for the following reasons. The standardisation of contracts does not permit a perfect cover of an open position. Since one can buy or sell only exact number of contracts, the exporter or importer will be compelled to either leave some amount uncovered or cover little more than his position. Besides, the number of maturities is limited to only four, i.e., March, June, September and December. Since all exposures cannot have only these dates as maturity dates, the cover obviously cannot be perfect. At least for a fraction of period, there will be open positions.

Question 6: Calculate the theoretical value of a Pound Futures contract maturing in 45 days with the following data:

Spot rate (US $/£): 1.690

45-day interest rates: US $: $\frac{513}{16}$ per cent p.a.

£: $7\frac{3}{8}$ per cent p.a.

Solution: Applying the Interest Rate Parity equation,

$$\text{Future rate} = \text{Spot rate} \times 1 + \frac{93}{16} \text{ per cent} \times \frac{45}{360}$$

$$1 + \frac{59}{8} \text{ per cent} \times \frac{45}{360}$$

$$= 1.690 \times 1 + \frac{93}{16} - \frac{59}{8} \text{ per cent} - \frac{45}{360}$$

$$= 1.686699$$

Question 7: Forward rate for the maturity of 20 December is US $ 0.5750/DM while December Future contract is quoting at US $ 0.5800/DM. What can an arbitrageur do with his DM 1 million?

Solution: As the price of the Future contract is higher than the price of Forward, the arbitrageur can make use of the difference to make a gain.

He will sell 8 DM Futures contracts and buy DM Forward and make a gain of

$ 1,25,000 × 8 × (0.5800 – 0.5750)

or

$ 5,000.

In practice, this gain will be a little different because of the maturity mismatch, as the date of the maturity of Forward contract is not the same as that of December Future.

Practical Questions and Answers on Options, Financial Derivatives, Futures and Swaps

INTRODUCTION

Q.1: An investor has purchased a 4-month call options on the equity shares of Birla Company for ₹ 5, it has a present market price per share of ₹ 112, exercise price of ₹ 120. At the end of 4-months, the investor expects the price of share to be in the following range of ₹ 90 to 170 with varying probabilities.

Expected price	₹ 100	₹ 110	₹ 125	₹ 150	₹ 170
Probability	0.10	0.25	0.30	0.25	0.10

From the above, you are required to answer the following:

1. What is expected value of share price 4-month hence ₹ What is the value of call option at its expiration (C_1) if the expected value of shares price prevails at the end of 4-months?
2. Determine the expected value of option price at maturity, assuming that the call option is held to this time. Why does it differ from the option value determined in part (i)?
3. What is the theoretical value of the option, at the beginning of 4-month period? Give comments on the market value of the call option in relation to its theoretical value.

Solution:

(i) Expected value of share at the end 4-months

Expected price (₹)	Probability	Expected value of share price (₹)
100	0.10	10.00
110	0.25	27.50
125	0.30	37.50

150	0.25	37.50
170	0.10	17.00
Expected value of share price		129.50

$C_1 = S_1 - E$

₹ 129.50 – ₹ 120 = ₹ 9.5

(ii) Expected value of call option

Expected price (₹)	Exercise price (₹)	Call value	Probability	Expected call value
100	100	0	0.10	0
110	120	0	0.25	0
125	120	5	0.30	1.50
150	120	30	0.25	7.50
170	120	50	0.10	5.00
				14.00

Expected call option value

Reason for difference: At share prices of less than ₹ 120, the call option has Zero value (as the call option cannot have negative value). This has enhanced the expected call option value (i.e., ₹ 14.00) *vis-à-vis* ₹ 9.5 in part (i), In part (i), calculation is based on negative call option values also as all the share prices have considered (from ₹ 100 to 170).

(iii) Theoretical value of call option = Max, (S0 – E, 0) = (₹ 112 – ₹ 120, 0) = 0. However, the call option has a positive value of ₹ 5. The reason is probability distribution of possible share prices (higher than exercise price) is relatively wide. This optimism of the market price of the share explains the positive call option price.

Q. 2: For facts given in Q. 1 answer the following:

(i) Determine the gain (loss) to the call option holder if the price of the share at the end of 4-month period ends up at ₹ 129.50.

(ii) Determine the price of share (on the expiry date of the call option contract) at which the call owner will be at the break-even.

(iii) Determine the maximum loss to the call owner.

(iv) Determine the maximum gain to the option holder and what is the probability?

(v) What is the maximum gain to the call writer and when will it be possible?

(vi) Determine the price of share (at the end of 4-months) at which the call writer will be at break-even.

(vii) State the major assumption in computing values from (i) to (vi).

Solution:

(i) Gain to the call-holder = S1 – (E + P) where, P = Call option premium

= ₹ 129.50 – (₹ 120 + ₹ 5) = ₹ 4.50

Alternatively, Gain = Value of call option, ₹ 9.50 – Option premium ₹ 5 = ₹ 4.50.

(ii) BEP = (Exercise price on maturity date of call option contract + Option premium paid) = ₹ 120 + ₹ 5 = ₹ 125.

(iii) Maximum loss to the call owner is limited to the call option premium of ₹ 5 per share.

(iv) The maximum gain to the call option holder = The maximum price of S1 on the date of maturity, ₹ 170 – (Exercise price ₹ 120 + Premium paid, ₹ 5) = ₹ 45. Its probability is 0.10.

(v) The maximum gain to the call writer is ₹ 5 (i.e., the call option premium received). It will be possible when the price of the share at the expiry date is equal to the exercise price of ₹ 1,210 or less.

(vi) BEP = Exercise price + Cell option premium received = ₹ 120 + ₹ 5 = ₹ 125.

(vii) There are no transaction costs of both call option buyer and call option writer.

Q.3: A call option at a strike price of ₹ 170 is selling at a premium of ₹ 15. At what share price on maturity will it break-even for the buyer of the option ₹ Will the writer of the option also break-even at the same price?

Solution:

(i) To recover the call option premium of ₹ 15, the share price on the date of expiration should rise to (₹ 15 + ₹ 170) = ₹ 185. The buyer of the call option would be at break-even if the share price (S1) ends-up at ₹ 185.

(ii) The option writer will also break-even at ₹ 185. This price is equal to ₹ 170 exercise price received from the buyer plus ₹ 15 option premium already received up-front.

Q.4: An investor is bullish about Cipla which trades in the spot market at ₹ 1,025.

He buys two-one month call option contracts (having a market lot of 100) on Cipla with strike price of ₹ 1,050 at a premium of ₹ 10 per call. Three-months later Cipla is selling at ₹ 1,080. Compute his profit on the position.

Solution:

Investor's profits = (₹ 1,080, S1 – ₹ 1,050, E – ₹ 10, P) × 2 × 100 = ₹ 4,000

Q.5: Prashant is Bullish about the index. Spot Nifty stands at ₹ 1,100. He decides to buy one-three month Nifty call option contract (having a market lot of 200) with a strike price of ₹ 1,160 at a premium of ₹ 15 per call. Three-months later, the index closes at ₹ 1,195. Determine the amount of profit (or loss) to Prashant.

Solution:

Prashant gains as on the date of maturity the Nifty Index is higher than the exercise price. His gain get reduced by the option premium paid. Accordingly, his gain is (₹ 1,195 – ₹ 1,160 – ₹ 15) × 200 lot size = ₹ 20 × 200 = ₹ 4,000.

Q.6: Vijay is Bullish about the index. Spot Nifty stands at ₹ 1,300. He decides to buy one-three month Nifty call option contract with a strike price of ₹ 1,350 at ₹ 50 a call. Three-months later, the index closes at ₹ 1,340. Determine the amount of profit (or loss) to Vijay. Assume the market lot is of 200.

Solution:

Vijay loses as the Nifty index on the day of maturity is lower (at ₹ 1,340) than the exercise price (₹ 1,350). He loses the entire sum of call premium (₹ 50 × 200 units) = ₹ 10,000.

Q.7: Akbar is Bearish about the index. Nifty stands at ₹ 1,250. He decides to buy a two-three month Nifty put option contract (having a market lot of 200) with a strike price of ₹ 1,275 at a premium of ₹ 40. Three-months later, the index closes at ₹ 1,225. Compute his pay-off on the position.

Solution:

Akram earns on the put option contract as the closing index is lower than the strike. His gain is (₹ 1,275, E – ₹ 1,225, S1 – ₹ 40, P) × 400 = ₹ 4,000.

Q.8: Maruti's share price is at present ₹ 120. After 6-months, its price will be either ₹ 150 with probability of 0.8 or ₹ 110 with probability of 0.20. An European call option exists with an exercise price of ₹ 130. Based on these facts, answer the following:

(i) As a call option writer, if you intend to create a perfectly hedged position, what will you do?

(ii) What will be the value of your hedged position in each of these two possibilities?

(iii) What is the expected value of call option price at the maturity date?

Solution:

(i) Hedge ratio = (Spread of possible call option prices, ΔAC/Spread of possible share prices, ΔS)

ΔC = (₹ 20 – 0); Δ5 = (₹ 150 – ₹ 110)

C1 = Max (S1 – E, 0) = ₹ 150 = ₹ 130 = ₹ 20 when share price is ₹ 150 and it is zero when share price is ₹ 110.

Hedge ratio = ₹ 20/₹ 40 = 0.5

The hedge ratio of 0.5 implies that the call option writer is to purchase one share of Maruti in a long position for every 2 call options sold (short position).

(ii) Value of hedged position at two share prices

	Particulars	**Amount**
(a)	When the share price is ₹ 150/Call option value is ₹ 20	
	Value of long position in shares (1 × ₹ 150)	₹ 150
	Less: Loss on exercising call option right on 2 calls by call option buyer (2 × ₹ 20)	40
	Value of hedged position	110
(b)	When share price is ₹ 10/Call option value is zero	
	Value of long position in share (1 × ₹ 110)	110
	Less: Value of call option	0
	Value of hedged Position	110

Thus, the value of the hedged position to the call option writer is the same respective of the share price of Maruti six-months hence.

(iii) Expected value of call option

Expected share price	Exercise price	Call value	Probability	Expected call option value
₹ 110	₹ 130	0	0.2	0
150	130	20	0.8	16

Q.9: An investor buys a put option at strike price of ₹ 30 for a premium at ₹ 6. The current market price of the share is ₹ 28. Find out the profits/loss profile of the investor if the market price of the share is ₹ 18, ₹ 26, ₹ 28, ₹ 31 or ₹ 39, on the/ expiration date. What will be his position if he buys the call option?

Solution:

The Profit/loss profile of the investor is as follows:

Case of Put option

Share Price	**₹ 18**	**₹ 26**	**₹ 28**	**₹ 31**	**₹ 39**
Premium Paid	–6	–6	–6	–6	–6
Sale of Share (Put)	+30	+30	+30	–	–
Cost of Share	–18	–26	–28	–	–
Net Pay-off	+6	–2	–4	–6	–6

Case of Call option

Share Price	**₹ 18**	**₹ 26**	**₹ 28**	**₹ 31**	**₹ 39**
Premium Paid	–6	–6	–6	–6	–6
Cost of Share (Call)	–	–	–	–30	–30
Sale of Share	–	–	–	+31	+39
Net Pay-off	–6	–6	–6	–5	+3

Q.10: The equity share of Ramacast Ltd. are being sold at ₹ 210. A 3-month call option is available for a premium of ₹ 6 per share and a 3-month put option is available for a premium of ₹ 5 per share. Find out the net pay-off of the option holder of the call option and put option given that — (i) the strike price in both cases is ₹ 220, and (ii) the share price on the exercise day is ₹ 200 or ₹ 210 or ₹ 220 or ₹ 230 or ₹ 240.

Solution:

The net pay-off for the call option holder may be shown as below:

Share Price on Exercise Day	**₹ 200**	**₹ 201**	**₹ 220**	**₹ 230**	**₹ 240**
Option Exercise	No	No	No	Yes	Yes
Outflow (Strike Price)	Nil	Nil	Nil	₹ 220	₹ 220
Outflow (Premium paid)	₹ 6	₹ 6	₹ 6	₹ 6	₹ 6
Total Outflow	₹ 6	₹ 6	₹ 6	₹ 226	₹ 226
Less: Inflow (Sale Proceed)	–	–	–	₹ 230	₹ 240
Net Pay-off	–₹ 6	–₹ 6	–₹ 6	₹ 4	₹ 14

The net pay-off for the put option holder may be shown as below:

Share Price on Exercise Day	₹ 200	₹ 201	₹ 220	₹ 230	₹ 240
Option Exercise	Yes	Yes	No	No	No
Inflow (Strike Price)	₹ 220	₹ 220	Nil	Nil	Nil
Less: Outflow (Premium Price)	₹ 200	₹ 201	–	–	–
Less: Outflow (Premium Paid)	₹ 5	₹ 5	₹ 5	₹ 5	₹ 5
Net Pay-off	₹ 15	₹ 5	₹ – 5	₹ – 5	₹ – 5

It may be observed that, in both the cases, the loss of the option holder is restricted to the amount of premium paid. But the profit (positive pay-off) depends upon the difference between the strike and the share price on the exercise day.

Q.11: Equity Shares of Casio Ltd. are being currently sold for ₹ 90 per share. Both the call option and the Put-option for a 3-month period are available for a strike price of ₹ 97 at a premium of ₹ 3 per share and ₹ 2 per share respectively. An investor wants to create a straddle position in this share. Find out his net pay-off at the expiration of the option period, if the share price on that day happens to be ₹ 90 or ₹ 105.

Solution:

A straddle position means that the investor will buy both the call option as well as the put option, and pay the premium of both. The net pay of position may be found as follows:

Total Premium paid = ₹ 3 + ₹ 2 = ₹ 5

If share price happens to be ₹ 90: (Call option will not exercised)

Net Pay of = Pay-off on Put – Premium paid

= (₹ 97 – ₹ 90) – ₹ 5

= ₹ 2

If share price happens to be ₹ 105: (Put option will not be exercised)

Net Pay of = Pay-off on Put – Premium paid

= (₹ 105 – ₹ 97) – ₹ 5

= ₹ 23

So, the investor will be benefited whether price is less than or more than the strike price on the expiry day.

Q.12: You are given three call options on a stock at exercise price (K) of ₹ 40, ₹ 45 and ₹ 50 with expiration date in 3-month and the premium of ₹ 4, ₹ 2 and ₹ 1 respectively. Show how the options can be used to create a butterfly spread. Construct a table with different market prices and show how profit changes with stock prices ranging from ₹ 30 to ₹ 60 for the butterfly spread.

Solution:

A butterfly spread can be constructed by buying a call option with a relatively low exercise price (₹ 40) and buying a call with a relatively high strike price (₹ 50) and also selling two call options with a strike price (₹ 45) in between the high (₹ 40) and low (₹ 50). The pattern of pay-off can be shown in tabular form as under:

Market Price	Pay-off (₹)			Net Premium - 4 + (2 × 2) -1	Total Pay-off
	K = ₹ 40, One option purchased	K = ₹ 45, Two option sold	K = ₹ 50, One option purchased		
₹ 30	0	0	0	−1	−1
32	0	0	0	−1	−1
34	0	0	0	−1	−1
36	0	0	0	−1	−1
38	0	0	0	−1	−1
40	0	0	0	−1	−1
42	+2	0	0	−1	+1
44	+4	0	0	−1	+3
45	+5	0	0	−1	+1
46	+6	−2	0	−1	−1
48	+8	−6	0	−1	−1
50	+10	−10	0	−1	−1
52	+12	−14	+2	−1	−1
54	+14	−18	+4	−1	−1
56	+16	−22	+6	−1	−1
58	+18	−26	+ 8	−1	−1
60	+20	−30	+10	−1	−1

The net pay of position of the investor, at different market prices on the due date, can also be shown diagrammatically as follows:

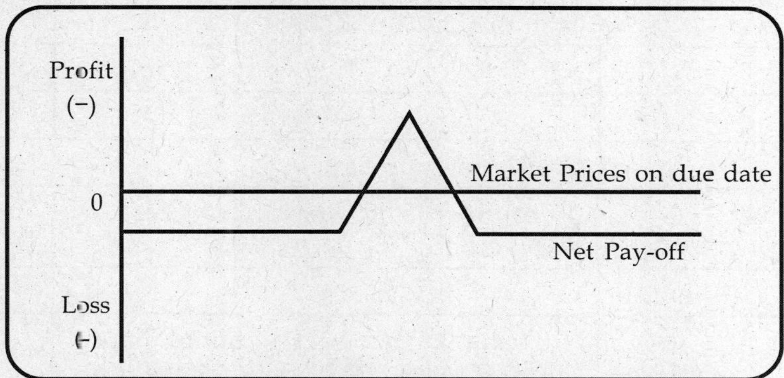

Q.13: On Nov. 15, when the spot price of Telco is ₹ 473 per share, Mr. X buys 15/ contracts of July Telco futures at 491. Assume that the initial margin for Telco futures is ₹ 800 per contract, and the maintenance margin is ₹ 600 per contract. Given that each contract is 50 shares. Daily settlement prices for the next few davs are as follows:

November 15	496
November 16	503
November 17	488
November 18	485
November 19	491

Assume that Mr. X withdraws profits from his margin account once, on November 16th, when he withdraws half the maximum amount allowed. Compute the Balance in the account at the end of each of these 5 days.

Solution:

15 – Nov.	Details	Amount
Opening Balance		
+ Initial Margin Paid	800/contract * 15 contracts	₹ 12,00.00
+ Profit/Loss Today	15 contracts * 50 shares/contract *5/ share	₹ 3,750.00
= Closing Balance		₹ 15,750.00
16 – Nov.		
Opening Balance	From previous day	₹ 15,750.00
+ Profit/Loss Today	15 contracts *5,000 shares/contract *7 share	₹ 5,250.00
= Balance before withdrawals		₹ 21,000.00

– Profit Withdrawn	Half of (21,000 – 12,000)	₹ 4,500.00
= Closing Balance		₹ 16,500.00
17 – Nov.		
Opening Balance	From previous day	₹ 16,500.00
+ Profit/Loss Today	15 contract *5,000 shares/contract *(-15)/share	₹ (11,250.00)
= Balance before Margin Call		₹ 5,250.00
+ Margin Call Paid	To bring Balance back to initial margin (since Balance fell below maintenance margin to 15*600 = 9,000)	₹ 6,750.00
= Closing Balance		₹ 12,000.00
18 – Nov.		
Opening Balance	From previous day	₹ 12,000.00
+ Profit/Loss Today	15 contracts *5,000 shares/contract *(-3)/share	₹ (2,250.00)
= Balance before Margin Call		₹ 9,750.00
+ Margin Call Paid	Non (since Balance in above maintenance margin of 12,000)	–
= Closing Balance		₹ 9,750.00
19 – Nov.		
Opening Balance	From previous day	₹ 9,750.00
+ Profit/Loss Today		₹ 14,250.00
= Closing Balance		₹ 14,250.00

Q.14: The current market price of an asset is ₹ 80(S). In One year's time from now, the price may be ₹ 100 (S_1) or ₹ 70 (S_2). A call option at the strike price of ₹ 80 is available for ₹ 20. However, call option price would be zero if the market price turns out to be ₹ 70. The risk-free rate of interest for the one period till expiration of call option is 10 per cent. Find out the fair value of the call option as per BM.

Solution:

In the given case, values of variables required for BM are:

Now, C_1 = ₹ 20

C_2 = 0

S = ₹ 80

S_1 = ₹ 100

S_2 = ₹ 70

r = .10

Now, u = $S_1 + S$ = 100/80 = 1.25

d = $S_2 + S$ = 70/80 = .875

Fair value of call option as per BM, using Equation 12.1 is:

$$C = \left[\frac{1+r-d}{u-d}\right]\left[\frac{C_1}{1+r}\right] + \left[\frac{u-1-r}{u-d}\right]\left[\frac{C_2}{1+r}\right]$$

$$= \left[\frac{1+.10-.875}{1.25-.875}\right]\left[\frac{20}{1+.10}\right] + \left[\frac{1.25-1-.10}{1.25-.875}\right]\left[\frac{0}{1+.10}\right]$$

= ₹ 10.90

It may be noted that in case of call option, C_2 is zero and in case of put option Cj is zero. There are two components in valuation of option. In the valuation of call option, the second component becomes zero while for put option valuation, the first component becomes zero. Further, in the formula for value of option, the V is not the annual rate of interest. Rather, it is the rate of interest for 1 period of option. For example, rate of interest is 10 per cent and period of option is 3-months, then interest for one period of option is 2.50 per cent and the value of r for the above equation is only .025.

The BM as discussed above is simple in its approach. But the basic assumption that there are only two possibilities for share price over next one period is impractical and hypothetical. Such a strategy may not work because there are more and more possibilities of share price. However, the number of possibilities is reduced as the time period is shortened. The Black & Scholes Model attempts to shorten the time period as well as the movement in share prices.

Q.15: The share of FM Ltd. is currently sold for ₹ 60. There is a call option available at strike price ₹ 56 for a period of 6-months. Finds out the value of the call option given that the rate of interest of the investor is 14 per cent and the standard deviation of the return of the share is 30 per cent. Use Black and Scholes Model.

Solution:

In order to apply the BSM, the values of d_1 and d_2 are to be calculated first, as follows:

$$d_1 = \frac{\text{In } (S/K) + (r + .5\sigma^2)t}{\sigma\sqrt{t}}$$

$$= \frac{\text{In } (60/56) + [.14 + .5\ (.09).5}{.3\sqrt{.5}}$$

$$= \frac{\text{In}(1.0714)+(.925)}{.2121}$$

$$= \frac{.0686 + .0925}{.2121}$$

$= .760$

$d_2 = d_1 - \sigma\sqrt{t}$

$= .760$

$= .548$

Now, $N(d_1)$ and $N(d_2)$ may be calculated. The values $N(d_1)$ and $N(d_2)$ represent the cumulative probabilities that the standard normal variable will assume for values less than d_1 and d_2 respectively. Using statistical terminology, the cumulative probability of 0 is 50 per cent or N(o) = .50. The cumulative probabilities for different values of d_1 and d_2 can be found with the help of Area Under Normal Curve Table. (Given as A – 5 in the Appendix III.)

Now $N(d_1)$ = N(.760) = .500 + .2764

= .7764

$N(d_2)$ = N (.548) = .500 + .2070

= .7070

The value of the call option can be calculated with the help of Equation 12.2 as follows:

Value = $SN(d_1)$ – Ke-rt $N(d_2)$

= 60 (.7764) – 56 × e-0.7 × .7070

= 60 (.7764) – 56 × .9324 × .7070

= 46.58 – 36.92 = ₹ 9.66

In the above-cited filedexample, the value oft has been taken as six-months or .5; the value of r is given as .14, so 'rt' is .5 × .14 = .07. Now, for the value of e-~-07, the Poisson distribution table may be referred to. The value of e-0.7 in this table is .9324. This value can also be calculated with the help of a scientific calculator.

Steps in BSM. Though the application of BSM requires a lot of calculations and reference to the statistical theory, the calculations may be taken as follows:

1. Find out the value of in terms of years. For example, for a call option of 6-months,

   t = .5; for a call option of 73 days, t – 73 365 = .2, and so on.

2. Find the value of rt by multiplying the rate of interest with the t.
3. Find the values of d_1 and d_2. The procedure for these two values has been explained in Example 12.1
4. Find out values of $N(d_1)$ and $N(d_2)$ with the help of Area under Normal Curve table.
5. Find out the value of a call by using Equation 12.2.

Note: The calculation of the value of d_1 requires natural log of S!K. In case, the natural log table is not available, the normal log table (base 10) can be used as follows: Suppose, In of number 'm' is to be found. This can be written as:

$$\text{In 'm'} = \frac{\log \text{'m'}}{\log e}$$

log e = log 2.7183 = .4343

$$\text{So, In 'm'} = \frac{\log \text{'m'}}{.1343}$$

Say, the In of 2.5 is to be found. This can be written as:

$$\text{In } 2.5 = \frac{\log 2.5}{.1343}$$

$$= \frac{\log 2.5}{.1343} = .9162$$

So, the In 2.5 (Natural log of 2.5) is .9162.

The natural log values can also be found with the help of a scientific calculator.

Q.16: shares of His Majesty Ltd. are being traded at ₹ 36. An investor buys a put Option at a strike price of ₹ 40 for a period of 6-months at a premium of ₹ 2. In order to cover his risk, he buys one share today by taking a loan @ 10 per cent p.a. Analyse the profit/loss profile of the investor.

The following quotes are available for 3-months options in respect of a share crrently traded at ₹ 31.

Strike Price	₹ 30
Gall Option	₹ 3
Put Option	₹ 2

Solution:

In this case, the strategy of the investor should be to borrow ₹ 38 (₹ 36 + ₹ 2) and buys one put option and a share. After 6-months, he would be required to pay an amount of ₹ 38 + Interest @ 10 per cent p.a.

Amount payable after 6-months ($38e^{.5 \times .1}$) ₹ 39.94

On the expiration date, if the market price is below ₹ 40, the investor should exercise the option to sell the share at ₹ 40 and make a profit of ₹ 0.06 (i.e., ₹ 40 – ₹ 39.94).

However, if the market price of the share on the expiration date is more than ₹ 40, he should sell the share in the market and make a profit of (Market Price – ₹ 39.94). So, in both the cases, the investor is able to make profits.

Q.17: An investor devises a strategy of burying a call and selling the share and a put option. Draw his profit/loss profits profile given that the rate of interest is 0 per cent p.a. What would be the position If the strategy adopted in selling a call and buying the put and the share.

Solution:

Strategy I: (Buying a call and selling a put and a share)

Initial Cash Inflow ₹ 31 – ₹ 3 + ₹ 2)	₹	30
Interest Rate		10 per cent
Amounts grows hi 3-months to (30 × e.1 × .25)	₹	30.76

After 3-months:

If the share price is greater than ₹ 30, he would exercise the call option and buy one share for ₹ 30 and his net profit is ₹ 0.76 (i.e., ₹ 30.76 – 30).

However, if the share price is less than ₹ 30, the counter – party would exercise the put sip-ion and the investor would buy one share at ₹ 30. The net profit to the investor is again He. 0.76.

Strategy II: (Selling a call and buying a put and a share)

In this case, the investor has to arrange a loan @ 10 per cent of ₹ 30 (i.e., ₹ 31 + 2 – 3)

This amount would be repaid after 3-months. Amount payable is:

$30 \times e^{.1 \times .25}$ ₹ 30.76

After 3-months, if the market price is more than ₹ 30, the counter – party would exercise the call option and the investor would be required to sell the share at ₹ 30. The loss to the investor would be ₹ 0.76 (i.e., ₹ 30.76 – 30).

However, if the rate is less than ₹ 30, the investor would exercise the put option and would get ₹ 30 from the rate of share. The loss to the buyer would again be ₹ 0.76.

Q.18: Internet Services Ltd. is a listed company and the share prices have been volatile. An investor expects that the share price may fall from the present level of ₹ 1,900 and wants to make profit by a suitable option strategy. He is short of shares at a price of ₹ 1,900 and wants to protect himself against any loss. The following option rates are available:

Strike Price	Call-Option	Put-Option
₹ 1,700	₹ 325	₹ 65
₹ 1,800	₹ 200	₹ 80
₹ 1,900	₹ 85	₹ 120
₹ 2,000	₹ 70	₹ 200
₹ 2,100	₹ 65	₹ 280

The investor decides to buy a call at a strike price of ₹ 1,800 and to write a put at a strike price of ₹ 2,000. find out the Profit/Loss profile of the investor if the share price on the expiration date is ₹ 1,600, ₹ 1,700, ₹ 1,800, ₹ 1,900, ₹ 2,000 or ₹ 2,100. Also make the diagrammatic presentation.

Solution:

In the given case, the investor has purchased a call at a premium of ₹ 200 and written (sold) a put at the premium of ₹ 200. So, net outflow on account of options would be zero. The net pay-off of the investor for different levels of share price are as follows:

Share Price	Gain on Call	Loss on Put	Spot Position	Net Position
₹ 1,600	—	–₹ 400	+₹ 300	–₹ 100
1,700	—	–₹ 300	200	–₹ 100
1,800	—	–₹ 200	100	–₹ 100
1,900	₹ 100	–₹ 100	—	—
2,000	200	—	–100	₹ 100
2,100	300	—	–200	₹ 100

The pay-off position can be diagrammatically shown as follows:

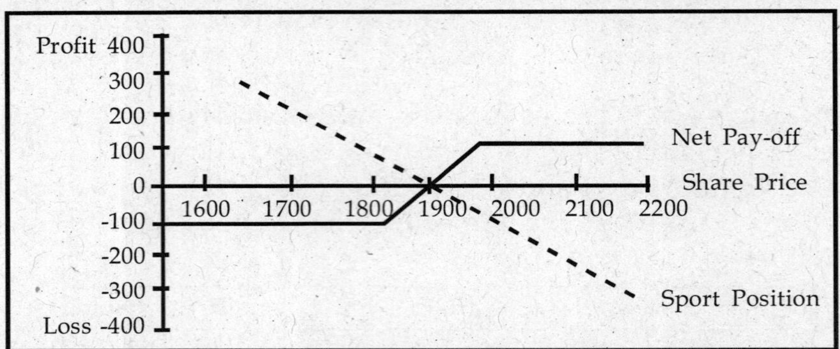

It may be noted that the strategy has also put a limit on the profit or loss position of the investor. His loss will not be more than ₹ 100 and his gain will also be restricted to ₹ 100 irrespective of movement in share prices.

Q.19: The Current market price of the equity shares of Redrey Ltd. is ₹ 70 per share. It may be either ₹ 90 or ₹ 50 after a year. A call option with a strike price of ₹ 66 (time 1 year) is available. The rate of interest applicable to the investor is 10 per cent. An investor wants to create a replicating portfolio in order to maintain his pay-off the call option for 100 shares.

Find out the hedge ratio, Amount of borrowing. Fair Value of the call and his cash-flow position after a year.

Solution:

The information given in the situation can be summarised as follows:

S = ₹ 70 $\quad$ S_1 = ₹ 90 $\quad$ S_2 = ₹ 50

K = ₹ 66

C_1 = (90 – 66) = ₹ 24 $\quad$ $C_2 = 0$

r = 10 per cent or .10

$$\Delta \text{ i.e., Hedge Ratio: } \frac{C_1 - C_2}{S_1 - S_2} = \frac{24 - 0}{90 - 50} = \frac{24}{40} = .60$$

Now, in order to create a replicating portfolio, he should buy .6 share for a call option of 1 share. So, he should buy 100 × .6 = 60 shares at the current market price of ₹ 70. His outflow would be 70 × 60 = ₹ 4,200.

Amount of Borrowing required: The amount of borrowing required for creating a replicating portfolio may be found as follows:

$$B = \frac{100}{1 + r100}(\triangle S_2 - C_2)$$

$$= \frac{100}{1+.10}(.6 \times 50 - 0)$$

$= ₹\ 2,727$

Value of the call (100 shares):

Value $= 100 \times \triangle \times S - B$

$= 100 \times\ 6 \times 70 - ₹\ 2,727$

$= ₹\ 1,473$

The value of the call may also be calculated as the difference between the purchase price of replicating shares now (₹ 4,200) minus the amount of borrowing (₹ 2,727).

Cash-flow position after a year: The cash-flow position of the investor in case the share price happens to be ₹ 90 or ₹ 50 can be summarised as follows:

Strategy	Pay-off after a year	
	If Share Price is ₹ 90	If Share Price is ₹ 50
I. Buy a call option (K = 66)	100 × (90 – 66) = ₹ 2,400	Nil
II. Buy 60 shares and borrow: Selling Price of 60 shares – Borrowing pay-off (2,727 × 1,10)	60 × 90 = ₹ 5,400 ₹ 3,000 ₹ 2,400 Nil	60 × 50 = ₹ 3,000 ₹ 3,000

So, by replicating the portfolio, the investor is able to have the same pay-off of ₹ 2,400 (if share price happens to ₹ 90) or ₹ NIL (if share price happens to be ₹ 50) in either strategy.

Q.20: On January 15, X bought a January Nifty futures contract that cost him ₹ 5,38,000. For this he had to pay an initial margin of, ₹ 43,040 to his broker. Each Nifty futures contract is for the delivery of 200-Nifties. On January 25, the index closed at 2,720. How much profit/loss did he make?

Solution:

X bought one futures contract costing him ₹ 5,38,000. At a market lot of 200, this means he paid ₹ 2,690 per Nifty future. On the futures expiration day, the futures price converges to the spot price. If the index closed at 2,720 this must be the futures close price as well. Hence, he would have made a profit of (₹ 2,720 – ₹ 2,690) × 200 = ₹ 6,000.

Q.21: X sold a January Nifty futures contract for ₹ 5,38,000. On January 15, for this he had to pay an initial margin of ₹ 43,040 to his broker. Each Nifty futures contract is for the delivery of 200 Nifties. On January 25, the index closed at 2,520. How much profit /loss did he make?

Solution:

X sold one futures contract costing in ₹ 5,38,000. At a market lot of 200, this works out to be ₹ 2,690 per Nifty future. On the futures expiration day, the futures price converges to the spot price. If the index closed at 2,520 this must be the futures close price as well. Hence, he would have made profit of (₹ 2,690 – ₹ 2,520) × 200 = ₹ 34,000.

Q.22: ABC Ltd., share price as on date is ₹ 200. It is expected that 50 per cent chances are that the share price will be ₹ 178 and 50 per cent chances are that the price will be ₹ 214 per share after 6-months. A call option of the share can be exercised at the end of the period at exercise price of ₹ 205 per share. The risk-free interest rate is 10 per cent p.a. (i.e., 5 per cent for 6-months). Find out the perfectly hedged situation through shares and the cell option. Compute value of holding in terms of hedged position as above. Estimate the option premium (option price) at the beginning based on given rate of interest assuming that share market is perfectly related to the rate of interest.

Solution:

(a) Perfectly hedged situation can be achieved by purchasing shares along with writing of call option. The hedge ratio, is:

$$\text{Hedge Ratio} = \frac{9-0}{214-178} = 0.25$$

One should purchase 0.25 share for every option of one share written.

(b) If the share price is ₹ 214 then value of purchased share will be:

Sales Proceeds of Investment (0.25 shares × ₹ 214)	53.50
Loss on account of short position (₹ 214 – 205)	–9.00
Net value of holding	44.50

If share price turns out to ₹ 178 then value of holding will be:

₹. 178 × 0.25 share = ₹ 44.50

Hence, it is same for the two alternatives.

(c) (Investment – Option premium) 1 + r = Final value of investment

(50 – V0) 1.05 = 44.50

V0 = 7.619, say ₹ 7.62

The same can also be calculated as under:

An investment of ₹ 53.50 will reduce to ₹ 44.50, and loss is ₹ 5.50

Total Loss = 5.50 + Interest cost (Interest on ₹ 50 @ 10 per cent for 6-months)

= 5.50 + 2.50 = ₹ 8

Present value of loss = $\frac{8}{1.05}$ = 7.62

Q.23: A share has a current market price of ₹ 40. One-month call is available at a strike price of ₹ 39. It is known that after 1-month the share price may be ₹ 42 or ₹ 38. Find out the value of the call as per BM if the risk-free rate is 8 per cent.

Solution:

In the given case, the binomial model is to be applied for finding out the value of the call. The rate of interest is 8 per cent p.a. and for one-month the interest is .0067. Various values for applying the BM are:

C_1 = After one-month, the price may be ₹ 42 against the current price of ₹ 40. The strike price for one-month call is ₹ 39. So C_1 = ₹ 42 – 39 = ₹ 3.

C_2 = If the market after two-month is ₹ 38, the value of the call would be zero.

The information can be presented as follows:

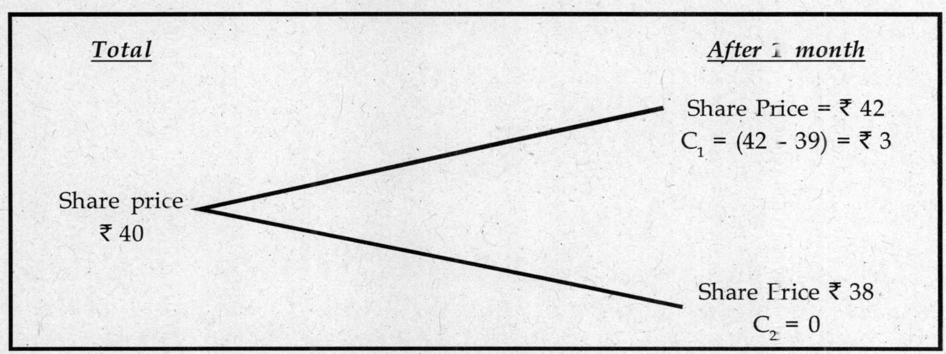

U = 42/40 = 1.05

d = 38/40 = 0.95

$$\text{The value of call} = \left[\frac{1+r-d}{u-d}\right]\left[\frac{C_1}{1+r}\right]$$

$$= \left[\frac{1+.0067-.95}{1.05-.95}\right]\left[\frac{3}{1+.0067}\right]$$

$$= \frac{.567}{.10} \times \frac{3}{1+.0067}$$

$$= \frac{.1701}{.10067} = 1.69$$

So, the value of the call should be ₹. 1.69

Q.24: Following information is available for a share:

S = ₹ 50	K = ₹ 50
S_1 = ₹ 55	r = 10 per cent p.a
S_2 = ₹ 45	T = 6-months

Find out the value of put as per BM

Solution:

r for 6-months = .05   u = 55/50 = 1.10

$C_1 = 0$ d = 45/50 = 0.90

C_2 = ₹ 50 – 45 = 5

$$\text{Value of Put} = \left[\frac{u - d - r}{u - d}\right]\left[\frac{C_2}{1 + r}\right]$$

$$= \left[\frac{1.1 - 1 - .05}{1.1 - .9}\right]\left[\frac{5}{1 + .05}\right]$$

$$= .25 \times 4.76$$

$$= 1.19$$

Q.25: ABC Ltd. is raising a loan at a floating rate of LIBOR + 20 basic points. It anticipates a rise in interest rates, and is considering to hedge against the interest rate risk. The loan is to be raised on 1-1-01 and the expected LIBOR for next two years with break of 6-months are:

1-1-2001	5.5 per cent
1-7-2001	7.0 per cent
1-1-2002	5.5 per cent
1-7-2002	3.5 per cent

Following Hedging strategies have been suggested:

(i) A two-year 5.5 per cent cap against LIBOR at a premium of 0.5 per cent

(ii) A two-year zero cost collar against LIBOR with a cap of 6.5 per cent and a floor of 4.5 per cent.

Find out the overall cost to the company for each six-month period for the years 2001 and 2002 under the situations:

(a) If No Hedge is taken up.

(b) Cap is purchased, and

(c) If collar is created.

Solution:

In the given situations, the total cost can be determined as follows:

No hedge: If the company does not take any hedge, then it would be required to pay the interest at LIBOR + .2 per cent.

Cap taken at 5.5 per cent: If the company has taken a cap, then it would be required to pay a premium of 0.5 per cent and the interest of 5.5 per cent or LIBOR + .2 per cent whichever is lower.

Collar at 4.5 per cent/6.5 per cent: In this case, the company has zero cost of creating a collar (given in the problem) and would be required to pay minimum interest of 4.5 per cent, the upper limit being lower of the LIBOR or 6.5 per cent.

Different strategies and the interest cost for different periods are:

	No Hedge	Cap	Collars
1.1.Y1	5.5 + .2 = 5.7 per cent	5.5 + .2 + .5 = 6.2 per cent	5.5 + .2 = 5.7 per cent
1.7.Y1	7.0 + .2 = 7.2 per cent	5.5 + .2 + .5 = 6.2 per cent	6.5 + .2 = 6.7 per cent
1.1.Y2	5.5 + .2 = 5.7 per cent	5.5 + .2 + .5 = 6.2 per cent	5.5 + .2 = 5.7 per cent
1.7.Y2	3.5 + .2 = 3.7 per cent	3.5 + .2 + .5 = 4.2 per cent	4.5 + .2 = 4.7 per cent
Average	5.575 per cent	5.7 per cent	5.7 per cent

Among the three situations, the first one, i.e., no hedge, is the best because average cost for two-years period is 5.575 per cent against 5.7 per cent of other two options.

Q.26: A call option is available at ₹ 6 per share of a period of 6-months at a strike Drice of ₹ 45 per share. The current market price of the share is ₹ 40 and the rate of interest is 10 per cent. The standard deviations for the share is 0.45. find out whether the call is rightly priced or not. Apply Black and Scholes Model.

Solution:

The value of the call option is given at ₹ 6. Whether it is fair value or not can be found with the help of Black and Scholes Model as follows:

$$d_1 = \frac{\text{In}\,(S/K) + (r + .5\sigma^2)t}{\sigma\sqrt{t}}$$

$$= \frac{\text{In } (40/45) + \left[.10 + .5(.45)^2\right].5}{.45\sqrt{.5}}$$

$$= \frac{-.1178 + .1006}{.3182} = -.054$$

$$d_2 = d_1 - \sigma\sqrt{t}$$

$$= -.054 - .45\sqrt{.5}$$

$$= -.372$$

Now, $N(d_1)$ = .4801

$N(d_2)$ = .3557

Value of call = $S \times N(d_1) - Ke\text{-}rt \times N(d_2)$

= 40 × .4801 – 45 × .9512 × .3557

= 19.20 – 15.23

= ₹ 3.97

The fair value of the call option is ₹ 3.97 whereas the current value of the option is ₹ 6. So, it is overprice.

Q.27: The flowing information about XYZ Company's shares and call options is available:

Current Share Price, S	₹ 165
Option exercise price, K	₹ 150
Risk-free interest rate	6 per cent
Time to option expiry	2 years
Totatility of share price (Standard deviation)	15 per cent

Calculate value of the option as per the BS Model.

Solution:

The value of the option, as per BS Model may be found by, first, calculating the values of d_1 and d_2 as follows:

$$d_1 = \frac{\text{In } 165/150 + \left[.06 + .5(.15)^2\right] 2}{.15\sqrt{2}}$$

$$= \frac{.095310 + .1425}{.212132} = 1.12104$$

$$d_2 = -d_1 - \sigma\sqrt{t}$$

$$= 1.12104 - .15\sqrt{2}$$

$$= .9089$$

$$N(d_1) = N(1.12104) = .8688$$

$$N(d_2) = N(.9089) = .8182$$

$$\text{Now Value of Option} = SN(d_1) - \frac{K}{e^{rt}}N(d_2)$$

$$= 165 \times (.8688) - \frac{150}{e^{(.06)(2)}}(.8182)$$

$$= 143.352 - \frac{150}{1.127497}(.8182)$$

$$= 143.352 - 108.8517$$

$$= ₹\ 34.50$$

Q.28: The equity share of ABC Ltd. is presently selling at ₹ 250. A call option with a period of 4-months and a strike price of ₹ 45 is available for ₹ 6 per share. Is the option correctly priced if (i) a dividend of ₹ 2 is expected in 2-months time, (ii) the variance of share price is 0.06, and (iii) the risk-free rate of interest is 3 per cent.

Solution:

In this case, the value of the call option may be found by applying the Black and Scholes model (adjusted for dividend) as follows:

Adjusted Share Price, Sa = Share Price – PV of Dividends

$$= ₹\ 50 - \frac{₹\ 2}{(1+.03)^{2/12}}$$

$$= ₹\ 50\ \frac{₹\ 2}{(1+.005)^{1}}$$

$$= ₹\ 48.01$$

Value of d_1 and d_2 may be found as follows:

$$d_1 = \frac{\text{In}(S_a IK) + (r + .5\sigma^2)t}{\sigma\sqrt{t}}$$

$$= \frac{\text{In}(48.01/45) + (.03 + .5 \times .06)4/12}{\sqrt{.06 \times 4/12}}$$

$$= \frac{.647 + .02}{.1414}$$

$$= .60$$

$$d_2 = .60 - .1414$$

$$= .4586$$

$$\text{Now, } N(d_1) = N(.6) = .7257$$

$$N(d_2) = N(.4586) = .6760$$

$$\text{Value of Call} = Sa \times N(d_1) - Ke^{-rt} \times N(d_2)$$

$$= ₹\ 48.01 \times .7257 - 45 \times .99 \times .6760$$

$$= 34.48 - 30.12$$

$$= ₹\ 4.72$$

Q.29: (I) The Shares of TIC Ltd. are currently priced at ₹ 415 and call option exercisable In three-months time has an exercise rate of ₹ 400. Risk-free interest rate is 5 per cent p.a. and standard deviation (Volatility) of share price is 22 per cent. Based on the assumption that TIC Ltd. is not going to declare any dividend over the next three-months, is the option worth buying for ₹ 25.

(II) Calculate value of aforesaid call option based on Block Scholes valuation model if the current price is considered as ₹ 380.

(III) What would be the worth of put option if current price is considered ₹ 380.

(IV) If TIC Ltd. share price at present is taken as ₹ 408 and a dividend of ₹ 10 is expected to be paid in the two-months time, then, calculate value of v., the call option.

Solution:

(i) Given: TIC Ltd. Current Price = ₹ 415

Exercise rate = 400

Risk-free interest rate is = 5 per cent p.a.

SD (Volatility) = 22 per cent

Based on the above bit is calculated value of an option based on Block Scholes Model

$$d_1 = \frac{I_n\left(\frac{415}{400}\right) + \left[.05 + \frac{1}{2}(.022)^2\right].25}{.22\sqrt{.25}}$$

$$= \frac{0.05129 + .01855}{.11}$$

$$= .5032727$$

$$d_2 = \frac{I_n\left(\frac{415}{400}\right) + \left[.05 + \frac{1}{2}(.022)^2\right].25}{.22\sqrt{.25}}$$

$$= \frac{.03681 + .00645}{.11}$$

$$= .3932727$$

$$N(d_1) = N\ (.50327) = 1\text{-}.3072 = .6928$$

$$N(d_2) = N\ (.39327) = 1\text{-}.3471 = .6529$$

$$\text{Value of Option} = 415\ (.6928) - \frac{400}{e^{(.05)\ (.25)}}(.6529)$$

$$= 287.512 - \frac{400}{1.012578}(.6529)$$

$$= 287.512 - 259.916$$

$$= ₹\ 27.60$$

NB N(.039327) can also be found as under:

Step 1: From table of area under normal curve find the area of variable 0.39, i.e., 0.6517

Step 2: From table of area under normal curve find the area of variable 0.40

Step 3: Find out the difference between above two variables and areas under normal curve

Step 4: Using interpolation method find out the value of 0.00327, which is as follows:

$$\frac{0.0037}{0.01} \times 0.00327 = 0.0012$$

Step 5: Add this value, computed above to the N(0.39). Thus N(0.39327) = 0.6517 + 0.0012 = 0.6529

Since market price of ₹ 25 is less than ₹ 27.60 (Blocks Scholes Valuation Model) indicate that option is underpricid, hence worth buying.

(ii) If the current price is taken as ₹ 380 the computations are as follows:

$$d_1 = \frac{\text{In}\left(\frac{380}{400}\right) + \left[,0.5 + \frac{1}{2}(.22)^2\right].25}{.22\sqrt{.25}}$$

$$= \frac{0.05129 + .01855}{.11}$$

$$= 0.297636$$

$$d_2 = \frac{\text{In}\left(\frac{380}{400}\right) + \left[,0.5 + \frac{1}{2}(.22)^2\right].25}{.22\sqrt{.25}}$$

$$= \frac{0.05129 + .00645}{.11}$$

$$= .0.407666$$

$$V_0 = V_s\, N(d_1) - \frac{E}{e^{rt}} N(d_2)$$

$N(d_1)$ = N(-0.297636) =.3830

$N(d_2)$ = N(-0.407666) =.3418

$$380\ (.3830) - \frac{400}{e^{(.05)\,(.25)}}(.3418)$$

$$145.54 - \frac{400}{1.012578}(.3418)$$

= 145.54 – 138.4397

= ₹ 7.10

(iii) Value of call option = ₹ 7.10

Current Market Value = ₹ 415

Present Value of Exercise Price = $\frac{400}{1.0125} = 395.06$

Vp = $V_s + V_s$ + PV (E)

Vp = 380 + 7.10 + 395.06

= 22.16

= ₹ 22.16 Ans,

(iv) Since dividend is expected to be paid in two-months we have to adjust the share price and the use Block & Scholes model to value the option:

Present Value of Dividend (using continuous discounting) = Dividend x e-rt

= ₹ 10 × $e^{-.05 \times .1666}$

= ₹ 10 × $e^{-.008333}$

= ₹ 9.917 (Please refer Exponential Table)

Adjusted price of shares is ₹ l 408 – 9.917 = ₹ .398.083

This can be used in Blocks & Scholes model.

$$d_1 = \frac{In\left(\frac{398.083}{400}\right) + \left[.05 + \frac{1}{2}(.22)^2\right].25}{.22\sqrt{.25}}$$

$$= \frac{-.00480 + 01855}{.11}$$

$$= .125$$

$$d_2 = \frac{In\left(\frac{398.083}{400}\right) + \left[.05 + \frac{1}{2}(.22)^2\right].25}{.22\sqrt{.25}}$$

$$= \frac{-.00480 + .00645}{.11}$$

$$= .015$$

$$N(d_1) = N(.125) = .5498$$

$$N(d_2) = N(.015) = .5060$$

$$\text{Value of Option} = 398.083\ (.5498) - \frac{400}{e^{(.0.5 \times .25)}}(.5060)$$

$$218.866 - \frac{400}{e^{.0125}}(.5060)$$

$$218.866 - \frac{400}{1.012578}(.5060)$$

$$= 218.866 - 199.8858$$

$$= ₹\ 18.98$$

Q.30: The following information is available for Nehra Ltd. a company that is not expected to pay dividend for a year:

S	K	R	T	O	0²
60	56	0.14	0.5	0.3	0.09

What is the value of the call option as per the Black and Scholes Model? Also find out the value of a put.

Solution:

$$\text{In}\ (S/K) = \text{In}\ (60/56) = 0.0687$$

$$d_1 = \frac{0.0687 + (0.14 + 0.045) \times (6/12)}{0.3 \times \sqrt{6 \div 12}} = 0.76$$

$$d_2 = 0.76 - 0.2121 = 0.5479$$

$$N(d_1) = 0.7764$$

$$N(d_2) = 0.7088$$

$$e^{-rt} = 0.9324$$

$$\text{Value of a call option} = 60 \times (0.7764) - 56 \times (0.9324) \times (0.7088) = 9.58$$

$$e^{-rt} = e^{.14 \times .5} = 1.0725$$

$$\text{Value of a Put} = (K/e^{rt}) + \text{Value of Call} - S$$

$$= (56/1.0725) + 9.58 - 60$$

$$= 1.80$$

Q.31: We have been given the following information about XYZ company's share and call options:

Current share price	= ₹ 165
Option exercise price	= ₹ 150
Risk-free interest rate	= 6 per cent
Time to option expiry	= 2 years
Volatility of Sharp price (standard deviation)	= 15 per cent

Calculate value of the option

Solution:

Applying Black & Scholes Model

$$d_1 = \frac{\text{In}\left(\frac{165}{150}\right) + \left[.06 + \frac{1}{2}(.15)^2\right].2}{.15\sqrt{.2}}$$

$$= \frac{-.095310 + .1425}{.212132}$$

$$= 1.12101$$

$$d_2 = \frac{\text{In}\left(\frac{165}{150}\right) + \left[.06 + \frac{1}{2}(.15)^2\right].2}{.15\sqrt{.2}}$$

$$= \frac{-.095310 + .0975}{.212132}$$

$$= .9089$$

$$N(d_1) = N(1.12104) = .8688$$

$$N(d_2) = N(.9089) = .8161$$

$$\text{Value of Option} = V_s N(d_1) - \frac{E}{e^n} N(d_2)$$

$$= 165 \times (.8688) - \frac{150}{e^{(.06 \times 2)}}(.8161)$$

$$143.352 - \frac{150}{e^{.12}}(.8161)$$

$$143.352 - \frac{150}{1.127497}(.8161)$$

$$= 143.352 - 108.5723$$

$$= ₹\ 34.779$$

$$= ₹\ 34.78$$

Q.32: The Equity share of VCC Ltd. is quoted at ₹ 210. A 3-month call option is available for a premium of ₹ 6 per share and a 3-month put option is available for a premium of ₹ 5 per share. Ascertain the net pay-offs to the option holder of a call option and put option.

(i) the strike price in both cases is ₹ 220, and

(ii) the share price on the exercise day is ₹ 200, 210, 220, 230, 240.

Also indicate the price range at which the call the put options may be gainfully exercised.

Solution:

Net pay-off for the holder of the call option (₹)

Strike price on exercise day	200	210	220	230	240
Option exercise	No	No	No	Yes	Yes
Outflow (Strike price)	Nil	Nil	Nil	220	220
Outflow (premium)	6	6	6	6	6
Total Outflow	6	6	6	226	226
Less infloe (Sales proceeds)	–	–	–	230	240
Net pay-off	-6	-6	-6	4	14

Net pay-off for the holder of the put option

Strike price on exercise day	200	210	220	230	240
Option exercise	Yes	Yes	No	No	No
Inflow (strike price)	220	220	Nil	Nil	Nil
Less outflow (premium)	5	5	5	5	5
Net pay-off	15	5	-5	-5	-5

The loss of the option holder is restricted to the amount of premium paid. The profit (Positive pay-off) depends on the difference between the strike price and the share price on the exercise day.

Q.33: Mr. A purchased a 3-month call option for 100 shares in XYZ Ltd. at a premium of ₹ 30 per share, with an exercise price of ₹ 550. He also purchased a 3-month I put option for 100 shares of the same company at a premium of ₹ 5 per share with an exercise price of ₹ 450. The market price of the share on the date of Mr. A's purchase of options, is ₹ 500. Calculate the profit or loss that Mr. A would make, assuming that the market price falls to ₹ 350 at the end of 3-months.

Solution:

Since, the market price at the end of 3-month falls to ₹ 250 which is below the exercise price under the call option, the call option will not be exercised. Only put option becomes variable.

The gain will be:	₹
Gain per share (₹ 450 – ₹ 350)	100
Total gain per 100 shares	10,000
Cost or premium paid (₹ 300 × 100) + (₹ 5 × 100)	3,500
Net gain	6,500

Q.34: A call and put exist on the same stock each of which is exercisable at trade for ₹ 60. The now trade for:

Market price of Stock or stock index	₹	55
Market price of call	₹	9
Market price of put	₹	1

Calculate the expiration date cash-flow, investment value, and net profit for

(i) Buy 1.0 call

(ii) Write 1.0 call

(iii) Buy 1.0 put

(iv) Write 1.0 put

For expiration date stock prices of ₹ 50, 55, ₹ 60, ₹ 65, ₹ 70.

Solution:

Expiration date cash-flows

Stock Prices	₹ 50	₹ 55	₹ 60	₹ 65	₹ 70
Buy 1.0 call	0	0	0	-60	-60
Write 1.0 call	0	0	0	60	60
Buy 1.0 put	60	60	0	0	0
Write 1.0 put	-60	-60	0	0	0

Expiration date investment value

Stock Prices	₹ 50	₹ 55	₹ 60	₹ 65	₹ 70
Buy 1.0 call	0	0	0	5	10
Write 1.0 call	0	0	0	-5	-10
Buy 1.0 put	10	5	0	0	0
Write 1.0 put	-10	-5	0	0	0

Expiration date investment value

Stock Prices	₹ 50	₹ 55	₹ 60	₹ 65	₹ 70
Buy 1.0 call	-9	-9	-9	-4	1
Write 1.0 call	9	9	9	4	-1
Buy 1.0 put	9	4	-1	-1	-1
Write 1.0 put	-9	-4	1	1	1

Q.35: Ramesh wants to invest in stock market. He has got the following information about individual securities.

Security	Excepted Return	Beta	O^2_{cl}
A	15	1.5	40
B	12	2	20
C	10	2.5	30
D	09	1	10
E	08	1.2	20
F	14	1.5	30

Market index variance is 10 per cent and the risk-free rate of return is 7 per cent. What should be the optimum portfolio assuming no short sales?

Solution:

Securities need to be ranked on the basis of excess return to beta ratio from highest to the lowest.

Security	R_i	β_1	$R_i - R_f$	$\frac{R_i - R_r}{\beta_1}$
A	15	1.5	8	5.33
B	12	2	5	2.5
C	10	2.5	3	1.2
D	9	1	2	2
E	8	1.2	1	0.83
F	14	1.5	7	4.67

Ranked Table

Security	$R_i - R_f$	β_1						C_1
A	8	1.5	40	0.30	0.30	0.056	0.056	1.923
F	7	1.5	30	0.35	0.65	0.075	0.131	2.814
B	5	2	20	0.50	1.15	0.20	0.331	2.668
D	2	1	10	0.20	1.35	0.10	0.431	2.542

CA = 10 × .0.3/[1 + (10 × 0.056)] = 1.923

CF = 10 × 0.65/[1 + (10 × 0.131)] = 2.814

CB = 10 × 1.15/[1 + (10 × 0.331)] = 2.668

CD = 10 × 1.35/[1 + (10 × 0.431)] = 2.542

CC = 10 × 1.60/[1 + (10 × 0.639)] = 2.165

CE = 10 × 1.66/[1 + (10 × 0.7111)] = 2.047

Cut-off point is 2.814

Q.36: The price of equity shares of Onida Picture Ltd. (a non-dividend paying Company) is ₹ 30. The risk-free rate is 12 per cent p.a. with continuous compounding An investor wants to enter into a 6-months forward contract. Find out the forward price.

Solution:

The forward price of a non-dividend paying share can be found as follows:

$F = S \times e^{rt}$

Where, F = Forward Price

S = Spot Price

r = Risk-free rate

t = time

Now, F = 30 × 2.71828.12 × .5

= ₹ 31.86

Q.37: The stock index is currently 350 and risk-free rate is 8 per cent. Find out the futures price for a 4-month contract if the dividend yield is 4 per cent.

Solution:

The futures price for a dividend yield index is:

$F = S \times e^{(r-q)t}$

= 350 × 2.71728 (.08 – 04).333

= ₹ 354.70

In this case, q is the dividend yield and the time is 4-month, i.e., .333.

Q.38: The Market price of equity shares of ABC Ltd. is ₹ 40. It has not been paying any dividend. The risk-free rate for the investor is 5 per cent. The 3-month forward rate for the share is ₹ 42. Should the investor enter into the 3-month future Contract?

Solution:

The futures price for the share of a non-dividend company may be found as follows:

$$F = S \times e^{rt}$$

$$\text{Now, } F = 40 \times 2.71825^{.05 \times .25}$$

$$= ₹\ 40.50$$

The equilibrium price of the futures is ₹ 40.50. however, if the market rate (of futures) is ₹ 42, the investor should sell the 3-months futures. He can borrow ₹ 40 now to purchase one share and to sell it in futures. Thereby, he can make a profit of ₹ 1.50 per share over a period of 3-months.

Q.39: The Debentures of ABC Ltd. are currently selling at ₹ 930 per debenture. The 4-month futures contract on this debenture is available at ₹ 945. There is no interest due during this 4-months period. Should the investor buy this future if the risk-free rate of interest is 6 per cent?

Solution:

In this case, the future price in equilibrium can be found with the help of the following equation:

$$F = S \times e^{rt}$$

$$\text{Now, } F = 930 \times 2.71828.06 \times .333$$

$$= ₹\ 948.79$$

As the futures is available at ₹ 945 only, the investor should buy the 4-months futures.

Q.40: She Spot price of a bond is ₹ 900 and one year's futures rate is ₹ 930. Interest payments of ₹ 40 are due after 6-months and after 1 year from today. The risk-free rate of interest for 6-months and 1 year period are 9 per cent and 10 per cent respectively. Find out the profit of the investor. What should be his strategy if he holdss one bond and the futures price is ₹ 905.

Solution:

The first payment of ₹ 40 is due after 6-months The present value of this amount @9 per cent for 6-months. The present value of this amount @9 per cent for 6-month's period (continuous compounding) is:

PV = ₹ 40 × $e^{-.09 \times .5}$

= ₹ 38.23

The investor should borrow ₹ 900 today to buy one-debenture. Out of ₹ 900, ₹ 38.23 is borrowed for 6-months, which together with interest @ 9 per cent continuous compounding, can be paid of ₹ 40 (first interest). The balance ₹ 861.77 is borrowed @10 per cent for 1 year which together with interest will become 861.77 × e.1 = ₹ 952.40.

After 1 year, he would receive ₹ 930 from the futures and ₹ 40 from the interest. Out of this total ₹ 970, he would pay ₹ 952.40 for loan. The profit of the invetor would be (₹ 970 – ₹ 952.40) i.e., ₹ 17.60. The strategy can be presented as follows:

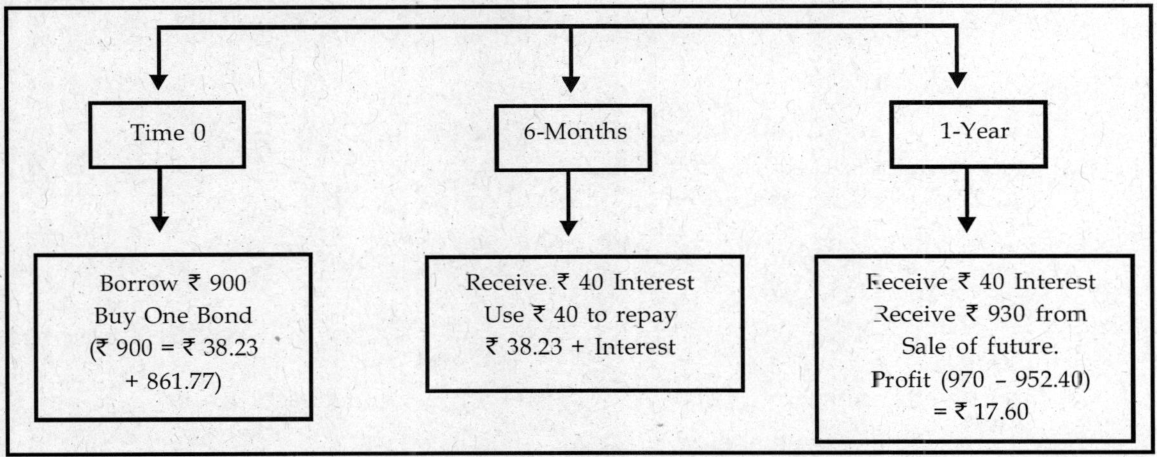

In case, he is holding one bond and the future price is ₹ 905, he should sell the bond now and buy one futures contract for one year. The strategy would be:

Out of ₹ 900 (received from the sale of one bond), ₹ 3.23 in invested @ 9 per cent for 6-months which will become ₹ 40 after 6-months, and ₹ 861.77 are invested @ 10 per cent for 1 year which will become ₹ 952.40. He is also foregoing ₹ 40 interest receivable from the company. So his net proceeds would be ₹ 912.40 and the payment on futures is ₹ 905, so his profit over a period of one year is ₹ 7.40.

Q.41: An investor buys a Sensex Futures at 5,500 in market lot of 200 futures. On the settlement date, the Sensex is 5,600. Find out his profit or loss for one lot of futures. What would be his position, if the Sensex is 5,450 on the settlement date?

Solution:

The investor has bought the Sensex Futures at 5,500. On the settlement date, the Sensex and the futures, both would coverge to the same level. As the Sensex on the settlement date is 5,600, the futures will also be 5,600. So, the profit to the investor is:

Profit = (5,600 – 5,500) × 200

= ₹ 20,000

However, if the Sensex on the settlement date is 5,450, the futures will also be 5,450 on that date. In this case, the loss to the investor would be:

Loss = (5,400 – 5,450) × 200

= ₹ 10,000

Q.42: An investor buys NIFTY Futures contract for ₹ 2,80,000 (Lot size 200 futures). On the settlement date, the NIFTY closes at 1,378. Find out his profit or loss, if he pays ₹ 1,000 as brokerage. What would be position, if he has sold the futures contract?

Solution:

In this case, the total value is ₹ 2,80,000 and the lot is 200, so, the NIFTY futures on the transaction date is 1,400 (i.e., 2,80,000 h-200). Now, on the settlement date, the NIFTY is 1,378. So, it has reduced by 22 points. The loss to the investor is:

Loss = (1,400 – 1,378) × 200 + 1,000

= ₹ 4,400 + ₹ 1,000

= ₹ 5,400

In case, he has sold the futures contract, his profit would have been:

Profit = (1,400 – 1,378) × 200 – ₹ 1,000

= ₹ 4,400 – ₹ 1,000

= ₹ 3,400

It may be noted that in both the cases, the brokerage of ₹ 1,000 would be payable.

Q.43: The Shares of Yellow Pages Ltd. are being traded at ₹ 250 on the BSE. Its in/sri Futures for 1-month, 2-months and 3-months are also available on the BSE. If the risk-free rate is 12 per cent p.a. and no dividends are expected during this period, what should be equilibrium price of these futures?

Solution:

The time period of these futures is 1-month, 2-months and 3-months, i.e., .083 year, .167 year, and .25 year. The spot price is ₹ 250 and the risk-free rate is 12 per cent. The equilibrium price for different futures would be:

1-months future: $F = S \times e^{rt}$

$= ₹\ 250 \times 2.71828^{.12 \times .083}$

= ₹ 252.50

2-moths future: F $= ₹\ 250 \times 2.71828^{.12 \times .167}$

$= ₹\ 255.05$

3-months future: F $= ₹\ 250 \times 2.71828^{.12 \times .25}$

$= ₹\ 257.62$

Q.44: The following data relate to ABC Ltd. share prices:

Current Market price per share	₹ 180
Price in futures market 6-months	₹ 195

It is possible to borrow money for securities transactions at the rate of 12 per cent p.a. Required:

(i) Calculate the theoretical minimum price of a 6-month forward contract.

(ii) Explain, if any, arbitrage opportunities exist.

Solution:

6-months forward price may be found as follows:

$F = S \times e^{rt}$

$= ₹\ 180 \times 2.71828^{.12 \times .5}$

$= ₹\ 180 \times 1.0618$

$= ₹\ 191.12$

So, the theoretical price of a 6-month forward contract is ₹ 191.12. As the actual price of a 6-month futures contract is ₹ 195, there is an arbitrage opportunity. In order to make gain, an investor may borrow funds @ 12 per cent to buy the shares now, and simultaneously, he should sell the share in the futures market @ 12 per cent to buy the shares now, and simultaneously, he should sell the share in the future market @ ₹ 195. He would be able to make a profit of ₹ 3.88 per share. The arbitrage opportunity will continue to exist so long as the actual market price is more than ₹ 191.12.

$$Z_A = \frac{1.5}{40}(5.33 - 2.814) \qquad = 0.08435$$

$$Z_F = \frac{1.5}{30}(4.67 - 2.814) \qquad = 0.0928$$

$X_A = 0.09435/[0.09435 + 0.0928] = 50.41$ per cent

$X_r = 0.0928 + 0.0928] = 49.59$ per cent

Funds to be invested in Security A & F are 50.41 per cent and 49.595 respectively.

Q.45: ABC Ltd wishes to borrow ₹ 100 crore for 5 years. It can borrow @ 14 per cent fixed or LIBOR + 1.25 per cent floating rate. There is another company Small Ltd. which also requires the same amount but because of lower credit rating can borrow either @ 15.75 fixed or LIBOR + 2 per cent floating. However, because of existing debt portfolio, ABC wants to borrow at floating rate and Small Ltd, wants to borrow" at fixed rate. If the savings is to be shares equally, is there a swap opportunity? Also find out the cash-flows in monetary amounts.

Solution:

The given information can be presented as follows:

	ABC Ltd.	Small Ltd.	Difference
Fixed Rate	14 per cent	15.75 per cent	1.75 per cent
Floating Rate	LIBOR + 1.25 per cent	LIBOR	.75 per cent
Potential Gain			1.00 per cent

It is evident that ABC Ltd. can borrow cheaper than Small Ltd. but it has comparative advantage in borrowing at fixed rate. In order to avail the potential gain of 1 per cent, ABC Ltd. should borrow at fixed rate and swap with Small Ltd.

There may be different swap arrangements to share the gains equally. One such arrangement could be as follows:

Small Ltd. should pay 15.25 per cent fixed to ABC Ltd. and ABC Ltd. should pay LIBOR + 2 per cent to Small Ltd. This can be presented as follows:

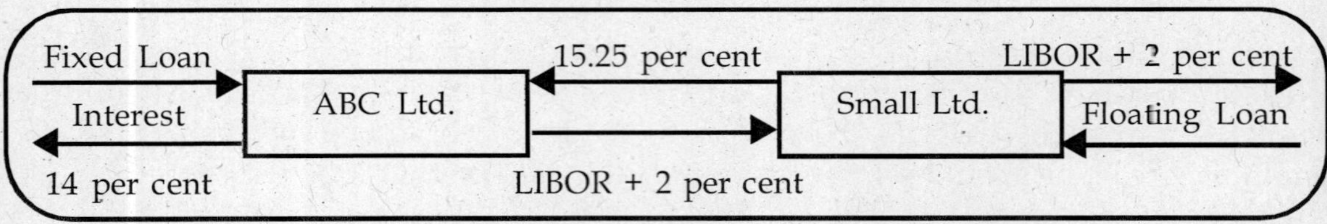

This distribution of potential gain between the two parties can be seen as follows:

ABC Ltd.	Fixed Loan	Pays to the lender	14.00 per cent		
		Receives from Small Ltd.	15.25 per cent	Gain	1.25 per cent
	Floating Loan	Pays to Small Ltd.	LIBOR + 2 per cent		
			LIBOR + 1.25 per cent	Loss	.75 per cent
Small Ltd.	Fixed Loan	Pays to ABC Ltd.		Net Gain	.50 per cent
		Opportunity Cost	15.25 per cent		
	Floating Loan	Pays to lender	15.75 per cent	Gain	.50 per cent
		Receives from ABC	LIBOR + 2 per cent		
			LIBOR + 2 per cent	Gain	0 per cent
				Net Gain	.50 per cent

Suppose, LIBOR is 12 per cent or 15 per cent. The above analysis can now be applied to find out the monetary cash-flows as follows:

		LIBOR 12 per cent	LIBOR 15 per cent
ABC Ltd.	Pay to lender	(₹ crores)	(₹ crores)
	Pays to Small Ltd.	14.00	14.00
	Receives from Small	14.00	17.00
	Net Cost	15.25	15.25
XYZ Ltd.	Pays to ABC Ltd.	12.75	15.75
	Receives from ABC Ltd.	14.00	17.00
	Net Cost	15,25	15.25
		14.00	17.00
		15.25	15,25

Whether LIBOR is 12 per cent or 15 per cent, in both cases, the two parties are able to reduce their cost from 14 per cent to 12.5 per cent and from 15.75 per cent to 15.25 per cent respectively for ABC and XYZ Ltd. So, swap is beneficial to both parties.

ABC Ltd. borrows a fixed rate loan even though it is serving (as is the wish of the company) the floating rate loan. Similarly, XYZ Ltd. is borrowing at floating rate but it servicing the fixed rate loan as it is the wish of the company.

Q.46: ABC Housing Finance Ltd. lends money to individuals @ 12 per cent p.a. and accepts deposits from investors at FR+1 per cent (Where FR is a floating rate). As the interest payment to investors is floating, it wants to hedge its risk, and has approached a swap dealer.

Another company XYZ Ltd. has also approached the swap dealer. XYZ Ltd. has to pay 12 per cent to the depositors but charges FR+2.25 per cent from its borrowers. You are required to devise a swap so that ABC Ltd., XYZ Ltd. and the dealer, all the three participants are benefited.

Solution:

ABC Housing Financing Ltd. wants to hedge against the floating rate liability and XYZ Ltd. wants to hedge against 12 per cent payable to the depositors. So, ABC Ltd. would be ady to swap its 12 per cent income against the interest liability plus some profit, say .805. Similarly, XYZ Ltd. would be ready to swap its floating income of FR + 2.25 per cent against the receipt of 12 per cent from the dealer. It also wants to gain, say .20 per cent out of swap. The swap arrangement can be structured as shown below:

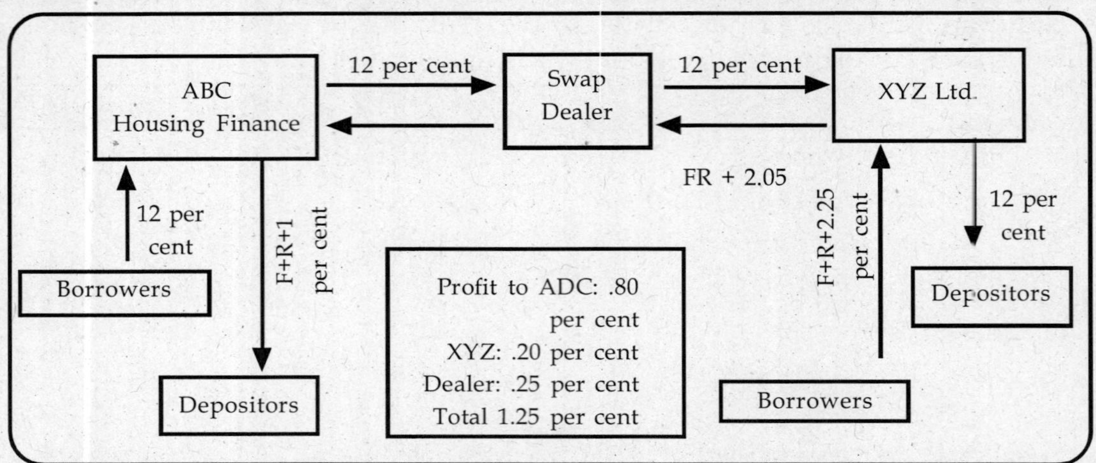

Q.47: Bacardi Ltd. has 12.5 per cent debt outstanding, payable after 4 years. The interest rates have come down and the risk-free rate is 8.5 per cent. Fixed to floating 4-years swaps are trading 75 bp above 8.5 per cent vs 6-months LIBOR. The present 6-months LIBOR is 8.25 per cent. The average LIBOR over next four years is likely to be much less than 12.5 per cent, how can the company benefit from it? To what extent, the funding cost could be reduced, how much is the gain and what are the risks involved?

Solution:

The swap position from the point of view of Bacardi Ltd. can be analysed as follows:

	Borrow at	Swap
Bacardi Ltd. Counter party	Fixed @12.5 per cent Floating @ LIBOR	Floating @ less than 12.5 per cent Fixed @ even higher than LIBOR

The swap may be entered into with a counterparty who borrows at floating LIBOR and waps with the Bacardi Ltd. so that both can benefit.

The cost of funds at floating rate is 8.25 per cent.

The present cost of fixed rate funds is 8.50 + 0.75 = 9.25 per cent.

The possible benefit is 9.25 – 8.25 = 1.00 per cent.

Assuming that the parties to the swap share the total benefit equally, the swap can be arranged as follows:

(i) Bacardi Ltd. borrows at 12.5 per cent fixed, lends to the counter party at 13 per cent fixed and borrows from it at LIBOR + 4.25 per cent.

(ii) The counterparty borrows at LIBOR, lends to Bacardi at LIBOR + 4.25 per cent and borrows from it at 13 per cent.

The cost of funds to Bacardi Ltd.	= –12.5 + 13.0 – (LIBOR + 4.25)
	= 12 per cent (as LIBOR is 8.25 per cent)
Saving	= 12.5 – 12.0 = 0.5 per cent
The cost of funds to the counterparty	= –LIBOR + (LIBOR + 4.25) –13
	= 8.75 per cent
Saving	= (8.50 + 0.75) – 8.75 = 0.5 per cent

So, both parties are benefited by 0.5 per cent.

Q.48: Integrated (India) Ltd. of India and Upper Class Ltd. of USA want to raise funds. However, the latter has a better credit rating and has an advantage in raising funds in both countries. Following are the rates of interest at which the funds can be raised by these companies in different markets:

Interest Rate

	INDIA	USA
Integrated (India) Ltd.	19 per cent	9 per cent
Upper Class Ltd.	18 per cent	6 per cent

Integrated (India) Ltd. wants dollar funds while Upper Class Ltd. wants rupee funds. Design a currency swap given that both companies require funds of ₹ 45 crores (or $ 1,00,00,000)

Solution:

The swap could be arranged through a dealer as follows:

(i) Integrated to borrow in India @ 19 per cent a sum of ₹ 45 crores.

(ii) Upper Class to borrow $ 1 crore in USA @ 6 per cent.

(iii) Integrated and Upper Class to exchange these receipts.

(iv) Integrated to pay to the dealer interest @ 8.5 per cent and received rupee interest @ 19 per cent from the dealer.

Q.49: XYZ Ltd. holds fixed rate bonds with coupon rate of 7 per cent. ABC Ltd., is a recipient of floating rate interest through floating rate bonds with coupons rate of LIBOR + 2 per cent. Both apprehend a fluctuation in interest rate in the coming years. ABC Ltd. and XYZ Ltd. enter Into a swap arrangement through a dealer, on the following terms:

- ABC Ltd. to pay floating rate interest of LIBOR + 2 per cent
- ABC Ltd. to receive from dealer fixed interest of 6.5 per cent

– XYZ Ltd. to pay a fixed Interest of 7 per cent.

– XYZ Ltd. to receive from the dealer in floating rate of LIBOR + 2 per cent

Show the cash-flow position of all the three parties.

Solution:

	Interest Inflow	Swap Inflow	Swap Outflow	Net Cash-flow
Dealer ABC Ltd. XYZ Ltd.	– + (LIBOR + 2 per cent) +7 per cent	+ (LIBOR .+ 2 per cent) from ABC + 7 per cent from XYZ + 6.5 per cent from dealer + (LIBOR + 2 per cent) from dealer	- 6.5 per cent to ABC - (LIBOR + 2 per cent) to XYZ - (LIBOR + 2 per cent) −7 per cent to dealer	+ 0.5 per cent + 6.5 per cent + (LIBOR + 2 per cent)

In this case, ABC Ltd. has hedged against the fall in interest and would be getting net 6.5 per cent fixed interest irrespective of the interest rate (which depends on LIBOR). On the other hand, XYZ Ltd. would be receiving net interest of LIBOR + 2 per cent. So, if there is a change in interest rates, then the cash inflow of XYZ Ltd. would also be affected.

Q.50: Higher Grade Ltd. (HG) and Lower Grade Ltd. (LG) have to borrow ₹ 100 lakh each. The relevant Interest rates are as follows:

	Fixed Rate	Floating Rate
Higher Grade Ltd.	12.0 per cent	LIBOR + 0.1 per cent
Lower Grade Ltd.	13.4 per cent	LIBOR + 0.6 per cent

HG is interested to borrow at floating rate while LG is interested to borrow at fixed rate obligations. You are required to design an appropriate swap. The swap dealer must get a commission of 0.1 per cent and profit be shared equally by two companies.

Solution:

HG has advantage over LG under fixed rate as well as the floating rate obligations. But it has separately higher advantage in fixed rate (12.4 per cent), as against .5 per cent in floating rate. The net gain of .9 per cent, .1 per cent is payable to the swap dealer. The remaining gain of .8 per cent may be shared eaually (.4 per cent) by HG and LG. The swap arrangement would be:

	Interest Inflow	Swap Inflow	Swap Outflow	Net Cash-flow
HG	12.0 per cent	12.4 per cent	LIBOR + .1 per cent	LIBOR – .3 per cent
LG	LIBOR + 6 per cent	LIBOR _ .1 per cent	12.5 per cent	13 per cent
Dealer	–	12.5 per cent	12.4 per cent	.1 per cent
		LIBOR + .1 per cent	LIBOR + .1 per cent	–

The swap arrangement helps HG to borrow at a net cost of LIBOR -3 per cent and LG to borrow at 13 per cent. So, both making a gain of 4 per cent. In the process, the swap dealer is getting a commission of .1 per cent.

Q.51: Equity Share of PQR Ltd., Is presently quoted at ₹ 320. The Market price of the share after 6-months has the following probability distribution:

Market Price	₹ 180	₹ 260	₹ 280	₹ 320	₹ 400
Probability	0.1	0.2	0.5	0.1	0.1

A put option with a strike price of ₹ 300 can be written.

You are required to find out expected value of option at maturity (i.e., 6-months)

Solution:

Expected Value of Option

(300 – 180) × 0 1	12
(300 – 260) × 0 2	8
(300 – 280) × 0 5	10
(300 – 320) × 0 1	Not Exercised
(300 – 400) × 0 1	Not Exercised
	30

* If the strike price goods beyond ₹ 300, option is not exercised at all.

In case of Put option, since Share price is greater than strike price Option Value would be Zero.

Q.52: Derivative Bank entered into a plain vanilla swap through on OIS (Overnight idex Swap) on a principal of ₹ 10 crores and agreed to receive MIBOR overnight floating rate for a fixed payment on the principal. The swap was entered into on Monday, 2nd August 2010 and was to commence on 3rd August 2010 and run for a period of 7 days.

Respective MIBOR rates for Tuesday to Monday were:

7.75 per cent, 8.15 per cent, 8.12 per cent, 7.95 per cent, 7.98 per cent, 8.15 per cent.

If the Derivative Bank received ₹ 317 net on settlement, calculate fixed rate and interest under both legs.

Notes:

(i) Sunday is Holiday

(ii) Work in rounded rupees and avoid decimal working.

Solution:

Day	Principal (₹)	MIBOR (per cent)	Interest (₹)
Tuesday	10,00,00,000	7.75	21,233
Wednesday	10,00,21,233	8.15	22,334
Thursday	10.00,43,567	8.12	22,256
Friday	10,00,56,823	7.95	21,795
Saturday & Sunday (*)	10,00,87,618	7.98	43,764
Monday	10,01,31,382	8.15	22,358
Total Interest @ Floating			1,53,740
Less: Net Received			317
Expected Interest @ fixed			1,53,423
Thus Fixed Rate of Interest			0.07999914 per cent
Approx.			8 per cent

(*) i.e., Interest for two days

Note: Alternatively, answer can also be calculated on the basis of 360 days in a year.

Q.53: A dealer quotes "All-in-cost" for a generic swap at 8 per cent against six-months LIBOR flat. If the notional principal amount of swap is ₹ 6,00,000.

(i) Calculate semi-annual fixed payment

(ii) Find the first floating rate payment for (i) above if the six-month period from the effective date of swap to the settlement date comprises 181 days and the corresponding LIBOR was 6 per cent on the effective date of swap.

(iii) In (ii) above if the settlement is on NET basis, how much the fixed rate payer would pay to the floating rate payer? Generic swap is based on 30/360 days.

Solution:

(i) Semi-Annual fixed payment = (N) (AIC) (Period)

Where, N = Notional Principal Amount = ₹ 6,00,000

All-In-Cost (AIC) = 8 per cent = 0.08

= ₹ 6,00,000 × 0.08 × 180/360

= ₹ 6,00,000 × 0.08 × 0.5

= ₹ 6,00,000 × 0.04 = ₹ 24,000

(ii) Floating rate payment = N(LIBOR) (dt/360)

= ₹ 6,00,000 × 0.06 × 181/360

= ₹ 6,00,000 × 0.06 × (o.502777)

= ₹ 18,100

(iii) Net Amount = (i) – (ii)

or = ₹ 24,000 – ₹ 18,100 = ₹ 5,900

Q.54: ABC Bank is seeking fixed rate funding. It is able to finance at a cost of six-months LIBGOR + ¼ per cent for ₹ 200 million for 5 years. The bank is able to swap into a fixed rate at 7.5 per cent versus syfmonth LJBOR treating six-months as exactly half a year.

(a) What will be the "all in cost" funds to ABC Bank?

(b) Another possibility being considered is the issue of a hybrid instrument which pays 7.5 per cent for first three years and LIBOR + ¼ per cent for remaining two years.

Given a three year swap rate of 8 per cent, suggest the methcd by which the bank should achieve fixed rate funding.

Solution:

(a) ABC Bank pays LIBOR + 0.25 per cent p.a. for 5 years. The swap involves payment of 7.5 per cent p.a. and receipt of LIBOR

Inflow	**Outflow**
LIBOR	LIBOR + 0.25 per cent + 7.5 per cent

Net interest payment 7.75 per cent

Cash-flows per six-month period

Inflow	**Outflow**
(LIBOR/2) × ₹ 200 million	(LIBOR/2) × ₹ 200 million
	+ ₹ 2,50,000 + ₹ 75,00,000

Therefore, All in cost of funds = ₹ 7,75,50,000.

Alternatively it can also be calculated as follows:

₹ 200 million × 7.75 per cent × 6 = ₹ 7.75 millions or ₹ 77,50,000

Q.55: The Following data relate to Anand Ltd.'s Share price:

Current Price Per share	₹ 1,800
6-months future's price/share	₹ 1,950

Assuming it is possible to borrow money in the market for transaction in securities at 12 per cent p.a. you are required:

(i) To calculate the theoretical minimum price of a 6-month forward purchases, and

(ii) To explain arbitrary opportunity.

Solution:

Anand Ltd.

(i) Calculation of theoretical minimum price of a 6-months forward contract –

Theoretical minimum price = ₹ 1,800 + (₹ 1,800 × 12/100 × 6/12) ₹ 1,908

(ii) Arbitrage Opportunity –

The arbitrageur can borrow money @ 12 per cent for 6-months and buy the shares at ₹ 1,800. At the same time he can sell the shares in the futures market at ₹ 1,950. On the expiry date 6-months later, he could deliver the share and collect ₹ 1,950 pay-off ₹ 1,908 and record a profit of ₹ 42 (₹ 1,950 – ₹ 1,908).

Q.56: XYZ established the following spread on the Delta Corporation's stock:

(i) Purchased one 3-month call option for 100 Nos. With a premium of ₹ 30 and an exercise price of ₹ 550.

(ii) Purchased one 3-month put option for 100 Nos. With a premium of ₹ 5 and an exercise price of ₹ 450.

The current price of Delta Corporations stock is ₹ 500, Determine XYZ profit or loss if the price of Delta Corporation:

(i) Stays at ₹ 500 after 3-months

(ii) Falls to ₹ 350 after 3-months

(iii) Rises to ₹ 600

Solution:

(i) Total premium paid on purchasing a call and put option

= (₹ 30 per share × 100) + (₹ 5 per share × 100).

= ₹ 3,000 + ₹ 500 = ₹ 3,500

In this case, XYZ exercises neither the call option nor the put option as both will result in a loss for her.

Ending value = – ₹ 3,500 + Zero gain

= – ₹ 3,500

i.e., Net loss = ₹ 3,500

(ii) Since the price of the stock is below the exercise price of the call, the call will not be exercised. Only put is valuable and is exercised.

Total premium paid = ₹ 3,500

Ending value = – ₹ 3,500 + ₹ [(450 – 350) × 100]

= – ₹ 3,500 + ₹ 10,000 = ₹ 6,500

i.e., Net gain = ₹ 6,500

(iii) In this situation, the put is worthless, since the price of the stock exceeds the put's exercise price. Only call option is valuable and is exercised.

Total premium paid = ₹ 3,500

Ending value = – ₹ 3,500 + ₹ [600 – 550] × 100]

Net Gain = – ₹ 3,500 + ₹ 5,000 = ₹ 1,500

Q.57: The Share of X Ltd. is currently selling for ₹ 300. Risk-free interest rate is 0.8 per cent per-month. A 3-months futures contract is selling for ₹ 312. Develop an arbitrage strategy and show what your riskless profit will be 3-month, hence assuming that X Ltd. will not pay any dividend in the next 3-months.

Solution:

The appropriate value of the 3-months future contract is –

Fo = ₹ 300 (1.008)3 = ₹ 307.26

Since the future price exceeds its appropriate value to do the following:-

Action	Initial Cash-flow	Cash-flow at time T (3-months)
Borrow ₹ 300 now and repay with interest	+ ₹ 300	– ₹ 300 (.1008)3
After 3-months		= – ₹ 307.26
Buy a share	– ₹ 300	ST
Sell a futures contract (Fo-312/-)	0	₹ 312 – ST
Total	₹ 0	₹ 474

Such an action would produce a risk less profit of ₹ 4.74

Q.58: Consider a two-year American call option with strike price of ₹ 50 on a stock the current price of which is also ₹ 50. Assume that there are two time periods of one year and in each year the stock price can move up or down by equal percentage of 20 per cent. The risk-free interest rate is 6 per cent. Using binomial option model, calculate the probability of price moving up and down. Also, draw a two-step binomial tree showing prices and pay-offs at each node.

Solution:

(a) Stock prices in the two step Binominal tree

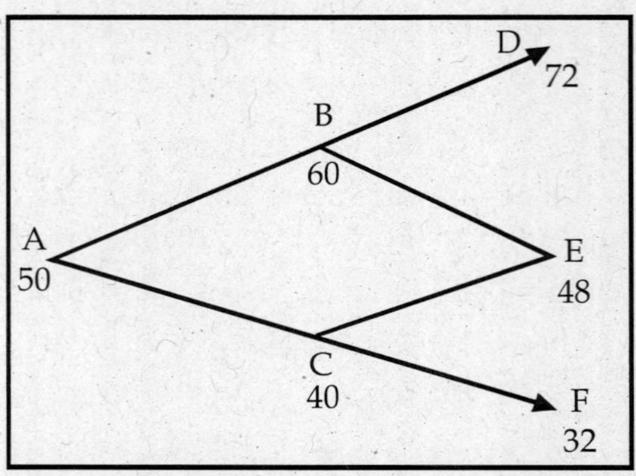

Using the single-period model, the probability of price increase is:

$$P = \frac{R-d}{U-d} = \frac{1.06-0.80}{1.20-0.80} = \frac{0.26}{0.40} = 0.65$$

therefore the p of price decrease = 1 – 0.65 = 0.35

The two step Binominal' tree showing price and pay-off

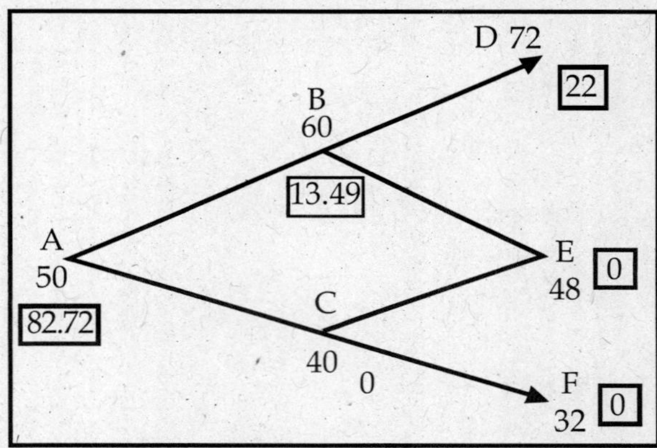

The value of an American call option at nodes D, E and F will be equal to the value of European option at these nodes and accordingly the call values at nodes D, E and F will be 22, 0 and 0 using the single period binomial model the value of call option at node B is:

$$C = \frac{Cup + Cd(1-p)}{R} = \frac{22 \times 0.65 + 0 \times 0.35}{1.06} = 13.49$$

At node B the pay-off from early exercise will pay ₹ 10, which is less than the value calculated using the single period binomial model. Hence, at node B, early exercise is not preferable and the value of American option at this node will be ₹ 13.49. If the value of.

Q.59: Consider the following data for Government Securities:

Face Value	Interest (Rate per cent)	Maturity (Years)	Current Price
1,00,000	0	1	91,000
1,00,000	10.5	2	99,000
1,00,000	11.0	3	99,500
1,00,000	11.5	4	99,900

Calculate the forward interest rates.

Solution:

To get forward Interest rates, begin with the one-year Government Security

₹ 91,000 = ₹ 1,00,000/(1 + r)

r = 0.099

Next consider the two year Government Security

₹ 99,000 = (₹ 10,500/1.099) + {₹ 1,10.500/(1.099)(1 + r)}

r = 0.124

Then consider the three year Government Security

₹ 99,500 = (₹ 11,000/1.099) + {(₹ 11,000/(1.099) (1.124)} + {₹ 1,11,000/(1.099)(1.124)(1 + r)

r = 0.115

Finally consider the four year Government Security

₹ 99,900 = (₹ 11,500/1.099) + {(₹ 11,500/(1.099)(1.124)} + {₹ 11,500/(1.099)(1.124)(1.115)} + {₹ 1.11,500/(1.099)(1.124) (1.115)(1 + r)

r = 0.128

Q.60: Calculate the price of M months PQR futures, if PQR (FV ₹ 10) quotes ₹ 220 on NSE and three-months future price quotes at ₹ 230 and the one-month borrowing rate is given as 15 per cent and the expected annual dividend yield is 25 per cent p.a. payable before expiry. Also examine arbitrage opportunities.

Solution:

Future's Price = Spot + Cost of carry – Dividend

F = 220 + 220 × 0.15 × 0.25 – 0.025** 10

= 225.75

** Entire 25 per cent dividend is payable before expiry, which is ₹ 2.50.

Thus, we see that futures price by calculation is ₹ 225.75 which is quoted at ₹ 230 in the exchange.

Analysis:

Fair value of Futures less than Actual futures Price:

Futures Overvalued Hence, it is advised to sell. Also do Arbitraging by buying stock in the cash market.

Step I:

He will buy PQR Stock at ₹ 220 by borrowing at 15 per cent for 3-months. Therefore his outflows are:

Cost of Stock	220
Add: Interest @ 15 per cent for 3-months, i.e., 0.25 years	8.25
(220 × 0.15 × 0.025)	
Total Outflows (A)	228.25

Step II:

He will sell March futures at ₹ 230. Meanwhile he would receive dividend for his stock.

Hence his inflow are	230
Total inflows (B)	2.50

Infloe – Outflow = Profit earned by Arbitrageur

= 232.5 – 228.25

= 4.25

Q.61: Following information is available for X Company's shares and call option:

Current share price	₹ 185
Option exercise price	₹ 170
Risk-free interest rate	7 per cent

Time of the expiry of option 3-years;

Standard deviation 0.18

Calculate the value of option using Black-Scholes formula.

Solution:

$$d_1 = \frac{I_n S/E + \left(r + \frac{\sigma^2}{2}\right)t}{\sigma\sqrt{t}}$$

$$= \frac{I_n(185/170) + \left(0.07 + \frac{0.18^2}{2}\right)3}{0.18\sqrt{3}}$$

$$= \frac{I_n\ 1.00882 + (0.07 + 0.0162)3}{0.18\sqrt{3}}$$

$$= \frac{0.08455 + 0.2586}{0.18\sqrt{3}}$$

$$= \frac{0.34315}{0.31177}$$

$$d_1 = 1.1006$$

$$d_2 = d_1 - \sigma\sqrt{t}$$

$$= 1.1006 - 0.31177 = 0.7888$$

$$N(d_1) = 0.8770 \text{ (from table)}$$

$$N(d_2) = 0.7848$$

$$\text{Value of option} = Vs\ (Nd_1) - \frac{E}{e^n}\ (Nd_2)$$

$$= 185\ (0.8770) - \frac{170}{e^{0.21}}\ (0.7848)$$

$$= 162.245 - \frac{170}{1.2336} \times 0.7848$$

$$= 162.245 - 108.151$$

$$= ₹\ 54.094$$

Q.62: Suppose a dealer quotes "All in Cost" for a generic swap at 8 per cent against six-month LIBOR flat. If the notional principal amount of swap is **₹ 5,00,000.**

(i) Calculate semi-annual fixed payment.

(ii) Find the first floating rate payment for: (i) above if the six-month period from the effective date of swap to the settlement date comprises 181 days and that the corresponding LIBOR was 6 per cent on the effective date of swap.

In (ii) above, if the settlement is on 'NET Basis' how much the fixed-rate payer would pay to the floating rate payer?

Generic swap is based on 30/360 days basis.

Solution:

(i) Semi-annual fixed payment

= (N) (AIC) (Period)

Where, N = Notional Principal amount = ₹ 5,00,000

AIC = All-in-cost = 8 per cent = 0.08

$$= 5{,}00{,}000 \times 0.08 \ \frac{(180)}{(360)}$$

$$= 5{,}00{,}000 \times 0.08\ (0.5)$$

$$= 5{,}00{,}000 \times 0.04$$

= ₹ 20,000

(ii) Floating Rate Payment

$$= \text{N (LIBOR)} \frac{(dt)}{(360)}$$

$$= 5{,}00{,}000 \times 0.06 \times \frac{181}{360}$$

$$= 5{,}00{,}000 \times 0.06\ (0.503) \text{ or } 5{,}00{,}000 \times 0.06\ (0.502777)$$

$$= 5{,}00{,}000 \times 0.03018 \text{ or } 0.30166$$

= ₹ 15090 or 15083

Both are correct

(iii) Net Amount

= (i) – (ii)

= ₹ 20,000 – 15,090 = 4,910

or = ₹ 20,000 – 15,083 = 4,917

Q.63: Mr. X established the following spread on the delta corporations stock:

(i) Purchased one 3-month call option with a premium of ₹ 30 and an exercise price of ₹ 550.

(ii) Purchased one 3-month put option with a premium of ₹ 5 and an exercise price of ₹ 450.

Delta corporation stock is currently selling at ₹ 500. Determine profit or loss if the price of Delta Corporations:

(i) Remains at ₹ 500 after 3-months

(ii) Falls to ₹ 350 after 3-months

(iii) Rises to ₹ 600

Assume the size option is 100 shares of delta corporation.

Solution:

(i) Expected return of the portfolio A and B

E (A) = (10 + 16)/2 = 13 per cent

E (B) = (12 + 18)/2 = 15 per cent

$$Rp = \sum_{1-1}^{N} x_i R_i = 0.4(13) + 0.6\ (15) = 14.2 \text{ per cent}$$

(ii) Stock A:

Variance = 0.5(10 – 13)2 + 0.5(16 – 13)2 = 9

Standard deviation = $\sqrt{9}$ = 3 per cent

Stock B:

Variance = 0.5 (12 – 15)2 + 0.5(18 – 15)2 = 9

Standard deviation = 3 per cent

(iii) Covariance of stocks A and B

Cov_{AB} = 0.5 (10 – 13) (12 – 15) + 0.5 (16 – 13) (18 – 15) = 9

(iv) Correlation coefficient

$$Tab = \frac{Cov_{AB}}{\sigma_A \sigma_B} = \frac{9}{3\chi 3} = 1$$

(v) Portfolio Risk

$$\sigma_p = \sqrt{X^2 A\sigma^2 A + X^2{}_{B\sigma} 2_B + 2X_A X_B(\sigma_A \sigma_B \sigma_{AB})}$$

$$= \sqrt{(0.4)^2 (3)^2 + (0.6)^2 (3)^2 + 2(0.4)(0.6)(3)(3)(1)}$$

$$= \sqrt{1.44 + 3.24 + 4.32} = 3 \text{ per cent}$$

Q.64 BSE 500

Value of Portfolio	**₹ 10,10,000**
Risk-free interest rate	**9 per cent p.a.**
Dividend yield on index	**6 per cent p.a.**
Beta of portfolio	**1.5**

We assume that a future contract on the BSE index with 4-months maturity is used to hedge the value of portfolio over next 3-months. One future contract is for delivery of 50 times the index.

Based on the above information calculate:

(i) Price of future contract

(ii) The gain on short futures position if index turns out to be 4,500 in 3-months.

Solution:

Note: It is assumed that the BSE Index on the day of hedging is 5,000 instead of 500 as printed in the question paper. The following working are based on this assumption.

(i) Current future price of the index = $5{,}000 + 5{,}000\,(0.09 - 0.06)\,\frac{4}{12}$

$= 5{,}000 + 50 = 5{,}050$

Price of the future contract = ₹ 50 × 5,050 = ₹ 2,52,500

(ii) Edge ratio $= \frac{1{,}01{,}000}{2{,}52{,}500} \times 1.5 = 6$ contracts

Index after 3-months turns out to be 4,500

Future price will be = 4,500 + 4,500 (0.09 – 0.06) × = 4,545

Therefore, gain from the short futures position is = 6 × (5,050 – 4,545) × 50

= ₹ 1,51,500

Alternative solution when BSE index is considered to be 500

(i) Current future price of index = $500 + 500\,(0.09 - 0.6)\,\frac{4}{12} = 500 + 5 = 505$

Price of the future contract = ₹ 50 × 505 = ₹ 25,250.

(ii) Hedge Ratio = $\frac{10{,}10{,}000}{25{,}250} \times 1.5 = 60$ contracts

Index after three-months turn out to be 4,500.

Future Price will be –

= 4,500 + 4,500 (0.09 – 0.06)/3 = 4,545

Therefore, gain from the short future position is

= 60 × (505 – 4545) × 50

= –12,12,00,00.

Q.65: The following table provides the prices of options on equity shares of X Ltd. and Y Ltd. the risk-free interest is 9 per cent. You as a financial planner are required to spot any mispricing in the quotations of options premium and stock prices.

Suppose, if you find any such mispricing then how you can take advantage of this pricing positions.

Share	Time to exercise	Exercise price (₹)	Share price (₹)	Gal price (₹)	Put price (₹)
X Ltd.	6-months	100	160	56	4
Y Ltd.	3-months	80	100	26	2

Solution:

1. In order to find out any mispricing we shall use Put Call Parity theorem

   Accordingly,

   Value of Call + PV (exercise price) = Value of Put + Share Price

   Thus,

   For shar of X Ltd.

   56 + 100 e-0.045 = 4 + 160

   56 + 95.60 = 164

The strategy to be adopted to take advantage of situation will be to buy call and sell put and share. The strategy will lead to cash-flow position as follows:

	Inflow ₹	Outflow ₹
Buying the Call	—	56
Selling put Short selling the share	4 160	—
Total Net Inflow	164 —	56 108
	164	164

Invest ₹ 108 for 6-months and get ₹ 108 × $e^{0.045}$ (₹ 108 × i.046)	₹ 112.97
After 6-months: Inflow from investment	₹ 112.97
Outflow due to exercise of option	₹ 100.00
Net Gain	₹ 12.97

Similarly for Share of Y Ltd.

26 + 80 $e^{0.045}$ = 2 + 100

26 + 76.48 = 102

102.48 = 102

Thus, there is a mismatch

The strategy to be adopted sell call and buy put and share. The position of cash-flows on the strategy adopted will be as follows:

	Inflow ₹	Outflow ₹
Buy the Share	–	100
Buy the Put	–	2
Sell the Call	26	–
Total	26	102
Net inflow	76	–
	102	102

This amount shall be borrowed for 3-months. After the 3-months the position will be as follows:

Repayment of borrowings (76 × $e^{0.045}$)	₹ 79.50
Inflow due to exercise of option Net Gain	₹ 80.00
	₹ 0.50

Q.66: The following details are related to the borrowing requirement of two companies ABC Ltd. and DEF Ltd.

Company	Requirement	Fixed Rates Offered	Loating Rates Offered
ABC Ltd.	Fixed Rupee rate	4.5 per cent	PLR + 2 per cent
DEF Ltd.	Floating Rupee rate	5.0 per cent	PLR + 3 per cent

Both companies are in need of ₹ 2,50,00,000 for a period of 5 years. The interest rates on the floating rate are reset annually. The current PLR for various period maturities are as follows.

Maturity (Years)	PLR (per cent)
1	2.75
2	3.00
3	3.20
4	3.30
5	3.375

DEF Ltd. has bought an Interest rate Cap at 5.625 per cent at an upfront premium payment of 0.25 per cent:

(a) You are required to exhibit how these two companies can reduce their borrowing cost by adopting swap assuming that gains resulting from swap shall be share equity among them.

(b) Further calculate cost of funding to these two companies assuming that expectation theory holds good for the 4 years.

Solution:

(a) The swap agreement will be as follows:

(i) ABC Ltd. will borrow at floating rate of PLR + 2 per cent and shall lend it to DEF Ltd. at PLR + 2 per cent and shall borrow from DEF Ltd. at Fixed Rate of 4.25 per cent.

(ii) DEF Ltd. shall borrow at 5 per cent and tend it to ABC Ltd. at 4.25 per cent and shall borrow from ABC Ltd at floating rate of PLR + 2 per cent.

Thus, net result will be as follows:

Cost to ABC Ltd. = PLR + 2 per cent – (PLR + 2 per cent) + 4.25 per cent = 4.25 per cent

Cost to DEF Ltd. = 5 per cent – 4.25 per cent + PLR + 2 per cent = PLR + 2.75 per cent

(b) Suppose if theory of expectations hold good, the cost of fund to DEF Ltd. will be as follows:

Year	Expected Annual PLR Rate	Loading	Effective Rate	Effective rate under Cap
1	2.75 per cent	275 per cent	5.50 per cent	5.50 per cent
2	(1.032 ? 1.0275) – 1 = 3.25 per cent	2.75 per cent	6.00 per cent	5.625 per cent
3	(1.0323 ? 1.032) – 1 = 3.60 per cent	2.75 per cent	6.35 per cent	5.625 per cent
4	(1.0334 ? 1.0323) – 1 = 3.60 per cent	2.75 per cent	6.35 per cent	5.625 per cent

Effective Cost = [(1.055) (1.05625)3] per cent –1 = 5.60 per cent

Q.67: The following information is available about standard gold.

Spot Price (SP)	₹ 15,600 per 10 gms
Future Price (FP)	₹ 17,100 for one year future contract
Risk-free interest rate (R)	8.5 per cent
Present value of storage cost	₹ 900 per year

From the above information you are requested to calculate the present value of Convenience yield (PVC) of the standard gold.

Solution:

$$\frac{FP}{(1+r_f)^t} = SP + PVS - PVC$$

$$PVC = SP + PVS - \frac{FP}{(1+r_f)^t}$$

Accordingly,

$$= ₹\ 15,600 + ₹\ 900 - \frac{₹\ 17,100}{(1+0.085)^1}$$

$$= ₹\ 15,600 + ₹\ 900 - ₹\ 15,760$$

$$= ₹\ 16,500 - ₹\ 15,760 = ₹\ 740$$

Q.68: ABC Technologic Is expecting' to receive a sum of US$ 4,00,000 after 3-months. The company decided to go for future contract to hedge against the risk. The standard size of future contract available in the market in the market is $ 1000. As on date spot and future $ contract are quoting at ₹ 44.00 and ₹ 45.00 respectively. Suppose after 3-months the company closes out its position futures are quoting at ₹ 44.50 and spot rate is also quoting at ₹ 44.50. You are required to calculate effective realization for the company while selling the receivable. Also calculate how the company has been benefited by using the future option.

Solution:

The company can hedge position by selling future contracts as it will receive amount from outside.

$$\text{Number of Contracts} = \frac{\$\ 4,00,000}{\$\ 1,000} = 40 \text{ contracts}$$

Gain by trading in futures = (₹ 45 – ₹ 44.50) 4,00,000 = ₹ 2,00,000

Net Inflow after 3-months = ₹ 44.50 × ₹ 4,00,000 + 2,00,000 = ₹ 1,80,000

$$\text{Effective Price realisation} = \frac{₹\ 1,80,000}{\$\ 4,00,000} = ₹\ 45 \text{ Per US \$z}$$

Q.69: XYZ borrows ₹ 20 million of 6-months LIBOR + 0.25 per cent fora period of two years. Toby, Treasury Manager of XYZ anticipates a rise in LIBOR and hence, proposes to buy a cap option from a ABC Bank at strike rate of 7 per cent. The lump sum premium is 1 per cent for the whole of the three resets period and the fixed rate of interest is 6 per cent p.a. The actual position of LIBOR during the forth coming reset period is as follows:

Reset Period	LIBOR
1	8.00 per cent
2	8.50 per cent
3	9.00 per cent

You are required to show how far interest rate risk is held through cap option.

Solution:

First of all we shall calculate premium payable to bank as follows:

$$= \frac{0.01}{(1/0.03) - \dfrac{1}{0.03 \times 1.03^4}} \times ₹\ 2,00,00,000$$

= ₹ 53,908

Now we see the net payment received from bank

Reset Period	Additional interest due to rise in interest rate (₹)	Amount received from bank (₹)	Premium paid to bank (₹)	Net Amt. received from bank (₹)
1	1,00,000	1,00,000	53,908	46,092
2	1,50,000	1,50,000	53,908	96,092
3	2,00,000	2,00,000	53,908	1,46,092
TOTAL	4,50,000	4,50,000	1,61,724	2,88,276

Thus, from above it can be seen that interest rate risk amount of ₹ 4,50,000 reduced to £ 2,88,276 by using of Cap option.

Q.70: X Ltd.'s share is currently trading at ₹ 220. It is expected that in 6-months 1 llbme if could double or halved (equipment to a 0 = 98 per cent). One year call option or T Ltd.'s share has an exercise price off ₹ 165. Assuming risk-free rate of interest be 20 per cent, calculate

(a) Value of call option on X Ltd.'s share

(b) Option delta for the second six-month, in case stock price rises to ₹ 440 or falls to ₹ 110.

(c) Now suppose in 6-months the share price is ₹ 110. How at this point we can replicate portfolio of call options and risk-free lending?

Solution:

The possible prices of X Ltd.'s share and the associated call option values shown below:

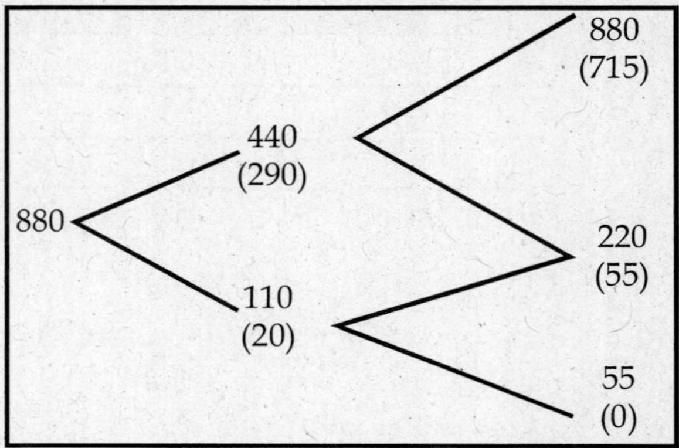

(a) Let p be the probability of a rise the stock price. Then, if investors are risk-neutral: p (1.0C) + (1 – p)(-0.50) = 0.10 p = 0,4

If the stock price in 6-month is ₹ 110, then the option wiil not be exercised. So expected value of call option is:

[(0.4 × ₹ 55) + (0.6 × ₹ O)]

And its worth to be:

[(0.4 × ₹ 55) + (0.6 × ₹ 0)]/1.10 = ₹ 20

Similarly, if the stock price is ₹ 440 in month 6, then, if it is exercised. The expected value of call option is:

[(0.4 × ₹ 715) + (0.6 × ₹ 55)]

And it will be worth:

[(0.4 × ₹ 715) + (0.6 × ₹ 55)]/1.10 = ₹ 290

Value of call today is:

[(0.4 × ₹ 290) + (0.6 × ₹ 20)]/1.10 = ₹ 116.36

(b) (i) If the price rises to ₹ 440:

$$\text{Delta} = \frac{₹715 - ₹55}{₹.880 - ₹220} = 1.0$$

(ii) If the price falls to ₹ 110:

$$\text{Delta} = \frac{₹\ 55 - 0}{₹\ 220 - ₹\ 55} = 0.33$$

(c) If the stock price is ₹ 110 at 6-months, the option delta is 0.33. Therefore, in order to replicate the stock, we buy three calls and lend, as follows:

	Initial Qutaly	**Stock Price = 55**	**Stock Price = 220**
Buy 3 calls	–60	0	165
Lend PV (55)	–50	+55	+55
	–110	+55	+220
This strategy is equivalent to:			
By stock	–110	+55	+220

Q.71: TMC Corporation entered into € 3.5 million notional principal interest rate swap agreement. As per the agreement TMC is to Pay a fixed rate and to receive a floating rate of LIBOR.

The payment will be made at the time of interval of 90 days for one year and it will be based on the adjustment factor 90/360. The term structure of LIBOR on the date of agreement is as follows:

Days	Rate (per cent)
90	7.00
180	7.25
270	7.45
360	7.55

You are required calculate fixed rate on the swap and first net payments on the swap.

Solution:

(i) The discount bond prices are as follows:

Term	Rate per cent	Discount Bond Price
90 days	7.00	B0(90) = 1/(1 + 0.07(90/360)) = 0.9828
180 days	7.25	B0(180) = 1/(1 + 0.0725(180/360)) = 0.9650
270 days	7.45	B0(270) = 1/(1 + 0.0745(270/360)) = 0.9471
360 days	7.55	B0(360) = 1/(1 + 0.0755(360/360)) = 0.9298

The fixed rate is:

$$\frac{(1-0.9298)}{(0.9828+0.9650+0.9471+0.9298)} \times \frac{(360)}{(90)} = 0.0734$$

(ii) The first net payment is based on a fixed rate of 7.34 per cent and a floating rate of 7 per cent.

Fixed payment ∊ 35,00,000(0.0734) (90/360) = ∊ 64,225

Floating payment: ∊ 35,00,000(0.07) (90/360) = ∊ 61,250

The net is that the party paying fixed makes a payment of ∊ 2,975

Q.72 Consider the following six cases of call option

	Cases					
	1	2	3	4	5	6
Spot price at expiration	80	90	100	110	120	130
Strike price	100	100	100	100	100	100

Find in each case (1) whether the option is in the money, at the money or out of the money and (2) value of option (to its owner) at expiration

Solution:

Cases	In, out or at	Value
1	Out	0
2	Out	0
3	At	0
4	In	10
5	In	20
6	In	30

Example (ii)

What will be your answers if the option in examples (i) are put options?

Case	In, out or at	Value
1	In	20
2	In	10
3.	At	0
4	Out	0
5	Out	0
6	Out	0

Four possibilities regarding possible prices

Possibilities	Possible Price	Probability
Up and by 10 per cent in first 6-months and again up by 10 per cent in next 6-months	100 × 1.10 × 1.10 = 121	0.70405 × 0.70505 = 0.4956
Up by 10 per cent in first 6-months and down by 10 per cent in next 6-months	100 × 1.10 × 0.90 = 99	0.70405 × 0.29595 = 0.2084
Down by 10 per cent in first 6-months and up by 10 per cent in next 6-months	100 × 0.90 × 1.10 = 99	0.29595 × 0.70405 = 0.2084
Down by 10 per cent in first 6-months and again down by 10 per cent in next 6-months	100 × 0.90 × 0.90 = 81	0.29595 × 0.29595 = 0.0886

Computation of value of ECO

Place on maturity	Gain	Probability	Expected gain
121	21	0.4956	10.41
99	0	0.4168	0
81	0	0.0876	0
		Total	10.41

Expected value of call on the date of maturity = ₹ 10.41

Value of option on the date of its writing: (10.41)e-0.08 = ₹ 9.61

Q.73: The equity share of Murari Ltd., is currently selling at ₹ 100. Find the value of 6-months maturity put option, strike price ₹ 101, risk-free rate of interest 12 per cent p.a. Over 3-month period, it is expected to go up by 10 per cent or go down by 10 per cent. Over next 3-month period, it is expected to go up by 8 per cent or go down by 6 per cent.

Solution:

$$P = \frac{110-90}{110-90} = 0.65$$

Probability pricing going up by 10 per cent over 3-months time – 0.65 Probability pricing going down by 10 per cent over 3-months time = 0.35 if at the end of 3-months the price is 10:

$$P = \frac{113.30-103.4}{118.8-103.4} = 0.6429$$

Probability pricing going up by 8 per cent over next 3-months time = 0.6429

Probability pricing going down by 6 per cent over next 3-months time = 0.3571

If at the end of 3-months the price is 90:

$$P = \frac{92.70 - 84.60}{97.20 - 84.60} = 0.6429$$

Probability pricing going up by 8 per cent over next 3-months time = 0.6429 Prob. pricing going down by 6 per cent over next 3-months time = 0.357 Four possibilities regarding possible prices:

Possibilities	Possible Price	Probability
Up by 10 per cent in first three-months and again up by 8 per cent in next 3-months	100 × 1.10 × 1.08 = 118.80	0.65 × 0.6429 = 0.4179

Possibilities	Possible Price	Probability
Up by the 10 per cent in first six-months and down in 6 per cent in next months	100 × 1.10 × 0.94 = 103.40	0.65 × 0.3571 = 0.2321
Down to 10 per cent in first 3-months and up by 8 per cent in next 3-months	100 × 0.90 × 1.08 = 97.20	0.35 × 0.6429 = 0.2250
Down by 10 per cent in first 3-months and again down by 6 per cent in next 3-month	100 × 0.90 × 0.94 = 84.60	0.35 × 0.3571 = 0.1250

Expect value of put in the date of maturity = ₹ 2.905

Value of option on the date of it writing: 2.905/1.06 = 2.7406

Q.74: You are given the following details about options currently traded on equity shares of Gopalji Ltd.

1 year maturity call: Strike priced ₹ 60: call Premium ₹ 12

1 year maturity put: Strike price ₹ 60: put Premium ₹ 3

If risk-free rate of return is 10 per cent p.a. find the spot price.

Solution:

As per PCPT: Spot price + per premium

= Call premium + present value of strike price

Spot price + 3 = 12 + 60(0.9048)

Spot price = 63.29

Q.75: X is holding of 5,00,000 ordinary shares of Y Ltd. H apprehends a decline in the prices of the shares and hence, he is thinking of selling these shares, though he is in quit sure that after 3-months, these shares will be the share Blanket's darling. His portfolio manager has suggested that the risk of Y Ltd.'s shares falling by more than 5 per cent from their current value could be protected against by buying option. The appropriate option maturity 3-months option is being traded for ₹ 11 million.

Other information:

(i) The current market price of Y's ordinary shares is ₹ 360.

(ii) The annual volatility (SD) of Y's shares for the last year was 50 per cent.

(iii) The risk-free rate is 10 per cent per year.

(iv) No dividend is expected to be paid by Y Ltd. during the next six-months.

Evaluate whether or not the price of the option is a fair price

Solution:

In case of (360/342) = (1.0526)

In case of (1.05) = 0.0488

In case of (1.06) = 0.0583

For LHS diff. of 0.01, RHS diff. is 0.0095

For LHS diff. of 0.0026, RHS diff. is: (0.0095/0.01) × 0.0026 i.e., 0.0025

In case of (1.0526) = 0.0488 + 0.0025 = 0.0513

$$d_1 = \frac{0.0513 + \left[0.10 + 0.50(0.50)^2\right] \times 0.25}{0.50 \times 0.50} = 0.4301$$

$$d_2 = \frac{0.0513 + \left[0.10 - 0.50(0.50)^2\right] \times 0.25}{0.50 \times 0.50} = 0.1801$$

Calculation of N (d_1)

For d_1 = 0.43, N(d_1) = 0.6664

For d_1 = 0.44, N(d_1) = 0.6700

When LHS ↑ by 0.01, RHS ↑ by 0.0036

When LHS ↑ by 1, RHS ↑ by 0.3600

When LHS ↑ by 0.0001, RHS ↑ by 0.3600 × 0.0001 i.e., by 0.000036

Hence, For d_1 = 0.4301, N (d_1) = 0.6664 + 0.000036 = 0.666436

Calculation of $N(d_2)$:

For d_2 = 0.18, $N(d_2)$ = 0.5714

For d_2 = 0.19, $N(d_1)$ = 0.5753

When LHS ↑ by 0.01, RHS ↑ by 0.0039

When LHS ↑ by 1, RHS ↑ by 0.39

When LHS T by 0.0001, RHS ↑ by 0.39 × .0001 i.e., by 0.000039

Hence, for d_2 = 0.1801, N (d_2) = 0.5714 + 0.000039 = 0.571439

Value of ECO = 360 × 0.666436 – 342 × e-10 × .25 × 0.571439 = 49.31

As per "Put Call Parity Theory"

Spot Price + put premium – call premium + PV of strike Price

As per perium = 49.31 + 342 × $e^{-10 \times .25}$

Value at ECO (also called as put premium) = ξ 22.87

As per premium on 5,00,000 shares = 5,00,000 × 22.87 = ξ 1,14,35,000.

The premium quoted in the market is fair (rather it is slightly less than the fair amount).

Q.76: A company borrows ₹ 1 billion at a floating rate of LIBOR + 0.60 per cent for 1 year, interest payable at the end of the year. The company apprehends that LIBOR may rise and hence, it is considering to hedge the interest rate. The company buys a cap at LIBOR 6.5 per cent for a premium of 1.15 per cent per year. Calculate the effective interest rates assuming the LIBOR rate for the next year is (i) 4.7 per cent (ii) 5.8 per cent, (iii) 7.3 per cent.

Solution:

	I	II	III
LIBOR	4.70	5.80	7.30
Addition	0.60	0.60	0.60
Cap perimum	1.15	1.15	1.15
Compensation from cal seller	–	–	–
Total	6.45	7.55	8.25

Q.77: Suppose today is 1st April 2007. A iMl Is to invest T 10,00,000 on 1st July 2007 for a period of 1 year. A Ltd. apprehends that the interest rates may decline by the time it will invest. At present the interest applicable to the investment for 1 year is 9.75 per cent p.a. A Ltd. approaches a bank for an FRA. The bank quotes the rate of 9.50 per cent p.a. The parties enter into an FRA on the basis of (1) the facts given in lie question and (2) the rate quoted by the bank. On reference date, the interest rate prevailing in the market is 9.00.

- Explain the execution of the FRA
- What amount will be invested by A Ltd. on 1st July 2007?
- What amount will be received by A Ltd. on 1st July 2007?

Solution:

(a) A Ltd. suffers loss on a account of interest rate decline. This loss will compensated by the bank. The bank will pay A Ltd. L

10,00,000 × 0.0005 × 1 × (1/1.09) = 4587.16

(b) A Ltd. shall deposit 10,04,587.16 for one year at 9 per cent

(c) A Ltd. will receive on maturity: 10,04,587.16 (1.09) = 10,95,000

Q.78: Madhav Ltd., Keshav Ltd. and Damodar Ltd. are planning to raise a loan of ₹ 10m each. Madhav is interested on fixed rate basis. Keshav on MIBOR-based floating rate and Damodar on treasury-based floating rate. They have been offered the loans on the following basis:

	Madhav	Keshav	Damodar
Fixed Rate	6 per cent	7 per cent	8 per cent
MIBOR Based Rate	M + 1	M + 3	M + 4
T. Bill Based Rate	T+3	T+5	T+5

An intermediary brings them to the table and an interest swap is arranged. The intermediary takes 0.10 of total savings as its commission and balance, i.e., 0.90 is shared equally by Madhav, Keshav and Damodar

Solution:

Various permutations of borrowing by their own choices

	Madhav	Keshav	Damodar
Own Choice	Fixed	M based	T bill based
Other Permutations:			
(i)	Fixed	T based	M based
(ii)	M based	Fixed	T based
(iii)	-do-	T based	Fixed
(iv)	T based	Fixed	M based
(v)	-do-	M based	Fixed

Various permutations of borrowing by their own choices

	Madhav	Keshav	Damodar	Total cost
Own Choice	6 per cent	M + 3	T + 5	M + T + 14
Other Permutation				
(i)	6 per cent	M + I	M+ I	T + 3
(ii)	T + 5	7 per cent	T + 5	796
(iii)	M + 4	T + 5	8 per cent	M + 4
(iv)	M + T + 15	M + T + 13	M + T + 14	M + T + 14
(v)	T + 3	M + 3	8 per cent	M + T + 14

Various Borrowing methods:

Madhav	M + 1
Keshav	7 per cent
Damodar	T + 5
Total cost as per recommended borrowings:	M + T + 13
Total Borrowing as per own choices:	M + T + 14
Savings	1 per cent
To be shared by:	
Intermediary	0.10
Madhav	0.30
Keshav	0.30
Damodar	0.30

Q.79: A Ltd. and B Ltd. want to raise a debt off 10 crore each. A'can borrow either at fixed rate of 8.50 per cent or at MIBOR + 0.50 per cent p.a. B can borrow either at 10.50 per cent p.a. or at MIBOR + 1.10 per cent. A is interested in floating rate while B wants fixed interest rate. An intermediary brings both the parties and suggests a swap for a commission of 0.10 per cent of the principals sum. The intermediary suggests that A should pay B at the rate if MIBOR + 0.10 while B should pay A at 9 per cent. Should the parties agree to this arrangement?

Solution:

A should borrow at fixed basis and B at floating basis.

A shall pay 8.50 + M 4 – 0.10 + 0.10 (commission) = M + 8.70. A shall receive 9 per cent. Net cost to A = M – 0.30 (had it borrowed as per its own choice the cost would have been M + 0.50 per cent).

B shall pay 9 + M + 1.10 –r 0.10 = M + 10.20. B receives M + 0.10. Net cost = 10.10 (had B borrowed as per its own choice, the cost would have been 10.50 per cent).

Savings to A: (M + 0.50) – (M - 0.30) = 0.80 per cent)

Savings to B: 10.50 per cent – 10.10 = 0.40 per cent

Commission income to Intermediary = 0.10 per cent + 0.10 per cent, i.e., 0.20 per cent of ₹ 10.00 crores.

Though the arrangement is in the interest of all the parties, it is more beneficial for A than B. The reason may be the fact that A's Credit rating is better than that of B. should try to negotiate to get the arrangement changed on its favour. Even if B does not get any gain from the negotiation, the arrangement should be accepted by all the parties including B.

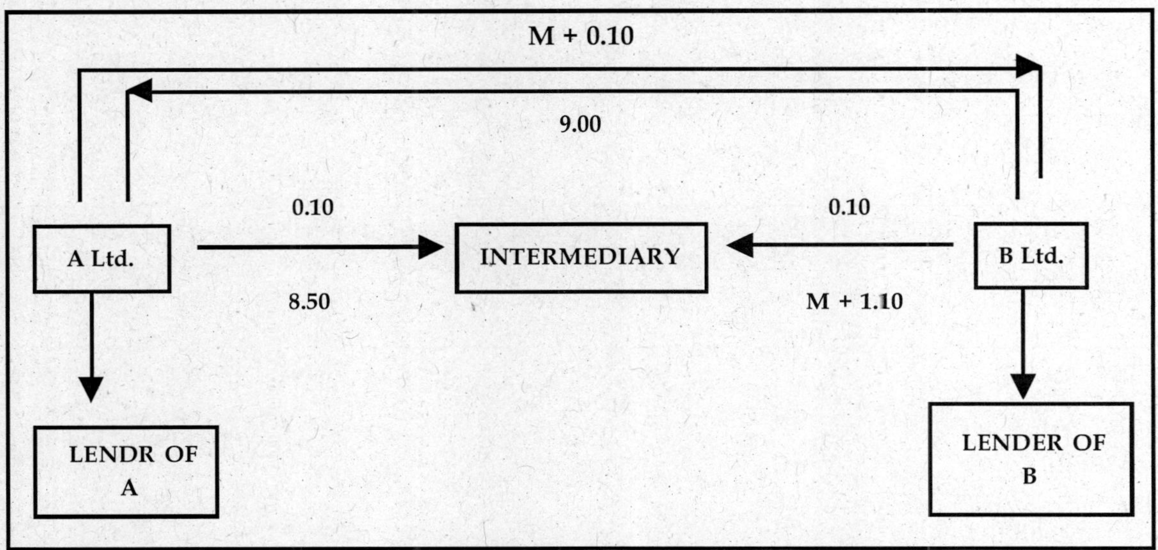

Q.80: Man Mohan Ltd. is to receive ₹ 1.04 million after 6-months from today. They plan deposit this amount with their bank for three-months immediately on receipt. They want to use this amount for purchasing a machine after 9-months from today. They apprehend decline in interest rates by the time they rephrase the money with the bank.

Currently interest rates are as follows:

3-months : 7 per cent – 8.50 per cent

6-months : 7.50 per cent – 8.50 per cent

9-months : 9 per cent – 10 per cent

How can the interest rate risk be hedged?

Solution:

(i) Borrow ₹ 1.04 million/1.04 i.e., ₹ 1 million for 6-months.

(ii) The borrowed amount plus interest that amount may be repaid using the business receipts of 1.4 million.

(iii) The borrowed amount may be invested at 9 per cent for 9-months. Investments proceeds ₹ 1 million (1.0675), i.e., ₹ 1.0675 million. Use this amount for purchasing the machine/other business purposes. Interest income = ₹ 1.0675 million – ₹ 1.04 million = ₹ 0.0275 million.

Q.81: Euro currently trades at ₹ 58. Two European options are currently quoted

Put A : Strike price ₹ 63, Premium ₹ 4

Put B : Strike price ₹ 68, Premium ₹ 10

Explain how the operator (say his name is X) arbitrage profit can be made.

Solution:

Buy A and Sell B

> ***Teaching note:*** For arbitrage profit, there should be profit in each and every situation. One such situation in the question is that neither of puts are exerxised, i.e., spot price on maturity is higher than 68; in this case the profit will be in form of savings of premiums. Savings of the premium as possible only if we buy A and sell B.

If price on maturity is? 63, say 62; both options will be exercised.

Profit: + 1 – 6 + 6 = 1

If price on maturity is 68, neither will be exercised. Profit: 6

Price 63 or more but up to 68

Price	Profit
63	0 – 5 + 6 = 1
64	0 – 4 + 6 = 2
65	0 – 3 + 6 = 3
66	0 – 2 + 6 = 4
67	0 – 1 + 6 = 5
68	0 – 0 + 6 = 6

Q.82: A biscuit Manufacturer has to purchase 1000 Quintal of "B Quality wheat" after 6-months from today, he apprehends a rise in the prices of the wheat during this period. An enquiry from the futures market reveals that 'B Quality Wheat' is not traded in the futures market, though 'A Quality Wheat' is being traded. His experience shows that 'B Quality Wheat' is always traded in the market at 80 per cent of 'A Quality wheat' price. How the manufacturer can hedge his risk?

Solution:

The manufacturer should enter into a futures 6-month maturity contract to purchase 800 Quintals of 'A Quality Wheat'. The profit from the futures contract of 'A Quality Wheat' will set off (more or less) the loss on actual purchase of B Quality Wheat'.

Q.83: M/s Yashodha Jewellery (YJ), a Gokul Based firm receives an export order from UK for supplying silver jewellery. The goods are to be supplied in 1-month. The export price is decided on the basis of the silver prices prevailing in the spot market on the date of receiving the order. YJ immediately purchased 50 kgs of silver for executing this order.

All of the sudden there was strike in their factory. It is expected to continue for 1-month. YJ communicates to the importer that it can supply the goods in 2-months' time. The importer agrees to changed supply schedule but with a condition. The condition is that the export price will be decided on the basis of the silver prices prevailing in the spot market on the date of shipment. YJ accepts this condition.

YJ apprehends fall in the silver prices. Suggest the action for hedging the risk relating to prices of silver. Ignore interest and warehousing costs.

Solution:

YJ may enter into a 2-month maturity futures contract of selling 50 kgms of silver. The profit from the futures contract will offset (more or less) the loss on account of decrease in export price.

Chapter 18 Accounting Aspects of Derivatives

In India there are currently no guidelines available for accounting of derivative transactions. In most cases in India, securities are valued at lower than cost or market value, applying the principles of conservatism. The Institute of Chartered Accountants of India (ICAI) has framed guidance note the same is not sufficient to account for different types of derivatives. India has issued Ind-ASs therefore, accounting guidance is available in Ind-AS 39 which is equivalent to corresponding IAS 39. However, the Ministry of Company Affairs (MCA) has not notified the effective date to implement Ind-ASs in India. Therefore, in India currently, the following accounting practices could be considered on conservatism basis:

- Unrealised losses on derivative transactions should be recognised, while unrealised profits should not be accounted until realisation.
- Realised profits and losses would be carried to the Profit & Loss Account.

Initial margins paid against Futures will be reflected as assets. Mere payment of margins will not qualify as profits or losses, though in most cases, the amounts of such margins will be based on the price movements of the futures in the market.

Accounting entry would be:

Initial Margin Account Dr.

To Bank/Cash

There is a controversy currently on whether daily payment of margins and daily 'settlement' amounts to daily 'realisation' of profits or losses for the purposes of accounting. If the daily 'settlement' is construed as daily 'realisation', then the question of 'unrealised' profits or losses will not arise.

ANNOUNCEMENT ON ACCOUNTING FOR DERIVATIVES

Looking at the current economic environment, the Council of the Institute of Chartered Accountants of India at its meeting held on March 27-29, 2008, made an announcement that the entities not opting for earlier adoption of AS 30, keeping in view the principle as enunciated in AS 1, Disclosure of Accounting Policies, are required to provide for losses with respect to all outstanding derivative contracts at the balance sheet date by marking them to market and make a separate disclosure of the losses provided. Those entities that have adopted the standard early have to disclose the amounts recognised in the in the financial statements. Can an entity that has gains from derivative transactions recognise those gains?

An entity that recognises gains from derivative transactions would be deemed to have adopted AS 30 early. Selective application of AS 30 is not possible. Hence, there is no prohibition on entities recognising gains on derivative transactions provided they also apply the categorisation, recognition, derecognition, initial and subsequent measurement, impairment and all other provisions of AS 30.

International Accounting Practices

International practices vary from country to country and could apply differently to various types of derivatives transactions, for example, those that seek to use index Futures as against those that attempt to protect cash-flow regularity. It is important to first recognise whether the index Future is a 'hedge' or not. If the transaction is not a 'hedge,' it would be treated as a 'trading' transaction.

Prior designation of hedging instrument and hedged item is essential to curb the scope for use of discretion for divergent interpretation and accounting treatment. This can be explained with the help of following illustration. Suppose a business entity is holding an investment and debt. The investment is earning fixed interest and interest on debt is payable in Libor. To achieve asset liability match the business entity enter in swap to designate either the fixed interest earning investment as hedging instrument and interest tied to Libor debt as hedged item or the fixed interest earning investment as hedged item and interest tied to Libor debt as hedging instrument. The former is fair value hedge and later is cash-flow hedge. The accounting treatment for fair value hedge is different from cash-flow hedge and should not be left to the discretion of business entity for designation at later date.

HEDGE ACCOUNTING

1. Fair Value Hedge Accounting

Query

Chew and Melt Ltd. (C&M) maintains an inventory of cocoa that it uses in the production of chocolate. C&M wants to hedge the risk of price changes in the cocoa inventory, and on 1 July 2005 enters into a forward derivative instrument that is indexed to cocoa. At 30 September 2005, there is no ineffectiveness. The fair value of the cocoa inventory has decreased by ₹ 50,000 and the fair value of the derivative increased by ₹ 50,000.

Answer: Accounting will be as follows as per Ind AS 39

Journal Entry: 1 July 2005

No entries are required because the forward was entered into at market (it has a fair value of zero).

Journal Entry: 30 September 2005

Forward Derivative Contract Debit	₹ 50,000	
Hedging Gain Credit		₹ 50,000

(To record the increase in the fair value of the derivative)

Journal Entry: 30 September 2005

Hedging Gain Debit	₹ 50,000	
Cocoa Inventory Credit		₹ 50,000

(To record the decrease in the fair value of the inventory)

In the above example, though the value of the inventory of cocoa has gone down, because the loss is fully hedged there is no charge to the income statement.

2. Cash-flow Hedge Accounting

Query

On January 4, 20x2, Pawan Ltd. has forecasted sale of 10,00,000 kg of chemical on or about 15 December 20x2 to Lohia Ltd. in UK. On January 4, 20x2, Pawan Ltd. designates the cash-flow of the forecast sale as a hedged item and enters into a forward exchange contract to sell 4 million pound based on the forecast receipt (10,00,000 kg at Pound 4 per kg). The forward contract locks in the value of the Pound to be received at a rate of 1 Pound = ₹ 80. At inception of the hedge, the derivative is on-market (i.e., fair value is zero).

On June 30, 20x2, the fair value of the forward contract is negative ₹ 1,00,000 because the forward rate has changed, reflecting the fact that the Rupees has weakened against Pounds. On December 31, 20x2 the transaction occurred as expected. The fair value of the forward is negative ₹ 1,50,000 as the Rupees continued to weaken against pound.

Answer: Accounting will be as follows as per Ind AS 39:

January 4, 20x2

No entries are required since the forward contract was entered "on-market", and therefore had a fair value of zero at inception.

June 30, 20x2

Dr. Equity	1,00,000	
Cr. Forward Contract		1,00,000

(To recognise the forward at fair value, reflecting that the forward contract is fully effective in hedging the forward rate of the forecast transaction)

December 31, 20x2

Dr. Equity	50,000	
Cr. Forward Contract		50,000

(To reflect further change in fair value of the forward)

Dr. Forward Contract	1,50,000	
Cr. Cash		1,50,000

(To reflect the cash paid in settling the forward contract)

Dr. Cash	3,20,150,000	
Cr. Sales		3,20,150,000

(To reflect receipt of 4 million pounds from the sale of chemical translated at the spot rate)

Dr. Sales	1,50,000	
Cr. Equity		1,50,000

(To reflect the cumulative effective portion of the hedging instrument included in equity that is released from equity to profit or loss when sales occurs.)

As can be seen from the above example, by applying cash-flow hedge, the loss of foreign exchange hedge is parked temporarily in equity and is recycled to the profit and loss account when the underlying transaction takes place at a gain. By doing so matching happens.

3. Net Investment Hedge Accounting

Example

Entity A, a UK entity with a Sterling functional currency, has a US subsidiary with a US dollar functional currency, Entity B. To finance this subsidiary, Entity A has a US$ 50 million US dollar loan with a third party bank. Entities A and B have the same 31 December year end and the net assets of Entity Bat 31 December 20x1 and 31 December 20x2 were US$ 70 million.

The loan is designated as a hedging instrument of the first US$ 50 million of net assets of Entity B. The designation is spot retranslation risk only. The hedge is determined to be highly effective. The US$/£ spot rate on 31/12/x1 is 1.6 and on 31/12/x2 it is 1.7.

On 31/12/x2 the entries are as follows:

Dr. Loan ₹ 1.84m

Cr. Other comprehensive income ₹ 1.84m

(To recognise the foreign exchange gain on the loan. This is the difference between US$ 50m translated at 1.6 and 1.7).

Dr. Other comprehensive income ₹ 2.57m

Cr. Net assets ₹ 2.57m

(To retranslate the net assets. This is the difference between US$ 70m translated at 1.6 and 1.7.)

The entire exchange difference on retranslating the net assets of the foreign operation is taken to other comprehensive income in accordance with Ind AS 21. The application of hedge accounting results in the remeasurement of the loanbeing recognised in other comprehensive income as opposed to profit or loss. No hedge in effectiveness has been recognised. Hedge in effectiveness would have arisen if the net assets of the foreign operation fell below US$ 50m at the period end.

Accounting for hedges differs significantly from regular accounting practices, as the recognition of profits or losses on hedge transactions are adjusted in the carrying amount of the underlying securities instead of being taken to the profit and loss account.

The application of hedge accounting principles will also depend on the method of valuation used for the underlying security. Where the underlying security is valued at cost, the hedge will also be valued at cost. Where the underlying security is marked-to-market, the hedge will also be marked-to-market. Where the underlying security is valued at lower of cost or market value, the hedge and the underlying security will be bundled together to ascertain the aggregate cost and market values respectively, and the lower of the two of the bundle will be considered for valuation.

Trading transactions

Internationally, trading transactions are marked-to-market. Accordingly, both unrealised losses and profits are taken to the profit & loss account. This is a significantly different practice, *vis-a-vis* the most common Indian conservative accounting practice of recognising only unrealised losses.

Trading transactions will include general hedges, i.e., those hedging transactions, which are not specifically related to specific assets or liabilities or commitments. Further, trading transactions will also include those specific hedge transactions, which do not meet all the defined criteria and hence, cannot follow hedge accounting principles.

Some examples are given below:

1. **First Year:** Underlying securities purchased for ₹ 2,00,000.
   - Index Futures sold for ₹ 2,00,000 and margin of ₹ 20,000 paid
   - Further margins of ₹ 5,000 paid from time-to-time
   - Year end values of underlying securities ₹ 1,90,000
   - Year end value of Futures ₹ 2,10,000.
2. **Second year:** the underlying securities are sold.
   - Underlying securities sold for ₹ 2,25,000
   - Futures contract has not expired and closing price comes to ₹ 2,05,000
   - Futures margin paid ₹ 8,000.
3. **Second Year:** the Futures transaction expires.
   Margins paid further ₹ 8,000
   - Futures contract expires at a closing value of ₹ 2,15,000
   - Amount receivable is immediately received.

Indian Accounting are as follows:

The accounting entries in the Indian context are given below:

1. First Year

	Debit	Credit
Debit Investments (Assets)	2,00,000	
Credit Bank		2,00,000
(Being Investment purchased)		
Debit Margins (Assets)	20,000	
Credit Bank		20,000
(Being margin money paid)		

Debit Margins (Assets)	5,000	
Credit Bank		5,000
(Being further margin money paid)		
Year End		
Debit Diminution in Investment (Expense)	10,000	
Credit Investments (Assets)		10,000
(Being loss on investment)		

Note: Unrealised gains on Futures ₹ 10,000 are not to be accounted as a matter of prudence concept.

Balance sheet impact

Investments will be reflected at ₹ 1,90,000

Profit & loss impact

Diminution in investments will reduce profits by ₹ 10,000

2. Second year

Debit Bank	2,25,000	
Credit Investments (Assets)		1,90,000
Credit Profit on sale of Investments (Gain)		35,000
(Being sale of investment)		

Note: No entry for Futures as no profits realised so far

Debit Margins (Assets)	8,000	
Credit Bank		8,000
(Being further margin money paid)		

3. Second year

Debit Margins	8,000	
Credit Bank		8,000
(Being further margin paid)		
Debit Bank	42,500	
Credit Profits on Futures		10,000
Credit Margins (released)		32,000

(2,15,000 – 2,05,000 = ₹ 10,000 profit on futures and received margin money)

Accounting for payments/receipts in respet of finitial margin is common for all types of Equity Derivative Instruments contracts.

Example 1: ACCOUNTING FOR INITIAL MARGIN

Suppose Mr. X enters into certain Equity Derivative Instruments contracts on March 28, 2003. The Initial Margin on these contracts, calculated as per the SPAN, is ₹ 30,000. The Margin for the sub-sequent days, calculated as per the SPAN, is as follows:

On 29th March, 2003	₹ 35,000
On 30th March, 2003	₹ 25,000
On 31st March, 2003	₹ 27,000

SUGGESTED ACCOUNTING TREATMENT

1. **The following entries may be passed for the payment/receipt of the Initial Margin:**

Date	Particulars		Dr. (₹)	Cr. (₹)
28/3/03	Initial Margin-Equity Derivative Inst. A/c	Dr.	₹ 30,000	
	To Bank A/c			₹ 30,000
	(Being initial margin paid on Equity Derivative Instruments contracts)			
29/3/03	Initial Margin-Equity Derivative Inst. A/c	Dr.	₹ 5,000	
	To Bank A/c			₹ 5,000
	(Being further margin paid to the exchange)			
30/3/03	Bank A/c	Dr.	₹ 10,000	
	To Initial Margin-Equity Derivative Inst. A/c			₹ 10,000
	(Being are fund of margin from the exchange)			
31/3/03	Initial Margin-Equity Derivative Inst. A/c	Dr.	₹ 2,000	
	To Bank A/c			₹ 2,000
	(Being further margin paid to the exchange)			

2. **The Initial Margin paid on Equity Derivative Instruments will be disclosed in the balance sheet as follows:**

   Extracts from the Balance Sheet

   Current Assets

   Initial Margin-Equity Derivative Instruments A/c ₹ 27,000

3. **Inrespect of initial margin, the following disclosure may be made in the notes to accounts:**

   'Initial Margin on Equity Derivative Instruments contracts has been paid in cash only.'

Example 2 (A): ACCOUNTING FOR EQUITY INDEX FUTURES

(A) Accounting for payment/receipt of Mark-to-Market Margin

1. Suppose Mr. A purchases the following units of Equity Index Futures:

Date of Purchase	Name of the Futures Contract	Expiry Date/ Series	Contract Price per Unit (₹)	Contract Multiplier (No. of Units)
28th March, 20x3	EF1	May 20x3	1,420	200
29th March, 20x3	EF2	June 20x3	4,280	50
29th March, 20x3	EF1	May 20x3	1,416	200

2. Daily Settlement Prices of the above units of Equity Index Futures are as follows:

Date	EF1 May Series (₹)	EF2 June Series (₹)
28/03/20x3	1,410	–
29/03/20x3	1,428	4,300
30/03/20x3	1,435	4,270
31/03/20x3	1,407	4,290

SUGGESTED ACCOUNTING TREATMENT

1. The amount of Mark-to-Market Margin Money received/paid due to increase/ decrease in Daily Settlement Prices is as below:

Date	EF1 May Series (₹)		EF2 June Series (₹)		Net Amount (₹)	
	Receive	Pay	Receive	Pay	Receive	Pay
28/03/20x3	–	2,000	–	–	–	2,000
29/03/20x3	6,000	–	1,000	–	7,000	–
30/03/20x3	2,800	–	–	1,500	1,300	–
31/03/20x3	–	11,200	1,000	–	–	10,200

2. The amount of Mark-to-Market Margin Money received/paid will be credited/ debited to 'Mark-to-Market Margin - EIF A/c' by passing the following entries:

Date	Particulars	L.F.	Debit (₹)	Credit (₹)
March 20x3				
8	Mark-to-Market Margin-EIF A/c Dr. To Bank A/c (Being net MTMM argin Money paid for day)		2,000	 2,000

29	Bank A/c Dr. To Mark-to-Market Margin-EIF A/c (Being net MTMM argin Money received)	7,000	7,000
30	Bank A/c Dr. To Mark-to-Market Margin-EIF A/c (Being net MTMM argin Money received)	1,300	1,300
31	Mark-to-Market Margin-EIF A/c Dr. To Bank A/c (Being net MTMM argin Money paid for day)	10,200	1,0200
	Total	20,500	20,500

3. On the above basis, 'Mark-to-Market Margin-EIF A/c' for the year will appear as follows in the books of Mr. A:

Mark-to-Market Margin-EIF A/c

Date	Particulars	Debit (₹)	Credit (₹)	Balance	
				Dr./Cr.	Amount (₹)
March					
28	To Bank	2,000		Dr.	2,000
29	By Bank		7,000	Cr.	5,000
30	By Bank		1,300	Cr.	6,300
31	To Bank	10,200		Dr.	3,900
31	By Balance c/d		3,900		
	Total	12,200	12,200		

(B) Accounting for Open Interests on the Balance Sheet date

SUGGESTED ACCOUNTING TREATMENT

1. Continuing example 2 (A) above, on 31st March, 20x3, Mark-to-Market (MTM) Margin Money received paid on all the contracts in each of the indexes is as follows:

   Amount paid on the contracts in respect of EF1 ₹ 4,400

   Amount received on the contracts in inrespect of EF2 ₹ 500

2. Keeping in view the consideration of prudence, a provision should be created for anticipated loss on open contracts in respect of EF1. equivalent to the a mount paid, by passing the following entry, whereas the amount received in open contracts in respect of EF2 would be ignored:

Profit & Loss A/c Dr. ₹ 4,400

To Provision for Loss-EIF A/c ₹ 4,400

(Being provision created for the amount paid to Clearing Member/Trading Member on account of movement in the prices of the contracts in respect of EF1)

3. In the balance sheet, the debit balance of 'Mark-to-Market Margin-EIF A/c' and 'Provision for Loss-EIFAccount' would be shown as follows:

Extracts from the Balance Sheet

Liabilities	Amount (₹)	Assets	Amount (₹)
Current Liabilities and Provisions		Current Assets, Loans and Advances:	
(A) Current Liabilities		(A) Current Assets	
(B) Provisions		(B) Loans and Advances	
Excess of Provision for Loss-EIF A/c		Mark-to-Market Margin-EIF A/c	3,900
over MTM-EIF A/c	500	*Less:* Prov. for Loss-EIF A/c	4,400
		Excess to besh own as Provision	500

4. In respect of open equity index futures contracts, the following disclosures should be made in the notes to accounts:

Detail of Open Interests in Equity Index Futures contracts

Name of Equity Index Future	No. of contracts	Units	
		Long	Short
EF1	2	400	
EF2	1	50	

(C) Accounting at the time of final settlement/squaring-up of the contracts

Continuing example 2 (A) above, the following further facts are provided:

1. Equity Index Futures contracts are squared-up at the Daily Settlement Price of the day on the following dates:
   - EF 2 June Series on 1st April, 20x3
   - 200 Units of EF1 May Series on 2nd April, 20x3
   - 200 Units of EF1 May Series on 3rd April, 20x3

2. Daily Settlement Prices of the units of Equity Index Futures, till squaring-up of the contracts, are as follows:

Date	EF1 May Series (₹)	EF2 June Series (₹)
01/04/20x3	1,415	4,250
02/04/20x3	1,430	–
03/04/20x3	1,442	–

SUGGESTED ACCOUNTING TREATMENT

1. The amount of Mark-to-Market Margin Money received/paid due to increase/decrease in Daily Settlement Prices is as below:

Date	EF1 May Series (₹)		EF2 June Series (₹)		Net Amount (₹)	
	Receive	Pay	Receive	Pay	Receive	Pay
01/04/20x3	3,200	–	–	2,000	1,200	–
02/04/20x3	6,000	–	–	–	6,000	–
03/04/20x3	2,400	–	–	–	2,400	–

2. The amount of profit/loss arising on squaring-up is calculated, using Weighted Average method, as follows:

Name of the Futures contract Series Date of Settlement	EF2 June 20x3 1st April, 20x3	EF1 May 20x3 2nd April, 20x3	EF1 May 20x3 3rd April, 20x3
Contract Price per unit (in ₹) Settlement Price per unit (in ₹) Profit (+)/Loss (–) per unit (in ₹) Number of Units	4,280 4,250 (–)30 50	1,418[1] 1,430 (+)12 200	1,418[1] 1,442 (+)24 200
Total Profit (+)/Loss (–)(in ₹)	(–)1,500	(+)2,400	(+)4,800

3. On the above basis, the following entries will be passed for the amount of Mark-to-Market Margin Money received/paid and profit/loss arising on the squaring-up:

Date	Particulars	L.F.	Debit (₹)	Credit (₹)
April 20x3				
01	Bank A/c Dr. To Mark-to-Market Margin-EIF A/c (Being net MTM Margin Money received)		1,200	 1,200
01	Profit & Loss A/c Dr. To Mark-to-Market Margin-EIF A/c (Being loss on squaring-up)		1,500	 1,500

02	Bank A/c Dr. To Mark-to-Market Margin-EIF A/c (Being net MTM Margin Money received)		6,000	6,000
02	Mark-to-Market Margin-EIF A/c Dr. To Profit & Loss A/c (Being profit on squaring-up of the contract)		2,400	2,400
03	Bank A/c Dr. To Mark-to-Market Margin-EIF A/c (Being net MTM Margin Money received)		2,400	2,400
03	Mark-to-Market Margin-EIF A/c Dr. To Profit & Loss A/c (Being profit on squaring-up of the contract)		4,800	4,800
	Total		18,300	18,300

[1]Weighted Average Price = (1,420* 200 + 1,416* 200)/400

4. In this case, 'Mark-to-Market Margin-EIF A/c' for the year will appear as follows in the books of Mr. A:

Mark-to-Market Margin-EIF A/c

Date	Particulars	Debit (₹)	Credit (₹)	Balance	
				Dr./Cr.	Amount (₹)
April 20×3					
01	To Balance b/d	3,900		Dr.	3,900
01	By Bank		1,200	Dr.	2,700
01	By Profit & Loss A/c		1,500	Dr.	1,200
02	By Bank	2,400	6,000	Cr.	4,800
02	To Profit & Loss A/c			Cr.	2,400
03	By Bank	4,800	2,400	Cr.	4,800
03	To Profit & Loss A/c				Nil
		11,100	11,100		

5. In case the contracts as above are not squared-up, but are settled on the final settlement date, the same entries as have been passed on squaring-up of the contracts, will be passed at the time of final settlement.

Example 3: ACCOUNTING FOR EQUITY STOCK FUTURES

Accounting for Equity Stock Futures which are settled in cash

The accounting treatment for Equity Stock Futures settled in cash would be the same as that in the case of Equity Index Futures. This is be cause in both the cases the settlement is done otherwise than by delivery of the underlying assets.

Accounting for Equity Stock Futures which are settled by delivery

Accounting for payment/receipt of Mark-to-Market Margin and for Open Interests as on the balance sheet date will be the same as that in case of cash-settled futures. The accounting at the time of final settlement of delivery-settled Equity Stock Futures contracts might be explained with the help of example given here under.

1. Suppose Mr. A purchases the following units of Equity Stock Futures (ESF):

Date of Purchase	ESF (Name of Company)	Expiry Date /Series	Contract Price per unit (₹)	Contract Multiplier (No. of Units)
28th March, 20×3	XYZ Ltd.	May, 20x3	1,420	200
29th March, 20×3	PQR Ltd.	June, 20x3	4,280	50
29th March, 20×3	XYZ Ltd.	May, 20x3	1,416	200

2. The contracts are settled through physical delivery of shares on the Settlement Date, i.e., both the contracts for shares of XYZ Limited (May 20x3 Series) are settled by purchasing the shares on the Settlement Date, viz., May 29, 20x3. Similarly, the contract for shares of PQR Limited (June 20x3 Series) is settled by purchasing the shares on the Settlement Date, viz., June 26, 20x3.
3 Net Mark-to-Market Margin received in respect of the contracts for shares of XYZ Limited (May 20x3 Series) till the Settlement Date is ₹ 4,000. Net Mark-to-Market Margin paid in respect of the contract for shares of PQR Limited (June 20x3 Series) till the Settlement Date is ₹ 3,500.

SUGGESTED ACCOUNTING TREATMENT

At the time of final settlement, the shares are required to be purchased/sold against the payment/receipt of the contract price. The amount paid/received earlier in the form of Mark-to-Market Margin will be adjusted against the amount payable/receivable. Accordingly, the following entries will be passed for purchase of shares on the final settlement of the contract:

Date	Particulars	L.F.	Debit (₹)	Credit (₹)
May 20x3				
29	Shares of XYZ Limited A/c Dr.		5,67,200	
	Mark-to-Market Margin-ESF A/c Dr.		4,000	
	To Cash/Bank A/c			5,71,200
	(Beings hares purchased on Settlement Date by payment of the net amount due in respect of the contracts)			

June 20x3 26	Shares of PQR Limited A/c Dr. To Cash/Bank A/c To Mark-to-Market Margin-ESF A/c (Beings hares received on settlement of contract by payment of the net amount due)		2,14,000	 2,10,500 3,500

Example 4: ACCOUNTING FOR EQUITY INDEX OPTIONS

(A) Accounting for Payment/Receipt of Premium and for Final Settlement of the Contracts

1. Suppose Mr. Abuys the following equity index options and the seller/writer of these options is Mr. B:

Date of Purchase	Type of the Options Contract	Expiry date	Premium unit (₹)	Contract Multiplier (No. of units)	Strike price (₹)
28th March, 20x3	S & PCNXNIFTY – Call	May 29, 20x3	15	200	880
28th March, 20x3	S & PCNXNIFTY – Put	May 29, 20x3	20	200	885

2. Mr. A. and Mr. B follow the calendar year as the accounting year.

SUGGESTED ACCOUNTING TREATMENT

In the books of the buyer/holder, i.e., Mr. A

1. The following entry may be passed to record the amount of premium paid:

   28/3/x3 Equity Index Option Premium A/c Dr. ₹ 7,000

   To Bank A/c ₹ 7,000

   (Being premium paid one quity Index options)

2. The following entries may be passed at the time of final settlement of the contracts:

Situation 1: Call Option May 20x3 Strike Price ₹ 880; price on expiry ₹ 875

29/5/x3 Profit and Loss A/c Dr. ₹ 3,000

To Equity Index Option Premium A/c ₹ 3,000

(Being the premium on the options contract written off on expiry of the option) Option will not be exercised in this situation.

Situation 2: Call Option May 20x3 Strike Price ₹ 880; price on expiry ₹ 890

Date	Particulars		Dr. (₹)	Cr. (₹)
29/5/x3	Bank A/c	Dr.	₹ 2,000	
	To Profit and Loss A/c			₹ 2,000
	(Being the profit on exercise of option received.)			
29/5/x3	Profit and Loss A/c	Dr.	₹ 3,000	
	To Equity Index Option Premium A/c.			₹ 3,000
	(Being the premium on the options contract written off on exercise of the option)			

Situation 3: Put Option May 20x3 Strike Price ₹ 885; price on expiry ₹ 875

Date	Particulars		Dr. (₹)	Cr. (₹)
29/5/x3	Bank A/c	Dr.	₹ 2,000	
	To Profit and Loss A/c			₹ 2,000
	(Being the profit on exercise of option received.)			
29/5/x3	Profit and Loss A/c	Dr.	₹ 4,000	
	To Equity Index Option Premium A/c			₹ 4,000
	(Being the premium on the options contract written off on exercise of the option)			

Situation 4: Put Option May 20x3 Strike Price ₹ 885; price on expiry ₹ 890

Date	Particulars		Dr. (₹)	Cr. (₹)
29/5/x3	Profit and Loss A/c	Dr.	₹ 4,000	
	To Equity Index Option Premium A/c			₹ 4,000
	(Being the premium on the options contract written off on expiry of the option) Option will not be exercised in this situation.			

In the books of the seller/writer, i.e., Mr. B

1. The following entry may be passed to record the amount of premium received:

Date	Particulars		Dr. (₹)	Cr. (₹)
28/3/x3	Bank A/c	Dr.	₹ 7,000	
	To Equity Index Option Premium A/c			₹ 7,000
	(Being the premium on option collected)			

2. The following entries may be passed at the time of final settlement of the contracts:

Situation 1: Call Option May 20x3 Strike Price ₹ 880; price on expiry ₹ 875

Date	Particulars		Dr. (₹)	Cr. (₹)
29/5/x3	Equity Index Option Premium A/c	Dr.	₹ 3,000	
	To Profit and Loss A/c			₹ 3,000
	(Being the premium on the options contract recognised as in come on expiry of the option) Option will not be exercised in this situation.			

Situation 2: Call Option May 20x3 Strike Price ₹ 880; price on expiry ₹ 890

29/5/x3	Profit and Loss A/c	Dr.	₹ 2,000	
	To Bank A/c			₹ 2,000
	(Being loss on exercise of option paid)			
29/5/x3	Equity Index Option Premium A/c	Dr.	₹ 3,000	
	To Profit and Loss A/c			₹ 3,000
	(Being the premium on the options contract recognised as income on exercise of the option)			

Situation 3: Put Option May 20x3 Strike Price ₹ 885; price on expiry ₹ 875

29/5/x3	Profit and Loss A/c	Dr.	₹ 2,000	
	To Bank A/c			₹ 2,000
	(Being loss on exercise of option paid)			
29/5/x3	Equity Index Option Premium A/c	Dr.	₹ 4,000	
	To Profit and Loss A/c			₹ 4,000
	(Being the premium on the options contract recognised as income on exercise of the option)			

Situation 4: Put Option May 20x3 Strike Price ₹ 885; price on expiry ₹ 890

29/5/x3	Equity Index Option Premium A/c	Dr.	₹ 4,000	
	To Profit and Loss A/c			₹ 4,000
	(Being the premium on the options contract recognised as income on expiry of the option) Option will not be exercised in this situation.			

(B) Accounting for Open Options at the end of an Accounting Period Countinuing with Example 4(A) above, except the following facts:

(a) Mr. A and Mr. B follow the financial year as the accounting year. Consequently, option sentered into in one accounting period are settled in an other accounting period.

(b) On 31st March, 20x3: For Call Option May 20x3 Strike Price ₹ 880, closing rate of premium ₹ 6 per unit. For Put Option May 20x3 Strike Price ₹ 885, closing rate of premium ₹ 28 per unit.

SUGGESTED ACCOUNTING TREATMENT

In the books of the buyer/holder, i.e., Mr. A

1. Net provision required to be made in the books of account would be computed as follows:

Call Option May 20x3 Strike Price	₹ 880
Premium paid	₹ 3,000
Less: Premium on the balance sheet date	₹ 1,200
Provision required	₹ 1,800
Put Option May 20x3 Strike Price	₹ 885
Premium paid	₹ 4,000
Less: Premium as on the balance sheet date	₹ 5,600
Provision required	₹ –1,600
Net provision to be made in the books of account:	₹ 200

2. The following entry may be passed to create provision for the above amount:

31/3/x3	Profit and Loss A/c	Dr.	₹ 200	
	To Provision for Loss on Equity Index Options A/c			₹ 200

(Being provision for loss on options as on 31-3-20x3)

3. In the balance sheet, the balance of 'Equity Index Options Premium Account' and 'Provision for Loss on Equity Index Options Account' would be shown as follows:

Extracts from the Balance Sheet

Current Assets:	₹
Equity Index Options Premium Account	7,000
Less: Provision for Loss on Equity Index Options	(200)
	6,800

4. In respect of the premium carried for ward (net of provisions), the following disclosure may be made in notes to accounts:

Name of Options (Equity index/stock)	Premium carried for ward as at the year-end net of provisions
S&PCNXNIFTY	₹ 6,800

5. At the time of final settlement of these contracts, the same entries would be passed as in the case of Example 4 (A) above.

In the books of the seller/writer, i.e., Mr. B

1. Net provision required to be made in the books of account may be computed as follows:

Call Option May 20x3 Strike Price	₹ 880
Premium as on the balance sheet date	₹ 1,200
Less: Premium received	₹ 3,000
Provision required	₹ –1,800
Put Option May 20x3 Strike Price	₹ 885
Premium as on the balance sheet date	₹ 5,600
Less: Premium received	₹ 4,000
Provision required	₹ 1,600
Net provision to be made in the books of account:	₹ NIL

(Since the net difference is negative.)

2. In the balance sheet, the balance of 'Equity Index Options Premium Account' would be shown as follows:

Extracts from the Balance Sheet

Current Liabilities and Provisions:	
Equity Index Options Premium Account	7,000
Provision for Losson Equity Index Options	NIL

3. In respect of the premium carried forward (including provisions), the following disclosure may be made in notes to accounts:

Name of Options (Equity index/stock)	Total Premium carried forward as at the year-end including provisions made
S&PCNXNIFTY	₹ 7,000

4. At the time of final settlement of these contracts, the same entries would be passed as in the case of Example 4 (A) above.

Example 5: ACCOUNTING FOR EQUITY STOCK OPTIONS

Accounting for Equity Stock Options which are settled in cash.

Accounting entries for Equity Stock Options settled in cash will be the same as that in the case of Equity Index Options. This is because in both the cases the settlement is done otherwise than by delivery of the underlying as sets.

Accounting for Equity Stock Options which are settled by delivery.

Accounting entries for the payment/receipt of premium and for open options at the balance sheet date will be the same as that in the case of cash settled options. The accounting entries at the time off in a settlement, presuming that options are exercised, will be as follows:

Suppose Mr. Abuys the following Equity Stock Options and the seller/writer of the options is Mr. B

Date of Purchase	Type of the Options contract	Expiry date	Market Lot	Premium per unit	Strike price (₹)
27th June, 20x3	XYZ Co. Limited-Call	August 28, 20x3	100	15	230
30th June, 20x3	ABC Co. Limited-Put	August 28, 20x3	200	20	275

SUGGESTED ACCOUNTING TREATMENT

In the books of the buyer/holder, i.e., Mr. A

1. The following entries may be passed at the time of exercise of the Call Option:

   Equity Shares of XYZ Limited A/c Dr. ₹ 23,000

   To Bank A/c ₹ 23,000

   (Being Call Option exercised and shares acquired)

   Profit and Loss A/c Dr. ₹ 1,500

   To Equity Stock Option Premium A/c ₹ 1,500

   (Being the premium on the options contract written off on exercise of the option)

2. The following entries may be passed at the time of exercise of the Put Option:

   Bank A/c Dr. ₹ 55,000

   To Equity Shares of ABC Ltd. A/c ₹ 55,000

   (Being Put Option exercised and shares delivered)

   Profit and Loss A/c Dr. ₹ 4,000

   To Equity Stock Option Premium A/c ₹ 4,000

   (Being the premium on the options contract written off on exercise of the option)

In the books of the seller/writer, i.e., Mr. B

1. The following entries may be passed at the time of exercise of the Call Option by the buyer:

   Bank A/c Dr. ₹ 23,000

   To Equity Shares of XYZ Limited A/c ₹ 23,000

   (Being shares delivered on exercise of the Call Option)

Equity Stock Option Premium A/c	Dr.	₹ 1,500	
To Profit and Loss A/c			₹ 1,500

(Being the premium on the options contract recognised as in come on exercise of the option)

2. The following entries may be passed at the time of exercise of the Put Option by the buyer:

Equity Shares of ABC Limited A/c	Dr.	₹ 55,000	
To Bank A/c			₹ 55,000

(Being shares acquired on exercise of the Put Option)

Equity Stock Option Premium A/c	Dr.	₹ 4,000	
To Profit and Loss A/c			₹ 4,000

(Being the premium on the options contract recognised as in come on exercise of the option) CORRIGENDUM

References

1. Guidance Note on Futures and Options – by ICAI
2. www.nsc.co.in
3. Jon-Hill

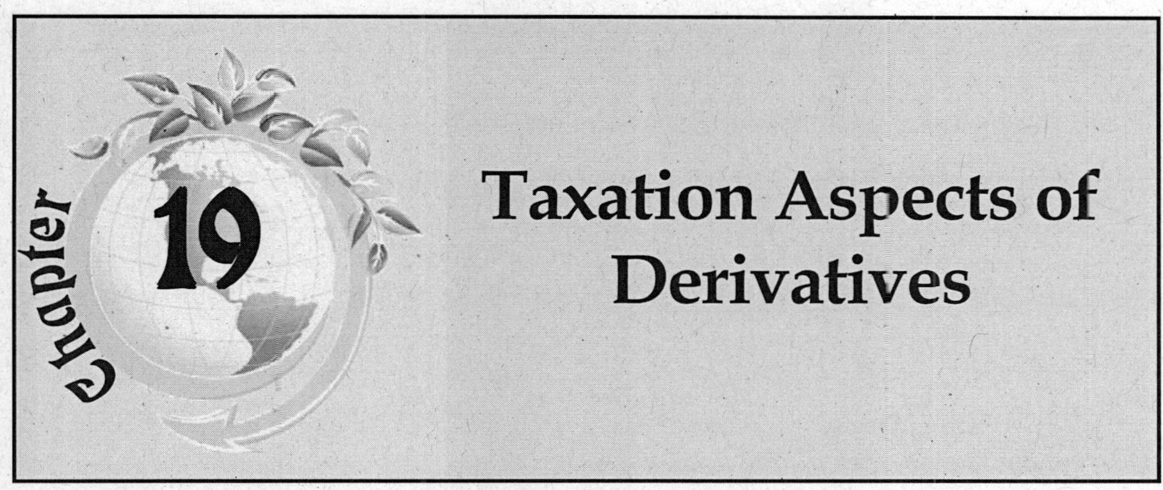

Taxation Aspects of Derivatives

Prior to Financial Year 2005-06, transaction in derivatives were considered as speculative transactions for the purpose of determination of tax liability under the Income Tax Act. This is in view of section 43(5) of the Income Tax Act, which defined speculative transaction as a transaction in which a contract for purchase or sale of any commodity, including stocks and shares, is periodically or ultimately settled otherwise than by the actual delivery or transfer of the commodity or scrips. However, such transactions entered into by hedgers and stock exchange members in course of jobbing or arbitrage activity were specifically excluded from the purview of definition of speculative transaction.

In view of the above provisions, most of the transactions entered into in derivatives by investors and speculators were considered as speculative transactions. The tax provisions provided for differential treatment with respect to set off and carry forward of loss on such transactions. Loss on derivative transactions could be set off only against other speculative income and the same could not be set off against any other income. This resulted in payment of higher taxes by an assessee.

Finance Act, 2005 has amended section 43(5) so as to exclude transactions in derivatives carried out in a 'recognised stock exchange' is not taxed as speculative income or loss. Thus loss on derivative transactions can be set off against any other income during the year. In case the same cannot be set off, it can be carried forward to subsequent assessment year and set off against any other income of the subsequent years. Such losses can be carried forward for a period of eight assessment years It may also be noted that securities transaction tax paid on such transactions is eligible as deduction under Income Tax Act, 1961.

As per Chapter VII of the Finance (No. 2) Act, 2004, Securities Transaction Tax (STT) is levied on all transactions of sale and/or purchase of equity shares and units of equity oriented fund and sale of derivatives entered into in a recognised stock exchange.

Sr. No.	Taxable Securities Transaction	Rate	Payable by
(a)	Sale of an option in securities	0.017 per cent	Seller
(b)	Sale of an option in securities, where option is exercised.	0.125 per cent	Purchaser
(c)	Sale of futures in securities	0.017 per cent	Seller

Consider an example: Mr. A. Sells a futures contract of M/s. XYZ Ltd. (Lot Size: 1,000) expiring on 29th September 2005, for ₹ 300. The spot price of the share is ₹ 290. The securities transaction tax thereon would be calculated as follows:

1. Total futures contract value = 1,000 × 300 = ₹ 3,00,000
2. Securities transaction tax payable thereon 0.017 per cent = 3,00,000 × 0.017 per cent = ₹ 51

Note: No tax on such a transaction is payable by the buyer of the futures contract.

CURRENT PROVISIONS SPECULATION LOSSES

Losses from speculation business can be set off only against profits of another speculation business. If speculation profits are insufficient, such losses can be carried forward for four years, and will be set off against speculation profits in these future years.

As we know that derivatives are powerful "Risk Management Tools". The markets of derivatives have popularly grown and it has assumed a very significant place in the capital market of our country. The Turnover of derivative segment has outnumbered the turnover of Cash Market segments on two leading Stock Exchanges of our country. Currently, Futures and Options are very popular contracts of a financial derivative market and are regularly traded on both these exchanges.

Futures Contracts-taxation aspect

Futures contract is an agreement to buy or sell an underlying asset at specified future date at specified future price. They are standardised contracts traded on the exchange. They are standardised in terms of size expiration date, settlement terms, etc. The price at which the contract will be settled in future is agreed upon at the time of entering into the contract and it casts an obligation on both the parties to fulfill the terms as specified in the contract.

Commodity futures contracts have the underlying assets as agricultural commodities, precious metals, etc., whereas financial futures contracts have financial assets like currency, bonds, shares, index equity stock, etc.

When an investor buys a futures contract from an exchange he is assuming a right and obligation to take the delivery as per terms of a contract on agreed future date and the *vice-a-versa* when he sells it. Futures contract, the underlying of which is a specific stock, is known as "Stock Futures" and in case the underlying is the stock index, it is known as "Index Futures". As on date Stock Exchanges permit trading in 3-months futures contracts, i.e., in the month of October 2005, the Futures, which can be traded, are October 2005, November 2005 and December 2005.

Options Contracts Options are type of derivative contracts where a person gets a "right" but not an 'obligation' to buy or sell an underlying asset at an agreed price on or before the specified future date. Under an options contract, the right (option) is purchased from the seller. This option may be the right relating to purchases (call option) or the right relating to sales (put option). The person who buys such right is called

'Buyer' or 'Holder' of the contract and the person who sells this right is known as 'Seller' or 'Writer' of the contract.

The buyer of the contract has a right but not an obligation to perform as per the terms of the contract and for acquiring this right, buyer has to pay 'Premium' to the seller. This premium amount is one time cost and not adjustable against final consideration. On the other hand, the seller has an obligation to buy or sell the specified underlying asset at an agreed price, if the buyer chooses to exercise the option, whether call or put.

There are two types of options, i.e., American Options and European Options. An American Options is an options contract that can be exercised at any time between the date of purchase and the date of expiry, whereas European Options is an options contract that can only be exercised on the expiration date. A person can buy either a call option or a put option. The rights and obligations of the parties involved in an options contract can be summarised in a tabular form, as under: The price at which the buyer has a right to buy or sell an underlying asset is known as 'Strike Price' or 'Exercise Price', which is agreed at the time of entering into a contract by both the parties. As on date Stock Exchanges have 3-months options contract with an underlying asset of either a Stock Index or a particular Stock. The index options contract is named such as to state the month expiry, call or put option, European or American Options and Strike price.

Option	Buyer or Holder	Seller or Writer
Call	Right but not an obligation to buy the underlying asset	Obligation but no right to sell the underlying asset.
Put	Right but not an obligation to sell the underlying asset	Obligation but no right to buy the underlying asset

Taxation Aspects of Futures and Options

The question as to whether the transaction has been entered into, as a "Trader" or "Investor" is first required to be answered, before one analyses the tax provisions relating to dealing in derivatives. Profit on dealing in contracts held as "Stock in trade" is taxed, as a "Business Income" and dealing in such contracts, which are held as an Investment, would be taxable as a "Capital Gain". The frequent and regular activities and also the motive of entering into a transaction can determine whether the activities relating to purchase or sale is a "Business activity" or an "Investment activity". Some indicative parameters are given hereunder, which however, requires to be examined on case-to-case basis.

(a) Motive/intention while purchase.

(b) Frequency of transaction.

(c) Regularity/continuity of transactions.

(d) Volume of transactions.

(e) Period of holding.

(f) Source of acquisition.

(g) Existence of other business.

(h) Object clause in Memorandum of Association.

(i) Percentage of volume between delivery based/non-delivery based transactions.

(j) Status/nature of activities in previous years.

Keeping in mind the demarcation of "Investment Activity" and "Business Activity", let us examine the taxation aspects relating to Derivatives for both:

(i) Investors

(ii) Traders

DERIVATIVE TRANSACTION FOR AN INVESTOR

Index Futures for an Investor

If an investor enters into transactions relating to purchase and sale of an "Index", the amount of profit or loss is taxable under the head "Capital Gain" or Otherwise? Any transaction on Capital Gain is primarily required to be examined with reference to the following factors:

(i) Whether the transaction relates to a "Capital Asset"?

(ii) If it relates to a Capital Asset, whether such asset is transferred or not?

In the given case one has to examine the transaction on the basis of following conditions:

(i) Whether Index Futures can be regarded as "Capital Asset"?

(ii) Whether settlement of Index Futures transactions involves "Transfer"?

Let us further examine both the conditions.

(i) Condition regarding Capital Asset:

Section 2(14) of Income Tax Act defines the Capital Asset as, "Capital Asset means property of any kind held by an assessee, whether or not connected with his business or profession.........".

Derivatives transactions (in Index Futures) are regarded as 'Securities' under the Securities Contracts (Regulation) Act, 1956. Index Futures contracts are contracts carrying rights that can be enforced in the market and they can be considered as a property carrying value. Under this premise Index Futures can be considered as a 'Capital Asset'.

(ii) Condition regarding transfer:

Section 2(47) of the Income Tax Act, defines 'Transfer' in relation to Capital Assets, To include 'the sale, exchange, or relinquishment of the asset, or extinguishments of any rights therein or..........'.

In case of Index Futures, settlement through deliveries do not take place and the differences are settled in cash. The rights under the contract expires, at the time of settlement or maturity. In practice, the situation is that the Investor buys the index at strike price and sells the same at prevailing market price on the settlement day. When the rights in the contract are worked out, it can be regarded as extinguishments or relinquishment of right. Here on settlement of the contract the relevant contract ceases to exist and under the circumstances it is arguable that the settlement of Index Futures contract falls within the definition of 'Transfer'.

CIT *vs.* Mrs. Grace Collis (2001) 248 ITR 323 (SC):

Extinguishments of rights are independent and otherwise than on account of transfer.

Anarkali Sarabhai *vs.* CIT 224 ITR 422 (SC):

Redemption of Preference Shares are also held as a 'transfer' under clause (i) of Section 2(47) of The Act. As both the prime conditions are satisfied, the gain or loss can qualify under the head 'Capital Gains'. Computation aspects as prescribed under Section 48 of the Act may not pose any peculiar problem as 'cost of purchase' and 'sales consideration' are available for computing capital gain, even though the contracts are getting settled through differences. The extreme view can be, the transactions in Index futures whether entered into for hedging or otherwise will always be in nature of business and hence, the profit/loss is taxed under 'Business Income'. However, one needs to examine whether there is any trade or adventure in the nature of trade.

In the case of Morgan Stanley & Co. International Ltd. (AAR) 142 Taxman 630, Authority for Advance Ruling, one can find the argument on both the side as to whether derivatives considered as 'Capital Asset' or 'Stock in Trade'.

Stock Futures for anInvestor

Currently 'Stock Futures' contracts are also cash-settled and its trading and settlement mechanisms are similar to those of Index Futures. The discussion made in above paragraphs with respect to conditions of 'Capital Asset' and 'Transfer' shall also apply to the contracts relating to 'Stock Futures'. As both the conditions are satisfied, the difference arising out of cash settled stock futures contracts also qualifies to be taxed under the head 'Capital Gains'. However, if the Stock Futures contracts become 'Delivery Settled' then the complications deepens. For example, if a person buys a Stock Futures contracts and allows it to be converted into delivery by paying a contracted price at the time of settlement, at what point of time the gain arises?

(a) At the time of 'Settlement of futures contract' or

(b) At the time of actually selling the underlying stock in future.

This issue can be examined by determining whether Derivative contract in Stock futures are independently existing or they are part and parcel of the same contract through which one purchases an underlying stock? Whether "Stock futures" contract merges with the underlying stock? (or) The stock futures contracts expires (settles) and the underlying stock is purchased thereafter? Trading mechanisms and various parameters set for Derivatives trading supports the arguments of 'Derivatives contracts having separate and independent existence'. The view can be further strengthened by the following points:

(i) Derivative segment and Cash Market segment on both the stock Exchanges have their independent existence.

(ii) Derivatives are separately defined as 'Securities' under Section 2(h) of Securities Contracts (Regulation) Act, 1956.

(iii) The contract of Stock futures expires on settlement day when delivery is actually taken. At no point of time 'stock futures contract' and its 'underlying stock' exist in parallel. The delivery of an underlying stock comes into being only on expiry of stock futures contract.

On the basis of above arguments, Stock Futures Contracts (Delivery Settled) can be considered as a separate and independent contract. However, once it is held to a separate and independent contract, issue pertaining to 'Year of Chargeability' arises. Example: Mr. A purchases a stock futures contract of a particular scrip at ₹ 600 per unit. On the date of settlement Market priceis ₹ 800 per unit and Mr.A decides to take delivery by making payment of ₹ 600 (contracted price). If derivative is held as an independent asset, the gain of ₹ 200 (₹ 800 – ₹ 600) canbe taxed as short-term capital gain out of Derivative contract.

However, question may arise whether capital gain tax is payable on notional gain. The other argument can be, that the delivery of stock shall always be givenat ₹ 600, i.e., at contracted price and mark to market margin of ₹ 200 is to be adjusted at the time of settlement, as if it has never been received. Under this situation, in the absence of any income the question of taxability does not arise. However, one will have to wait till the futures market of derivatives becomes delivery based in our country.

OPTIONS CONTRACTS FOR INVESTORS

Two basic questions which arise here are, (i) If the option is exercised, whether premium paid shall be added to the cost of the shares or allowed to be reduced from sales consideration? (ii) If the option is not exercised what will be the treatment of premium paid? Let us examine these issues: The term 'cost' is not defined in the Income Tax Act, 1961 The 'cost of acquisition' referred to in Section 48 of the Income Tax Act not only contemplates the purchase cost but also all the incidental expenses necessary to bring in the asset into a state which enables the owner to put the asset in 'Ready' or 'Deliverable' stage. Expenses like brokerage, stamp duty, D'mat charges, etc. certainly forms part of cost of acquisition.

On the same premise, the premium can also form part of cost of acquisition and can be added to the cost (*vice versa* can be reduced from sales consideration).

If contract of derivatives is considered as a separate and independent contract, the treatment of tax will be different and the premium may not be allowed to be added to the cost or reduced from the sales consideration, as the case may be. Under this situation, options will be held as independent capital asset and the difference of either premium or the contracted price and the prevailing market price may be brought under the tax net. However, proper examination can be done only on implementation of delivery-based options in the capital market of our country. The second issue is about the treatment of premium paid by the investor, when options are not exercised. In this case, whether loss can be considered as a 'Capital Loss' or it is a loss of Capital, which is not deductible under Income Tax Act.

As discussed in previous paragraphs, two prime conditions for chargeability of income under the head "Capital Gains" are: (a) There has to be capital asset, and (b) There has to be transfer Options contracts of derivatives arerecognised as 'Securities' under the Securities Contracts (Regulation) Act, 1956. They carry rights, which are enforceable in the market by the holder of the contract. As the options contracts are property-carrying value it will certainly qualify as a 'Capital Asset' as defined under Section 2(14) of the Income Tax Act. When the options contracts are not exercised; i.e., if they are lapsed then there are extinguishments of right attached therein. The definition of "Transfer" under section 2(47) of the Income Tax includes "extinguishments" of rights and, hence, the second condition is also satisfied. Observations made in Vania Silk Ltd. vs. CIT 191 ITR 647, has no bearings on this issues as the same has been overruled by other pronouncements such as CIT vs. TISCO 206 ITR 196, Kartikeyasarabhai vs. CIT (1997) 228 ITR 163.

Therefore, amount of premium paid can be claimed as a "Capital Loss". The other view can be that Options contracts are the tools made only for traders and not for Investors and transactions entered into Options contracts are always in capacity as a "Traders". However, for determining the same one has to keep in mind the various parameters and also the arguments given in the case of Morgan Stanley & Co. International Ltd. (AAR) 142 Taxman 630.

Traders – Taxability of Futures & Options Contract

Finance Act, 2005, has brought in an important insertion in Section 43(5), clarifying the tax treatment of Derivative transaction under Income Tax Act. Section 43(5) as amended has been reproduced as below which has come into effect from 1.4.2005 "Speculative transaction" means a transaction in which a contract for the purchase or sale of any commodity, including stocks and shares, is periodically or ultimately settled otherwise than by the actual delivery or transfer of the commodity or scrips: Provided that for the purposes of this clause –

(a) A contract in respect of raw materials or merchandise entered into by a person in the course of his manufacturing or merchanting business to guard against loss through future price fluctuations in respect of his contracts for actual delivery of goods manufactured by him or merchandise sold by him; or

(b) A contract in respect of stocks and shares entered into by a dealer or investor therein to guard against loss in his holdings of stocks and shares through price fluctuations; or

(c) A contract entered into by a member of a forward market or a stock exchange in the course of any transaction in the nature of jobbing or arbitrage to guard against loss which may arise in the ordinary course of his business as such member; [or]

(d) An eligible transaction in respect of trading in derivatives referred to in clause (aa) of section 2 of the Securities Contracts (Regulation) Act, 1956 (42 of 1956) carried out in a recognised stock exchange; shall not be deemed to be a speculative transaction;

Explanation – For the Purposes of this Clause, the Expressions

(i) "Eligible transaction" means any transaction, –

(A) Carried out electronically on screen-based systems through a stock broker or sub-broker or such other intermediary registered under section 12 of the Securities and Exchange Board of India Act, 1992 (15 of 1992) in accordance with the provisions of the Securities Contracts (Regulation) Act, 1956 (42 of 1956) or the Securities and Exchange Board of India Act, 1992 (15 of 1992) or the Depositories Act, 1996 (22 of 1996) and the rules, regulations or bye-laws made or directions issued under those Acts or by banks or mutual funds on a recognised stock exchange; and

(B) Which is supported by a time stamped contract note issued by such stock broker or sub-broker or such other intermediary to every client indicating in the contract note the unique client identity number allotted under any Act referred to in sub-clause (A) and permanent account number allotted under this Act;

(ii) "Recognised stock exchange" means a recognised stock exchange as referred to in clause (f) of section 2 of the Securities Contracts (Regulation) Act, 1956 (42 of 1956) and which fulfills such conditions as may be prescribed and notified by the Central Government for this purpose;

Whether the insertion is clarificatory in nature (or) it applies only from A.Y. 2006-07?

The insertion seems to be clarificatory in nature as there are no new conditions prescribed for excluding derivative transactions from the clutches of Section 43(5) of the Act. The transactions entered into prior to 1.4.2005 were similar in nature and also fulfilling the conditions given in the definition of "eligibletransaction". There cannot be different set of treatment for the transactions of a similar nature. One can also possibly argue that even in the pre-amendment scenario, Derivatives, not being a commodity (including Stock and Shares) could always have been excluded from the definition of "Speculative transaction" given in Section 43(5).

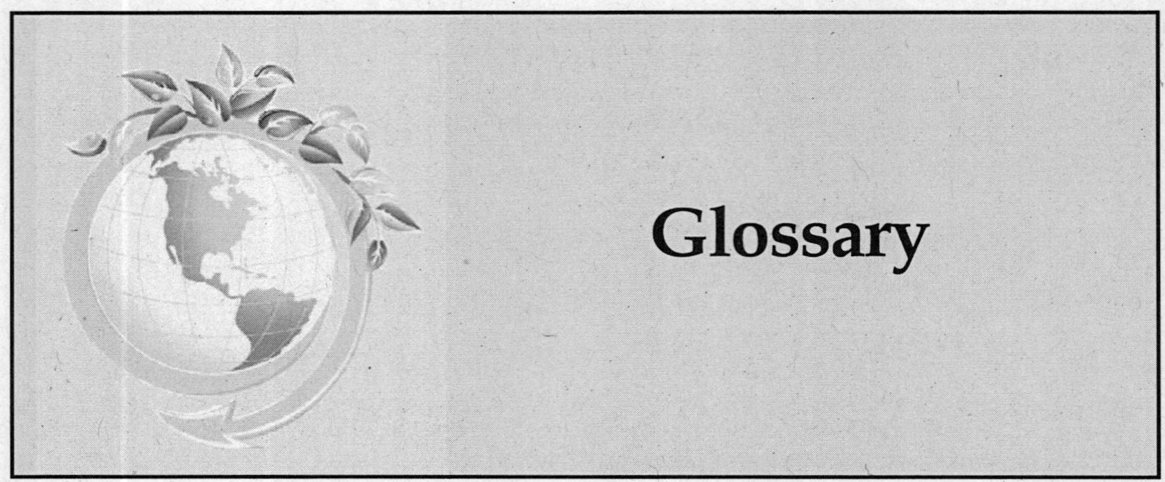

Glossary

In this book the following terms are used with the meanings specified:

Call Option: A Call Option is an Option to buy the specified underlying asset on or before the Expiry Date.

Clearing Corporation/House: Clearing Corporation/House means the Clearing Corporation/House approved by SEBI for clearing and settlement of trades on the Derivatives Exchange/Segment.

Clearing Member: Clearing Member means a member of the Clearing Corporation and includes all categories of Clearing Members as may be admitted as such by the Clearing Corporation to the Derivatives Segment.

Client: A Client means a person, on whose instructions and, on whose account, the Trading Member enters into any contract for the purchase or sale of any contractor does any actinrelation thereto.

Contract Month: Contract Month, inrelation to a futures contract, means the month in which the exchange/Clearing Corporation rules require a contract to be finally settled, and inrelation to an options contract, means the month in which the Expiry Datefalls.

Daily Settlement Price: Daily Settlement Priceis the closing price of the equity index/stock futures contract for the day or such other price as may be decided by the Clearing House from time-to-time.

DERIVATIVES: DERIVATIVES INCLUDE

(a) A security derived from a debt instrument, share, loan, whether secured or unsecured, risk instrument or contract for differences or any other form of security;

(b) A contract which derives its value from the prices, or index of prices, of underlying securities.

Derivative Exchange/Segment: Derivative Exchange means an Exchange approved by SEBI as a Derivative Exchange. Derivative Segment means Segment of an existing Exchange approved by SEBI as Derivative Segment.

Exercise Date: Exercise Date is the date on which the buying/selling right in the Option is actually exercised by the Option Buyer/Holder.

Exercise of an Option: Exercise of an Option means enforcing the right by the Option Buyer/Holder available under the option contract of buying or selling the underlying asset at the Strike Price.

Expiry Date: Expiry Date is the last date on or up to which the Option can be exercised.

Final Settlement Price: Final Settlement Price is the closing price of the Equity Derivative Instruments contract on the last trading day of the contract or such other price as may be specified by the Clearing Corporation, from time-to-time.

Long Position: Long Position means outstanding purchase obligations in respect of equity index/stock futures contracts at any point of time.

Open Interest: Open Interest means the total number of Equity Derivative Instruments contracts that have not yet been offset and closed by an opposite contract nor fulfilled either by delivery of cash or by actual delivery of underlying security.

Option: Option is a contract, which gives the buyer/holder the right, but not the obligation, to buy or sell as pecified underlying as set at a predetermined price.

Option Buyer/Holder: Option Buyer/Holder is the person who buy sa Call or a Put Option.

Option Premium: Option Premium is the price paid by the Option Buyer/Holder to the Option Seller/Writer to acquire the right in the Option.

Option Seller/Writer: Option Seller/Writer is the person who sells a Callora Put Option.

Put Option: Put Optionis an Option to sell the specified underlying asset on or before the Expiry Date.

Settlement Date: Settlement Date means the date on which the outstanding obligations in an equity index/stock futures contract are required to be settled as provided in the bye-laws of the Derivatives Exchange/Segment.

Short Position: Short Position means outstanding sell obligations inrespect of equity index/stock futures contracts at any point of time.

Strike Price/Exercise Price: Strike Price/Exercise Price is the price specified in the option contract at which the underlying asset may be purchased or sold by the buyer/holder.

Trading Member: Trading Member means amember of the Derivatives Exchange/ Segment and registered with SEBI.

Part – II

Financial Instruments

Financial Instruments (Ind AS 39, IAS 39 and AS 30)

INTRODUCTION

The objective of Ind AS 39 is to establish principles for recognising and measuring financial assets, financial liabilities and some contracts to buy or sell non-financial items. Requirements for presenting information about financial instruments are in Ind AS 32, Financial Instruments: Presentation. Requirements for disclosing information about financial instruments are in Ind AS 107 Financial Instruments: Disclosures.

This Standard shall be applied by all entities to all types of financial instruments except:

(a) Those interests in subsidiaries, associates and joint ventures that are accounted for under Ind AS 27 Consolidated and Separate Financial Statements, Ind AS 28 Investments in Associates or Ind AS 31 Interests in Joint Ventures. However, entities shall apply this Standard to an interest in a subsidiary, associate or joint venture that according to Ind AS 27, Ind AS 28, or Ind AS 31 is accounted for under this Standard. Entities shall also apply this Standard to derivatives on an interest in a subsidiary, associate or joint venture unless the derivative meets the definition of an equity instrument of the entity in Ind AS 32.

(b) Rights and obligations under leases to which Ind AS 17 Leases applies. However:

(i) Lease receivables recognised by a lessor are subject to the derecognition and impairment provisions of this Standard (see paragraphs 15-37, 58, 59, 63-65 and Appendix A paragraphs AG36-AG52 and AG84-AG93);

(ii) Finance lease payables recognised by a lessee are subject to the derecognition provisions of this Standard (see paragraphs 39-42 and Appendix A paragraphs AG57-AG63); and

(iii) Derivatives that are embedded in leases are subject to the embedded derivatives provisions of this Standard (see paragraphs 10-13 and Appendix A paragraphs AG27-AG33).

(c) Employers' rights and obligations under employee benefit plans, to which Ind AS 19 Employee Benefits applies.

(d) Financial instruments issued by the entity that meet the definition of an equity instrument in Ind AS 32 (including options and warrants) or that are required to be classified as an equity instrument in accordance with paragraphs 16A and 16B or paragraphs 16C and 16D of Ind AS 32. However, the holder of such equity instruments shall apply this Standard to those instruments, unless they meet the exception in (a) above.

(e) Rights and obligations arising under (i) an insurance contract as defined in Ind AS 104 Insurance Contracts, other than an issuer's rights and obligations arising under an insurance contract that meets the definition of a financial guarantee contract in paragraph 9, or (ii) a contract that is within the scope of Ind AS 104 because it contains a discretionary participation feature. However, this Standard applies to a derivative that is embedded in a contract within the scope of Ind AS 104 if the derivative is not itself a contract within the scope of Ind AS 104 (see paragraphs 10-13 and Appendix A paragraphs AG27-AG33 of this Standard). Moreover, if an issuer of financial guarantee contracts has previously asserted explicitly that it regards such contracts as insurance contracts and has used accounting applicable to insurance contracts, the issuer may elect to apply either this Standard or Ind AS 104 to such financial guarantee contracts (see paragraphs AG4 and AG4A). The issuer may make that election contract by contract, but the election for each contract is irrevocable.

(f) Any forward contract between an acquirer and a selling shareholder to buy or sell an acquiree that will result in a business combination at a future acquisition date. The term of the forward contract should not exceed a reasonable period normally necessary to obtain any required approvals and to complete the transaction.

(g) Loan commitments other than those loan commitments described in paragraph 4. An issuer of loan commitments shall apply Ind AS 37 Provisions, Contingent Liabilities and Contingent Assets to loan commitments that are not within the scope of this Standard. However, all loan commitments are subject to the derecognition provisions of this Standard (see paragraphs 15-42 and Appendix A paragraphs AG36-AG63).

(h) Financial instruments, contracts and obligations under share-based payment transactions to which Ind AS 104 Share-based Payment applies, except for contracts within the scope of paragraphs 5-7 of this Standard, to which this Standard applies.

(i) Rights to payments to reimburse the entity for expenditure it is required to make to settle a liability that it recognises as a provision in accordance with Ind AS 37, or for which, in an earlier period, it recognised a provision in accordance with Ind AS 37.

The following loan commitments are within the scope of this Standard:

(a) Loan commitments that the entity designates as financial liabilities at fair value through profit or loss. An entity that has a past practice of selling the assets resulting from its loan commitments shortly after origination shall apply this Standard to all its loan commitments in the same class.

(b) Loan commitments that can be settled net in cash or by delivering or issuing another financial instrument. These loan commitments are derivatives. A loan commitment is not regarded as settled net merely because the loan is paid out in instalments (for example, a mortgage construction loan that is paid out in instalments in line with the progress of construction).

(c) Commitments to provide a loan at a below-market interest rate. Paragraph 47(d) specifies the subsequent measurement of liabilities arising from these loan commitments.

This Standard shall be applied to those contracts to buy or sell a non-financial item that can be settled net in cash or another financial instrument, or by exchanging financial instruments, as if the contracts were financial instruments, with the exception of contracts that were entered into and continue to be held for the purpose of the receipt or delivery of a non-financial item in accordance with the entity's expected purchase, sale or usage requirements.

There are various ways in which a contract to buy or sell a non-financial item can be settled net in cash or another financial instrument or by exchanging financial instruments. These include:

(a) When the terms of the contract permit either party to settle it net in cash or another financial instrument or by exchanging financial instruments;

(b) When the ability to settle net in cash or another financial instrument, or by exchanging financial instruments, is not explicit in the terms of the contract, but the entity has a practice of settling similar contracts net in cash or another financial instrument or by exchanging financial instruments (whether with the counterparty, by entering into offsetting contracts or by selling the contract before its exercise or lapse);

(c) When, for similar contracts, the entity has a practice of taking delivery of the underlying and selling it within a short period after delivery for the purpose of generating a profit from short-term fluctuations in price or dealer's margin; and

(d) When the non-financial item that is the subject of the contract is readily convertible to cash.

A contract to which (b) or (c) applies is not entered into for the purpose of the receipt or delivery of the non-financial item in accordance with the entity's expected purchase, sale or usage requirements and, accordingly, is within the scope of this Standard. Other contracts to which paragraph 5 applies are evaluated to determine whether they were entered into and continue to be held for the purpose of the receipt or delivery of the non-financial item in accordance with the entity's expected purchase, sale or usage requirements and, accordingly, whether they are within the scope of this Standard.

A written option to buy or sell a non-financial item that can be settled net in cash or another financial instrument, or by exchanging financial instruments, in accordance with paragraph 6(a) or (d) is within the scope of this Standard. Such a contract cannot be entered into for the purpose of the receipt or delivery of the non-financial item in accordance with the entity's expected purchase, sale or usage requirements.

Definitions

Financial instrument: a contract that gives rise to a financial asset of one entity and a financial liability or equity instrument of another entity.

Financial asset: any asset that is:

- Cash;
- An equity instrument of another entity;
- A contractual right:
  - To receive cash or another financial asset from another entity or
  - To exchange financial assets or financial liabilities with another entity under conditions that are potentially favourable to the entity or
- A contract that will or may be settled in the entity's own equity instruments and is:
  - A non-derivative for which the entity is or may be obliged to receive a variable number of the entity's own equity instruments or
  - A derivative that will or may be settled other than by the exchange of a fixed amount of cash or another financial asset for a fixed number of the entity's own equity instruments. For this purpose the entity's own equity instruments do not include instruments that are themselves contracts for the future receipt or delivery of the entity's own equity instruments; they also do not include puttable financial instruments

Financial liability: any liability that is:

- A contractual obligation:
  - To deliver cash or another financial asset to another entity; or
  - To exchange financial assets or financial liabilities with another entity under conditions that are potentially unfavourable to the entity; or

- A contract that will or may be settled in the entity's own equity instruments and is:
  - A non-derivative for which the entity is or may be obliged to deliver a variable number of the entity's own equity instruments or
  - A derivative that will or may be settled other than by the exchange of a fixed amount of cash or another financial asset for a fixed number of the entity's own equity instruments. For this purpose the entity's own equity instruments do not include: instruments that are themselves contracts for the future receipt or delivery of the entity's own equity instruments or puttable instruments

Common Examples of Financial Instruments Within the Scope of IND AS 39

- Cash
- Demand and time deposits
- Commercial paper
- Accounts, notes, and loans receivable and payable
- Debt and equity securities. These are financial instruments from the perspectives of both the holder and the issuer. This category includes investments in subsidiaries, associates, and joint ventures
- Asset backed securities such as collateralised mortgage obligations, repurchase agreements, and securitised packages of receivables
- Derivatives, including options, rights, warrants, futures contracts, forward contracts, and swaps.

A derivative is a financial instrument:

- Whose value changes in response to the change in an underlying variable such as an interest rate, commodity or security price, or index;
- That requires no initial investment, or one that is smaller than would be required for a contract with similar response to changes in market factors; and
- That is settled at a future date.

EXAMPLES OF DERIVATIVES

Forwards: Contracts to purchase or sell a specific quantity of a financial instrument, a commodity, or a foreign currency at a specified price determined at the outset, with delivery or settlement at a specified future date. Settlement is at maturity by actual delivery of the item specified in the contract, or by a net cash settlement.

Interest Rate Swaps and Forward Rate Agreements: Contracts to exchange cash-flows as of a specified date or a series of specified dates based on a notional amount and fixed and floating rates.

Futures: Contracts similar to forwards but with the following differences: futures are generic exchange-traded, whereas forwards are individually tailored. Futures are generally settled through an offsetting (reversing) trade, whereas forwards are generally settled by delivery of the underlying item or cash settlement.

Options: Contracts that give the purchaser the right, but not the obligation, to buy (call option) or sell (put option) a specified quantity of a particular financial instrument, commodity, or foreign currency, at a specified price (strike price), during or at a specified period of time. These can be individually written or exchange-traded. The purchaser of the option pays the seller (writer) of the option a fee (premium) to compensate the seller for the risk of payments under the option.

Caps and Floors: These are contracts sometimes referred to as interest rate options. An interest rate cap will compensate the purchaser of the cap if interest rates rise above a predetermined rate (strike rate) while an interest rate floor will compensate the purchaser if rates fall below a predetermined rate.

Embedded Derivatives

Some contracts that themselves are not financial instruments may nonetheless have financial instruments embedded in them. For example, a contract to purchase a commodity at a fixed price for delivery at a future date has embedded in it a derivative that is indexed to the price of the commodity.

An embedded derivative is a feature within a contract, such that the cash-flows associated with that feature behave in a similar fashion to a stand-alone derivative. In the same way that derivatives must be accounted for at fair value on the balance sheet with changes recognised in the income statement, so must some embedded derivatives. IND AS 39 requires that an embedded derivative be separated from its host contract and accounted for as a derivative when:

- The economic risks and characteristics of the embedded derivative are not closely related to those of the host contract,
- A separate instrument with the same terms as the embedded derivative would meet the definition of a derivative, and
- The entire instrument is not measured at fair value with changes in fair value recognised in the income statement.

If an embedded derivative is separated, the host contract is accounted for under the appropriate standard (for instance, under IND AS 39 if the host is a financial instrument). Appendix A to IND AS 39 provides examples of embedded derivatives that are closely related to their hosts, and of those that are not.

Examples of embedded derivatives that are not closely related to their hosts (and therefore, must be separately accounted for) include:

- The equity conversion option in debt convertible to ordinary shares (from the perspective of the holder only).
- Commodity indexed interest or principal payments in host debt contracts.
- Cap and floor options in host debt contracts that are in-the-money when the instrument was issued.
- Leveraged inflation adjustments to lease payments.
- Currency derivatives in purchase or sale contracts for non-financial items where the foreign currency is not that of either counterparty to the contract, is not the currency in which the related good or service is routinely denominated in commercial transactions around the world, and is not the currency that is commonly used in such contracts in the economic environment in which the transaction takes place. IND AS 39 requires that an embedded derivative be separated from its host contract, but the entity is unable to measure the embedded derivative separately, the entire combined contract must be designated as a financial asset as at fair value through profit or loss).

Classification as Liability or Equity

Since IND AS 39 does not address accounting for equity instruments issued by the reporting enterprise but it does deal with accounting for financial liabilities, classification of an instrument as liability or as equity is critical. Ind AS 32 Financial Instruments: Presentation addresses the classification question.

Classification of Financial Assets

IND AS 39 requires financial assets to be classified in one of the following categories:

- Financial assets at fair value through profit or loss
- Available-for-sale financial assets
- Loans and receivables
- Held-to-maturity investments.

Those categories are used to determine how a particular financial asset is recognised and measured in the financial statements.

Financial assets at fair value through profit or loss: This category has two subcategories:

Designated: The first includes any financial asset that is designated on initial recognition as one to be measured at fair value with fair value changes in profit or loss.

Held for trading: The second category includes financial assets that are held for trading. All derivatives (except those designated hedging instruments) and financial assets acquired or held for the purpose of selling in the short term or for which there is a recent pattern of short-term profit taking are held for trading.

Available-for-sale financial assets (AFS): are any non-derivative financial assets designated on initial recognition as available for sale or any other instruments that are not classified as as (a) loans and receivables, (b) held-to-maturity investments or (c) financial assets at fair value through profit or loss. AFS assets are measured at fair value in the balance sheet. Fair value changes on AFS assets are recognised directly in equity, through the statement of changes in equity, except for interest on AFS assets (which is recognised in income on an effective yield basis), impairment losses and (for interest-bearing AFS debt instruments) foreign exchange gains or losses. The cumulative gain or loss that was recognised in equity is recognised in profit or loss when an available-for-sale financial asset is derecognised.

Loans and receivables: are non-derivative financial assets with fixed or determinable paymentsthat are not quoted in an active market, other than held for trading or designated on initial recognition as assets at fair value through profit or loss or as available-for-sale. Loans and receivables for which the holder may not recover substantially all of its initial investment, other than because of credit deterioration, should be classified as available-for-sale. Loans and receivables are measured at amortised cost.

Held-to-maturity investments: are non-derivative financial assets with fixed or determinable payments that an entity intends and is able to hold to maturity and that do not meet the definition of loans and receivables and are not designated on initial recognition as assets at fair value through profit or loss or as available for sale. Held-to-maturity investments are measured at amortised cost. If an entity sells a held-to-maturity investment other than in insignificant amounts or as a consequence of a non-recurring, isolated event beyond its control that could not be reasonably anticipated, all of its other held-to-maturity investments must be reclassified as available-for-sale for the current and next two financial reporting years. Held-to-maturity investments are measured at amortised cost.

Classification of Financial Liabilities

IND AS 39 recognises two classes of financial liabilities:

- Financial liabilities at fair value through profit or loss.
- Other financial liabilities measured at amortised cost using the effective interest method.

The category of financial liability at fair value through profit or loss has two sub-categories:

- ***Designated.*** A financial liability that is designated by the entity as a liability at fair value through profit or loss upon initial recognition.
- ***Held for trading.*** A financial liability classified as held for trading, such as an obligation for securities borrowed in a short sale, which have to be returned in the future.

INITIAL RECOGNITION

IND AS 39 requires recognition of a financial asset or a financial liability when, and only when, the entity becomes a party to the contractual provisions of the instrument, subject to the following provisions in respect of regular way purchases.

Regular way purchases or sales of a financial asset. A regular way purchase or sale of financial assets is recognised and derecognised using either trade date or settlement date accounting. The method used is to be applied consistently for all purchases and sales of financial assets that belong to the same category of financial asset as defined in IND AS 39 (note that for this purpose assets held for trading form a different category from assets designated at fair value through profit or loss). The choice of method is an accounting policy.

IND AS 39 requires that all financial assets and all financial liabilities be recognised on the balance sheet. That includes all derivatives. Historically, in many parts of the world, derivatives have not been recognised on company balance sheets. The argument has been that, at the time the derivative contract was entered into, there was no amount of cash or other assets paid. Zero cost justified non-recognition, notwithstanding that as time passes and the value of the underlying variable (rate, price, or index) changes, the derivative has a positive (asset) or negative (liability) value.

Initial Measurement

Initially, financial assets and liabilities should be measured at fair value (including transaction costs, for assets and liabilities not measured at fair value through profit or loss).

Measurement Subsequent to Initial Recognition

Subsequently, financial assets and liabilities (including derivatives) should be measured at fair value, with the following exceptions:

- Loans and receivables, held-to-maturity investments, and non-derivative financial liabilities should be measured at amortised cost using the effective interest method.
- Investments in equity instruments with no reliable fair value measurement (and derivatives indexed to such equity instruments) should be measured at cost.
- Financial assets and liabilities that are designated as a hedged item or hedging instrument are subject to measurement under the hedge accounting requirements of the IND AS 39.
- Financial liabilities that arise when a transfer of a financial asset does not qualify for derecognition, or that are accounted for using the continuing-involvement method, are subject to particular measurement requirements.

Fair value is the amount for which an asset could be exchanged, or a liability settled, between knowledgeable, willing parties in an arm's length transaction. IND AS 39 provides a hierarchy to be used in determining the fair value for a financial instrument:

- Quoted market prices in an active market are the best evidence of fair value and should be used, where they exist, to measure the financial instrument.
- If a market for a financial instrument is not active, an entity establishes fair value by using a valuation technique that makes maximum use of market inputs and includes recent arm's length market transactions, reference to the current fair value of another instrument that is substantially the same, discounted cash-flow analysis, and option pricing models. An acceptable valuation technique incorporates all factors that market participants would consider in setting a price and is consistent with accepted economic methodologies for pricing financial instruments.
- If there is no active market for an equity instrument and the range of reasonable fair values is significant and these estimates cannot be made reliably, then an entity must measure the equity instrument at cost less impairment.

Amortised cost is calculated using the effective interest method. The effective interest rate is the rate that exactly discounts estimated future cash payments or receipts through the expected life of the financial instrument to the net carrying amount of the financial asset or liability. Financial assets that are not carried at fair value though profit and loss are subject to an impairment test. If expected life cannot be determined reliably, then the contractual life is used.

IND AS 39 Fair Value Option

IND AS 39 permits entities to designate, at the time of acquisition or issuance, any financial asset or financial liability to be measured at fair value, with value changes recognised in profit or loss. This option is available even if the financial asset or financial liability would ordinarily, by its nature, be measured at amortised cost – but only if fair value can be reliably measured.

IND AS 39 restricts the use of the option to designate any financial asset or any financial liability to be measured at fair value through profit and loss (the fair value option). The revisions limit the use of the option to those financial instruments that meet certain conditions:

- the fair value option designation eliminates or significantly reduces an accounting mismatch, or
- a group of financial assets, financial liabilities or both is managed and its performance is evaluated on a fair value basis by entity's management.

Once an instrument is put in the fair-value-through-profit-and-loss category, it cannot be reclassified out with some exceptions. The amendments permit reclassification of some financial instruments out of the fair-value-through-profit-or-loss category (FVTPL) and out of the available-for-sale category. In the event of reclassification, additional disclosures are required under Ind AS 107. On reclassification of a financial asset out of the 'fair value through profit or loss' category, all embedded derivatives have to be (re)assessed and, if necessary, separately accounted for in financial statements.

IND AS 39 Available for Sale Option for Loans and Receivables

IND AS 39 permits entities to designate, at the time of acquisition, any loan or receivable as available for sale, in which case it is measured at fair value with changes in fair value recognised in equity.

IMPAIRMENT

A financial asset or group of assets is impaired, and impairment losses are recognised, only if there is objective evidence as a result of one or more events that occurred after the initial recognition of the asset. An entity is required to assess at each balance sheet date whether there is any objective evidence of impairment. If any such evidence exists, the entity is required to do a detailed impairment calculation to determine whether an impairment loss should be recognised. The amount of the loss is measured as the difference between the asset's carrying amount and the present value of estimated cash-flows discounted at the financial asset's original effective interest rate.

Assets that are individually assessed and for which no impairment exists are grouped with financial assets with similar credit risk statistics and collectively assessed for impairment.

If, in a subsequent period, the amount of the impairment loss relating to a financial asset carried at amortised cost or a debt instrument carried as available-for-sale decreases due to an event occurring after the impairment was originally recognised, the previously recognised impairment loss is reversed through profit or loss. Impairments relating to investments in available-for-sale equity instruments are not reversed through profit or loss.

Financial Guarantees

A financial guarantee contract is a contract that requires the issuer to make specified payments to reimburse the holder for a loss it incurs because a specified debtor fails to make payment when due.

Under IND AS 39 as amended, financial guarantee contracts are recognised:

- Initially at fair value. If the financial guarantee contract was issued in a stand-alone arm's length transaction to an unrelated party, its fair value at inception is likely to equal the consideration received, unless there is evidence to the contrary.
- Subsequently at the higher of (i) the amount determined in accordance with Ind AS 37 Provisions, Contingent Liabilities and Contingent Assets and (ii) the amount initially recognised less, when appropriate, cumulative amortisation recognised in accordance with Ind AS 18 Revenue. (If specified criteria are met, the issuer may use the fair value option in IND AS 39. Furthermore, different requirements continue to apply in the specialised context of a 'failed' derecognition transaction.)

Some credit-related guarantees do not, as a precondition for payment, require that the holder is exposed to, and has incurred a loss on, the failure of the debtor to make payments on the guaranteed asset when due. An example of such a guarantee is a credit derivative that requires payments in response to changes in a specified credit rating or credit index. These are derivatives and they must be measured at fair value under IND AS 39.

Derecognition of a Financial Asset

The basic premise for the derecognition model in IND AS 39 is to determine whether the asset under consideration for derecognition is:

- An asset in its entirety or
- Specifically identified cash-flows from an asset or
- A fully proportionate share of the cash-flows from an asset or
- A fully proportionate share of specifically identified cash-flows from a financial asset.

Once the asset under consideration for derecognition has been determined, an assessment is made as to whether the asset has been transferred, and if so, whether the transfer of that asset is subsequently eligible for derecognition.

An asset is transferred if either the entity has transferred the contractual rights to receive the cash-flows, or the entity has retained the contractual rights to receive the cash-flows from the asset, but has assumed a contractual obligation to pass those cash-flows on under an arrangement that meets the following three conditions:

- The entity has no obligation to pay amounts to the eventual recipient unless it collects equivalent amounts on the original asset,
- The entity is prohibited from selling or pledging the original asset (other than as security to the eventual recipient),
- The entity has an obligation to remit those cash-flows without material delay.

Once an entity has determined that the asset has been transferred, it then determines whether or not it has transferred substantially all of the risks and rewards of ownership of the asset. If substantially all the risks and rewards have been transferred, the asset is derecognised. If substantially all the risks and rewards have been retained, derecognition of the asset is precluded.

If the entity has neither retained nor transferred substantially all of the risks and rewards of the asset, then the entity must assess whether it has relinquished control of the asset or not. If the entity does not control the asset then derecognition is appropriate; however if the entity has retained control of the asset, then the entity continues to recognise the asset to the extent to which it has a continuing involvement in the asset.

Derecognition of a Financial Liability

A financial liability should be removed from the balance sheet when, and only when, it is extinguished, that is, when the obligation specified in the contract is either discharged or cancelled or expires. Where there has been an exchange between an existing borrower and lender of debt instruments with substantially different terms, or there has been a substantial modification of the terms of an existing financial liability, this transaction is accounted for as an extinguishment of the original financial liability and the recognition of a new financial liability. A gain or loss from extinguishment of the original financial liability is recognised in profit or loss.

HEDGE ACCOUNTING

IND AS 39 permits hedge accounting under certain circumstances provided that the hedging relationship is:

- Formally designated and documented, including the entity's risk management objective and strategy for undertaking the hedge, identification of the hedging instrument, the hedged item, the nature of the risk being hedged, and how the entity will assess the hedging instrument's effectiveness and
- Expected to be highly effective in achieving offsetting changes in fair value or cash-flows attributable to the hedged risk as designated and documented, and effectiveness can be reliably measured and
- Assessed on an ongoing basis and determined to have been highly effective.

Hedging Instruments

Hedging instrument is an instrument whose fair value or cash-flows are expected to offset changes in the fair value or cash-flows of a designated hedged item.

All derivative contracts with an external counterparty may be designated as hedging instruments except for some written options. A non-derivative financial asset or liability may not be designated as a hedging instrument except as a hedge of foreign currency risk.

For hedge accounting purposes, only instruments that involve a party external to the reporting entity can be designated as a hedging instrument. This applies to intragroup transactions as well (with the exception of certain foreign currency hedges of forecast intragroup transactions - see below). However, they may qualify for hedge accounting in individual financial statements.

Hedged Items

Hedged item is an item that exposes the entity to risk of changes in fair value or future cash-flows and is designated as being hedged.

A hedged item can be:

- A single recognised asset or liability, firm commitment, highly probable transaction or a net investment in a foreign operation
- A group of assets, liabilities, firm commitments, highly probable forecast transactions or net investments in foreign operations with similar risk characteristics
- A held-to-maturity investment for foreign currency or credit risk (but not for interest risk or prepayment risk)
- A portion of the cash-flows or fair value of a financial asset or financial liability or
- A non-financial item for foreign currency risk only for all risks of the entire item
- In a portfolio hedge of interest rate risk (Macro Hedge) only, a portion of the portfolio of financial assets or financial liabilities that share the risk being hedged.

In April 2005, the IASB amended IAS 39 to permit the foreign currency risk of a highly probable intragroup forecast transaction to qualify as the hedged item in a cash-flow hedge in consolidated financial statements - provided that the transaction is denominated in a currency other than the functional currency of the entity entering into that transaction and the foreign currency risk will affect consolidated financial statements.

On 30 July 2008, the IASB amended IAS 39 to clarify two hedge accounting issues:

- Inflation in a financial hedged item, and
- A one-sided risk in a hedged item.

EFFECTIVENESS

IND AS 39 requires hedge effectiveness to be assessed both prospectively and retrospectively. To qualify for hedge accounting at the inception of a hedge and, at a minimum, at each reporting date, the changes in the fair value or cash-flows of the hedged item attributable to the hedged risk must be expected to be highly effective in offsetting the changes in the fair value or cash-flows of the hedging instrument on a prospective basis, and on a retrospective basis where actual results are within a range of 80 per cent to 125 per cent.

All hedge ineffectiveness is recognised immediately in profit or loss (including ineffectiveness within the 80 per cent to 125 per cent window).

Categories of Hedges

A fair value hedge is a hedge of the exposure to changes in fair value of a recognised asset or liability or a previously unrecognised firm commitment or an identified portion of such an asset, liability or firm commitment, that is attributable to a particular risk and could affect profit or loss. The gain or loss from the change in fair value of the hedging instrument is recognised immediately in profit or loss. At the same time the carrying amount of the hedged item is adjusted for the corresponding gain or loss with respect to the hedged risk, which is also recognised immediately in net profit or loss.

A cash-flow hedge is a hedge of the exposure to variability in cash-flows that (i) is attributable to a particular risk associated with a recognised asset or liability (such as all or some future interest payments on variable rate debt) or a highly probable forecast transaction and (ii) could affect profit or loss. The portion of the gain or loss on the hedging instrument that is determined to be an effective hedge is recognised in other comprehensive income.

If a hedge of a forecast transaction subsequently results in the recognition of a financial asset or a financial liability, any gain or loss on the hedging instrument that was previously recognised directly in equity is 'recycled' into profit or loss in the same period(s) in which the financial asset or liability affects profit or loss.

If a hedge of a forecast transaction subsequently results in the recognition of a non-financial asset or non-financial liability, then the entity has an accounting policy option that must be applied to all such hedges of forecast transactions:

- Same accounting as for recognition of a financial asset or financial liability – any gain or loss on the hedging instrument that was previously recognised in other comprehensive income is 'recycled' into profit or loss in the same period(s) in which the non-financial asset or liability affects profit or loss.
- 'Basis adjustment' of the acquired non-financial asset or liability – the gain or loss on the hedging instrument that was previously recognised in other comprehensive incomeis removed from equity and is included in the initial cost or other carrying amount of the acquired non-financial asset or liability.

A hedge of a net investment in a foreign operation as defined in Ind AS 21 is accounted for similarly to a cash-flow hedge.

A hedge of the foreign currency risk of a firm commitment may be accounted for as a fair value hedge or as a cash-flow hedge.

Discontinuation of Hedge Accounting

Hedge accounting must be discontinued prospectively if:

- The hedging instrument expires or is sold, terminated, or exercised
- The hedge no longer meets the hedge accounting criteria – for example it is no longer effective
- For cash-flow hedges the forecast transaction is no longer expected to occur, or
- The entity revokes the hedge designation.

For the purpose of measuring the carrying amount of the hedged item when fair value hedge accounting ceases, a revised effective interest rate is calculated.

If hedge accounting ceases for a cash-flow hedge relationship because the forecast transaction is no longer expected to occur, gains and losses deferred in other comprehensive income must be taken to profit or loss immediately. If the transaction is still expected to occur and the hedge relationship ceases, the amounts accumulated in equity will be retained in equity until the hedged item affects profit or loss.

If a hedged financial instrument that is measured at amortised cost has been adjusted for the gain or loss attributable to the hedged risk in a fair value hedge, this adjustment is amortised to profit or loss based on a recalculated effective interest rate on this date such that the adjustment is fully amortised by the maturity of the instrument. Amortisation may begin as soon as an adjustment exists and must begin no later than when the hedged item ceases to be adjusted for changes in its fair value attributable to the risks being hedged.

Receivables and payables

Often the fair value of a debt instrument that does not have a quoted rate or price can be determined by scheduling the cash-flows and discounting them using the applicable current market interest rate for debt instruments that have substantially the same terms and characteristics (similar remaining maturity, cash-flow pattern, credit quality, currency risk, collateral, and interest basis) for which quoted rates in active markets exist. These and other techniques for determining fair value are discussed in finance and valuation textbooks.

When goods or services are sold, the seller often gives the buyer some specified time to pay the invoice amount, such as 60 days, with no stated interest. This means that the seller obtains a short-term receivable and that the buyer obtains a short-term payable that meet the definition of financial instruments and are accounted for under IND AS 39. Conceptually, such a receivable or payable should be measured at its present value (i.e., the present value of the invoice amount discounted using applicable current market interest rates). In that case, interest would be accrued over the term of the receivable for the difference between the initial present value and the invoice amount. As a practical accommodation, however, IND AS 39 permits measuring short-term receivables and short-term payables with no stated interest at the original invoice amount if the effect of discounting is immaterial. For longer-term receivables or payables that do not pay interest or pay a below-market interest, IND AS 39 does require measurement initially at the present value of the cash-flows to be received or paid

Difference between Ind AS 39 and Existing AS 30

(Ind AS 39 vs. Existing AS 30)

Ind AS 39, Financial Instruments: Recognition and Measurement and the existing AS 30,

Financial Instruments: Recognition and Measurement

(i) The financial instruments to which Ind AS 39 does not apply include financial instruments issued by the entity that meet the definition of an equity instrument in Ind AS 32 (including options and warrants) or that are required to be classified as an equity instrument in accordance with paragraphs 16A and 16B or paragraphs 16C and 16D of Ind AS 32. The existing standard does not exclude the latter. (Paragraph 2 (d) of Ind AS 39).

(ii) As per Paragraph 2 (f) of AS 30, the contracts for contingent consideration in a business combination in case of acquirers are exempted from the scope of the Standard. However, Ind AS 39 does not include this exemption.

(iii) Paragraph 8.2 (a) (ii) of AS 30 states that a financial asset or financial liability at fair value through profit or loss is classified as held for trading if 'it is part of a portfolio of identified financial instruments that are managed together and for which there is evidence of a recent actual pattern of short-term profit-taking'. IND AS 39 states that a financial asset or financial liability at fair value through profit or loss is classified as held for trading if 'on initial recognition it is part of a portfolio of identified financial instruments.........'. The existing standard does not use the words 'on initial recognition'.

(iv) Ind AS 39 does not include the paragraph this would normally be relevant in case of a venture capital organisation, mutual fund, unit trust or similar entity whose business is investing in financial assets with a view to profiting from their total return in the form of interest or dividends and changes in fair value corresponding to paragraph 8.2 (b) (ii) of AS 30 when a group of financial assets, financial liabilities or both is managed and its performance is evaluated on a fair value basis, in accordance with a documented risk management or investment strategy.

(v) Ind AS 39 states that 'an entity shall not reclassify any financial instrument out of the fair value through profit or loss category if upon initial recognition it was designated by the entity as at fair value through profit or loss; and may, if a financial asset is no longer held for the purpose of selling or repurchasing it in the near term (notwithstanding that the financial asset may have been acquired or incurred principally for the purpose of selling or repurchasing it in the near term), reclassify that financial asset out of the fair value through profit or loss category if the requirements in paragraph 50B or 50D are met.' AS 30 prohibits any financial instruments into or out of the category of financial instruments designated at fair value through profit or loss. (Paragraph 50 (b) of Ind AS 39)

(vi) AS 30 states that 'an entity should not reclassify a financial instruments into or out of the fair value through profit or loss category while it is held or issued ' while Ind AS 39 states that 'an entity shall not reclassify a derivative out of the fair value through profit or loss category while it is held or Issued.' (Paragraph 50 of Ind AS 39).

(vii) Ind AS 39 (Application Guidance on effective interest rate) specifically states that 'if a financial asset is reclassified in accordance with paragraphs 50B, 50D or 50E, and the entity subsequently increases its estimates of future cash receipts as a result of increased recoverability of those cash receipts, the effect of that increase shall be recognised as an adjustment to the effective interest rate from the date of the change in estimate rather than as an adjustment to the carrying amount of the asset at the date of the change in estimate.' AS 30 does not specify so. (AG 8 of Ind AS 39).

(viii) The following paragraph has been added in Ind AS 39: 'if an entity is unable to measure separately the embedded derivative that would have to be separated on reclassification of a hybrid (combined) contract out of the fair value through profit or loss category, that reclassification is prohibited. In such circumstances the hybrid (combined) contract remains classified as at fair value through profit or loss in its entirety.' (Paragraph 12, of Ind AS 39)

(ix) Ind AS 39 modifies paragraph 2 (g) of the existing standard as 'any forward contracts between an acquirer and a selling shareholder to buy or sell an acquiree that will result in a business combination at a future acquisition date. The term of the forward contract should not exceed a reasonable period normally necessary to obtain any required approvals and to complete the transaction.' (Paragraph 2 (g), of Ind AS 39) (Changes shown in bold)

(x) Paragraph 80 of AS 39 states that 'for hedge accounting purposes, only assets, liabilities, firm commitments or highly probable forecast transactions that involve a party external to the entity can be designated as hedged items. It follows that hedge accounting can be applied to transactions between entities or segments in the same group only in the individual or separate financial statements of those entities or segments and not in the consolidated financial statements of the group.' The words 'or segments' have been deleted in Ind AS 39. (Paragraph 80 of Ind AS 39, paragraph 89 of AS 30)

(xi) Paragraph 97 of Ind AS 39 modifies paragraph 108 of AS 30 to state 'if a hedge of a forecast transaction subsequently results in the recognition of a financial asset or a financial liability, the associated gains or losses that were recognised in other comprehensive income in accordance with paragraph 95 shall be reclassified from equity to profit or loss as a reclassification adjustment (see Ind AS 1) in the same period or periods during which the hedged forecast cash-flows affects profit or loss (such as in the periods that interest income or interest expense is recognised). However, if an entity expects that all or a portion of a loss recognised in other comprehensive income will not be recovered in one or more future periods, it shall reclassify into profit or loss as a reclassification adjustment the amount that is not expected to be recovered.' (Paragraph 97 of Ind AS 39, AS 30, paragraph 108 of AS 30) (Changes shown in bold)

(xii) The financial instruments to which Ind AS 39 does not apply include financial instruments issued by the entity that meet the definition of an equity instrument in Ind AS 32 (including options Differences between Ind ASs and Existing Ass 52 and warrants) or that are required to be classified as an equity instrument in accordance with paragraphs 16A and 16B or paragraphs 16 C and 16 D of Ind AS 32. The existing standard does not refer to the latter. (Paragraph 2 (d) of Ind AS 39).

(xiii) Ind AS 39 does not exempt contracts for contingent consideration in a business combination from its scope while the existing standard provides an exemption. In the existing standard, the exemption applies only to the acquirer. (Paragraph 2(f) of Ind AS 39).

(xiv) Ind AS 39 provides that in determining the fair value of the financial liabilities, which, upon initial recognition, are designated at fair value through profit or loss, any change in fair value consequent to changes in the entity's own credit risk shall be ignored. AS 30, however, requires all changes in fair values in case of such liabilities to be recognised in profit or loss.

(xv) Ind AS 39 gives guidance on – (i) Reassessment of Embedded Derivatives (ii) Hedges of a Net Investment in a Foreign Operation and Extinguishing Financial Liabilities with Equity Instruments. AS 30 does not give such guidance.

Difference between Ind AS and IFRS

(Ind AS 39 vs. IAS 39)

1. A provisio has been added to paragraph 48 of Ind AS 39 that in determining the fair value of the financial liabilities which upon initial recognition are

designated at fair value through profit or loss, any change in fair value consequent to changes in the entity's own credit risk shall be ignored. IAS 39 requires all changes in fair values in such liabilities to be recognised in profit or loss.

2. IAS 39 does not change the requirements relating to employeebenefit plans that comply with IAS 26, Accounting and Reporting by Retirement Benefit Plans. Ind AS 39 does not mention so as IAS 26 is not relevant for companies.
3. The transitional provisions given in IAS 39 and IFRIC 6, IFRIC 16 and IFRIC 19 have not been given in Ind AS 39, since Accounting Standard corresponding to IFRS 1, First-time Adoption of International Financial Reporting Standards, will deal with the same. The transitional provisions given in IAS 39 and IFRIC 6, IFRIC 16 and IFRIC 19 have not been given in Ind AS 39, since all transitional provisions related to Ind ASs, wherever considered appropriate have been included in Ind AS 101, First-time Adoption of Indian Accounting Standards corresponding to IFRS 1, First-time Adoption of International Financial Reporting Standards.
4. Different terminology is used, as used in existing laws, e.g., the term 'balance sheet' is used instead of 'Statement of financial position' and 'Statement of profit and losses' is used instead of 'Statement of comprehensive income'.
5. The following paragraph numbers appear as 'Deleted' in IAS 39. In order to maintain consistency with paragraph numbers of IAS 39, the paragraph numbers are retained in Ind AS 39:
   (i) paragraph 2 (f)
   (ii) paragraph 3

Analysis of main differences

As per IFRS

IAS 39 requires all changes in fair values in case of financial liabilities designated at fair valuethrough Profit and Loss at initial recognition shall be recognised in profit or loss. IFRS 9 which will replace IAS 39 requires these to be recognised in 'other comprehensive income'.

Carve out

A proviso has been added to paragraph 48 of Ind AS 39 that in determining the fair value of thefinancial liabilities which upon initial recognition are designated at fair value through profit or loss, any change in fair value consequent to changes in the entity's own credit risk shall be ignored.

Reasons

It is felt that recognition of gain in profit or loss or in 'other comprehensive income' on deterioration of own credit risk is not proper because such deterioration ordinarily occurs when an entity is incurring losses. Thus, if an entity is allowed to recognise gain on deterioration of its own credit risk, it will book gains when its performance is not up to the mark. In the recent financial crisis in USA, it was noted that some banks booked gains while they were incurring losses due to the crisis.

Example 1

This example illustrates the application of IND AS 39 to items other than financial instruments.

Entity A enters into a contract to purchase 5 million pounds of copper for a fixed price at a future date.Copper is actively traded on the metals exchange and is readily convertible to cash. Discuss whether this contract falls within the scope of IND AS 39.

Solution:

This contract potentially is within the scope of IND AS 39 because it is a contract to buy or sell a nonfinancial item (copper) and the contract is subject to potential net settlement. Under IND AS 39, a contract is considered to be subject to potential net settlement if the nonfinancial item that will be delivered is readily convertible to cash. This condition is met in this case because the nonfinancial item is traded on an active market.

Therefore, the contract is within the scope of IND AS 39 unless it is a "normal purchase or sale." There is not sufficient information in the question to determine whether it is a "normal purchase or sale." The contract would be considered to be a normal purchase or sale if the entity intends to settle the contract by taking delivery of the nonfinancial item and has no history of:

- Settling net;
- Entering into offsetting contracts; or
- Selling shortly after delivery in order to generate a profit from short-term fluctuations in price or dealer's margin.

Example 2

This examples illustrates how to classify a financial asset or financial liability into one of the categories of financial assets or financial liabilities.

Entity A is considering how to classify these financial assets and financial liabilities:

(a) An accounts receivable that is not held for trading.

(b) An investment in an equity instrument quoted in an active market that is not held for trading.

(c) An investment in an equity instrument that is not held for trading and does not have a quoted price, and whose fair value cannot be reliably measured.

(d) A purchased debt security that is not quoted in an active market and that is not held for trading.

(e) A purchased debt instrument quoted in an active market that Entity A plans to hold to maturity. If market interest rates fall sufficiently, Entity A will consider selling the debt instrument to realize the associated gain.

(f) A "strategic" investment in an equity instrument that is not quoted in an active market. Entity A has no intention to sell the investment.

(g) An investment in a financial asset that is held for trading.

Indicate into which category or categories each item can be classified. Please note that some of the items can be classified into more than one category.

Solution:

(a) An accounts receivable that is not held for trading should be classified into the category of loans and receivables, unless the entity elects to designate it as either at fair value through profit or loss or available for sale.

(b) An investment in an equity instrument that has a quoted price and that is not held for trading should be classified as an available-for-sale financial asset, unless the entity elects to designate it as at fair value through profit or loss.

(c) An investment in an equity instrument that is not held for trading and does not have a quoted price, and whose fair value cannot be reliably measured, should be classified as an available for-sale financial asset.

(d) A purchased debt security that is not quoted in an active market and that is not held for trading should be classified into the category loans and receivables unless the entity designates it as either at fair value through profit or loss or available for sale.

(e) This purchased debt instrument should be classified as available for sale unless the entity elects to designate it as at fair value through profit or loss. Even though the debt instrument is quoted in an active market and Entity A plans to hold it to maturity, Entity A cannot classify it as held to maturity because Entity A will consider selling the debt instrument if market interest rates fall sufficiently.

(f) A "strategic" investment in an equity instrument that is not quoted in an active market and for which there is no intention to sell should be classified as available for sale unless Entity A designates it as at fair value through profit or loss.

(g) An investment in a financial asset that is held for trading should be classified into the category of financial asset at fair value through profit or loss.

Example 3

This examples illustrates the application of the principle for recognition of a financial asset or financial liability.

Entity A is evaluating whether each of the next items should be recognized as a financial asset or financial liability under IND AS 39:

(a) An unconditional receivable.

(b) A forward contract to purchase a specified bond at a specified price at a specified date in the future.

(c) A planned purchase of a specified bond at a specified date in the future.

(d) A firm commitment to purchase a specified quantity of gold at a specified price at a specified date in the future. The contract cannot be net settled.

(e) A firm commitment to purchase a machine that is designated as a hedged item in a fair value hedge of the associated foreign currency risk.

Help Entity A by indicating whether each of the above items should be recognised as an asset or liability under IND AS 39.

Solution:

(a) Entity A should recognise the unconditional receivable as a financial asset.

(b) In principle, Entity A should recognise the forward contract to purchase a specified bond at a specified price at a specified date in the future as a financial asset or financial liability. However, the initial carrying amount may be zero because forward contracts usually are agreed on terms that give them a zero fair value at inception.

(c) Entity A should not recognise an asset or liability for a planned purchase of a specified bond at a specified date in the future, because it does not have any present contractual right or obligation.

(d) Entity A should not recognise an asset or liability for a firm commitment to purchase a specified quantity of gold at a specified price at a specified date in the future. The contract is not a financial instrument but is instead an executory contract. Executory contacts are generally not recognised before they are settled under existing standards. (Firm commitments that are financial instruments or that are subject to net settlement, however, are recognised on the commitment date under IND AS 39.)

(e) Normally, a firm's commitment to purchase a machine would not be recognised as an asset or liability because it is an executory contract. Under the hedge accounting provisions of IND AS 39, however, Entity A would recognise an asset or liability for a firm commitment that is designated as a hedged item in a fair value hedge to the extent there have been changes in the fair value of the firm commitment attributable to the hedged risk (i.e., in this case, foreign currency risk).

Example 4

This example illustrates the application of the principle for derecognition of financial assets.

During the reporting period, Entity A has sold various financial assets:

(a) Entity A sells a financial asset for ₹ 10,000. There are no strings attached to the sale, and no other rights or obligations are retained by Entity A.

(b) Entity A sells an investment in shares for ₹ 10,000 but retains a call option to repurchase the shares at any time at a price equal to their current fair value on the repurchase date.

(c) Entity A sells a portfolio of short-term account receivables for ₹ 1,00,000 and promises to pay up to ₹ 3,000 to compensate the buyer if and when any defaults occur. Expected credit losses are significantly less than ₹ 3,000, and there are no other significant risks.

(d) Entity A sells a portfolio of receivables for ₹ 10,000 but retains the right to service the receivables for a fixed fee (i.e., to collect payments on the receivables and pass them on to the buyer of the receivables). The servicing arrangement meets the pass-through conditions.

(e) Entity A sells an investment in shares for ₹ 10,000 and simultaneously enters into a total return swap with the buyer under which the buyer will return any increases in value to Entity A and Entity A will pay the buyer interest plus compensation for any decreases in the value of the investment.

(f) Entity A sells a portfolio of receivables for ₹ 1,00,000 and promises to pay up to ₹ 3,000 to compensate the buyer if and when any defaults occur. Expected credit losses significantly exceed ₹ 3,000.

Help Entity A by evaluating the extent to which derecognition is appropriate in each of the above cases.

Solution:

(a) Entity A should derecognise the transferred financial asset, because it has transferred all risks and rewards of ownership.

(b) Entity A should derecognise the transferred financial asset, because it has transferred substantially all risks and rewards of ownership. While Entity A has retained a call option (i.e., a right that often precludes derecognition), the exercise price of this call option is the current fair value of the asset on the repurchase date. Therefore, the value of call option should be close to zero. Accordingly, Entity A has not retained any significant risks and rewards of ownership.

(c) Entity A should continue to recognise the transferred receivables because it has retained substantially all risks and rewards of the receivables. It has kept all expected credit risk, and there are no other substantive risks.

(d) Entity A should derecognise the receivables because it has transferred substantially all risks and rewards. Depending on whether Entity A will obtain adequate compensation for the servicing right, Entity A may have to recognise a servicing asset or servicing liability for the servicing right.

(e) Entity A should continue to recognise the sold investment because it has retained substantially all the risks and rewards of ownership. The total return swap results in Entity A still being exposed to all increases and decreases in the value of the investment.

(f) Entity A has neither retained nor transferred substantially all risks and rewards of the transferred assets. Therefore, Entity A needs to evaluate whether it has retained or transferred control. Assuming the receivables are not readily available in the market, Entity A would be considered to have retained control over the receivables. Therefore, it should continue to recognise the continuing involvement it has in the receivables, that is, the lower of

(1) The amount of the asset (₹ 1,00,000) and

(2) The maximum amount of the consideration received it could be required to repay (₹ 3,000).

Example 5

This example illustrate the application of the principle for derecognition of financial liabilities.

(a) A put option written by Entity A expires.

(b) Entity A owes Entity B ₹ 50,000 and has set aside that amount in a special trust that it will not use for any purpose other than to pay Entity B.

(c) Entity A pays Entity B ₹ 50,000 to discharge an obligation to pay ₹ 50,000 to Entity B.

Evaluate the extent to which derecognition is appropriate in each of the above cases.

Solution:

(a) Derecognition is appropriate because the option liability has expired. Therefore, the entity no longer has an obligation and the liability has been extinguished.

(b) Derecognition is not appropriate because Entity A still owes Entity B ₹ 50,000. It has not obtained legal release from paying this amount.

(c) Derecognition is appropriate because Entity A has discharged its obligation to pay ₹ 50,000.

Example 6

This example sillustrate how to measure a financial asset or financial liability on initial recognition.

During 20x5, Entity A acquires and incurs these financial assets and financial liabilities:

(a) A debt security that is held for trading is purchased for ₹ 50,000. Transaction costs of ₹ 200 are incurred.

(b) Equity securities classified as at fair value through profit or loss are purchased for ₹ 20,000. The dealer fee paid is ₹ 375.

(c) A bond classified as available for sale is purchased at a premium to par. The par value is ₹ 1,00,000 and the premium is ₹ 1,000 (such that the total amount paid is ₹ 1,01,000). In addition, transaction costs of ₹ 1,500 are incurred.

(d) A bond measured at amortised cost is issued for ₹ 30,000. Issuance costs are ₹ 600.

Determine the initial carrying amount of each of these financial instruments.

Solution:

(a) The initial carrying amount is ₹ 50,000. The transaction costs of ₹ 200 are expensed. This treatment applies because the debt security is classified as held for trading and, therefore, measured at fair value with changes in fair value recognised in profit or loss.

(b) The initial carrying amount is ₹ 20,000. The dealer fee of ₹ 375 is expensed as a transaction cost. This treatment applies because the equity securities are classified as at fair value with changes in fair value recognised in profit or loss.

(c) The initial carrying amount is ₹ 1,02,500 (i.e., the sum of the amount paid for the securities and the transaction costs). This treatment applies because the bond is not measured at fair value with changes in fair value recognised in profit or loss.

(d) The initial carrying amount is ₹ 29,400 (i.e., the amount received from issuing the bond less the transaction costs paid). For liabilities, transaction costs are deducted, not added, from the initial carrying amount. This treatment applies because the bond is not measured at fair value with changes in fair value recognised in profit or loss.

Example 7

This example illustrate when an investment would be measured at cost.

During 20x6, Entity A acquired these financial instruments:

(a) A share quoted on a stock exchange

(b) A bond quoted in an active bond market

(c) A bond that is not quoted in an active market

(d) A share that is not quoted in an active market but whose fair value can be estimated using valuation techniques

(e) A share that is not quoted in an active market and whose fair value cannot be measured reliably

(f) A derivative that is linked to and must be settled by an unquoted equity instrument whose fair value cannot be measured reliably.

Indicate which of the above items would be measured at cost.

Solution:

Only (e) and (f) would be measured at cost.

(a) A share quoted on a stock exchange would always be measured at fair value, assuming the market is active.

(b) A bond quoted in an active bond market would be measured at fair value or amortised cost, depending on its classification.

(c) A bond that is not quoted in an active market would be measured at fair value or amortised cost, depending on its classification.

(d) A share that is not quoted in an active market, but whose fair value can be estimated using valuation techniques, would always be measured at fair value.

(e) A share that is not quoted in an active market and whose fair value cannot be measured reliably would be measured at cost.

(f) A derivative that is linked to and must be settled by an unquoted equity instruments whose fair value cannot be measured reliably would be measured at cost.

Example 8

This example illustrate how to determine the fair value of a financial instrument.

Entity A is considering how to determine the fair value of the following financial instruments:

(a) A share that is actively traded on a stock exchange

(b) A share for which no active market exists but for which quoted prices are available

(c) A loan asset originated by the entity

(d) A bond that is not actively traded but whose fair value can be determined by reference to quoted interest rates for government bonds

(e) A complex derivative that is tailor-made for the entity.

In each of these cases, discuss whether fair value would be determined using a quoted market price or a valuation technique under IND AS 39.

Solution:

(a) The fair value of a share that is actively traded on a stock exchange equals the quoted market price.

(b) The fair value of a share for which no active market exists, but for which quoted prices are available, would be determined using a valuation technique.

(c) The fair value of a loan asset originated by the entity would be determined using a valuation technique.

(d) The fair value of a bond that is not actively traded, but whose fair value can be determined by reference to quoted interest rates for government bonds, would be determined using a valuation technique.

(e) The fair value of a complex derivative that is tailor-made to the entity would be determined using a valuation technique.

Example 9

This example illustrates how to account for impairment of loans and receivables.

Entity A has a loan asset whose initial carrying amount is ₹ 1,00,000 and whose effective interest rate is 8 per cent. On January 1, 20x5, Entity A determines that the borrower will probably enter into bankruptcy, and expects to collect only ₹ 20,000 of remaining principal and interest cash-flows. Entity A expects to recover this amount at the end of 20x5.

Determine the amount that Entity A should record as an impairment loss during 20x5 and the amount of interest income that would be reported during 20x5, if any.

Solution

On January 1, 20x5, Entity A should recognise an impairment loss of ₹ 81,481. The present value of the estimated future cash-flows is ₹ 18,519 (= ₹ 20,000/1.08). The difference between the previous carrying amount of the asset (₹ 100,000) and the present value of the estimated future cash-flows (₹ 18,519) is ₹ 81,481. The journal entry is

Dr. Impairment loss	81,481	
Cr. Loans and receivables		81,481

During 20x5, Entity A should recognise interest income of ₹ 1,481. This is computed by multiplying the original effective interest rate with the carrying amount (= 8 per cent × 18,519). The journal entry is

Dr. Loans and receivables	₹ 1,481	
Cr. Interest income		₹ 1,481

Example 10

This example illustrates how to account for derivatives.

On January 1, 20x6, Entity A enters into a forward contract to purchase on January 1, 20x8, a specified number of barrels of oil at a fixed price. Entity A is speculating that the price of oil will increase and plans to net settle the contract if the price increases. Entity A does not pay anything to enter into the forward contract on January 1, 20x6. Entity A does not designate the forward contract as a hedging instrument. At the end of 20x6, the fair value of the forward contract has increased to ₹ 4,00,000. At the end of 20x7, the fair value of the forward contract has declined to ₹ 3,50,000.

Prepare the appropriate journal entries on January 1, 20x6, December 31, 20x6, and December 31, 20x7.

Solution:

The journal entries are:

January 1, 20x6

No entry is required.

December 31, 20x6

Dr. Derivative asset	4,00,000	
Cr. Gain		4,00,000

December 31, 20x7

Dr. Loss	50,000	
Cr. Derivative asset		50,000

Example 11

This example illustrates when to separate embedded derivatives.

Entity A is seeking to identify embedded derivatives that are required to be separated under IND AS 39. It is considering whether these contracts contain embedded derivatives:

(a) An investment in a bond whose interest payments are linked to the price of gold. The bond is classified as at fair value through profit or loss.

(b) An investment in a bond whose interest payments are linked to the price of silver. The bond is classified as available for sale.

(c) An investment in a convertible debt instrument that is classified as available for sale.

(d) A lease contract that has a rent adjustment clause based on inflation.

(e) An issued convertible debt instrument.

Identify any embedded derivatives in these cases and, in each case, determine whether any identified embedded derivative requires separate accounting.

Solution:

(a) An investment in a bond whose interest payments are linked to the price of gold contains an embedded derivative on gold. However, because the bond is classified as at fair value through profit or loss, the embedded derivative should not be separated.

(b) An investment in a bond whose interest payments are linked to the price of silver contains an embedded derivative on silver. Because the bond is not measured at fair value with changes in fair value recognised in profit or loss and a commodity derivative is not closely related to a host debt contract, the embedded derivative is separated and accounted for as a derivative.

(c) An investment in a convertible debt instrument that is classified as available for sale contains an embedded equity conversion option. Because the bond is not measured at fair value with changes in fair value recognised in profit or loss and an equity conversion option is not closely related to a host debt contract, the embedded derivative is separated and accounted for as a derivative.

(d) A lease contract that has a rent adjustment clause based on inflation contains an embedded derivative on inflation. However, the embedded derivative is not separated from the lease contract because a rent adjustment clause based on inflation is considered to be closely related to the host lease contract.

(e) An issued convertible debt instrument contains an embedded equity conversion option. However, the equity conversion option generally is not accounted for as a derivative but is separated as an equity component in accordance with IAS 32 and accounted for as own equity.

Example 12

This example considers the reasons and conditions for hedge accounting.

Required

(1) Describe the three types of hedging relationships specified by IND AS 39.

(2) Discuss in what circumstances entities may want to apply hedge accounting.

(3) Discuss the conditions for hedge accounting.

Solution:

(1) IND AS 39 identifies three types of hedging relationships:

(a) Fair value hedges are hedges of the exposure to changes in fair value of a recognised asset or liability or an unrecognised firm commitment that is attributable to a particular risk and that could affect profit or loss. Under fair value hedge accounting, if the hedged item is otherwise measured at cost or amortised cost, the measurement of the hedged item is adjusted for changes in its fair value attributable to the hedged risk. These changes are recognised in profit or loss. If the hedged item is an available-for-sale financial asset, changes in fair value that would otherwise have been included in equity are recognised in profit or loss.

(b) Cash-flow hedges are hedges of the exposure to variability in cash-flows that is attributable to a particular risk associated with a recognised asset or liability or a highly probable forecast transaction and could affect profit or loss. Under cash-flow hedge accounting, changes in the fair value of the hedging instrument attributable to the hedged risk are deferred as a separate component of equity to the extent the hedge is effective (rather than being recognised immediately in profit or loss).

(c) Hedges of net investments in foreign operations are accounted for like cash-flow hedges.

(2) Entities may want to use hedge accounting to avoid mismatches in the recognition of gains and losses on related transactions. When an entity uses a derivative (or other instrument measured at fair value) to hedge the value of an asset or liability measured at cost or amortized cost or not recognised at all, accounting that is not reflective of the entity's financial position and financial performance may result because of the different measurement bases used for the hedging instrument and the hedged item. The normally applicable accounting requirements would include the changes in fair value of a derivative in profit or loss but not the changes in fair value of the hedged item in profit or loss. In addition, when an entity uses a derivative (or other instrument measured at fair value) to hedge a future expected transaction, the entity would like to defer the recognition of the change in fair value of the derivative until the

future transaction affects profit or loss. Otherwise, the changes in fair value of a derivative hedging instrument would be recognised in profit or loss without a corresponding offset associated with the hedged item.

(3) The hedge accounting conditions are:

(a) There is formal designation and documentation of the hedging relationship and the entity's risk management objective and strategy for undertaking the hedge. Hedge accounting is permitted only from the date such designation and documentation is in place.

(b) The hedge is expected to be highly effective in achieving offsetting changes in fair value or cash-flows attributable to the hedged risk.

(c) The effectiveness of the hedge can be measured reliably.

(d) The hedge is assessed on an ongoing basis and determined actually to have been highly effective throughout the financial reporting periods for which the hedge was designated.

(e) For cash-flow hedges, a hedged forecast transaction must be highly probable and must present an exposure to variations in cash-flows that could ultimately affect profit or loss.

Example 13

This example illustrates the accounting for a fair value hedge.

Entity A has originated a 5 per cent fixed rate loan asset that is measured at amortised cost (₹ 1,00,000). Because Entity A is considering whether to securitise the loan asset (i.e., to sell it in a securitisation transaction), it wants to eliminate the risk of changes in the fair value of the loan asset. Thus, on January 1, 20x6, Entity A enters into a pay-fixed, receive-floating interest rate swap to convert the fixed interest receipts into floating interest receipts and thereby offset the exposure to changes in fair value. Entity A designates the swap as a hedging instrument in a fair value hedge of the loan asset. Market interest rates increase. At the end of the year, Entity A receives ₹ 5,000 in interest income on the loan and ₹ 200 in net interest payments on the swap. The change in the fair value of the interest rate swap is an increase of ₹ 1,300. At the same time, the fair value of the loan asset decreases by ₹ 1,300.

Required

Prepare the appropriate journal entries at the end of the year. Assume that all conditions for hedge accounting are met.

Solution:

Dr. Cash	5,000	
Cr. Interest income		5,000

(To record interest income on the loan)

Dr. Cash	200	
Cr. Interest income		200

(To record the net interest settlement of the swap)

Dr. Derivative	1,300	
Cr. Hedging gain		1,300

(To record the increase in the fair value of the swap)

Dr. Hedging loss	1,300	
Cr. Loan asset		1,300

(To record the decrease in the fair value of the loan asset attributable to the hedged risk)

Example 14

This example illustrates the accounting for a cash-flow hedge.

Entity A is a producer of widgets. To hedge the risk of declines in the price of 100 widgets that it expects to sell on December 31, 20x8, Entity A on January 1, 20x7, enters into a net-settled forward contract on 100 widgets for delivery on December 31, 20x8. During 20x7, the change in the fair value of the forward contract is a decrease of ₹ 8,000. During 20x8, the change in the fair value of the forward contract is an increase of ₹ 2,000. On December 31, 20x8, Entity A settles the forward contract by paying ₹ 6,000. At the same time, it sells 100 widgets to customers for ₹ 93,000.

Prepare the appropriate journal entries on January 1, 20x7, December 31, 20x7, and December 31, 20x8. Assume that all conditions for hedge accounting are met and that the hedging relationship is fully effective (100 per cent).

Solution:

January 1, 20x7

No entry required.

December 31, 20x7

Dr. Equity	8,000	
Cr. Derivative liability		8,000

(To record the decrease in fair value of the hedging instrument)

December 31, 20x8

Dr. Derivative liability	2,000	
Cr. Equity		2,000

(To record the increase in fair value of the hedging instrument)

Dr. Derivative liability	6,000	
Cr. Cash		6,000

(To record the settlement of the hedging instrument)

Dr. Cash	93,000	
Cr. Equity		6,000
Cr. Sales revenue		87,000

(To record the sale and the associated amount deferred in equity related to the hedge of the sale)

QUESTIONS

1. The scope of IND AS 39 includes all of the following items except:
   (a) Financial instruments that meet the definition of a financial asset.
   (b) Financial instruments that meet the definition of a financial liability.
   (c) Financial instruments issued by the entity that meet the definition of an equity instrument.
   (d) Contracts to buy or sell nonfinancial items that can be settled net.

   Answer: (c)

2. Which of the following is not a category of financial assets defined in IND AS 39?
   (a) Financial assets at fair value through profit or loss.
   (b) Available-for-sale financial assets.
   (c) Held-for-sale investments.
   (d) Loans and receivables.

   Answer: (c)

3. All of the following are characteristics of financial assets classified as held-to-maturity investments except:
   (a) They have fixed or determinable payments and a fixed maturity.
   (b) The holder can recover substantially all of its investment (unless there has been credit deterioration).
   (c) They are quoted in an active market.
   (d) The holder has a demonstrated positive intention and ability to hold them to maturity.

   Answer: (b)

4. Which of the following items is not precluded from classification as a held-to-maturity investment?
   (a) An investment in an unquoted debt instrument.
   (b) An investment in a quoted equity instrument.
   (c) A quoted derivative financial asset.
   (d) An investment in a quoted debt instrument.

Answer: (d)

5. All of the following are characteristics of financial assets classified as loan and receivables except:
   (a) They have fixed or determinable payments.
   (b) The holder can recover substantially all of its investment (unless there has been credit deterioration).
   (c) They are not quoted in an active market.
   (d) The holder has a demonstrated positive intention and ability to hold them to maturity.

Answer: (d)

6. What is the principle for recognition of a financial asset or a financial liability in IND AS 39?
   (a) A financial asset is recognised when, and only when, it is probable that future economic benefits will flow to the entity and the cost or value of the instrument can be measured reliably.
   (b) A financial asset is recognised when, and only when, the entity obtains control of the instrument and has the ability to dispose of the financial asset independent of the actions of others.
   (c) A financial asset is recognised when, and only when, the entity obtains the risks and rewards of ownership of the financial asset and has the ability to dispose the financial asset.
   (d) A financial asset is recognised when, and only when, the entity becomes a party to the contractual provisions of the instrument.

Answer: (d)

7. In which of the following circumstances is derecognition of a financial asset not appropriate?
   (a) The contractual rights to the cash-flows of the financial assets have expired.
   (b) The financial asset has been transferred and substantially all the risks and rewards of ownership of the transferred asset have also been transferred.

(c) The financial asset has been transferred and the entity has retained substantially all the risks and rewards of ownership of the transferred asset.

(d) The financial asset has been transferred and the entity has neither retained nor transferred substantially all the risks and rewards of ownership of the transferred asset. In addition, the entity has lost control of the transferred asset.

Answer: (c)

8. Which of the following transfers of financial assets qualifies for derecognition?

(a) A sale of a financial asset where the entity retains an option to buy the asset back at its current fair value on the repurchase date.

(b) A sale of a financial asset where the entity agrees to repurchase the asset in one year for a fixed price plus interest.

(c) A sale of a portfolio of short-term accounts receivables where the entity guarantees to compensate the buyer for any losses in the portfolio.

(d) A loan of a security to another entity (i.e., a securities lending transaction).

Answer: (a)

9. Which of the following is not a relevant consideration when evaluating whether to derecognise a financial liability?

(a) Whether the obligation has been discharged.

(b) Whether the obligation has been canceled.

(c) Whether the obligation has expired.

(d) Whether substantially all the risks and rewards of the obligation have been transferred.

Answer: (d)

10. At what amount is a financial asset or financial liability measured on initial recognition?

(a) The consideration paid or received for the financial asset or financial liability.

(b) Acquisition cost. Acquisition cost is the consideration paid or received plus any directly attributable transaction costs to the acquisition or issuance of the financial asset or financial liability.

(c) Fair value. For items that are not measured at fair value through profit or loss, transaction costs are also included in the initial measurement.

(d) Zero.

Answer: (c)

11. In addition to financial assets at fair value through profit or loss, which of the following categories of financial assets is measured at fair value in the balance sheet?
    (a) Available-for-sale financial assets.
    (b) Held-to-maturity investments.
    (c) Loans and receivables.
    (d) Investments in unquoted equity instruments.

Answer: (a)

12. What is the best evidence of the fair value of a financial instrument?
    (a) Its cost, including transaction costs directly attributable to the purchase, origination, or issuance of the financial instrument.
    (b) Its estimated value determined using discounted cash-flow techniques, option pricing models, or other valuation techniques
    (c) Its quoted price, if an active market exists for the financial instrument.
    (d) The present value of the contractual cash-flows less impairment.

Answer: (c)

13. Is there any exception to the requirement to measure at fair value financial assets classified as at fair value through profit or loss or available for sale?
    (a) No. Such assets are always measured at fair value.
    (b) Yes. If the fair value of such assets increases above cost, the resulting unrealised holding gains are not recognised but deferred until realised.
    (c) Yes. If the entity has the positive intention and ability to hold assets classified in those categories to maturity, they are measured at amortised cost.
    (d) Yes. Investments in unquoted equity instruments that cannot be reliably measured at fair value (or derivatives that are linked to and must be settled in such unquoted equity instruments) are measured at cost.

Answer: (d)

14. What is the effective interest rate of a bond or other debt instrument measured at amortized cost?
    (a) The stated coupon rate of the debt instrument.
    (b) The interest rate currently charged by the entity or by others for similar debt instruments (i.e., similar remaining maturity, cash-flow pattern, currency, credit risk, collateral, and interest basis).

(c) The interest rate that exactly discounts estimated future cash payments or receipts through the expected life of the debt instrument or, when appropriate, a shorter period to the net carrying amount of the instrument.

(d) The basic, risk-free interest rate that is derived from observable government bond prices.

Answer: (c)

15. Which of the following is not objective evidence of impairment of a financial asset?

 (a) Significant financial difficulty of the issuer or obligor.

 (b) A decline in the fair value of the asset below its previous carrying amount.

 (c) A breach of contract, such as a default or delinquency in interest or principal payments.

 (d) Observable data indicating that there is a measurable decrease in the estimated future cash-flows from a group of financial assets although the decrease cannot yet be associated with any individual financial asset.

Answer: (b)

16. Under IND AS 39, all of the following are characteristics of a derivative except:

 (a) It is acquired or incurred by the entity for the purpose of generating a profit from short-term fluctuations in market factors.

 (b) Its value changes in response to the change in a specified underlying (e.g., interest rate, financial instrument price, commodity price, foreign exchange rate, etc.).

 (c) It requires no initial investment or an initial net investment that is smaller than would be required for other types of contracts that would be expected to have a similar response to changes in market factors.

 (d) It is settled at a future date.

Answer: (a)

17. Under IND AS 39, is a derivative (e.g., an equity conversion option) that is embedded in another contract (e.g., a convertible bond) accounted for separately from that other contract?

 (a) Yes. IND AS 39 requires all derivatives (both freestanding and embedded) to be accounted for as derivatives.

 (b) No. IND AS 39 precludes entities from splitting financial instruments and accounting for the components separately.

 (c) It depends. IND AS 39 requires embedded derivatives to be accounted for separately as derivatives if, and only if, the entity has embedded the derivative in order to avoid derivatives accounting and has no substantive business purpose for embedding the derivative.

(d) It depends. IND AS 39 requires embedded derivatives to be accounted for separately if, and only if, the economic characteristics and risks of the embedded derivative and the host contract are not closely related and the combined contract is not measured at fair value with changes in fair value recognised in profit or loss.

Answer: (d)

18. Which of the following is not a condition for hedge accounting?

   (a) Formal designation and documentation of the hedging relationship and the entity's risk management objective and strategy for undertaking the hedge at inception of the hedging relationship.

   (b) The hedge is expected to be highly effective in achieving offsetting changes in fair value or cash-flows attributable to the hedged risk, the effectiveness of the hedge can be reliably measured, and the hedge is assessed on an ongoing basis and determined actually to have been effective.

   (c) For cash-flow hedges, a forecast transaction must be highly probable and must present an exposure to variations in cash-flows that could ultimately affect profit or loss.

   (d) The hedge is expected to reduce the entity's net exposure to the hedged risk, and the hedge is determined actually to have reduced the net entity-wide exposure to the hedged risk.

Answer: (d)

19. What is the accounting treatment of the hedging instrument and the hedged item under fair value hedge accounting?

   (a) The hedging instrument is measured at fair value, and the hedged item is measured at fair value with respect to the hedged risk. Changes in fair value are recognised in profit or loss.

   (b) The hedging instrument is measured at fair value, and the hedged item is measured at fair value with respect to the hedged risk. Changes in fair value are recognised directly in equity to the extent the hedge is effective.

   (c) The hedging instrument is measured at fair value with changes in fair value recognised directly in equity to the extent the hedge is effective. The accounting for the hedged item is not adjusted.

   (d) The hedging instrument is accounted for in accordance with the accounting requirements for the hedged item (i.e., at fair value, cost or amortised cost, as applicable), if the hedge is effective.

Answer: (a)

20. What is the accounting treatment of the hedging instrument and the hedged item under cash-flow hedge accounting?

    (a) The hedged item and hedging instrument are both measured at fair value with respect to the hedged risk, and changes in fair value are recognised in profit or loss.

    (b) The hedged item and hedging instrument are both measured at fair value with respect to the hedged risk, and changes in fair value are recognised directly in equity.

    (c) The hedging instrument is measured at fair value, with changes in fair value recognised directly in equity to the extent the hedge is effective. The accounting for the hedged item is not adjusted.

    (d) The hedging instrument is accounted for in accordance with the accounting requirements for the hedged item (i.e., at fair value, cost or amortised cost, as applicable), if the hedge is effective.

Answer: (c)

References: Ind AS 39, Existing AS 30 and IAS 39

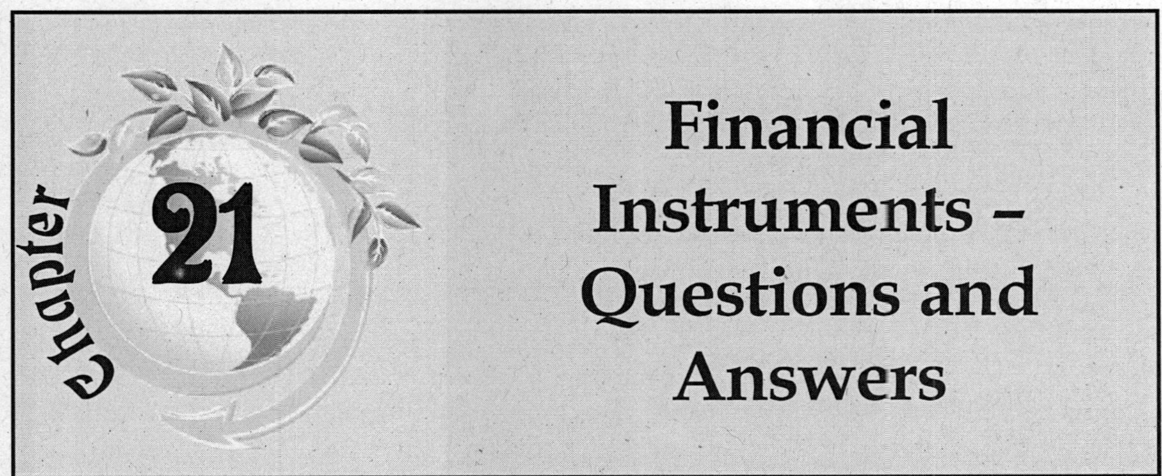

Financial Instruments – Questions and Answers

Question 1:

Aakshaya Ltd. has given a 12.50 per cent fixed-rate loan to its subsidiary Shaya Ltd. Aakshaya Ltd. Measures this loan at an amortised cost of ₹ 2,50,000. Aakshaya Ltd. has plans to hive off the receivable at a later stage and as a measure to safeguard against fall in value of its dues enters into a pay-fixed, receive floating interest rate swap to convert the fixed interest receipts into floating interest receipts. Aakshaya Ltd. Designates the swap as a Hedging instruments in a fair value hedge of the Loan Asset.

Over the following months, market interest rates increase and Aakshaya Ltd. earns interest income of ₹ 25,000 on the loan and ₹ 1,000 as net interest payments on the swap. The fair value of the loan assets decrease by ₹ 5,000 while that of the interest rate swap increases by ₹ 5,000. You are informed that all conditions required for the Hedge Accounting are satisfied. You are required to pass Journal Entries with suitable narrations in the books of Aakshaya Ltd., to record the above transactions.

Answer:

In the books of Aakshaya Ltd.

Journal Entities

	₹	₹
Cash Account Dr. To Interest Account (Being the receipt of interest income on the loan asset)	25,000	25,000
Derivative Account Dr. To Hedging Gain Account (Being increase in the fair value of the interest rate swap)	5,000	5,000

Hedging Loss Account To Loan to Shaya Ltd. Account (Being decrease in the fair value of loan to Shaya Ltd. attributable to the hedged risk recorded)	Dr.	5,000	 5,000
Cash Account To Interest Account (Being the entry to record the interest settlement of the swap as increase ininterest income)	Dr.	1,000	 1,000

Question 2:

Friendly Ltd. granted ₹ 100 lakhs as loan to its employees on 1st Jaunary 2009 at a concessional rate of interest of 4 per cent per annum on the condition that the loan is to be repaid in five qual annual installments along with interest thereon. You are informed that the prevailing lending rate for such risk profiles is 10 per cent p.a. You are required to find out what value the loan should be recognised initially and the amount of annual amortisation till closure thereof. Show journal Entries with appropriate narrations that will be recorded in the company's books in the year 2009.

[Present value of an Indian Rupee at a discount rate of 10 per cent per annum will be .9090, .8263, .7512, .6829 and .6208 which is to be adopted for purpose of calculation.]

Answer:

(1) Caluation of initial recognition amount of loan to employees

Year ended	Cash-flows		Total ₹	P.V. Factor @ 10%	Present Value ₹
	Principal ₹	Interest @ 4% ₹			
2009	20,00,000	4,00,000	24,00,000	0.9090	21,81,600
2010	20,00,000	3,20,000	23,20,000	0.8263	19,17,016
2011	20,00,000	2,40,000	22,40,000	0.7512	16,82,688
2012	20,00,000	1,60,000	21,60,000	0.6829	14,75,064
2013	20,00,000	80,000	20,80,000	0.6208	12,91,264

(2) Calculation of amortised cost of loan to employees

Year	Amortised cost (opening Balance) [1] ₹	Interest to be recognised @10% [2] ₹	Repayment (including interest) [3] ₹	Amortised cost (closing balance) [4]=[1]+[2]-[3]
2009	85,47,632	8,54,763	24,00,000	70,02,395
2010	70,02,395	7,00,240	23,20,000	53,82,635
2011	53,82,635	5,38,264	22,40,000	36,80,899
2012	36,80,899	3,68,090	21,60,000	18,88,989
2013	18,88,989	1,91,011*	20,80,000	Nil

*The difference of ₹ 2,112 (₹ 1,91,011 – ₹ 1,88,899) is due to approximation incomputations.

(3) Journal Entries in the books of Friendly Ltd. For the year ended 31st December, 2009 (regarding loan to employees)

Particulars	Dr. Amount	Cr. Amount
Staff Loan A/c Dr. To Bank A/c (Being the disbursement of loans to staff)	1,00,00,000	 1,00,00,000
Staff cost A/c (1,00,00,000 – 85,47,632) Dr. To Staff Loan A/c* (Being the write off of excess of loan balance over present value thereof in order to reflect the loan at its present value of ₹ 85,47,632)	14,52,368	 14,52,368
Staff Loan A/c Dr. To Interest on staff loan A/c (Being the charge of interest @ market rate of 10 per cent on the loan)	8,54,763	 8,54,763
Bank A/c Dr. To Staff Loan A/c (Being the repayment of first installment with interest for the year)	24,00,000	 24,00,000
Interest on staff loan A/c Dr. To Profit and Loss A/c (Being transfer of balance of staff loan interest account to profit and loss account)	8,54,763	 8,54,763
Profit and Loss A/c Dr. To Staff cost A/c (Being transfer of balance of staff cost account to profit and loss account)	14,52,368	 14,52,368

*Loans and receivables should be measured at amortized cost using the effective interest method as per AS-30 'Financial Instruments: Recognition and Measurements'.

Question 3:

On 1st April 2008 Sigma Ltd. issued 6 per cent Convertible debentures of face value of ₹ 100 per debentures at par. The debentures are redeemable at a premium of 10 per cent on 31/03/2010 or these maybe converted into ordinary shares at the option of the holder, the interest rate for equivalent debentures without conversion rights would have been 10 per cent. Being a compound financial instrument. You are required to seprate equity and debts portions as on 01-04-2008. Equity portion is ₹ 1,85,400. Find out the debts portion [Debenture amount]. The present value of ₹ 1 receivable at the end of each year based on discount rates of 6 per cent and 10 per cent can be taken as:

End of year	6 per cent	10 per cent
1	0.94	0.91
2	0.89	0.83
3	0.84	0.75
4	0.79	0.68

Answer:

Assume that total proceeds of the issue is = ₹ M

Hence, interest payable every year = 6 per cent on ₹ M = .06M

Present Value of interest (at 10 per cent discount) = 0.06M × cumulative discount factor of 4 years

= 0.06M × 3.17 = 0.1902M

Amount refundable (as amount have to be redeemed at 10 per cent premium) – 1.10 × M

Present Value of 1.10M at 4th year = 1.10M × 0.68 = 0.748 M

Therefore, total present value of debentures = 0.1902M + 0.748 M = 0.9382 M

Hence, amount of equity = M – 0.9382M = ₹ 1, 85,400

0.0618M = ₹ 1,85,400

M = 1,85,400/0.0618 = ₹ 30,00,000

Therefore, total proceeds of the issue is ₹ 30,00,000

Debt Portion = ₹ 30,00,000 – ₹ 1,85,400 = ₹ 28,14,600

Question 4:

At the beginning of year 1, an enterprise issued 20000 convertible debentures with face value of ₹ 100 per debentures at par. The debentures have six year term. The interest at annual rate of 9 per cent is paid half-yearly. The bondholders have an option to convert half of the face value of debentures into 2 ordinary shares at the end of year 3. The bondholders not exercising the conversion option will be repaid at par to the extent of ₹ 50 per debentures at the end of year 3. The non-convertible portion will be repaid at 10 per cent premium at the end of year 6. At the time of issue, the prevailing market interest rate for similar debt without conversion option was 10 per cent. Complete value of embedded derivative.

Answer:

Half Year	Cash-flows	DF	PV
1 - 6	₹ 000 (5 per cent) ₹ 000 / 90	5.076	456.84

7 – 12	45	3.787	170.41
12	1,100	0.557	612.70
Value of host (Liability component)			1,239.95
Value of embedded derivative (Equity component)			760.05
Issue Proceeds			2,000.00

Question 5:

Certain callable convertible debentures are issued at ₹ 60. The value of similar debentures without call or equity conversion option ₹ 57. The value of call as determined using Black and Scholes model for pricing is ₹ 2.

Determine values of liabilities and equity component.

Answer:

A callable bond is one that gives the issuer a right to buy the bond from the bondholders at a specified price. This feature in effect is a call option written by the bondholder. The option premium (Value of call) is payable by the Issuer.

Liability component (disregarding the call) = ₹ 57

Value of call payable by issuer = ₹ 2

Liability component = ₹ 57 – ₹ 2 = ₹ 55

Equity component = ₹ 60 – ₹ 55 = ₹ 5

Question 6:

On February 1, 2009, Future Ltd. entered into a contract with Son Ltd. to receive the fair value of 1,000 Future Ltd.'s own equity shares outstanding as on 31/01/2010 in i.e., exchange for payment of ₹ 1,04,000 in cash i.e., ₹ 104 per share The contract will be settled in net cash on 31.01.2010.

The fair values of this forward contract on the different dates were:

(1) Fair value of forward on 01-02-09 Nil

(2) Fair value of forward on 31-12-09 6300

(3) Fair value of Forward on 31-01-10 2000

Presuming that future ltd closes its books on 31st December each year, pass entries:

(1) If net settled in cash

(2) If net is settled by Son Ltd by delivering of Future Ltd.

Answer:

(1) If net settled in Cash

On 01-02-2009: No entry is required because fair value of derivative is zero and no cash is paid or received.

On 31-12-2009:

Forward Asset A/c	Dr.	6,300	
To Gain A/c			6,300

On 31-01-2010

Loss A/c	Dr.	4,300	
To Forward Asset A/c			4,300
Cash A/c	Dr.	2,000	
To Forward Asset A/c			2,000

(2) If net settled by delivery of shares

First three entries will be the same, only the last entry will change as under:

Equity A/c	Dr.	2,000	
To Forward Asset A/c			2,000

Question 7:

Comforts Ltd. granted ₹ 10,00,000 loan to its employees on Juanuary 1, 2009 at a concessional interest rate of 4 per cent per annum Loan is to be repaid in five equal annual installments along with interest. Market rate of Interest for such loan is 10 per cent per annum. Following the principals of recognition and measurement as laid down in AS 30 'Financial Instruments: Recognition and Measurement', record the entries for the year ended 31st December 2009 for the loan transaction, and also calculate the value of loan initially to be recogninsed and amortised cost for all the subsequent years. The present value of ₹ 1 receivable at the end of each year based on discount factor of 10 per cent can be taken as:

Year end	1	0.9090
	2	0.8263
	3	0.7512
	4	0.6829
	5	0.6208

Answer:

Workings:

1. Principal repayment each year will be 10,00,000/5 = ₹ 2,00,000
2. Concession in interest rate is 10 per cent market rate minus 4 per cent actual rate = 6 per cent

Calculation of initial recognition amount of loan to employees

Year end	Cash Inflow		Total ₹	P.V. Factor	Present Value ₹
	Principal ₹	Interest @ 4 per cent ₹			
2009	2,00,000	40,000	2,40,000	0.9090	2,18,160
2010	2,00,000	32,000	2,32,000	0.8263	1,91,702
2011	2,00,000	24000	2,24,000	0.7512	1,68,269
2012	2,00,000	16,000	2,16,000	0.6829	1,47,506
2013	2,00,000	8,000	2,08,000	0.6208	1,29,126
				Present value	8,54,763

Calculation of amortised cost of Loan to employees

Year	Amortised Cost (Opening Balance) (1)	Interest to be Recognised @ 10 per cent (2)	Repayment (Including intt.) (3)	Amortised cost (closing balance) (4) [1+2-3]
2009	8,54,763	85,476	2,40,000	7,00,239
2010	7,00,239	70,024	2,32,000	5,38,263
2011	5,38,263	53,826	2,24,000	3,68,089
2012	3,68,089	36,809	2,16,000	1,88,898
2013	1,88,898	19,102	2,08,000	Nil

Journal Entries in the books of Comfort Ltd.

For the year ended 31st December, 2009

		Debit ₹	Credit ₹
Staff loan A/c To bank Loan (Being the disbursement of loans to staff)	Dr.	10,00,000	 10,00,000
Staff Cost A/c (10,00,000 – 8,54,763) To Staff Loan A/c (Being the write off of excess of Loan balance over present value thereof, in order to reflect the Loan at its present value of ₹ 8,54,763)	Dr.	1,45,237	 1,45,237

Staff Loan A/c To Interest on Staff Loan A/c (Being the charge of interest @ market rate of 10 per cent to the Loan)	Dr.	85,476	85,476
Bank A/c To Staff Loan (Being the repayment of first installment with interest for the year)	Dr.	2,40,000	2,40,000
Interest on staff Loan A/c To Profit and Loss A/c (Being transfer of balance in staff Loan interest account to Profit and loss A/c)	Dr.	85,476	85,476
Profit and Loss A/c To Staff Loan A/c (Being transfer of balance in staff cost account to profit and loss account)	Dr.	1,45,237	1,45,237

Question 8:

Danu Ltd. holds ₹ 1,00,000 of loans yielding 18 percent interest per annum for their estimated lives of 9 years. The fair value of these loans, after considering the interest yield is estimated at ₹ 1,10,000.

The company securitises the principal component of the loan plus the right to receive interest at 14 per cent to Susovana Corporation, a special purpose vehicle, for 1,00,000.

Out of the balance interest of 4 per cent, it is stipulated that half of such balance interest, namely 2 per cent, will be due to Danu Ltd. as fees for continuing to service the loans. The fair value of their servicing asset so created is estimated at 3,500. The remaining half of the interest is due to Danu Ltd. As an interest strip receivable, the fair value of which is estimated at 6,500.

Give the accounting treatment of the above transactions in the form of Journal entries in the books of originator.

Answer:

Workings

1. Fair Value of securitised component of Loan

	₹	₹
Fair value of Loan		1,10,000
Less: Fair Value of servicing asset	3,500	
Less: Fair Value of interest strip	6,500	10,000
Fair Value of Loan		1,00,000

2. Apportionment of carrying amount based on relative fair values

Particulars	Fair Value ₹	Per cent based on total Fair value	Carrying amount/ cost
Securitised component of the Loan	1,00,000	90.91 per cent	90,910
Servicing Asset	3,500	3.18 per cent	3,180
Interest Strip Receivable	6,500	5.91 per cent	5,910
Total	1,10,000	100.00 per cent	1,00,000

3. Profit on Securitisation ₹

Net proceeds from securitization	1,00,000
Less: Cost (apportioned carrying amount) of securitised Component of Loan)	90,910
Profit	**9,090**

Journal entries in the books of originator

	Debit	Credit
Bank A/c Dr.	1,00,000	
To Loans A/c (Cost of securitization of principal amount and right to receive interest at 14 per cent interest rate)		90,910
To Profit on Securitisation A/c		9,090
(being securitisation of principal amount and right to receive interest at 14 per cent interest rate)		
Servicing Asset A/c Dr.	3,180	
Interest Strip A/c Dr.	5,910	
To Loans A/c		9,090
(Being creation of servicing asset and interest strip receivable)		

Question 9:

Accounting for interest rate swap

Raj Limted wants to borrow 5-year fixed-rate rupee funding to finance an expansion project. Its credit rating is BBB (not very high). It finds that it will have to pay interest @ 11 per cent if it borrows at fixed-interest rate. In the floating rate market, it can issue floating rate notes at margin of 0.75 per cent over the prime rate, which is 10 per cent.

On the other hand, Vijay Ltd., a large unit, is looking for floating rate note but finds that it will have to pay prime rate, while in the fixed rate market it can raise 5 Year funds at 9.50 per cent due to AAA rating and BBB rating is 150 bp in fixed rate segment and 75 bp in floating rate segment. The requirements and access of the two parties are summarised below:

Particulars	Raj Ltd. (BBB Rating)	Vijay Ltd. (AAA Rating)
Cost of Fixed Loan	11 per cent	9.50 per cent
Cost of Floating Loan	Prime rate + 0.75 per cent	Prime rate (10 per cent)

Give the accounting treatment for interest rate swaps. Assume equal sharing of gains between swap bank and the parties to the swap arrangement, and an underlying principal of ₹ 100 lakhs, is exchanged at the beginning. At the end of the year , fair value of the swap is estimated as ₹ 1.25 lakhs, net gain to Vijay Ltd.

Answer:

1. How the swap arrangement can be structured: An effective swap arrangement can be structured, only if Vijay Limited. (the stronger company) opts for an interest rate scheme in which it has maximum comparative advantage. Therefore, Vijay Limited should opt for fixed loan (advantage of 1.5 per cent vs. 0.75 per cent in floating rate), and Raj Limited would go for a floating rate scheme at prime rate + 0.75 per cent.
2. Sharing of gain: Total gain = difference between swap points of fixed rate and floating rate = 1.50 per cent - 0.75 per cent = 0.75 per cent. Therefore, each party will gain 0.25 per cent
3. Effective Interest rate and structure of swap can be presented through diagram:

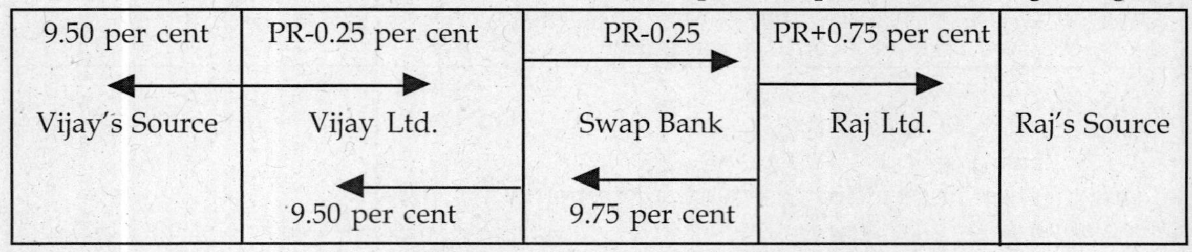

Effective Rate PR-0.25 per cent

Effective Rate 10.75 per cent

Journal entries in the books of Vijay Limted

Date	Particulars		Debit	Credit
1.	Cash A/c To Loan A/c (Being amount borrowed from Financial Institutions)	Dr.	1,00,00,000	 100,00,000
2.	Interest A/c To Bank A/c (Being interest liability for the year paid for 100 lakhs * 9.50 per cent)	Dr.	9,50,000	 9,50,000
3.	Interest A/c To Swap Bank A/c (Being Interest payable to swap bank under swap arrangement made due = 100 lakhs * 9.75 per cent, e.g., PR-0.25 per cent)	Dr.	9,75,000	 9,75,000
4.	Swap Bank A/c To Bank (Being interest paid to swap bank)	Dr.	9,75,000	 9,75,000
5.	Swap bank A/c To Interest A/c (Being Interest payable by swap bank under the swap arrangement = ₹ 100 Lakhs * 9.50 per cent)	Dr.	9,50,000	 9,50,000
6.	Bank A/c To Swap Bank A/c (Being interest received from swap bank under swap arrangenment (9,50,000* 5)	Dr	47,50,000	 47,50,000
7.	Swap Asset A/c To gain on Swap A/c (Profit and Loss)	Dr.	1,25,000	 1,25,000

Question 10: Accounting for Interest Rate Swap-Gain/Loss

On April 1, 2006, A Ltd borrowed ₹ 10 lakh at annual fixed interest rate of 7 per cent payable half-yearly. The life of the loan is 4 years with no pre-payment permitted. The Company expected the interest rate to fall and on the same day, it entered into an Interest Rate swap arrangement, whereby the company would pay 6-month LIBOR and would receive annual fixed interest of 7 per cent every half year. The swap effectively converted the Company's fixed rate obligation to floating rate obligation. The value of swap and debt are ₹ 0.2 lakh (positive) and ₹ 10.2 lakh on 1.10.2006 and (₹ 0.1 lakh) and ₹ 9.9 lakh on 31.03.2007 respectively. Six-month LIBOR on April 1, 2006 was 6 per cent and that on October 1, 2006 was 8.5 per cent. Show important accounting entries for the first year.

Journal Entries in the books of A Ltd

Date	Particulars	Debit	credit
01.04.06	Bank A/c Dr. To 7 per cent Term Loan A/c (Term loan borrowed at 7 per cent annual interest rate payable half yearly)	10,00,000	10,00,000
30.09.06	Interest A/c Dr. To Bank A/c (Interest on Term Loan for the first half year = ₹ 10 lakhs * 7 per cent* 6/12 months)	35,000	35,000
30.09.06	Loss on Valuation of Debt A/c Dr. To 7 per cent Term Loan A/c (Increase in value of debt recognised due to restatement based on fair value. Fair value ₹ 10,20,000 Less book value ₹ 10,00,000)	20,000	20,000
30.09.06	Swap Hedge A/c Dr. To Gain on swap hedge A/c (Increase in value of swap recognised)	20,000	20,000
30.09.06	Bank A/c Dr. To Interest A/c (Swap settlement received for first half year 2006-07. Gain on underlying principal received ₹ 10 lakhs * 6/12 *(7 per cent contracted rate - 6 per cent swap agreed interest rate.)	5,000	5,000
31.03.07	Interest A/c Dr. To Bank A/c (Interest on term Loan for the second half year = ₹ 10 lakhs * 7 per cent * 6/12)	35,000	35,000
31.03.07	Loan A/c Dr. To Gain on Valuation of debt A/c (Decrease in value of debt recognised due to restatement based on fair value. Fair value ₹ 9,90,000 – Book value ₹ 10,20,000)	30,000	30,000
31.03.07	Loss on Swap Hedge A/c Dr. To Swap Hedge A/c (Cumulative loss on swap recognised. Value as at 31.03.07 ₹ 20,000 loss Less value already recognised gain ₹ 10,000 = 20,000 – 10,000)	30,000	30,000

31.03.07	Interest A/c Dr. To Bank A/c (Swap settlement paid for second half year 2006-07. ₹ 10 lakhs * (8.5 per cent – 7 per cent) * 6/12	7,500	7,500

Question 11:

On 31.03.2006 fair value per Ordinary shares of A Ltd. Was ₹ 45. On this date, B Ltd., committed to buy 10,000 of these shares at fair value. B Ltd. paid the price and accepted delivery of these shares on April 3, 2006. B Ltd. closed its Annual Accounts on March 31, 2006. Fair Value of A Ltd. Shares was ₹ 45.40 on March 31, 2006 and ₹ 45.30 on April 3, 2006.

Show Journal Entries in the Books of B Ltd. In respect of above in the following three cases:

(a) B Ltd. classifies its investment in A Ltd. as 'Financial Asset held to maturity'.

(b) B Ltd. classifies its investment in A Ltd. as 'Financial Asset available for sale'.

(c) B Ltd. classifies its investment in A Ltd. as 'Financial Asset at Fair Value through Profit or Loss'.

Answer:

(a) B Ltd. classifies its investment in A Ltd. as 'Financial Asset held to maturity'

Date	Particulars	Debit	Credit
30.03.2006	Investment A/c Dr. To Payable A/c (Commitment to purchase the shares of A Ltd.)	4,50,000	4,50,000
03.04.2006	Payable A/c Dr. To Bank A/c (Amount paid for purchase of Investment)	4,50,000	4,50,000

(b) B Ltd. classifies its investment in A Ltd. as 'Financial Asset available for sale'

Date	Particulars	Debit	Credit
30.03.2006	Investment A/c Dr. To Payable A/c (Commitment to purchase the shares of A Ltd)	4,50,000	4,50,000

31.03.2006	Investment A/c Dr. To Fair Value Adjustment A/c (Carrying amount of investments restated to represent current market value of ₹ 4,54,000 by adjusting the book value)	4,000	4,000
31.03.2006	Fair value Adjustment A/c Dr. To Investment Revaluation Reserve A/c (Increase in the value of Investment recognised in revaluation reserve Account)	4,000	4,000
03.04.2006	Payable A/c Dr. To Bank A/c (Amount paid for purchase of investment)	4,50,000	4,50,000
03.04.2006	Fair Value Adjustment A/c Dr. To Investment A/c (Being fair value adjustment 4,54,000 minus 4,53,000)	1,000	1,000
31.03.2007	Investment Revaluation Reserve A/c. Dr. To Fair Value Adjustment A/c	1,000	1,000

Note: It is presumed that investment have the same fair value as on 31.03.2007 and they have not been sold.

(c) B Ltd. classifies its investment in A Ltd as 'Financial Asset at Fair Value through Profit or Loss'

Date	Particulars	Debit	Credit
30.03.2006	Investment A/c Dr. To Payable A/c (Commitment to purchase the shares of A Ltd.)	4,50,000	4,50,000
31.03.2006	Investment A/c Dr. To Fair Value Adjustment A/c (Carrying amount of investments restated to represent current market value of ₹ 4,54,000 by adjusting the book value)	4,000	4,000
31.03.2006	Fair value Adjustment A/c Dr. To Profit and Loss A/c (Increase in the value of Investment recognised in profit and loss Account)	4,000	4,000
03.04.2006	Payable A/c Dr. To Bank A/c (Amount paid for purchase of investment)	4,50,000	4,50,000

03.04.2006	Fair Value Adjustment A/c To Investment A/c (Being fair value adjustment 4,54,000 minus 4,53,000)	Dr.	1,000	1,000
03.04.2006	Profit and Loss A/c To Fair Value Adjustment A/c (Increase in the value of Investment recognised in profit and Loss A/c)	Dr.	1,000	1,000

Question 12: Securitised Financial Instruments

A Ltd. has lent ₹ 50,000 yeilding 18 per cent Interest p.a. for 10 years. The company transferred the right to receive Principal ₹ 50,000 on maturity and the right to receive 14 per cent Interest per year. Of the balance 4 per cent interest, 2 per cent is due to the transferor, i.e., A Ltd. as service fee for collection of principal and interest. The expected cost of collection etc is ₹ 400. A Ltd. has retained the right to receive the remaining 2 per cent interest per year. Assume expected yield rate of 13 per cent per annum Show Journals.

Answer:

Computation of fair value of the Components **Amount (₹)**

Particulars	Cash-flow	Time Period	DF @ 13%	Fair \Value
Interest Transferred (50,000 * 14 per cent)	7,000	1- 10	5.426	37,982
Principal Transferred	50,000	10	0.295	14,750
Interest Retained (50,000 * 2 per cent)	1,000	1- 10	5.426	5,426
Service Fee (50,000 * 2 per cent – Cost ₹ 400)	6,00	1- 10	5.426	3,256
Total				**61,424**

Allocation of carrying amount

Particulars	Computation	Carrying Amount
Interest Transferred	37,982/61,424 x 50,000	30,918
Principal Transferred	14,750/61, 424 x 50,000	12,007
Interest Retained (Interest strip)	5,426/61,424 x 50,000	4,417
Service Fee	3,256/61,424 x 50,000	2,658
	Carrying Amount	**50,000**

Journal Entries in the books of A Ltd

S.No.	Particulars		Debit	Credit
1.	Bank A/c (37,982 + 14,750)	Dr.	52,732	
	To Loan Receivable A/c (30,918 + 12,007)			42,925
	To Profit and loss A/c			9,807
	(Being right to receive principal and interest up to 14 per cent there of transferred at fair value. Consideration ₹ 37,982 + 14,750 = ₹ 52,732. Carrying amount transferred 30,918 + 12,007 = ₹ 42,925			
2.	Servicing asset A/c	Dr.	2,658	
	Interest Strip A/c	Dr.	4,417	
	To Loan Receivable A/c			7,075
	(Being service fee and interest receivable from original debtor)			

Question 13: Securitised Financial Instruments

A Ltd. lent ₹ 20,000 for 8-years at 8 per cent interest payable annually. At the time, the fair value of the loan at effective annual interest rate of 10.2 per cent was ₹ 17,670. The borrower had the option to prepay the loan. After 3-years, when amortised cost of the loan was ₹ 18,100, the company transferred its right to receive principal to the extent of 90 per cent and interest to the extent of 9.5 per cent in favour of B Ltd. The consideration for the transaction was ₹ 16,700. The other particulars of the transcations were as below:

(a) Fair value of the loan at the time of transaction at effective interest rate of 10 per cent was ₹ 18,484. A Ltd. retained the excess spread of 0.5 per cent Principal transferred.

(b) A Ltd. retained the right to receive collection of Principal to the extent of ₹ 2,000 plus interest thereon. Defaults if any are deductible from the Company's claim in the principal, subject to maximum 2000.

(c) The estimated fair value of the excess Spread of 0.5 per cent is ₹ 38.

(d) Collections from prepayments are to be allocated between A Ltd. and transferee proportionately in ratio of 1 : 9.

Show Journal Entry to record the transfer.

Answer:

Evaluation of Appropriate Approach: The company has transferred the significant prepayment risk but has retained control over the loan. It has also retained significant default risk, giving credit enhancement for the transferee. The continuing involvement approach in this case is appropriate.

1. Allocation of carrying amount of Loan

Component of Loan	Fair Value	Proportion	Carrying amount allocated (₹)
Amount Transferred	16,636	90 per cent	18,100 * 90 per cent = 16,290
Amount retained	1,848	10 per cent	18,100 * 10 per cent = 1,810
	18,484		18,100

2. Allocation of Carrying Amount of Loan	**Amount**
Fair Value of part transferred	16,636
Less: Proportionate carrying amount of part transferred	16,290
Gain from part transferred	**346**
Carrying amount of part retained	1,810
Consideration received from the transferee	16,700
Less: Fair value of part transferred	16,636
Value of credit enhancement	**64**
Add: Value of interest strip	38
Income recognised in subsequent periods on time proportionate basis	**102**

Note: In respect of principal not transferred, the company should recognise ₹ 2,000/- as asset as well as liability (for the possibility of default) for continued involvement.

Value of liability for continued involvement = Principal retained + deferred income = ₹ 2,102

Journal Entry in the books of A Ltd.

Particulars		Debit	Credit
Bank A/c	Dr.	16,700	
Financial asset for continued involvement A/c	Dr.	2,000	
Interest strip A/c	Dr.	38	
To Loan A/c			16,290
To Profit and Loss A/c (gain on transfer)		346	
To Financial Liability for continued involvement A/c			2,102
(Being debt securitisation recorded)			

Note: In the company will recognise interest on balance of loan in subsequent periods by effective interest method.

Question 14:

On the basis of the following information related to trading in Options, you are required to pass relevant Journal Entries (at the time of inception and at the time of final settlement) in the books of Mr. X (buyer) and Mr. Y (seller). Assume that the price on expiry is ₹ 950 and both Mr. X and Mr. Y follow the calendar year as accounting year.

Date of Purchase	Option Type	Expiry Date	Premium per Unit	Contract Multiplier	Strike Price
29.03.2004	Equity Index, call	31.05.2004	₹ 10	200	₹ 850

Answer:

Date	Particulars		Debit	Credit
29.3.04	Equity index option premium A/c	Dr.	2,000	
	To Bank A/c			2,000
	[Being premium paid on equity stock options] (200*10)			
31.5.04	Profit and Loss A/c	Dr.	2,000	
	To Equity index stock option A/c			2,000
	[Being premium on option written off on expiry]			
31.5.04	Bank A/c	Dr.	20,000	
	To Profit and Loss A/c			20,000
	(Being profit earned on exercise of option) ((950– 850) * 200)			
29.3.04	Bank A/c	Dr.	2,000	
	To Equity index option premium A/c			2,000
31.5.04	Equity index option premium A/c	Dr.	2,000	
	To Profit and Loss A/c			2,000
31.5.04	Profit and Loss A/c	Dr.	20,000	
	To Bank A/c			20,000

Question 15:

Mr. Investor buys a stocks option of ABC Ltd. in July 2004 with a strike price on 30.07.2004 of ₹ 250 to be expired on 30.08.2004. The premium is ₹ 20 per unit and the market lot is 100. The margin to be paid is ₹ 120 per unit.

Show the accounting treatment in the books of buyer when:

1. The option is settled by delivery of the asset and
2. The option is settled in cash and the stock price is ₹ 260 per unit.

Answer:

Journal entries in the books of buyer

Date	Particulars		Debit	Credit
2004 July	**At the time of inception**			
	Stock option premium A/c	Dr.	2,000	
	To Bank A/c			2,000
	(Being premium paid to buy a stock option i.e., ₹ 20 * 100)			
	At the time of settlement			
2004 August	**1. Option settled by delivery of the asset**			
	Shares of ABC Ltd. A/c	Dr.	25,000	
	To Bank A/c			25,000
	(Being option exercised and shares acquired i.e. ₹ 250 * 100)			
	Profit and Loss A/c	Dr.	2,000	
	To Stock option premium A/c			2,000
	(Being the premium transferred to profit and loss account on exercise of option)			
	2. Option is settled in cash			
	Profit and Loss A/c	Dr.	2,000	
	To Stock option premium A/c			2,000
	(Being the premium transferred to profit and loss account)			
	Bank A/c (₹ 10 * 100)	Dr.	1,000	
	To Profit and Loss A/c			1,000
	(Being profit on exercise of option)			

Question 16:

A buyer buys a stock option of New Light Company Ltd. on 30th August, 2006 with a strike price of ₹ 150 per unit to be expired on September 30, 2006. The premium is ₹ 10 per unit and the market lot is of 100. The margin to be paid is ₹ 60 per unit.

Show how the transaction will appear in the books of the seller, when:

(1) The option is settled by delivery of the Asset and

(2) The option is settled in cash and the index price is ₹ 160 per unit.

Answer:

Date	Particulars	Debit	Credit
2006 30th Aug	**At the time of inception** Bank A/c Dr. To Stock option premium A/c (Being premium received on sale of stock option i.e., ₹ 10 * 100)	1,000	1,000
2006 30th Sep	**At the time of settlement:** **1. Option settled by delivery of the asset** Bank A/c Dr. To Shares of New light comp Ltd. A/c (Being shares delivered on exercise of call option)	1,500	1,500
2006 30th Sep	Stock option premium A/c Dr. To Profit and Loss A/c (Being the premium on the options contract recognised as income on exercise of the option i.e., 10 * 100)	1,000	1,000
	2. Options settled in cash Stock option premium A/c Dr. To Profit and Loss A/c (Being the premium on options contract recognized as income on exercise of the option i.e., ₹ 10 * 100)	1,000	1,000
	Loss on option A/c Dr. To Bank A/c (Being the loss on exercise of the option paid i.e., 100 @ ₹ 10 (₹ 160 – ₹ 150)	1,000	1,000
	Profit and Loss A/c Dr. To Loss on option A/c (Being the transfer of loss on options)	1,000	1,000

Question 17:

A Ltd. borrows ₹ 10 Lakh from B Ltd. under the following terms:

(a) The loan will carry 5 per cent annual rate of interest. Payable at the end of each year.

(b) A Ltd. will make immediate payment of an organization fee of ₹ 70,000 to B Ltd.

(c) The principal will be repaid in two installments. ₹ 4 lakh at the end of year 3 and ₹ 6 lakh at the end of year 5.

Show the Loan A/c in the books of B Ltd.

Answer:

Fair value of the loan = ₹ 10 lakh

Transaction cost = origination fee = ₹ 70,000

Fair value, net of transaction cost = ₹ 9.30 lakh

The loan taken is recognised initially at ₹ 9.30 lakh

Effective interest rate is discounting rate at which present value of interest and principal payments over 5 years is equal to ₹ 9.30 lakh. This rate is determined by trial and error as shown below:

Present value at guessed rate 6 per cent

Year	Cash-flow ₹ 000	DF 6 per cent	PV ₹ 000
1	50	0.943	47
2	50	0.890	44
3	450	0.839	378
4	30	0.792	24
5	630	0.747	471
			964

Present value at guessed rate 8 per cent

Year	Cash-flow ₹ 000	DF 8 per cent	PV ₹ 000
1	50	0.926	46
2	50	0.857	43
3	450	0.794	357
4	30	0.735	22
5	630	0.680	429
			897

Effective Interest rate (by interpolation) = 6 per cent + 8 – 6 × (964 – 930) = 7 per cent (964 – 897).

Computation of Interest cost - Figures in (000)

Year	Amortised Cost	Interest cost at 7 per cent	Cash paid	Amortised cost -Closing Balance
1	930	65	50	945
2	945	66	50	961
3	961	67	450	578
4	578	41	30	589
5	589	41	630	Nil

In the books of A Ltd.

Loan Account (₹ 000)

Year	Particulars	Amount	Year	Particular	Amount
Year 1	To Bank	70	Year 1	By Bank	1000
	To Bank	50		By Interest	65
	To Balance c/d	945			
		1065			**1065**
Year 2	To Bank	50	Year 2	By Balance b/d	945
	To Balance c/d	961		By Interest	66
		1011			**1011**
Year 3	To Bank	450	Year 3	By Balance b/d	961
	To Balance c/d	578		By Interest	67
		1028			**1028**
Year 4	To Bank	30	Year 4	By Balance b/d	578
	To Balance c/d	589		By Interest	41
		619			**619**
Year 5	To Bank	630	Year 5	By Balance b/d	589
				By Interest	41
		630			**630**

Question 18:

XYZ Ltd. needs $3,00,000 on May 1, 2009, for payment of loan installment and interest. As on December 1, 2008, It appears to the company that the dollar may be dearer as compared to the exchange rate prevailing on that date, say $1 = ₹ 43.50. Accordingly, XYZ Ltd. may enter into a forward contract with a banker for $3,00,000. The forward rate maybe higher or lower than the spot rate prevailing on the date of the forward contract. Assume forward rate as on December 1, 2008 was $1 = ₹ 44 as against the spot rate of ₹ 43.50. As on the future date, i.e., May 1,2009 the banker will pay XYZ Ltd. $ 3,00,000 at ₹ 44 irrespective of the spot rate as on that date. Assume that the spot rate is on that date is $1 = ₹ 44.80. Journalise in the books of XYZ Ltd.

Answer:

Working Notes:

1. Payment to be made as per forward contract: ($ 3,00,000 × ₹ 44) = ₹ 1,32,00,000
2. Amount payable had the forward contract not been in place: ($ 3,00,000 × ₹ 44.80) = ₹ 1,34,40,000
3. Gain arises (1,34,40,000 – 1,32,00,000) = ₹ 2,40,000

Journal entries in the books of XYZ Co. Limited

Date	Particulars		Debit	Credit
1.12.2008	Premium on FCE A/c To Swap Bank (Being the recognition of premium – 3,00,000 × 44-43.5)	Dr.	1,50,000	 1,50,000
1.12.2008	Profit & Loss A/c To Premium on FEC (Being written of premium for 121 days that is 121/152 * 1,50,000 = 1,19,608 Balance ₹ 30,392 to be written off	Dr.	1,19,608	 1,19,608
1.05.2009	Loan A/c Exchange Difference A/c To Bank (Being settlement of liability $ 300000 × 44)	Dr. Dr.	1,30,50,000 3,90,000	 1,34,40,000
1.05.2009	Swap Bank A/c To Exchange Difference A/c (Being transfer of amount of exchange difference)	Dr.	3,90,000	 3,90,000
1.05.2009	Bank A/c To SWAP bank A/c (Being swap settled)	Dr.	2,40,000	 2,40,000
1.05.2009	Profit and Loss A/c To premium on FEC (Premium written off)	Dr.	30,392	 30,392

Question 19:

On 24 January 2006, Chinnaswamy of Chennai sold goods to Watson of Washington, USA for an invoice price of $40,000 when the spot market rate was ₹ 44.20 per US$. Payment was to be received after 3-months on 24th April 2006. To mitigate the risk of loss from decline in the exchange rate on the date of receipt of payment, Chinnaswamy immediately acquired forward contract to sell on 24th April 2006 US$ 40,000 @ ₹ 43.70. Chinnaswamy closed his books of account on 31st March 2006, when the spot rate was ₹ 43.20 per US$. On 24th April 2006 the date of receipt of money by Chinnaswamy to record the effect of all the above mentioned events.

Answer:

Date 2006	Particulars		Debit	Credit
Jan 24	Watson a/c To Sales account (Being credit sales made to Watson of Washington USA for $40,000 recorded at spot matket rate of ₹ 44.20 per US $)	Dr.	17,68,000	 17,68,000

Jan 24	Forward (₹) contract receivable A/c Deferred discount A/c To Forward ($) contract payable A/c (Being forward contract acquired to sell on 24th April, 2006 US $ 40,000 @ ₹ 43.70) Deferred discount (43.70 – 43.20) × 40,000 = 20,000	17,48,000 20,000	 17,68,000
March 31	Exchange loss A/c Dr. To Watson A/c (Being record of exchange loss @ ₹ 1 per US $ (44.20-43.20) × 40000	40,000	 40,000
March 31	Forward ($) Contract Payable A/c Dr. To Exchange gain A/c (Being decrease in liability on forward contract due to fall in exchange rate)	40,000	 40,000
March 31	Discount account A/c Dr. To deferred discount account A/c (Being record of proportionate discount expense for 66 days out of 90 days that is 66/90 × 20000 = ₹ 14667)	14,667	 14,667
April 24	Bank A/c Dr. Exchange loss A/c Dr. To Watson A/c (Being receipt of $ 40,000 from Watson, USA customer @ ₹ 43.70 per US $ (17,48,000 – 40,000 exchange loss already booked), exchange loss being ₹ (43.70 – 43.20) × 40,000 = ₹ 20,000.	17,08,000 20,000	 17,28,000
April 24	Forward ($) contract payable A/c Dr. To Exchange gain A/c To Bank A/c (Being settlement of forward contract by payment of $ 40,000)	17,28,000	 20,000 17,08,000
April 24	Bank A/c Dr. To Forward (₹) contract receivable A/c (Being receipt of cash in settlement of forward contract receivable $ 40,000 × 43.70 = ₹ 17,48,000)	17,48,000	 17,48,000
April 24	Discount A/c Dr. To deferred discount A/c (Being recording of discount expense for 24 days ₹ 20,000 × 24 days/90 days = ₹ 5,333	5,333	 5,333

Question 20:

Mr. A purchases the following units of equity Index Futures (EIF)

Date of Purchase	Name of Future	Expiry Date /series	Contract Price per unit (₹)	Contract Multiplier (No. of Units)
28th March 2003	EF1	May 2003	1420	200
29th March 2003	EF2	June 2003	4280	50
29th March 2003	EF1	May 2003	1416	200

Daily Settlement Prices of the above units of Equity Index Futures were as follows:

Date	EF1 May Series (₹)	EF2 June Series (₹)
28/03/2003	1,410	0
29/03/2003	1,428	4.300
30/03/2003	1,435	4.270
31/03/2003	1,407	4.290
01/04/2003	1,415	4.250
02/04/2003	1,430	0
03/04/2003	1,442	0

For the sake of convenicence, it has been assumed that the above contracts were settled on the following dates:

(a) EF2 June Series on 1st April, 2003

(b) A contract of 200 Units of EF1 May Series on 2nd April, 2003

(c) The other contract of EF1 May Series on 3rd April, 2003.

Prepare necessary accounts.

Answer:

1. The amount of mark-to-market margin money received/paid due to increase/ decrease in daily settlement prices is as below:

Date	EF 1 may Series (₹)		EF 2 June Series (₹)		Net Amount (₹)	
	Receive	Pay	Receive	Pay	Receive	Pay
28/03/03		2,000*				2,000
29/03/03	6,000**		1,000		7,000	
30/03/03	2,800			1,500	1,300	
31/03/03		11,200	1,000			10,200

* Pay 1,420 –1,410 = 10 × 200 = ₹ 2,000

** Receive (1,428 – 1,416) × 200 = ₹ 2,400 + (1,428 – 1,410) × 200 = ₹ 3,600 = ₹ 6,000

3. The amount of Mark-to-Market Margin money received/paid will be credited/debited to Mark-to-Market margin-EIF A/c by passing the following entries:

Journal Entries

Date	Particulars	Debit	Credit
28/03/03	Mark-to-Market Margin-EIF A/c Dr. To Bank A/c (Being net MTM Margin money paid for the day)	2,000	2,000
29/03/03	Bank A/c Dr. To Mark-to-Market Margin-EIF A/c (Being net MTM Margin money received)	7,000	7,000
30/03/03	Bank A/c Dr. To Mark-to-Market Margin-EIF A/c	1,300	1,300
31/03/03	Mark-to-Market Margin-EIF A/c Dr. To Bank A/c	10,200	10,200

4. On the above basis, Mark-to-Market Margin-EIF A/c for the year will appear as follows in the books of Mr. A:

Mark-to-Market Margin-EIF A/c

Date	Particulars	Debit	Credit	Dr./Cr. Balance	Balance Amount
March 2003 28	To bank	2,000		Dr.	2,000
29	By bank		7,000	Cr.	5,000
30	By bank		1,300	Cr.	6,300
31	To bank	10,200		Dr.	3,900
31	By balance c/d		3,900		
	Total	12,200	12,200		

On 31st March 2003, Mark-to-Market (MTM) Margin money received/paid on all the contracts in each of the indexes is as follows:

Amount paid on the contracts in respect of EF 1 (13,200 – 8,800)	₹ 4,400
Amount received on the contracts in respect of EF 2 (20,00 – 15,00)	₹ 500

(a) Keeping in view the consideration of prudence, a provision should be created for anticipated loss on open contracts in respect of EF 1, equivalent to the amount paid, by passing the following entry, whereas the amount received in open contracts in respect of EF 2 would be ignored:

31.03.2003	Profit and Loss A/c	Dr.	₹ 4,400	
	To Provision for Loss- EIF A/c			4,400

(Being provision created for the amount paid to clearing member on account of movement in the prices of the contracts in respect of EF 1)

(b) In respect of open equity index futures contracts, the following disclosures should be made in the notes to accounts:

Details of open interests in equity Index Futures contracts

Name of equity Index Futures	No. of contracts	Long (in units)	Short (in units)
EF 1	2	400	
EF 2	1	50	

In the next year 2003-04

1. The amount of Mark-to- market, margin money received/paid due to increase/decrease in daily settlement prices is as follows:

Date	EF 1 May Series (₹)		EF 2 June Series (₹)		Net Amount (₹)	
	Receive	Pay	Receive	Pay	Receive	Pay
1/4/03	3,200			2,000	1,200	
2/4/03	6,000				6,000	
3/4/03	2,400				2,400	

2. The amount of profit/loss arising on squaring-up is calculated, using weighted average method, as follows:

Name of the future contract	EF 2	EF 1	EF 1
Series	**June 2003**	**May 2003**	**May 2003**
Date of settlement	**1st April 2003**	**2nd April 2003**	**3rd April 2003**
Contract price per unit (in ₹)	4,280	1,418*	1,418*
Settlement price per unit (in ₹)	4,250	1,430	1,442
Profit (+)/Loss (-) per unit (in ₹)	-30	+12	+24
Number of Units	50	200	200
Total profit/loss	-1,500	+2,400	+4,800

* (1,420 + 1,416)/2 = ₹ 1,418

Journal Entries

Date	Particulars		Debit	Credit
April 2003 1	Bank A/c To Mark-to-Market Margin-EIF A/c (Being net MTM margin money received)	Dr.	1,200	1,200
1	Profit and Loss A/c To Mark-to-Market Margin-EIF 2 A/c (-30 × 50 = ₹ 1,500 being loss on squaring up)	Dr.	1,500	1,500
2	Bank A/c To Mark-to-Market Margin-EF 1 (Being net MTM Margin money received)	Dr.	6,000	6,000
2	Mark-to-Market Margin-EIF 1 A/c To Profit & Loss A/c (Being profit on squaring up of the contract)	Dr.	2,400	2,400
3	Bank A/c To Mark-to-Market A/c (Being net MTM margin money received-EF 1)	Dr.	2,400	2,400
3	Mark-to-Market Margin-EIF 1 A/c To Profit and Loss A/c (Being profit on squaring up of the contract-EF 1)	Dr.	4,800	4,800

3. In this case, Mark-to-Market Margin-EIF A/c for the year will appear as follows in the books of Mr. A

Mark-to-Market Margin-EF A/c

Date	Particulars	Debit	Credit	Dr./Cr.	Balance
2003 April 1	To Balance b/d	3,900		Dr.	3,900
1	By Bank		1,200	Dr.	2,700
1	By Profit and Loss A/c		1,500	Dr.	1,200
2	By Bank		6,000	Cr	4,800
2	To Profit and Loss A/c	2,400		Cr.	2,400
3	By Bank		2,400	Cr	4,800
3	To Profit and Loss A/c	4,800			
	Total	**11,100**	**11,100**		

Note: In case the contracts as above are not squared-up, but are settled on the final settlement date, the same entries as have been passed on squaring-up of the contracts, will be passed at the time of final settlement.

Question 21:

Mr. X enters into certain equity derivatives instruments contracts on March 28, 2003. The initial Margin on these contracts calculated as per the SPAN, is ₹ 30,000. The margin for the subsequent days calculated as per SPAN' s are as follows:

On 29th March 2003 ₹ 35,000

On 30th March 2003 ₹ 25,000

On 31st March 2003 ₹ 27,000

Journalise.

Answer: 1. Journal Entries

Date	Particulars	Debit	Credit
28/03/03	Initial Margin-equity Derivative Instruments A/c Dr. To Bank A/c (Being initial margin paid)	30,000	30,000
29/03/03	Margin -equity Derivative Instrument A/c Dr. To Bank A/c (35,000 – 30,000 = 5,000 Further margin money paid to the exchange)	5,000	5,000
30/03/03	Bank A/c Dr. To Margin-equity derivative Instrument A/c (25,000 – 35,000 = 10,000 Being refund of margin money)	10,000	10.000
31/03/03	Margin-equity derivative Instrument A/c Dr. To Bank A/c (27,000 – 25,000 = 2,000 further margin money paid)	2,000	2,000

2. ***Extracts from the Balance Sheet*** Assets Side

   Current Assets

   Initial margin-equity derivative Instruments ₹ 27.000

3. ***Disclosure:*** In respect of initial margin, the following disclosure may be made in the notes to accounts:

   "Initial Margin on equity derivative instruments contracts has been paid in cash only".

Question 22:

Dravid Investment Ltd. deals in equity derivatives. Their current portfolio comprises of the following instruments:

Infosys ₹ 5,600 Call Expiry June 2004, 2000 unit bought at ₹ 197 each (cost)

Infosys ₹ 5,700 Call Expiry June 2004, 3600 unit bought at ₹ 131 each (cost)

Infosys ₹ 5,400 Put Expiry June 2004, 4000 unit bought at ₹ 81 each (cost)

What will the profit or loss to Dravid Investments Ltd. in the following situation?

(a) Infosys closes on the expiry day at ₹ 6,041

(b) Infosys closes on the expiry day at ₹ 5,812

(c) Infosys closes on the expiry day at ₹ 5,085

Answer:

1. Pay-off/unit at Infosys Closing price

Instrument	Units	Cost	Strike	At 6041	At 5812	At 5085
5600 Call	2000	197	5600	441	212	NIL
5700 Call	3600	131	5700	341	112	NIL
5400 Put	4000	81	5400	NIL	NIL	315

2. Per unit profit and total amount of profit

Instrument	At 6041	At 5812	At 5085	At 6041	At 5812	At 5085
5600 Call	244	15	-197	4,88,000	30,000	-3,94,000
5700 Call	210	-19	-131	7,56,000	-68,400	-4,71,600
5400 Put	-81	-81	234	-3,24,000	-32,4000	9,36,000
		Total	9,20,000	-3,62,400	70,400